INTERPRETING LITERATURE
WITH CHILDREN

D1004459

INTERPRETING LITERATURE WITH CHILDREN

Shelby A. Wolf
*University of Colorado
at Boulder*

LAWRENCE ERLBAUM ASSOCIATES, PUBLISHERS
2004   Mahwah, New Jersey   London

Director, Editorial:	Lane Akers
Executive Assistant:	Bonita D'Amil
Cover Design:	Shelby A. Wolf
Cover Layout:	Kathryn Houghtaling Lacey
Textbook Production Manager:	Paul Smolenski
Full-Service Compositor:	TechBooks
Text and Cover Printer:	Sheridan Books, Inc.

This book was typeset in 10/13.5 pt. ITC Garamond, Italic, Bold, and Bold Italic.
The heads were typeset in ITC Garamond, Italic and Bold.

Lawrence Erlbaum Associates, Inc., Publishers
10 Industrial Avenue
Mahwah, New Jersey 07430
www.erlbaum.com

Library of Congress Cataloging-in-Publication Data

Wolf, Shelby Anne.
  Interpreting literature with children / Shelby A. Wolf.
    p.   cm.
  Includes bibliographical references (p.   ) and indexes.
  ISBN 0-8058-4513-5 (casebound)—ISBN 0-8058-4514-3 (pbk.)
    1.Literature—Study and teaching (Elementary)—United States.   2. Children—Books
and reading—United States.   I. Title.
  LB1575.5.U5W65   2004
  372.64—dc22

                                                              2003017992

Books published by Lawrence Erlbaum Associates are printed on
acid-free paper, and their bindings are chosen for strength and
durability.

Printed in the United States of America
10 9 8 7 6 5 4 3 2 1

Once upon a time there were two sets of sisters
Martha and Karen
&
Lindsey and Ashley
And they meant more than words can tell

Contents

III: Ways of Doing Literature

Acknowledgments

Wilbur never forgot Charlotte. Although he loved her children and grandchildren dearly, none of the new spiders ever quite took her place in his heart.
She was in a class by herself.

  It is not often that someone comes along who is a true friend and a good
writer. Charlotte was both.

—*Charlotte's Web*, E. B. White (1952, p. 184)

Throughout my life I have been blessed by books, which at their best bring
good writers and true friends together. Thus, I must first acknowledge the
authors, the illustrators, the critics, and the scholars of children's literature
who have given me language, image, and thought, and more important, given
these gifts to children.

And children give back to books. My daughters, Lindsey and Ashley, were
the first to instruct me. Lindsey's drama and Ashley's humor showed me
the profound insights and intriguing connections children make between
literature and life. The many school children I've taught, observed, and learned
from over the years have only deepened my understanding, for children see
the light in literature, and their writing, their drama, their art, and their lives
illuminate the words on the page.

There are many adults to thank as well. First and foremost, Shirley Brice
Heath, my academic mentor and hero, true friend and fairy godmother, offered both critical commentary and constant support. She is in a class by
herself. Pat Enciso, children's literature expert extraordinaire and all around
pal, challenged me to think even more broadly about the work. Leslie Maniotes, a literacy scholar and fellow lover of literature, was one of the first to
see early drafts, and her encouraging words kept me on my path of thinking
and writing about children and their literature.

My editor, Lane Akers, stood by to help me with any aspect of the book, from the largest of insights into college textbook publishing to the smallest, but not insignificant, details of acquiring permissions. And the permissions to use multiple quotes from children's literature would still be floating in the Neverland between fax, email, and phone messages if it weren't for Lisa Loranger, whose patience and persistence brought me much peace of mind. I also want to thank my fellow authors—Patty Anders and Barbara Guzetti, Kathy Au, Freddy Hiebert, Taffy Raphael and P. David Pearson, Steven Stahl and Bill Nagy, and especially Sheila Valencia—who will be contributing their own volumes to this literacy series, and who graciously invited me into their company.

Still, this volume would be slight without the teachers, whose creative and critical classroom examples help to highlight children's connections with books. They were my students at the University of Colorado at Boulder, and I was theirs. Rather than hide their names under the guise of pseudonyms, they have granted me the best of permissions—to use their real names in this text. So, to Darcy Ballentine, Jill Brown, Stephanie Brown, Kathryn Buhler, Rebecca Ervin, Jeannie Finch, Cathy Glaab, Sybil Hall, Kirsten Ames Kahn, Susan Kandyba, Jessica Levitt Knorr, Jennifer Mayer, Unna Montoya-Trunkenbolz, Karen Musick, Erika Norman, Sandy Quezada, María Ramírez, Lorynda Sampson, Amy Schackman, Christy Shoemaker, Diane Starkey, Shannon Suedkamp, Kerri Therriault, Sandra Vazquez, and Jessica Whitelaw, I owe a world of thanks. It's not often that teachers come along who are true friends and good writers. You were both.

Prologue:
Engagement Beyond the Edges
of the Earth

Once upon a crisp autumn day, I was in a classroom observing a group of children reading a short tradebook about maps. The text described the prevailing view of the populace who believed the earth was flat, but then explained how a few brave thinkers suggested the spherical shape of the planet. Finally, the tradebook summarized the voyage of Magellan, who set out to prove the new theory by circumnavigating the globe. The children—a group of confident, worldly 9- and 10-year-olds—laughed over the image of the earth as flat. I suggested that even though the theory seemed amazing to us now, they should try to imagine the courage of those who set out into their own unknown. I explained that in ancient times, people said, "At the edges of the earth, there be dragons." The boy sitting next to me immediately jerked around in his seat, looked me square in the eye, and exclaimed, "You talk just like a book!"

Of course, the book he meant was not the expository tradebook before us, but *literature*. Yet what in my statement triggered his exclamation? Possibly it was the alliterative quality in "edges of the earth" with the repetition of the letter *e* in such close proximity. It could be, perhaps, the more archaic construction of "there be" instead of "there were." But I think the most likely reason of all may have been the presence of dragons, who live and breathe fire into a number of children's tales, from the terrifying creature in *Saint George and the Dragon* (Hodges, 1984) to Hagrid's careful, but ultimately catastrophic, attempt to raise a baby dragon in *Harry Potter and the Sorcerer's Stone* (Rowling, 1998). From an old classic to a 21st century publishing phenomenon, dragons seem a sure bet for drawing children into literature. Still,

1

the range of children's literature extends well beyond fantasies that feature dragons, and it's up to you, as a teacher of literature, to help children and young adolescents engage with prose and poetry.

Ruined by Reading

One way to do that is to first consider your own reading habits. Do you like to read? Is it a life-long, everyday habit or an every-once-in-a-while thing? Do you have certain authors you admire or certain genres you prefer? Do you belong to a book club or look for opportunities to share your ideas about books with friends? Now consider who you are as a teacher or future teacher of literature. How can you help children connect with literary text? Through daily read-alouds? Through literature discussion groups? Through a careful selection of stories that you know will get children talking about literature and life? And beyond talking about text, how can you provide opportunities for children to express their literary response through writing, the visual arts, and drama? In other words, how can you communicate a love of reading to children?

As someone who has been accused of "talking like a book," I admit I love reading, and children's literature is my particular passion. I have been teaching for 30 years, initially as a Peace Corps volunteer, then as an elementary classroom teacher, and now as a university professor. But I am, first and foremost, a student of children's literature and literary interpretation. I am, in a phrase facetiously coined by Lynn Schwartz (1996), "ruined by reading."

My ruination began later in life. Although I'd done my fair share of reading as a child, my real love of reading began with my first day of teaching first grade. I had decided to read "Snowdrop," a version of Snow White from a Grimm Brothers' (1973) edition of fairy tales. I practiced the story in advance, testing out various accents and intonations, as well as gathered the props I felt were necessary to a dramatic delivery. Once in class, with my children leaning in close, I pulled a mirror from my pocket and imitated the deep and dangerous voice of the evil queen as she stepped before her mystic mirror. Holding my own mirror high, I intoned, "Mirror, Mirror on the wall,/Who is the fairest of us all?" (p. 7).

Several children began to imitate my gestures, staring haughtily into the palms of their hands and chanting the familiar words with me as the story advanced. I pulled out a bright ribbon for Snowdrop's lacings, a tortoise shell barrette for the poisoned comb, and a shiny red apple for Snowdrop's destiny. After I cut the apple in two, I held out one section, and my children instinctively drew back. "Don't do it!" one small boy shouted, flinging his arm out to prevent Snowdrop from making her ill-fated decision. It was an auspicious beginning to my elementary teaching career, for I had been able to lure my children into the language of narrative and, I hoped, begin their own ruination by reading.

A Recipe for Engagement

My goal in this book is to spark your own passion for reading or to fan the flames if you're already well on your way. Over my years of teaching both children and adults, I've learned a few things about how to encourage children's engagement with literature, and I want to share what I've learned with you.

It's an intriguing mixture, really—one that involves a healthy understanding of literary theory, with a generous portion devoted to genre and its impact on the other narrative components of character, setting, plot, theme, point of view, style, and tone. Each of these components shifts and changes depending on the critical perspective. But the study of literary forms, even with the added zest of the various types of criticism, would make a poor formula for the classroom if children's transactions with text weren't invited into the mix, especially their views of culture, class, and gender. Indeed, who children are is inextricably blended with how they will engage in literature, and it will affect their talk, their writing, their drama, and even their art as they construct meaning from text.

The brief recipe for literary response that I've outlined calls to mind another book about dragons: Robin McKinley's (1984) *The Hero and the Crown.* In this Newbery-award winner, the heroine—Aerin—is determined to slay dragons, and in her reading she comes across an ancient recipe for an ointment that protects the slayer against the heat of a dragon's fire. The recipe requires a number of esoteric ingredients, and it is many weeks and several burnt fingers before Aerin perfects the mixture and rides out to test its effectiveness. In my own reading and research, I've come across several formulas for literary response, and through my own trial and error, this book represents the best combination I know for encouraging children's engagement with literature.

An Outline for the Book

Designed for preservice as well as practicing teachers who want to learn more about how to teach literature, the upcoming chapters focus on those who teach or hope to teach kindergarten through the eighth grade (typically children from 5 to 14 years of age). The first section of the book—"Salutations! Learning about Literature"—will start the conversation. In chapter 1, "Critical Perspectives," I define literature and literary interpretation as well as delineate some essential ideas that can help to expand children's engagement in text. I then discuss the prevailing views of several types of literary criticism, and I show how the critic's stance determines how he or she will analyze its content. I also make the argument that combining critical perspectives is an effective way to aid children's enthusiasm for literary analysis. Throughout chapter 1, I showcase E. B. White's (1952) *Charlotte's Web* to demonstrate key ideas as well as how literary critics might approach this classic text. Although it would be helpful for you to read this text before reading chapter 1, it's not a requirement. Still, if you haven't read or reread White's masterpiece in awhile, you're in for a treat.

In chapter 2, "Literary Elements in Prose and Poetry," I explore each of the common components of narrative in turn—genre, theme, character, setting, plot, point of view, style, and tone—to establish a foundation for literary teaching. Here I lean on two other touchstone texts: *The Watsons Go to Birmingham—1963*, a novel by Christopher Paul Curtis (1995), and *Hansel and Gretel*, a picture book illustrated by Anthony Browne and written by the Grimm Brothers (1981). Although I include examples from a number of other texts, you might want to have these books by your side as you read through this section. In addition, I explore the typical features of poetry, using pieces that relate well to the two narrative texts.

The second section of the book is entitled "Ways of Taking from Literature," and here I emphasize the importance of language, culture, class, and gender in how children understand and talk about text. Because talk is central to interpretation, in chapter 3 I concentrate on "Talking about Literature," reminding teachers and their children of the power of expressive language as they engage in literary discussion and criticism. When given opportunities to talk about text in critical ways, children grow not only in understanding the text on the page but the texts of their lives. This leads directly to chapter 4, "Culture & Class in Children's Literature," and chapter 5, "Gender in Children's Literature," where I demonstrate the social influences on children's literary interpretations. In all of the chapters in this section, I showcase literature that gets children talking—provocative, puzzling, and pleasurable books that encourage children's reflection and critical conversations. But don't feel constrained by my choices. You, no doubt, have your own ideas for books that would be effective in upping the ante on the social and political dimensions of response.

In addition, I share classroom examples from teachers I admire—teachers who have been in my classes at the university and are building their expertise in interpreting literature with children. They have graciously allowed us to listen in on their classroom conversations and shared their children's insights and illustrations, in the hope that in reading about their work you will be tempted to try out some of your own techniques.

The third and final section of this book is entitled "Ways of Doing Literature." Talk is certainly a way to *do* literature. Indeed, it's a time-honored tradition to place dialogue at the forefront of literary interpretation. Yet, verbal expression is only one of many "languages" available to children as they interpret text. An emphasis on talk may actually silence children, particularly non-mainstream and/or non-native English-speaking children, because all cultures do not emphasize verbal displays of knowledge that school teachers have come to see as "normal." The same may be said of mainstream children who are known for their dramatic and artistic interpretations of literature at home, but who lose opportunities for such expressive modes once they enter school. The focus on alternate modes of expression is not meant to eliminate verbal forms; rather, these artistic modes extend what can be accomplished verbally.

The end result is a literary tool kit that will allow children, young adolescents, and teachers to develop a wide range of tools for constructing literary engagement. As Wertsch (1991) argued, "In terms of the tool kit approach . . . some tools are more powerful and efficacious for certain activities or spheres of life, and others are more powerful and efficacious for others" (p. 102). Depending on the book, and certainly depending on the child (or group of children) as well as the context, other tools of response may be more or less effective. Thus, the chapters in this section focus on several mediational means for literary response. Chapter 6 concentrates on interpreting literature through writing, chapter 7 on the visual arts, and chapter 8 on drama. Again, these chapters feature intriguing books as well as exemplary teachers' classroom examples of interpretive work and play. In the epilogue, I look back to provide a summary of the book as well as look forward to discuss future directions you might take in your own journey to encourage and enhance your students' literary engagement.

"At the edges of the earth, there be dragons." Not really, as it turns out. But dragons still hold sway in the hearts and minds of children as well as in the thoughts and actions of a number of literary characters in the books that children read. Still, we know that much lies well past the places where dragons dwell, and if we let the threat of their fire hold us back and cancel our journeys in the fear of getting singed or worse, we would never discover the rich, round world of interpreting literature with children—a world that exists beyond traditional edges. And so, our journey begins.

Boulder, Colorado, 2003

I

Salutations!
Learning About Literature

> Literature transforms and intensifies ordinary language, deviates systematically from everyday speech. . . . This, in effect, was the definition of the "literary" advanced by the Russian formalists. . . . [In their thinking], the literary work was neither a vehicle for ideas, a reflection of social reality nor the incarnation of some transcendental truth: it was a material fact, whose functioning could be analysed rather as one could examine a machine. (pp. 2–3)

But E. B. White, deft as he was, was no machinist. No. His fine-tuning of language was made for a purpose: to *communicate*, to talk of friendship, love, and uplifting life; the foibles of foolish humans; the compassionate wit of spiders, the radiance of pigs, and the humor in rats; the rich, loamy smell of a barn in spring; the rush of freedom in a barn swing; and the ultimate "glory of everything" (p. 183). True to his word, when White was once asked about his purposes for writing, he said, "All that I hope to say in books, all that I ever hope to say, is that I love the world" (Neumeyer, 1994, p. xxix).

Clearly, White hoped that children would participate in that passion as well, and he had enough respect for children to know that they could take up whatever he gave them:

> Anyone who writes down to children is simply wasting his time. You have to write up, not down. Children are demanding. They are the most attentive, curious, eager, observant, sensitive, quick, and generally congenial readers on earth. They accept, almost without question, anything you present them with, as long as it is presented honestly, fearlessly, and clearly. . . . Some writers for children deliberately avoid using words they think a child doesn't know. This emasculates the prose and, I suspect, bores the reader. Children are game for anything. I throw them hard words, and they backhand them over the net. (p. 242)

Critical to understanding this quote is the idea that White not only threw them "hard words" but complex ideas. What is life? What does it mean to be a true friend? What is death, and how do we move on in the face of terrible loss?

Charlotte's Web was one of the first children's books to discuss death in such clear, honest, and fearless prose, but rather than repel them, generations of children were drawn to it. Most likely, they knew that here was a writer who would *write up* to them rather than down. Even when they felt overwhelmingly saddened by the death, White had too much respect for children and life to falsely let Charlotte live on and on. And his editor, Ursula Nordstrom, who supported him in this stance, answered one child's lament about the death of Charlotte by writing:

> When I read the manuscript I felt exactly the way you now feel. I didn't want Charlotte to die, and I too cried over her death. What I think you and I both should keep in mind is that Charlotte had a good and worthwhile life. And she was a true friend to Wilbur. And something to be glad about is that she had all those children. I think the author knows that in due course a spider such as Charlotte does die, but her children live, and so will her children's children. (Marcus, 1998a, pp. 340–341)

And *Charlotte's Web* lives as well, proving this essential point: Children's uptake of literature depends on there being something substantive to take up! If the books are smooth and saccharine, there's hardly anything to chew on, to contemplate, to question, or even to criticize. If the language is ordinary, what's there to backhand across the net? And if the ideas are simple, why talk about them at all? If we want our children to be engaged in literature, we have to give them something to think about.

Limiting Engagement

Some parents and teachers choose texts for children based on their heart-felt notions of children as innocent and in vast need of protection from the harsh realities of life. Katherine Paterson's (1978) novel *The Great Gilly Hopkins* was banned for profanity because Gilly said "damn." *The Light in the Attic* by Shel Silverstein (1981) came under fire because it reputedly encouraged children to be disobedient. Trina Schart Hyman's version of the Grimm Brothers (1983) *Little Red Riding Hood* was banned because she carried a bottle of wine to her grandmother rather than a basket of goodies. Even during their lifetimes, Jacob and Wilhelm Grimm both chose and were forced to tone down the violence in their texts. Indeed, a recent review of a book on the Brothers Grimm explained how the brothers were challenged again and again to revise their texts. Some, with an excess of violence, were eliminated. Others tales were expurgated, "Wilhelm himself did the work, but he wrote, in some exasperation, 'You can fool yourself into thinking that what can be removed from a book can also be removed from real life'" (Zarin, 2001, p. 29).

One of the most famous cases of adult attempts to shield children from potentially disturbing images occurred with the publication of Maurice Sendak's (1970) *In the Night Kitchen*. Some librarians, shocked at Mickey's full frontal nudity, drew shorts on the tiny figure, diapered him in white paint, or removed the book from their shelves. Ursula Nordstrom, who was also Sendak's editor, received a letter from an adult who had burned a copy of the text! Distressed, Ursula wrote, "I assume it is the little boy's nudity which bothers you. But truly, it does not disturb children! It is only adults who ever feel threatened by Sendak's work" (Marcus, 1998a, p. 326).

In a letter she wrote to Sendak, Nordstrom explained how she had to face some similar issues with *Charlotte's Web*.

> I have engaged in "a dialogue" with a woman who hated *Charlotte's Web* because the spider loved drinking the fly's blood. So this woman wouldn't give the book to her 8 year old niece.... I wrote her an impassioned letter saying that it was in the nature of spiders to drink the blood of flies, and that indeed in the book Wilbur shared her (the woman's) distaste at Charlotte's eating habits. But I begged her to give the little girl the book, to give the book a chance. Etc. etc. Blood all over the typewriter. Well, she wrote back and said if I were a gambling woman she would bet me the price of the book that the niece would hate the book. I told her that gambling was the one bad habit I did not indulge in, but please to try it anyway. Happy ending: she had the decency to write me that the niece loved the book and she took back what she'd written. Which is why I always like to answer insane letters. We are in the field of wanting to communicate so I must be consistent and try to communicate. (pp. 323-324)

As teachers of literature, we are also in the field of wanting to communicate, so we must work to expand literary engagement rather than limit it.

Expanding Engagement

Although there are many ways of limiting children's interactions with text, in the classrooms of capable teachers, children's engagement with text expands exponentially. As I've taught and observed in schools, I've come to believe that there are at least four essential ideas to know about children and literature. I'll try to state them simply and directly, and they may at first seem like common sense. Still, if you look at the alternatives, you'll realize that ignoring these principles may put you in peril of not really connecting the children in your classrooms with books.

Children Are Smart.   All too often, children are characterized as innocent, egocentric, and in much need of guidance and protection—considerations that have much to do with the information on banning and distorting texts that I shared previously. Still, far more insidious than shielding children from bottles of wine and bloodthirsty spiders is protecting them from complex ideas. As Perry Nodelman (1996) eloquently explained:

> Children become what we believe they are; assumptions about childhood have the potential to become self-fulfilling prophecies. The more we believe that children are limited in various ways, the more we deprive them of experiences that might make them less limited. If we believe that children have short attention spans, we won't expose them to long books. If we believe they cannot understand complicated language, we will give them only books with limited vocabularies. If we believe they are susceptible, we will keep them away from interesting books that may contain potentially dangerous ideas or attitudes. And if we believe they like only certain kinds of books, we will not give them access to other kinds. Deprived of the experience of anything more than the little we believe them capable of, children often do learn to be inflexible, intolerant of the complex and the unconventional. (p. 80)

Highlighting the intelligence of children is essential, and if you give them a chance, children will let their engagement shine through. For example, a preservice teacher in one of my classes followed an 8-year-old boy's response to *Tuck Everlasting* (Babbitt, 1975), a story rich in figurative language. While reading the story to her case-study child, she stopped to admire Babbitt's use of similes. At first, she thought the boy was too young to understand the literary concept, but when he demanded a definition, she provided it and asked him to look for similes in their subsequent reading. He picked up on the concept right away, much to the surprise of the preservice teacher, who wrote:

> I was amazed—he picked out almost every one—even ones that I didn't notice. He picked out "the meadows like foam on a painted sea" and "three armchairs and a rocker stood about aimlessly, like strangers at a party, ignoring each other" [as well as many others]. I learned a lesson from this—children are smart and can and want to learn things. (Wolf, Carey, & Mieras, 1996, p. 140)

This preservice teacher's initial assumption was that similes were too complex for a child so young. He was, after all, only 8-years-old. Yet, when the boy challenged her to reveal how the language was crafted for effect, she was "amazed" with how easily he grasped the concept and was able to recognize quite different comparisons.

Children Are Unique. Theories of development that suggest that children's learning moves through increasingly complex stages to full fruition as an adult have been applied to cognitive, moral, social, and linguistic development. Yet, when you talk with and listen to children, they'll often demonstrate their flexibility outside the scope and sequence of knowledge that adults might think developmentally appropriate. As Huck, Hepler, Hickman, and Kiefer (1997) wrote,

> The whole idea of stages . . . suggests a progression of development that might be far more orderly than what occurs in real life. Some feel that the theory fails to describe the intricacy and complexity of children's thinking and might lead teachers to focus on what children are supposedly not able to do, thus falsely lowering expectations. (p. 47)

If we believe that story understanding, metaphor making, and genre shaping apply universally to children, we fail to recognize the power of experience in a child's life that may offset stage-model predictions.

Angela Carey, a preservice teacher in one of my classes, followed the responses of two little boys to fairy tales. Even though one child was younger, he had more experience in literature. He had been read to extensively and had his own library. The older child had few books in his home and little experience with the bedtime story. The differences in how the boys responded to stories appeared as soon as they began reading fractured fairy tales. These tales often break the rules of a familiar fairy tale or retell it from another's point of view, and they imply a reader who is quite knowledgeable of the original tale. When Angela read Scieszka's (1989) *The True Story of the 3 Little Pigs!*, the older child expressed confusion. Angela wrote:

> At first I overlooked this as trivial information until I read him *The Frog Prince Continued* [1991]. In this book, the frog is confronted by many witches borrowed from other fairy tales. The interesting part of this reading to me was that the 7-year-old didn't relate any of the witches to any of the fairy tales that

they belonged to. I had gone through the same procedure as I had for the 5-year-old child when I came upon a new witch. Before I turned the page I would ask him which fairy tale the witch belonged to. The only one that he was close to was "The one with the little boy and little girl" meaning *Hansel and Gretel*. On the other hand, the 5-year-old was able to tell me in great detail the events that took place. He loved the witches that were along the Prince's path, and had no problems recognizing them. (Wolf, Carey, & Mieras, 1996, p. 152)

The irony and humor of multiple fairy tale characters appearing in the same place, but using props, words, and insinuations from other times and places, falls flat without experience with the original stories. As Angela later wrote, "Without the wealth of background knowledge, the language play—with sarcasm and humor a part—is not recognized by the child with little reading experience, but it is relished by the other." Ultimately, Angela came to realize that not all children enjoy 1,000 hours of book reading with friends and family prior to school, but that doesn't mean they are already lost to the system. Instead, a substantial part of her job as a future teacher of literature would be to provide the multiple readings and extended conversations that could help children build connections among texts both on and off the page.

Literary Engagement Is Cognitive Work.   People often argue that pleasure and the stirring of the imagination are the fundamental offerings of children's literature. But pleasure is only a part of literature's potential. Instead, it's essential to look at literature in terms of children's intellectual engagement. Otherwise it might be easily dismissed. On the national scene, literature has taken a back seat to a strong emphasis on *learning to read* rather than *reading to learn*.

Two linked publications demonstrate this point. First, the National Research Council (1998) published *Preventing Reading Difficulties in Young Children*, a highly influential book lauded by newspapers and national experts as the definitive text on early reading. For example, Richard Riley, the U. S. Secretary of Education at the time, suggested that it ". . . clearly defines the key elements all children need in order to become good readers." Yet, literature and literary interpretation are not even listed in the index. Even when the text slips towards storybook reading, the implication is that the end result is enjoyment, "Children who learn from their parents that literacy is a source of enjoyment may be more motivated to persist in their efforts to learn to read despite difficulties they may encounter during the early years" (p. 143). Although the report has many fine points regarding early reading, the place of literature as merely a pleasant motivator to help children get past the difficulties of decoding is troublesome at best.

Following quickly on the heels of this text was the National Reading Panel's (2001) report on *Teaching Children to Read: An Evidence-Based Assessment of the Scientific Research Literature on Reading and Its Implications for Reading Instruction.* Their congressional charge was to follow up on the National Research Council's work and specifically address how reading is most effectively taught. Members of the National Reading Panel broke into sub-groups to study "alphabetics" (with an emphasis on systematic phonics instruction), "fluency" (with an emphasis on children's ability to read with "speed, accuracy, and proper expression"), and "comprehension" (with an emphasis on vocabulary development and comprehension strategy instruction). Again, the place of literature and literary interpretation was woefully absent.

To argue literature from the standpoint of pleasure runs the risk of diminishing its power as rich cognitive work. Even Perry Nodelman (1996)—whose book is entitled *The Pleasures of Children's Literature*—argued that these pleasures represent recognition, connection, and reflection. For example, he discussed "the pleasure of recognizing forms and genres—of seeing similarities between works of literature" as well as "the pleasure of understanding—of seeing how literature not only mirrors life but comments on it and makes us consider the meaning of our own existence" (p. 21). And while Lukens (2003) listed pleasure as the first reward of literature, she quickly moved to the other rewards, such as literature's ability to show human motivation and provide a coherent shape for experience.

Still, I worry that the preeminent place of pleasure may do more harm than good. How easy for people less knowledgeable than Lukens or Nodelman to dismiss literature when it seems most closely associated with fun and games or merely a stepping stone to the real work of learning to read. As Huck, Hepler, Hickman, and Kiefer (1997) suggested, "Because children naturally take such delight in books, we sometimes need to remind ourselves that books can do more for children than entertain them" (p. 8).

Literature Is an Available & Ready Resource.   When we think of children and adults reading together, we're sometimes reminded of the stability of literature because storybooks and the time we set aside for their reading place a double stop-action on the pace of the world:

> The first stop-action comes from the fact that the time for book-reading halts the normal flow of activity of both adult and child.... A second stop-action results from the fact that, unlike the continual and relatively undesignated pace of everyday life, storybooks frame page-by-page words and pictures to make them hold still indefinitely and stand ready for repeated revisits. (Wolf & Heath, 1992, pp. 84–85)

Even though the life of the classroom is stilled during read-alouds and the words and pictures of books remain stable for subsequent viewings, how children take up literature changes with each rereading. The words of written texts are available and ready resources for children's unique connections to other words, altered meanings, and new settings. As Anatole Broyard suggested, "a good book is never finished; it goes on whispering to you from the wall" (Sutton, 2001, p. 281). And those whispers have real life applications, even for very young children.

A preservice teacher in one of my classes followed her five-year-old daughter's connections among books read and life experienced. Her daughter, who loved to be read to, exclaimed, "Read to me, Mom. Read and read and read and read. Wouldn't it be great if we could climb into the book and run around the story?" At age five, her daughter was particularly interested in witches—their physical characteristics, their motivations, and most important, how they could be defeated. She weighed the deaths of three witches—being pushed in the oven as in *Hansel and Gretel* (Grimm Brothers, 1988), jumping into water as in *Heckedy Peg* (Wood, 1987), and being doused with water as in *The Wizard of Oz* (Baum, 1900)—and ultimately was able to make use of this information. Her mother wrote:

> One Saturday morning we had to wait for quite some time for the doors to open at the downtown post office. When both the east and south doors opened at once, people streamed in and merged to form one line in front of the counter. One particularly stressed-out woman loudly and shrewishly began complaining that people had jumped in front of her in line. She then shoved her way in front of several shocked patrons. My daughter pulled me down so she could whisper in my ear. "*Mom, we should throw some water on her.*" It took me a second to make the connection—MELT THE WITCH! We laughed so hard we had tears

flooding our eyes. Other people in line must have thought we'd taken leave of our senses.

Together, my daughter and I have experienced worlds of imagination, animal homes and witches' lairs, problem solving, and the neutralization of real-life shrews. Besides bringing us closer as parent and child, I believe our shared reading has enabled her to gain a greater ability to merge literature, language and thought, and to some degree helped her see that literature brings with it the tools she will need to empower her in life. I feel that just as she requested, we did indeed, "climb into the book and run around the story," and we have both climbed out a little stronger and a little wiser. (Wolf, Carey, & Mieras, 1966, p. 152)

A central part of climbing into a book and running around the story is the ability to make connections among texts on and off the page. More important than the connections themselves, however, is the emphasis on what the act of making connections actually does. Thus, the experience of reading children's literature with adults extends far beyond the precise moments of reading to grasping the creative and continuing possibilities of literary language, character, setting, plot, and theme for children's own literary inventions and their relations with friends, family, and even frightening strangers.

Critical Perspectives

The idea of grasping the creative possibilities of literature brings us to the multiple and unique ways in which literary theorists analyze text. Each theorist, depending on his or her stance, interprets literature in an attempt to construct meaning. There are numerous ways of parsing out and presenting critical views. Anna Soter (1999), for example, presented an overview of 13 critical perspectives and an analysis of several young adult novels viewed through selected stances. She cautioned that the reasoning behind aligning particular novels with particular perspectives is based on her central question, *"What do I want my students to learn from this experience?"* (p. 13). Similarly, Deborah Appleman (2000) looked at carefully selected high school English texts through a variety of critical lenses, and she argued that secondary students should learn about literary theory to become more adept in their interpretations.

I'd like to make the same argument for younger children, because limiting children's access to theory underestimates their intelligence. At the beginning of Appleman's chapter on multiple perspectives, she quoted Bertolt Brecht, "A man with one theory is lost. He needs several of them, or lots! He should stuff them in his pockets like newspapers" (p. 12). Children, too, should be encouraged to stuff their pockets.

The image of children and pockets brings us back to *Charlotte's Web* (White, 1952). In another scene from the novel, Fern (who originally rescued Wilbur from the ax) and her brother Avery have just been pestering their aunt for a piece of blueberry pie. She feeds them and then scoots them out of the house, and Fern, with a crown of daisies in her hair, and Avery, with a frog stuffed in his pocket, climb to the hayloft to ride the barn swing:

> Mr. Zuckerman had the best swing in the county. It was a single long piece of heavy rope tied to the beam over the north doorway. At the bottom end of the rope was a fat knot to sit on. It was arranged so that you could swing without being pushed. You climbed a ladder to the hayloft. Then, holding the rope, you stood at the edge and looked down, and were scared and dizzy. Then you straddled the knot, so that it acted as a seat. Then you got up all your nerve, took a deep breath, and jumped. For a second you seemed to be falling to the barn floor far below, but then suddenly the rope would begin to catch you, and you would sail through the barn door going a mile a minute, with the wind whistling in your eyes and ears and hair. Then you would zoom upward into the sky, and look up at the clouds, and the rope would twist and you would twist and turn with the rope. Then you would drop down, down, down out of the sky and come sailing back into the barn almost into the hayloft, then sail out again (not quite so far this time), then in again (not quite so high), then out again, then in again, then out, then in; and then you'd jump off and fall down and let somebody else try it.
>
> Mothers for miles around worried about Zuckerman's swing. They feared some child would fall off. But no child ever did. Children almost always hang onto things tighter than their parents think they will. (pp. 68–69)

As you read this passage a number of things may have occurred to you. You may have wondered about White's own experiences with barn swings and children. You may have admired the craft of White's prose, or you might have thought of other written texts that have similar writing styles or points to make. You may have even remembered a time in your life when you had a similarly thrilling experience. Or perhaps you wondered about the perspective, especially the contrast between children's and parents' views of Zuckerman's swing.

Kinds of Criticism

These ways of thinking about a literary passage align with particular forms of literary criticism: (a) *genetic criticism* with a focus on the author, (b) *formal criticism* with highly specific attention to the text itself, (c) *text-to-text criticism* with an emphasis on how one written text fits within the larger body of literature, (d) *transactional criticism* with an eye on the reader's interaction with the text, and (e) *sociocultural criticism* with an emphasis on cultural, political, and social-historical perspectives. Although criticism takes many forms, I believe these five have special strengths that make them especially effective in classrooms for young people. In the following sections, I define each type of criticism and demonstrate the analytic stance each kind of critic would take towards White's swing passage in the context of the entire text of *Charlotte's Web*. I also offer you a potential "tool" to help you "see" from that point of view. (See Table 1.1).

Genetic Criticism. This critical stance emphasizes a view of the literary work as primarily a reflection of the author's life and times, and the term calls to mind images of heredity and lineage from the author to his or her work. Keesey (1987) explained, "Poems are caused by people.... To ask what a poem means is, on this view, to ask what the author meant when he or she created it" (p. 9). Still, he continued:

> ... the inquiry widens to include a great deal more than the strictly biographical. For the genetic critic, after all, is by definition a student of causes, and if a poem is the product of an author and the author is the product of an age, then nothing less than a full understanding of that age—the author's entire political, social, and intellectual milieu—is required if we are to fully understand that author's art. (p. 11)

In relation to White's swing passage as well as the larger job of interpreting the entire book, the tool I would offer you is a copy of *The Annotated Charlotte's Web* by Peter Neumeyer (1994). If you had this book at hand, you could look at pictures of E. B. White, read annotations of the swing passage, and peruse the other annotations as well as several of White's essays. In your reading, you would discover that as a boy White spent time in a neighbor's barn, swinging on a rope swing from the loft. You would learn about his vast respect for youth, especially in his essay, "On Writing for Children." And you would read

TABLE 1.1

Key Forms of Literary Criticism

Criticism	Definition	Tools
Genetic	Genetic criticism emphasizes a view of the literary work as primarily a reflection of the author's life and times. Keesey (1987) explained, "Poems are caused by people.... To ask what a poem means is, on this view, to ask what the author meant when he or she created it" (p. 9).	*Annotations & essays of E. B. White for author study* *The* ANNOTATED CHARLOTTE'S WEB *Introduction and Notes by* PETER F. NEUMEYER
Formal	Formal criticism depends on close readings in order to understand how textual elements work together to create a unified whole. Clearly avoiding the "intentional" as well as the "affective" fallacies, formal critics believe that the meaning of a text lies in the *language* of the text itself.	*Swing passage & markers for a "close reading"* Then you would drop down, down, down out of the sky and come sailing back into the barn almost into the hayloft, then sail out again (not quite so far this time), then in again (not quite so high), then out again, then in again, then out, then in; and then . . . (White, 1952, p. 69)
Text-to-Text	Text-to-text criticism suggests that interpretation depends on how a text fits within the larger body of literature. Such comparisons look at texts by the same author, in the same genre, using similar stylistic devices, or at myriad other potential connections among *written* as well as *media* texts	*Other literary texts for comparison and contrast* Amos & Boris by William Steig Meet Danitra Brown by Nikki Grimes
Transactional	Rosenblatt (1994) developed transactional criticism in which the reader brings individual life experience to the text that acts as a guide. The "poem" is the result—a new understanding that becomes a "part of the ongoing stream of [the reader's] life experience" (p. 12).	*A mirror for reflecting on reader response*
Sociocultural	Sociocultural criticism concentrates on the political and socio-historical dimensions of response. Within this view, critics interrogate literature in terms of whose perspectives, values, and norms are voiced and whose views are silenced. Questions of power and authority are key.	*A doll for developing a view of the child* *What's the perspective on children?*

about how, as an adult, White raised and butchered his own pigs, but he was increasingly bothered by his "double-dealing." He wrote, "It used to be clear to me, slopping a pig, that as far as the pig was concerned I could not be counted on, and this, as I say, troubled me. Anyway, the theme of *Charlotte's Web* is that a pig shall be saved, and I have an idea that somewhere deep inside me there was a wish to that effect" (p. 237). One of White's most famous essays is entitled "Death of a Pig," which recounts a much more realistic and dismal outcome than Wilbur's.

My students also learn that White discovered his own Aranea Cavatica on his farm and studied her for several days as she spun her egg sac and deposited her eggs inside. He even packed her and the egg sac up when he returned to New York, and when the babies hatched they built their webs across his bedroom dresser:

> They strung tiny lines from my comb to my brush, from my brush to my mirror, and from my mirror to my nail scissors. They were very busy and almost invisible, they were so small. We all lived together happily for a couple of weeks, and then somebody whose duty it was to dust my dresser balked, and I broke up the show. (p. 238)

In genetic criticism, the tiny lines between the author's biography and the work exist not only in reality, but also in the imagination. Authors stretch beyond what they've actually experienced to the myriad possibilities available both in life and in dreams.

In your classroom, you can make extensive use of genetic criticism. You can ask your students to do author studies, and there are myriad sources available for discovering the details of authors' lives as well as insights into their motivations for writing particular texts (Jenkins, 1999). One extensive collection, Anita Silvey's (1995) *Children's Books and Their Creators*, offered biographical details on twentieth-century authors and illustrators from A to Z, and her newer, paperback *Essential Guide* (2002) is even more accessible. The Horn Book Association for Library Service to Children (2001) compiled biographical sketches and acceptance speeches for Newbery and Caldecott winners. Conferences and celebrations compile insightful reflections from famous authors such as Betsy Hearn's (1993) edited volume of essays by such luminaries as Virginia Hamilton, Maurice Sendak, Katherine Paterson, and Trina Schart Hyman. The recent influx of online sites exploring the lives and times of authors past and present as well as the colorful home pages designed by or for authors and illustrators offer you and your children the opportunity to access information in a twinkling if the technology is available.

Still, there are problems with genetic criticism. It's hard to know what authors are hoping to accomplish in their prose, especially when they are not sure themselves. For example, E. B. White wrote with more than a little tongue in cheek, "I haven't told why I wrote the book, but I haven't told why I sneeze, either. A book is a sneeze" (Neumeyer, 1994, p. 238). While I'd argue that White knew a lot about why he wrote the book, getting into the mind of an author is not a straightforward task. As Terry Eagleton (1983) cautioned, "There are obvious problems with trying to determine what is going on in somebody's head. . . . For one thing, a great many things are likely to be going on in an author's head at the time of writing" (p. 68).

On the other hand, genetic criticism can be vastly informative, as long as it's not viewed as the one and only way of approaching a text. Rosenblatt (1994) argued, "What is more natural than to sense the author behind the words to which we have vividly responded?" (p. 112). Reading about E. B. White is wonderfully informative, but it's not the end all and be all to interpreting *Charlotte's Web* with children. It's an angle, not the whole view. Thus, in maintaining your seat on a swing as well as in incorporating theoretical views into your classroom life, the question is largely one of balance.

Formal Criticism. In formal criticism, readers rely on "close readings" in order to understand how the text works in both smaller passages and larger structural chunks to create a unified whole. Keesey (1987) suggested that this stance argues for the "'objective' study of poetic art free from the entangling difficulties and irrelevancies of author and reader psychology" (p. 73). Indeed, formal critics would dismiss any discussion of the author's mindset as an "intentional fallacy" because you can't really know the author's intentions. They'd also reject any talk of the reader's personal response as an "affective fallacy" because your emotions would blur your ability to see your way through to a "correct" interpretation of literature. For formal critics, the meaning lies in the language of the text itself. According to Eagleton (1983), "To think of literature as the Formalists do is really to think of all literature as *poetry*" (p. 6). Keesey (1987) agreed with this characterization: "What is the meaning of an image, a motif, a symbol, of a character or a pattern or a scene? In each case we must see how the element fits into its context, how it functions in the poem. To investigate these relationships and the meanings they produce is the chief task of formal analysis" (p. 75).

The tool I would give you for this critical stance would be the swing passage itself and a highlighting marker. At first, you might feel a little stumped by the task, but as you leaned closer and closer into the text, you'd start to see the extraordinary skill with which White crafted this piece. It would help you even more if you were to read it aloud, breathlessly reading through the rush of words as long as the length of the rope swing itself, and then pause, taking in White's shortened phrases separated by parenthetical comments, semi-colons, and commas, as the swing slowed to a final stop. White's writing is renown, but this passage is particularly famous for how the prose mimics the action of the swing. Once you discover it, you might be more convinced that close readings have much to reveal.

All too often, criticism like this is reserved for the work of A.P. English students in high school. Teachers of young children often content themselves with the textual elements of character, setting, and plot, whereas those with older children tentatively add theme to this traditional trio. Experts in children's literature, however, have long paid attention to the style and tone associated with the specific language of a text. And expert teachers know that a focus on language is key in helping children learn how to appreciate quality writing as well as craft their own narrative pieces.

Indeed, the increased interest in how to help children with their writing has been the impetus for a number of attempts to link published literature with children's authorial accomplishments. The argument is that children's writing will improve if they are given multiple opportunities to talk analytically about text. Writing assessment programs such as "6-Trait Writing" (Spandel, 2000) lean heavily on literature to make their points about "voice," "word choice," "organization," and the like. Most recently, Katie Wood Ray (1999) has given us *Wondrous Words*, making the connections between reading and writing even clearer with its focus on authors' craft. I discuss these arguments in more detail in chapter 6, but it's important to understand the critical links between formal criticism and what it can do for young readers and writers.

As with every form of criticism, there is a downside. First and foremost, formal criticism had a stranglehold on classrooms for decades, especially in high schools and universities. The grip was particularly pernicious in its dependence on "classic" literature—shutting out alternative voices and perspectives. For example, Arthur Applebee (1991) conducted a survey of secondary schools, asking the chairs of English departments to list the books they required. The results were disheartening, for the most frequently required books included *Romeo and Juliet, Macbeth, Huckleberry Finn*, and other very familiar titles. On these results, Applebee pointed out:

> All but one of these are the work of white, male, Anglo-Saxon authors—a situation that has changed not at all since [an earlier] survey in 1907.... Although it was discouraging to see so little diversity in the top 10 titles, it was even more discouraging to find a similar homogeneity in the top 30 and top 50. (p. 233)

My own choice of using White's *Charlotte's Web* as a touchstone book for this chapter could easily be accused of the same flaw, but as you look across the totality of texts I reference and explore in this volume, you'll see much more variety.

A second legitimate complaint against formal criticism was based on the fact that teachers often stood in front of their classrooms and expounded on the meaning of a text, positioning their students as passive recipients of text interpretation. As Marshall (2000) explained, "the teacher's goal, through an insistence on closer reading of the formal structures in a text, was to help develop particular, socially valuable kinds of response" (p. 386). And, of course, when only certain kinds of responses are valued, it becomes difficult for anyone but experts to interpret.

Still, the potential oppression in formal criticism should not lead you to dismiss the power of looking closely at a text's language. How an author selects and places words and phrases to craft character, reveal setting, process plot, and unveil theme is an art, and it deserves close inspection. The trick to applying this criticism in classrooms, however, is to open the museum doors to alternative voices and multiple possibilities in interpretation. Teachers cannot be curators of text—keeping children at a distance with velvet ropes and glass cases. Instead, you should invite children to help set up the exhibits and discuss the varying interpretations that could be applied to each piece of art.

Text-to-Text Criticism.   Text-to-text criticism suggests that interpretation depends on how a text fits within the larger body of literature. Rosenblatt (1994) explained, "Sometimes we find ourselves comparing the potentialities of this text with other texts by the same author, sometimes with other texts of the same genre, sometimes with the whole body of remembered readings" (p. 152). Thus, "text-to-text" criticism focuses on comparisons and contrasts in an author's body of work, or in the same genre, or in the stylistic devices selected, or in the vast array of other potential connections among written as well as media texts.

The tools I would give you for this stance are two picture books, and I would ask you to look across the books in search of deep connections. *Meet Danitra Brown* (Grimes, 1994) is a delightful set of poems about two friends, Zuri Jackson and Danitra Brown, who stick with each other through good times and bad. Although their unsentimental devotion provides an apt link to *Charlotte's Web*, you will find the books are also similar in their poetic celebration of the glory of everyday life. Although the illustrations in the two texts are very different, you will also find there is gentleness in both that captures the action as well as the affection.

Amos & Boris (Steig, 1971) offers a second textual link to *Charlotte's Web* because of the improbable friendship between two animal characters—Amos the mouse and Boris the whale. Amos is traveling in search of himself when he tumbles off the deck of his boat and nearly drowns. Boris saves him and the two become fast friends though they are destined to part. The ending of the story has close and tender parallels to Charlotte and Wilbur's parting. The story is also wonderfully linked in writing style and love of nature, for like White, Steig is a wizard with words and is fascinated by the beauty of the surrounding world. Consider the following: "One night, in a phosphorescent sea, he marveled at the sight of some whales spouting luminous water; and later, lying on the deck of his boat gazing at the immense, starry sky, the tiny mouse Amos, a little speck of a living thing in the vast living universe, felt thoroughly akin to it all."

As a teacher of literature, you may feel thoroughly akin to text-to-text criticism, and if you adopt this stance, you would carefully select texts in literature units to reiterate and emphasize potential connections. You would typically choose a central text and then select other stories that complement it. Regie Routman (2000) called the initial texts "anchor books that would be supported by conceptually related supplemental books" (p. 65). She argued: "Supplemental books would be used to expand key concepts as well as to provide instructional reading material at a student's reading level. In that way, all students in any particular grade level would be discussing similar concepts and themes, but they would be reading a variety of books" (p. 66).

In considering text-to-text criticism, it may be useful to think of a building. You begin with an anchor book that serves as a foundation for the building of

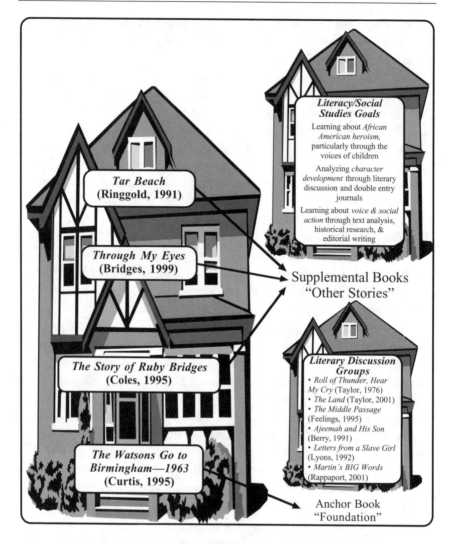

FIG. 1.1. "Building" a Literacy/Social Studies Unit on African American Heroism.

a literacy unit, and then you select supplemental books to add on the other stories, both literally and metaphorically. Figure 1.1 offers an example of a literacy/social studies unit on African American heroism designed for 10- to 14-year old students. In this unit, *The Watsons Go to Birmingham—1963* (Curtis, 1995) serves as our foundation text. The other stories or supplemental texts build up from there, and note that *The Story of Ruby Bridges* (Coles, 1995), *Through my Eyes* (Bridges, 1999), and *Tar Beach* (Ringgold, 1991) are all picture books. If we continued building up, many more stories could be added, and some exemplary titles are listed in the box for "Literary Discussion Groups." Concentrating on African American heroism, particularly through children's voices, would be our central goal, but analyzing character development and learning about voice and social action are critical as well.

Almost all of these books feature a child protagonist who meets racism and prejudice and then makes heroic efforts to make positive changes in his or her world. The foundation text from Curtis (1995) served as our inspiration. In the epilogue to his powerful novel, he wrote about "true American heroes. They are the boys and girls, the women and men who have seen that things are wrong and have not been afraid to ask 'Why can't we change this?'" (p. 210). All of our complementary texts were carefully selected to let Curtis's question echo through the hearts and minds of the children we teach—children we hope will be our new heroes.

According to Hartman and Hartman (1993), literary texts can be arranged in several ways:

- **Companion texts** are intended by the author to be read as a collection.
- **Complementary texts** . . . can be assembled to explore various aspects of a topic or theme.
- **Synoptic texts** . . . [allow you] to select a single story, idea, or event and read across the versions, variations, and accounts of it.
- **Disruptive texts** present conflicting or alternative perspectives on the same topic, theme, event, or idea.
- **Rereading texts** . . . is to ask students to visit and revisit the same text. (pp. 204–206)

There are, no doubt, other ways to arrange texts, but this list offers a good variety.

What might be the negatives of text-to-text criticism when there are so many positive features? The most important one is the possibility that the connections among texts are only tentative or made "in name only." An example might be linking texts simply because they are about African Americans or about friendship. If a teacher selects texts solely on the superficial aspects of a topic or theme, the connections might stay on the surface rather than explore the deeper possibilities. Because associations among written texts are so critical in aiding children's interpretations, you must choose both your anchor books and supplemental texts with great care.

Transactional Criticism. Louise Rosenblatt (1994) is generally recognized as the first voice in transactional criticism. In this stance, the reader brings individual life experience to the text that acts as a guide, and the result is what Rosenblatt calls a "poem," although her view of the poem is quite different from that of a formal critic.

> The poem, then, must be thought of as an event in time. It is not an object or an ideal entity. It happens during a coming-together, a compenetration, of a reader and a text. The reader brings to the text his past experience and present personality. Under the magnetism of the ordered symbols of the text, he marshals his resources and crystallizes out from the stuff of memory, thought, and feeling a new order, a new experience, which he sees as the poem. This becomes part of the ongoing stream of his life experience, to be reflected on from any angle important to him as a human being. (p. 12)

The transactional process between text and reader is active and highly personal. It is an aesthetic experience in which individual readers' life experiences help to shape textual understandings.

Rosenblatt placed the reading event on a continuum from *efferent* reading to *aesthetic* reading (see Fig. 1.2). She based her argument on the differences between expository texts (e.g., textbooks, newspaper articles, formulas, recipes) and literary works (e.g., poetry, plays, fantasy, realistic fiction). She also differentiated the reader's involvement in these varying texts. In efferent reading, "the reader's attention is focused primarily on what will remain

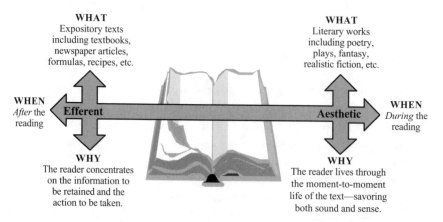

FIG. 1.2.   Rosenblatt's Continuum.

as the residue *after* the reading—the information to be acquired" (p. 23). In contrast, in aesthetic reading, "the reader's primary concern is with what happens *during* the actual reading event" (p. 24).

In children's literature, a case in point is the way you might approach *Charlotte's Web*. In reading White's text, you're not so interested in the information about spiders, even though White offers many scientific facts about this species, including the technical names for their leg parts, their eating habits, the ways they build a web, and their sheer variety. Instead, you are intrigued by the language, and how it inscribes the relationship between Wilbur and Charlotte (who also happens to be a spider). And as you read, you're constantly connecting the text to your own experiences.

Still, it is a critical tenet of this book to stress the importance of the aesthetic reading event past the actual physical contact with the story—for the meeting of reader and text involves not only what we bring to the text, but also what we take from it. And this residue does not have to be limited to factual information. Those who love *Charlotte's Web* carry away images of pastoral life and loyalty as well as lyrical language. In my observations of children, I've seen them carry texts around in their heads far beyond any direct contact with a particular book. Through verbal references, metaphorical connections, and socio-dramatic play, children extend literature into their emerging identities, their worlds of friends and family, and their encounters with future written and oral texts.

When studying transactional criticism, the "tool" I would give you is a mirror, and you could read the "swing passage" with your own personal experiences in mind. True, you might attend to the rhythm of the language, but rather than lean in closer to analyze just how White accomplishes this rhythm (as a formal critic would), you would lean out to capture the rush of your own memories. You might recall your experiences as a child—the motion of a swing, the feel of a rope in your hand, or other sensations of freedom and movement. As you continue to reflect, you might think of stories of how your mother and father tried to protect you from dangerous activities and laugh at some of your daring exploits. If you're a parent, you might marvel at how you have now taken on the role of protective parent yourself, and how hesitant you'd be to let your own children jump from a hayloft with only a rope between them and the barn floor below.

The mirror has its limitations as a tool, however, for it could be misinterpreted as placing too much weight on the individual reader, stressing that his or her reflection is the only thing that matters. This view is more closely associated with those reader-response critics who are interested in the psychology of the reader. Perhaps that's why Rosenblatt prefers the term "transactional," because her emphasis is on the encounter between the reader and the text. Both are necessary to the aesthetic experience, and both are changeable depending on shifts in context. Rosenblatt (1994) explained:

> "The poem" comes into being in the live circuit set up between the reader and "the text." As with the elements of an electric circuit, each component of the reading process functions by virtue of the presence of the others. A specific reader and a specific text at a specific time and place: change any of these, and there occurs a different circuit, a different event—a different poem. (p. 14)

So what are the negative aspects of transactional criticism? I believe there are three, though unfortunately they stem from misinterpretations of Rosenblatt's intent rather than her actual stance. The first has to do with an exaggerated preeminence of the reader, which might lead you to believe that *any* response from a child is as good as another. Rosenblatt never meant to espouse an atmosphere of "anything goes." Although she clearly argued that there could never be a single or "correct" text interpretation, she stressed that readers should be able to return to the text in order to substantiate and justify their conclusions.

A second negative aspect is related to the first, and has to do with the preeminence of this kind of criticism—especially the focus on *reader response* rather than *transaction*. While formal criticism held sway in classrooms for years, the pendulum has shifted in the last two decades. Teachers are far more likely to look for ways to help children and young adolescents connect personally and emotionally to text than to introduce them to other kinds of criticism. A teacher in one of my classes told me of a worksheet she'd seen that asked students to read a passage and then list "five feelings" as well as "five connections" to their own life experiences. This kind of over-the-top swing to personal response fails to take into account how a child's connection to a text could be heightened by a study of the author, by a closer look at the language of the text, or by links to other written and media texts—forms of criticism that I discussed in previous sections.

Another negative aspect could be found in the interpretation of "self" in its most narrow sense, because when you look in the mirror, it's not you alone that you see. Instead, you are reflected in terms of culture, class, and gender, living in a particular time, place, and situation. Rosenblatt was well aware of the social and political positioning of the reader, but critics who initially looked solely at the reader are now looking beyond the immediate reflection to the wider world. And for that perspective, I turn to our fifth and final kind of criticism.

Sociocultural Criticism. This last critical stance focuses on the political and sociohistorical dimensions of response. Within this view, critics interrogate literature in terms of whose perspectives, values, and norms are voiced and whose views are silenced. Questions of power and authority are key—as critics push against the hidden assumptions of a text and resist the status quo. And a huge part of this resistance occurs in the continuing canon wars:

> On the one hand are those who argue that the canon has been established on primarily aesthetic grounds—that the texts located there are of proven literary value—and should be studied because they represent, in [Matthew] Arnold's phrase, "the best that has been thought and said." ... On the other hand are those who argue that the canon represents an elitist, highly selective group of texts that grossly underrepresents those who have traditionally been without political or cultural visibility (primarily women and minorities) and that serves best those with already established economic and political power (primarily white men). ... (Marshall, 2000, pp. 383–384)

As I explained earlier, the texts taught at the secondary level have changed little over the last century, and this lack of change is at the heart of the canon conflict.

The situation is only slightly better in classrooms for children and young adolescents. In 1972, Nancy Larrick wrote an article entitled "The all-white world of children's books" to demonstrate the dominance of a Eurocentric view. Though there have been times of hope and upward swings in multicultural children's literature, the downward shift often seems to be sadly inevitable, and of the 5,000 children's books published a year, very few are devoted to diversity.

The "one step forward, two steps back" progression in the children's book world also applies to issues of class and gender. Children in stories are portrayed all too often as safe and secure in their two-parent family households, surrounded by books and toys in their own well-appointed rooms. Boys are still three times more likely to appear in award-winning books than girls (Hurley & Chadwick, 1998) as well as be three times more active than girls in children's literature in general (Kortenhaus & Demarest, 1993). I discuss issues of culture, class, and gender in greater detail in chapters 4 and 5, but for now, it is enough to say that sociocultural critics often question the stereotypical representations of children in literature.

When studying sociocultural criticism, the tool I would give you is a little stuffed doll. Imagine that she is European American; she is blonde; she has sky blue eyes; and she is dressed in a starched pink frock with an apron tied around her waist. Pinned to her apron is a question: "What's the perspective on children?" Using the doll as a metaphor, you could begin to look closely at Fern and her brother, Avery, in *Charlotte's Web* and notice that the children take on expected gender roles. When they come into their aunt's kitchen, Avery is carrying a frog and Fern has flowers in her hair. Fern scolds Avery when his frog jumps into her aunt's soapy dishpan and for the fact that he manages to get pie all over himself. When the aunt scoots them out the door, Avery suggests a swing in the barn, and Fern follows without question. Avery takes a swing first, with frog in tow in his pocket, and Fern has to yell at him to get her turn. After an hour taking turns on the swing, Avery suggests building a tree house for his frog, but Fern wants to visit Wilbur, and this time Avery follows.

As you look closely at the text, you might come to question some of the givens in the book. Fern and Avery are European American, living in a two-parent household just down the road from their aunt and uncle. Their existence is one of rather idyllic farm life, and they have the leisure time to swing on a rope, collect frogs, and sit on a stool watching the animals for hours. When Fern speaks to her mother about the animals' conversations, Ms. Avery has the time as well as the inclination to visit the male family doctor for some sage advice. Each time Ms. Avery frets about Fern, she is given wise council by either her husband or Dr. Dorian. In one of the most startling shifts in the book, however, Fern gives up her link with her imaginative life to ride the Ferris wheel with Henry Fussy. She neither attends Wilbur's triumphant award ceremony, nor comments on Charlotte's death. Indeed, after she runs off to meet Henry a second time, she disappears from the book entirely, except for the smallest aside.

The stereotypical representations of Fern and Avery might spur you to analyze *why* these portrayals are so predictable. You might consider the date of publication and reflect on the gendered expectations in the 1950s as well as the fact that multicultural literature was almost nonexistent at the time. On the other hand, you might notice how Fern defies certain expectations in terms of her dress, how she spends her time, and especially her willingness to stand up for her beliefs. You might concentrate on the metaphorical implications of White's ending statement for the swing passage, "Children almost always hang onto things tighter than their parents think they will." And it might cause you to wonder if White, though constrained by his own culture, class, and gender as well as the time in which he wrote, wasn't pushing against established notions of children as innocent, naïve, and in need of constant protection.

The debate arising from sociocultural criticism is one of the hottest in education today. In particular, E. D. Hirsch (1987) has sent out dire warnings of what might happen if we fail to teach the "classics," arguing that such a dangerous step would deny children the common knowledge they need to be educated citizens in contemporary American society. His numerous follow-up books take individual grade levels and list out details of what every child "needs to know." The difficulty in this stance, however, is: Who gets to decide what children need to know? If certain books are elevated, what books are denied publication? If certain views are celebrated, whose voices are silenced? And if certain virtues are extolled (Bennett, 1993), whose values are rendered invisible?

I debated these questions long and hard in selecting *Charlotte's Web* as the central text for this chapter. The book is, after all, over 50 years old, and its representations of children's lives are at quite a distance from many contemporary children today. Even more important, there are any number of magnificent texts that I could have used instead—books with well-drawn characters, absorbing plots, deeply rendered themes, and jewel-like craft in terms of language. Mildred Taylor's (1976) *Roll of Thunder, Hear My Cry* or her latest masterpiece *The Land* (2001) come immediately to mind, but so does Gary Soto's (1990) *Baseball in April and Other Stories*, especially for his extraordinary use of metaphor and the contemporary nature of his tales. I might have chosen An Na's (2001) new award winner, *A Step from Heaven*, for its achingly beautiful images of Korean American immigrant life or Louise Erdrich's *The Birchbark House* for its astonishing portrayal of a Native American family's life and love as well as their strength in the face of adversity. I might have decided on Jacqueline Woodson's (1994) tale of two friends, Lena and Marie, in *I Hadn't Meant to Tell You This*, for they manage to cross the boundaries of class and culture in order to connect. (See the "Recommended Tradebooks" section at the end of this chapter for brief annotations of each of these books.)

All of these books could be viewed easily from the range of critical stances I offer here. In terms of genetic criticism, these are famous authors and much has been written about them. Though An Na is new to the scene, it would be fascinating to find out more about her. All of these writers have exquisite craft, making their books fine candidates for formal criticism. With the exception that *A Step from Heaven* is An Na's first novel, the authors are prolific, and many have built-in text-to-text connections. Taylor's many novels center on the life of one African American family, and Erdrich's *The Birchbark House* is the first of a series of four novels. Woodson's (1999) sequel, *Lena*, tells what happened when she and her sister ran away from home, and Soto's many books—from novels to picture books to poetry—concentrate on the lives of contemporary Mexican Americans. Of course, text-to-text criticism could extend far beyond what the authors themselves have written. For example, you can look back at Fig. 1.1 for an idea on how Taylor's books would mesh with several other texts on African American heroism.

Turning to transactional criticism, children would have no trouble relating to these novels, and even if the situations and scenes were far distanced from their own lives, the emotional quality of the characters' dilemmas would help them to connect. Finally, in terms of sociocultural criticism, the interplay of culturally and historically situated meanings in these novels and short stories would lead children into deep discussion.

Still, as much as I love these books (and others!), I chose *Charlotte's Web*, mainly because it is a book I have loved my whole life. In your own selection of books for your children, be guided by your own affection for particular texts, but don't let that keep you from widening your repertoire, especially because what you like may not always match what might be inspirational books for your children. Keeping children at the forefront of your text selection will make their engagement in literature even deeper, especially when the texts allow them to enter into conversations about the sociocultural world around them.

Keep in mind, however, there are drawbacks to sociocultural criticism, and one is the overanalysis of texts for stereotypes—ferreting out any faults in the portrayal of culture, class, and gender, and potentially taking a stance in the shadow of censorship. Critics who have very different views toward texts—from the political left as well as the right—often come perilously close to denying children access based on their own critical rejection of the voices and values portrayed. When feminist critics chop at *The Giving Tree* (Silverstein, 1964) for representing the tree as a female who gives and gives and gives (McClure, 1995), you might find yourself defensive about a text you love. And when critics trumpet the sexist, racist, and colonial defects in De Brunhoff's (1931) *The Story of Babar, the Little Elephant* (Kohl, 1995), you might put your foot down. "Enough," you cry. "For goodness sake! He's just an elephant in a nice green suit!"

Charmingly attired or not, books have remarkable power to leave a lasting impression. As Kohl explained:

> I wouldn't ban or burn *Babar*, or pull it from libraries. But buy it? No. I see no reason to go out of one's way to make *Babar* available to children, primarily because I don't see much critical reading going on in the schools, and children don't need to be propagandized about colonialism, sexism, or racism. . . . I believe *Babar* would best be relegated to the role of collector's item, an item in a museum of stereotypes. . . . If there were only a few books a child had access to, it would be foolish to select any that have racial, class, or sexual bias woven into their content and imagery as positive things, no matter how charming or "classic" they are. (pp. 28–29)

Still, I believe the key phrase to consider in Kohl's quote is "critical reading," and sociocultural critics are strong advocates of just this kind of conversation. According to Rudine Sims Bishop (1997), even the most offensive of books "can offer opportunities for careful, sensitive, critical discussions of their derogatory images and the purposes they serve" (p. 18).

Analyzing *Charlotte's Web* in terms of culture, class, and gender does not persuade me to love the book less. Instead, I place my affection for this classic text in a sociocultural context, and I look for ways I can open up critical conversations with children. Conversations centered on more problematic books can be harder. Your skill as a teacher is more in demand, and the harm that might come to children who see themselves cast as stereotypes is more likely. However, if you handle these books with care, such conversations can help all students to "reflect on [literature] in all its rich diversity, to prompt them to ask questions about who we are now as a society and how we arrived at our present state, and to inspire them to actions that will create and maintain social justice" (Bishop, 1997, p. 19).

Summary

In this chapter, I offer an overview of literary interpretation, defining literature through sound, metaphor, and structure, but I move well beyond the delivery system to look at how we limit as well as expand children's engagement with text. I also present five kinds of criticism for consideration in K–8 classrooms. Each critical approach has its own strengths and weaknesses, but a central tenet of this chapter is that if you combine critical perspectives (depending on the child, the text, and the context), you will enhance children's uptake of literature. Even Louise Rosenblatt (1994), who feels you must begin with transactional criticism, saw the benefit of looking through other critical lenses:

> Coming to the critic after one's own transaction with the text, one can be helped to realize more keenly the character of that experience. Like other readers, critics may reveal the text's potentialities for responses different—perhaps more sensitive and more complex—from our own. The critic may have developed a fuller and more articulate awareness of the literary, ethical, social, or philosophic concepts that [s/]he brings to the literary transaction, and may thus provide us with a basis for uncovering the assumptions underlying our own responses. In this way, critics may function not as stultifying models to be echoed but as teachers, stimulating us to grow in our own capacities to participate creatively and self-critically in literary transactions. (p. 148)

It's true that authors can be surprised by or even skeptical of how critics interpret their work. In reading a critical analysis of *Charlotte's Web,* E.B. White said, "It is an extraordinary document, any way you look at it, and it makes me realize how lucky I was (when I was writing the book) that I didn't know what in hell was going on" (Neumeyer, 1994, p. xv).

Still, figuring out what's going on in a book and how it connects to the author (genetic criticism), the language (formal criticism), other written and media texts (text-to-text criticism), the self (transactional criticism), and the world (sociocultural criticism) is exactly what makes literary engagement so essential and so exciting. Think of it in terms of White's swing passage. He eloquently captures the exhilaration of childhood—riding a swing with the wind in our hair and eyes and ears—and then slowly, slowing us down to a full stop, with the satisfactory suggestion that despite adult worries, children inevitably know how to hang on. Expanding literary uptake through critical analysis is complex to be sure, but I assure you: Children know how to hang on.

BOOKS FOR THE PROFESSIONAL

Neumeyer, P. F. (1994). *The annotated Charlotte's web.* New York: HarperCollins. If you love *Charlotte's Web,* you'll love this book, for it annotates the children's classic with rich detail. It also includes informative essays by E.B. White about the creation of the book as well as his views on children and writing.

Nodelman, P. (1996). *The pleasures of children's literature.* New York: Longman. A notable scholar in children's literature, Perry Nodelman outlines common assumptions about children that often deprive them of opportunities for substantive engagement in literature. He presents a powerful argument for reversing this trend. Each chapter also includes "explorations" in which he invites the reader to argue with him, making the book all the more engaging.

Marcus, L. S. (1998). *Dear genius: The letters of Ursula Nordstrom.* New York: HarperCollins. This is a marvelous collection of letters written by Ursula Nordstrom, one of the 20th century's most famous children's book editors. Innovative, witty, and a savvy business woman to boot, her letters to Margaret Wise Brown, Maurice Sendak, E. B. White, and John Steptoe (just to name a few) are both entertaining and enlightening.

Rosenblatt, L. M. (1994). *The reader, the text, the poem: The transactional theory of the literary work.* Carbondale, IL: Southern Illinois University Press. This is a new edition of Louise Rosenblatt's classic, first written in 1978. Here, Rosenblatt offers an extended theoretical explanation of how readers *transact* with text.

Soter, A. (1999). *Young adult literature & the new literary theories: Developing critical readers in middle school.* New York: Teachers College Press. Anna Soter makes a compelling plea for adolescents to experience critical analysis. Using examples from several well-known pieces of young adult literature, her book is both practical and provocative.

Chapter Touchstone Text

White, E. B. (1952). *Charlotte's web*, illustrated by Garth Williams. New York: Harper & Row. One of the classic texts of our time, *Charlotte's Web* is the story of a surprising friendship between a pig named Wilbur and a large, grey spider named Charlotte A. Cavatica. The friendship ostensibly begins and builds on the issue of survival. Charlotte is determined to save Wilbur from death by cleverly weaving words into her web and tricking the gullible humans into believing that Wilbur is too special to kill. Moving from "Some Pig" to "Terrific" to "Radiant" and ultimately to "Humble," Charlotte's web words have the desired effect and Wilbur is saved. Still, the text hardly reached classic status for its plot. Instead, it is the word web that E. B. White himself weaves that makes the book an astonishing masterpiece.

Recommended Tradebooks for Critical Perspectives

Erdrich, Louise. (1999). *The birchbark house.* New York: Scholastic. A National Book Award Honor book, Erdrich's novel gives voice to a tale rarely heard in textbook versions of American history as we follow an Ojibwa family's life in the face of relentless change and the specter of smallpox. Gently illustrated and lyrically written, this book is a song "like a shining needle" to "sew up a broken heart." (See chapter 4 for more insights on this novel.)

Na, An. (2001). *A step from heaven.* Asheville, NC: Front Street. The winner of the 2002 Michael Printz Award for Excellence in Young Adult Literature, this poignant narrative details the life of Young Ju, from her immigration to America from Korea at the age of four until she begins college. In her youth, Young Ju believed that America was heaven. Her uncle explains that while America is not paradise, perhaps it is just a step away. But the journey Young Ju has to travel makes it clear that the distance is far wider. Faced with language difficulties and crushing poverty, Young Ju's family struggles to survive. Her father loses the battle and becomes an alcoholic whose violence erupts against his family until a climactic scene when Young Ju calls the police. This stunning first novel is sure to grip the minds and hearts of adolescents as they discuss a world that is far more than a step from heaven.

Soto, Gary. (1990). *Baseball in April and other stories.* San Diego: Harcourt Brace Jovanovich. Soto's set of short stories was one of the first to explore modern-day Mexican American youth culture. Recalling his own upbringing in California's Central Valley, he reveals big themes through the small events of daily life. Filled with humor, his stories perceptively show us the differences between the illusions and realities in young people's lives.

Taylor, Mildred D. (2001). *The land.* New York: Phyllis Fogelman Books/Penguin Putnam. A prequel to *Roll of Thunder, Hear My Cry,* Taylor's latest novel won the Coretta Scott King Award in 2002. It details the life of Paul-Edward, the son of a white slave owner and an enslaved African-Indian woman. Beautifully crafted, the novel exemplifies how an individual's determination to make his or her own way is always affected by culture and class. (See chapter 4 for more information on Mildred Taylor.)

Woodson, Jacqueline. (1994). *I hadn't meant to tell you this.* New York: Delacorte. This tale upends stereotypes in a complex dance of human issues and relationships. As Woodson (1995) explains, "In [my story], Marie and Lena, two mother-less twelve-year-old girls—one black, one white; one rich, the other poor—find a common ground across lines of color and class and ignore the world beyond this ground." Woodson is a gifted writer who is "committed to changing the way the world thinks, one reader at a time" (p. 711).

2

Literary Elements
in Prose & Poetry

"Let's let the children go off by themselves," suggested Mr. Arable. "The Fair only comes once a year." Mr. Arable gave Fern two quarters and two dimes. He gave Avery five dimes and four nickels. "Now run along!" he said. "And remember, the money has to last *all day*. Don't spend it all the first few minutes. And be back here at the truck at noontime so we can all have lunch together. And don't eat a lot of stuff that's going to make you sick to your stomachs."

"And if you go in those swings," said Mrs. Arable, "you hang on tight! You hang on *very* tight. Hear me?"

"And don't get lost!" said Mrs. Zuckerman.

"And don't get dirty!"

"Don't get overheated!" said their mother.

"Watch out for pickpockets!" cautioned their father.

"And don't cross the race track when the horses are coming!" cried Mrs. Zuckerman.

The children grabbed each other by the hand and danced off in the direction of the merry-go-round, toward the wonderful music and the wonderful adventure and the wonderful excitement, into the wonderful midway where there would be no parents to guard them and guide them, and where they could be happy and free and do as they pleased. Mrs. Arable stood quietly and watched them go. Then she sighed. Then she blew her nose.

"Do you really think it's all right?" she asked.

"Well, they've got to grow up some time," said Mr. Arable. "And a fair is a good place to start, I guess."

—White (1952, pp. 131–133)

The Garth Williams' illustration that accompanies this passage from *Charlotte's Web* shows Fern and Avery walking towards "the wonderful midway" of the county fair. Neither looks back. They're holding hands and heading straight towards a large and alluring Ferris wheel. When I look at this illustration, I think of the Ferris wheel as a metaphor, for almost all of children's literature spins on the idea that in order to mature, children must do it by themselves. Their parents are relegated to the sidelines. And while they're generally shouting a long litany of admonitions, ultimately they have to wave good-bye.

Maurice Sendak once said that what interests him most in writing for children "is what children do at a particular moment in their lives where there are no rules, no laws, when emotionally they don't know what is expected of them." He continued:

> Children make crucial decisions at that point, ... and it happens in the wink of an eye. It's those crucial seconds when the mother and father can't watch. This was so absolutely, beautifully, rendered for me when I was very young and I saw "The Wizard of Oz." There's a scene ... near the end of the movie, when Dorothy is imprisoned in the room with the Wicked Witch, and the witch takes the hourglass and turns it over and says: "You see that? That's how much longer you've got to be alive."
>
> And Dorothy says, "I'm frightened, I'm frightened." and then the crystal ball shows Auntie Em, and Auntie Em is saying, "Dorothy, Dorothy, where are you?" and Dorothy hovers over it and says: "I'm locked up in the witch's castle. Don't go away, I'm frightened." And I remember that when my sister took me I burst into tears. I knew just what it meant, which was that a mother and child can be in the same room and want to help each other, and they cannot. Even though they were face to face, the crystal ball separated them. Something separates people now and then. And I think it's that moment that interests me, and compels me. (Rothstein, 1988, p. C24)

Sendak's stories consistently focus on this compelling moment. In his famous trilogy of texts, Max sails off to *Where the Wild Things Are* (1963) leaving his mother behind, Mickey falls *In the Night Kitchen* (1970) when his parents are sleeping, and Ida enters *Outside Over There* (1981) to rescue her baby sister on her own. When Sendak illustrated *Dear Mili*, the last-known tale of Wilhelm Grimm (1988), he painted one of the most poignant portrayals in all of children's literature. Rather than have her daughter face the terrors of war, a mother sends her into the forest alone. The mother is on her knees, grasping her child, holding her in a direct gaze while she gives her last instructions. While the mother's embrace is strong and true, it's clear that she must let go.

Sendak is not alone in his interest in this moment, for most children's literature revolves around issues of separation. The child in *Dear Mili* is just one of many children sent into the forest—think of Red Riding Hood, Snow White, and Hansel and Gretel. Even when a forest is not available—stories are built around moments when children must face their fates alone. For example, the 14-year-old heroine of *Jazmin's Notebook* (Grimes, 1998) has to figure out on her own how to exit from a party scene that gets much too intense. And in *A Step from Heaven* (Na, 2001) Young Ju must separate herself from her family in order to save it. Although the young people in these fairy tales and novels return home at the end of their stories, they are changed. Perry Nodelman (1996) called this basic pattern "home-away-home" and described it as a circle, "A child or childlike creature, bored by home, wants the excitement of adventure; but since the excitement is dangerous, the child wants the safety of home—which is boring, and so the child wants the excitement of danger—and so on" (p. 157).

For me, this idea is best captured in the symbol of the Ferris wheel, for the circle of motion indicates that after the thrill of the ride, the child will be back on stable ground—safe, shaken perhaps, different no doubt—but home once more. Figure 2.1 offers an image of the Ferris wheel with a sampling of ten stories that follow the basic home-away-home pattern. Among these stories, there are vast differences in how the pattern plays out. For example, in Mildred Taylor's (2001) *The Land*, Paul Edward does not return home but creates a home of his own. Still, in E. B. White's words all the children represented here have "got to grow up sometime," and to do it they must set out on their ventures alone.

In this chapter, I follow children on their various paths to explore the literary elements in prose and poetry in a number of representative texts. With the prose texts, I analyze the elements of (a) genre, (b), theme (c) character, (d) setting, (e) plot, (f) point of view, (g) style, and (g) tone. These eight components are the ones most often explored by formal critics who look to texts for close readings. While I talk about a number of texts in this chapter, I focus on two in particular. In the first, we go into the woods with *Hansel and Gretel* (Grimm Brothers, 1981). I use an adaptation of the text illustrated by the award-winning Anthony Browne, well known for its modern interpretation. The children in this version are not dressed in German peasant clothes but

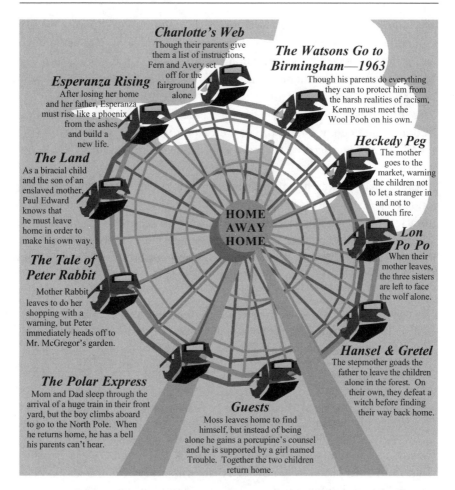

Charlotte's Web
Though their parents give them a list of instructions, Fern and Avery set off for the fairground alone.

The Watsons Go to Birmingham—1963
Though his parents do everything they can to protect him from the harsh realities of racism, Kenny must meet the Wool Pooh on his own.

Esperanza Rising
After losing her home and her father, Esperanza must rise like a phoenix from the ashes and build a new life.

The Land
As a biracial child and the son of an enslaved mother, Paul Edward knows that he must leave home in order to make his own way.

Heckedy Peg
The mother goes to the market, warning the children not to let a stranger in and not to touch fire.

The Tale of Peter Rabbit
Mother Rabbit leaves to do her shopping with a warning, but Peter immediately heads off to Mr. McGregor's garden.

HOME
AWAY
HOME

Lon Po Po
When their mother leaves, the three sisters are left to face the wolf alone.

The Polar Express
Mom and Dad sleep through the arrival of a huge train in their front yard, but the boy climbs aboard to go to the North Pole. When he returns home, he has a bell his parents can't hear.

Guests
Moss leaves home to find himself, but instead of being alone he gains a porcupine's counsel and he is supported by a girl named Trouble. Together the two children return home.

Hansel & Gretel
The stepmother goads the father to leave the children alone in the forest. On their own, they defeat a witch before finding their way back home.

FIG. 2.1. "Well, they've got to grow up some time!"

wear the shirts, sweaters, and dresses of our own time. Gretel wears Mary Jane shoes, and her hair is cut in a bob. Hansel wears striped pajamas out into the garden to gather his stones, and he's able to see them all the better because he wears glasses! The woods in this story are fantastically ominous, with faces and figures seeming to jump out of the howling knotholes and gnarled limbs. Thus, while the children literally enter the forest, they symbolically tread on dangerous ground, for they are abandoned by their parents, captured by a wicked witch, and they must find their way home again on their own.

In our second text, we go into the woods in an even more metaphorical mode. The young protagonist, Kenny, in Christopher Paul Curtis's (1995) astonishing novel, *The Watsons Go to Birmingham—1963*, never literally enters the forest. However, he and his family—a family of immense humor and greater courage—leave their home in Michigan to travel south towards "one of the darkest moments in America's history." In Birmingham, they witness the 1963 bombing of the Sixteenth Avenue Baptist Church in which four little girls were murdered during Sunday school. In Curtis's fictionalized account, Kenny enters the church alone where he meets the "Wool Pooh," a symbolic specter who represents death and the evil of racism in the world.

Unlike many children's tales, Kenny's story is not an imaginary adventure, a ride on a Ferris wheel, a walk in the woods with terrifying, but often temporary, dangers. No. His story reveals the real horrors of the world—a place where adults would murder children to preserve segregation. The Wool Pooh is emblematic of this evil, and when Kenny asks his brother, Byron, to help him understand the motivation of the murderers, Byron explains:

> I don't know, Kenny. Momma and Dad say they can't help themselves, they did it because they're sick, but I don't know. I ain't never heard of no sickness that makes you kill little girls just because you don't want them in your school. I don't think they're sick at all, I think they just let hate eat them up and turn them into monsters. (pp. 199–200)

Like the many dragons I mentioned in the Prologue, monsters are common in literature, but their forms are fluid and shape shifting. Wolves, witches, wizards, and wild things predominate the pages of children's books, but they range from the monster under the bed that turns out to be nothing more than a bathrobe in *Bedtime for Francis* (Hoban, 1960) to the vicious Voldemort in *Harry Potter* (Rowling, 1998). Still, the monstrous Wool Pooh in *The Watsons* represents the real world where the woods are dark and darker still, and some of the inhabitants are eaten up by hate. Children who enter these woods have extraordinary lessons to teach us about the sheer strength it takes to come home again, safe but altered, and current books for youth show us far more complex and wide-ranging characters, subjects, and situations (Dresang, 1999).

From an analysis of the literary elements in our prose texts, I turn to poetry, selecting poems with close text-to-text links with *The Watsons* as well as *Hansel and Gretel* to demonstrate the features of poetry including rhyme, rhythm, figurative language, and compactness among others. In this chapter,

I purposefully selected only a few texts to explore because my preservice and practicing teachers tell me that when they read textbooks that list book after book, example after example, they tire. There are so many books they don't know, and they tend to lose the central thread of the explanation in the maze of books. Still, there could be problems with my decision to narrow the number of books, especially if you believe the analysis I provide applies only to *Hansel and Gretel*, *The Watsons*, and a smattering of text-to-text poetry. It's critical for you to look at the upcoming analysis not only in terms of the designated texts, but also in terms of how it could be applied to any piece of prose or poetry. Don't let the limited examples limit your ability to stretch out beyond these texts and see the applications for your work with literature in general. Let's begin with prose.

Literary Elements in Prose

A succinct way of looking at the analysis of narrative is *actors* and *arenas for action*, but a stripped-down version of character, setting, and plot would make a poor story. Writers craft characters by revealing their intentions, motivations, and emotional responses through careful choices of style, tone, and point of view. They move characters through time, space, and situation by selecting genre, setting, and plot. And all of the elements work together to deliver particular themes.

Developing an understanding of the components of narrative will enable you and your children to communicate with a common language. I designed the Components of Narrative chart (Table 2.1) to provide you with a framework for literary analysis. It is not comprehensive, for narrative is far more complex. Yet, the chart provides quick reference to the definition of each element, the technical vocabulary associated with each, and potential ways of talking about the components with children using the kinds of criticism discussed in chapter 1.

Of course, the separation of the components—indicated by the lines and boxes in Table 2—is an artificial choice. Indeed, a quick look at the chart might lead you to believe I advocate a traditional interpretation of narrative instruction that is clichéd and constraining. My intention here, however, is to emphasize how narrative components are orchestrated, rather than break them up into bits. A strong character may fall flat in an underdeveloped plot. Exquisite writing style may not carry a themeless set of episodes. The eight narrative components must work in sync for an author to develop a powerful

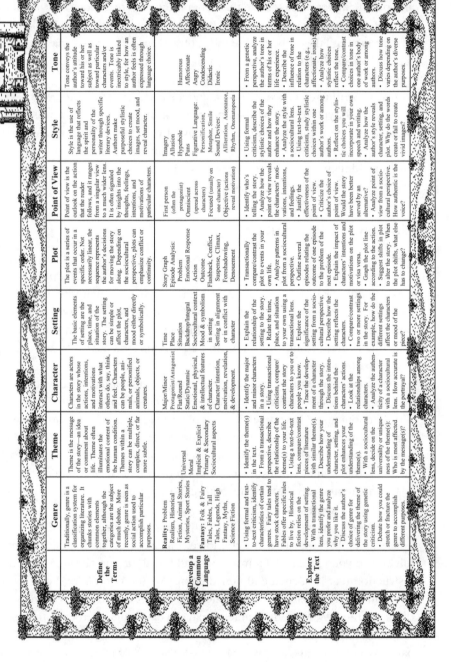

TABLE 2.1
Components of Narrative

	Genre	Theme	Character	Setting	Plot	Point of View	Style	Tone
Define the Terms	Traditionally, genre is a classification system for organizing literature. It chunks stories with common elements together, although the categories are the subject of much debate. More recently, genre is seen as social action used to accomplish particular purposes.	Theme is the message of the story—an idea or comment about life. Theme often illuminates the emotional content of the human condition. Themes within a story can be multiple, complex, direct, or far more subtle.	Characters are actors in the story whose actions, intentions, and motivations interact with what others do, say, think, and feel. Characters can be people, animals, or personified animals, objects, or creatures.	The basic elements of setting are the place, time, and situation of the story. The setting can be simple or affect the plot, characters, and mood either directly or symbolically.	The plot is a series of events that occur in a specific order. Not necessarily linear, the sequence represents the author's decisions for moving the story along. Depending on the sociocultural perspective, plots can emphasize conflict or continuity.	Point of view is the outlook on the action that the reader follows, and it ranges from a singular view to a much wider lens. It is often signaled by insights into the thoughts, feelings, intentions, and motivations of particular characters.	Style is the use of language that reflects the spirit and personality of the writer through specific literary devices. Authors make purposeful stylistic choices to create images, set mood, and reveal character.	Tone conveys the author's attitude toward his or her subject as well as toward particular characters and/or events. Tone is inextricably linked to style, for how an author feels is often expressed through language choice.
Develop a Common Language	**Reality:** Problem Realism, Historical Fiction, Animal Stories, Mysteries, Sport Stories **Fantasy:** Folk & Fairy Tales, Fables, Tall Tales, Legends, High Fantasy, Myths, Science Fiction	Universal Moral Implicit & Explicit Primary & Secondary Sociocultural aspects	Major/Minor Protagonist/Antagonist Flat/Round Static/Dynamic Emotional, physical, & intellectual features of character. Character intention, motivation, revelation, & development.	Time Place Situation Backdrop/Integral Sociocultural context Mood & symbolism in setting Setting in alignment or in conflict with character	Story Graph Episode Analysis: Problem Emotional Response Action Outcome Flashback, Conflict, Suspense, Climax, Foreshadowing, Denouement	First person (often the protagonist) Omniscient (spread across characters) Focused (usually on one character) Objective (actions reveal motivation)	Imagery Allusion Hyperbole Puns Figurative Language: Personification, Metaphor, Simile Sound Devices: Alliteration, Assonance, Rhythm, Onomatopoeia	Humorous Affectionate Angry Condescending Didactic Ironic
Explore the Text	• Using formal and text-to-text criticism, identify characteristics of certain genres. Fairy tales tend to have stock characters. Fables offer specific rules to live by: Historical fiction relies on the development of setting. • With a transactional lens, identify the genre you prefer and analyze why you like it. • Discuss the author's choice of genre for delivering the theme of the story using genetic criticism. • Debate how you could stretch or fracture the genre to accomplish different purposes.	• Identify the theme(s) in the text. • From a transactional perspective, describe the relationship of the theme(s) to your life. • Using a text-to-text lens, compare/contrast with similar theme(s). • Describe how your understanding of character, setting, and plot enhances your understanding of the theme(s). • With a sociocultural lens, decide on the universality or uniqueness of the theme(s): Who is most affected by the message(s)?	• Identify the major and minor characters in a story. • Using transactional criticism, compare/ contrast the story characters to you or to people you know. • Trace the development of a character through the story. • Discuss the intentions behind the characters' actions. • Look at the relationships among characters. • Analyze the authenticity of a character with a sociocultural lens. How accurate is the portrayal?	• Explain the relationship of the setting to the story. • Relate the time, place, and situation to your own using a transactional lens. • Explore the significance of the setting from a socio-cultural perspective. • Describe how the setting reflects the characters. • Compare/contrast two or more settings in the story. For example, how do the different settings affect the characters or mood of the piece?	• Transactionally compare/contrast the plot to events in your own life. • Analyze patterns in plot from a sociocultural perspective. • Outline several episodes relating the outcome of one episode to the problem of the next episode. • Explain the impact of characters' intentions and motivations on the plot or vice versa. • Graph the plot line according to the action. • Suggest shifts in plot to alter the story. When the plot shifts, what else has to change?	• Identify who's telling the story. • Analyze how the point of view reveals the characters' motivations, intentions, and feelings. • Justify the effectiveness of the point of view. • Criticize the author's choice of point of view. Would the story have been better served by an alternative? • Analyze point of view from a socio-cultural perspective. How authentic is the voice?	• Using formal criticism, analyze the stylistic choices of the author and how they enhance the story. • Analyze the style with a sociocultural lens. • Using text-to-text criticism, study stylistic choices within one author's work or among authors. • Reflect on the stylistic choices you will incorporate in your own speech and writing. • Analyze how the author's style reveals character, setting, and plot. Why do the words create or fail to create vivid images?	• From a genetic perspective, analyze the author's tone in terms of his or her life experience. • Describe the influence of tone in relation to the characters (e.g., affectionate, ironic). • Analyze how stylistic choices reflect the tone. • Compare/contrast choices in tone in one author's body of work or among authors. • Discuss how tone varies depending on the author's diverse purposes.

story. Furthermore, literary uptake depends on powerful teaching, and you need a strong foundation in the fundamental language of narrative to enhance your children's engagement in literature.

The following sections are designed to provide you with an overview of well-known and relatively well-understood literary elements. I briefly outline each of the narrative components by (a) offering a definition, (b) suggesting some key questions that teachers and children can explore, and (c) providing illustrative examples from literature, particularly from the touchstone texts for this chapter: *Hansel and Gretel* and *The Watsons Go to Birmingham— 1963*. The necessary orchestration across elements will build as we progress through the individual components. We begin with genre, for this element often determines how the orchestration of the other components will play.

Genre

Genre provides the frame for the story. It typecasts the tale, sending signals to prepare the reader for what lies ahead. The rounding of character, functions of setting, predictability of plot, and explicitness of theme are often determined by genre. Traditionally, genre provides a classification system for organizing literature, although the characteristics of certain "categories" are not set in stone. Indeed, the boundaries appear to be more porous than solid, as stories float among specific categories. More recently, genre is seen as social action used to accomplish particular purposes. As a result, when we think of genre today we tend to think not so much about what kind of book it is, but what it does to help children understand and transform their worlds (McGinley & Kamberelis, 1992). In thinking about genre, there are several questions that you and your children can consider: Using formal and text-to-text criticism, what patterns in the story make you think it's a specific genre? Can the story cross over to more than one category? What would happen if the tale were written in a different genre? From a sociocultural perspective, what is the author trying to accomplish in using, stretching, or breaking a particular genre? And from a transactional perspective, what is it about this genre that you like or dislike?

Very general lines separate fantasy from reality. Realistic tales include those that center on personal and social problems, historical fiction, sports stories, mysteries, or tales that follow real animals in authentic situations. Although historical fiction places emphasis on the authenticity of setting, problem realism centers on character development. In a text like *The Watsons Go to Birmingham—1963*, which could arguably fit in both subgenres, Kenny struggles to understand the impact of a horrific historical event on his own life and family.

On the other hand, fantasy opens the door to the rich world of make-believe. Although the problems may be as "real" as those portrayed in realistic fiction, the vehicle is as different as a magical royal coach from an ordinary garden pumpkin. Subgenres of fantasy include folk and fairy tales, fables, myths, legends, science fiction, and high fantasy. Folk and fairy tales are well known for their predictability—stories painted in black and white. There is little gray in the world of the folk tale: characters are either good or evil, the setting a dark forest or a shining castle, the hero victorious and the nemesis defeated. Quite often the plot cycles around the number three. There are three brothers, three questions to be answered, and three nights to be spent spinning straw into gold. In terms of *Hansel and Gretel*, many of these patterns are apparent. Both the witch and the stepmother are clearly evil antagonists, while the children are forces for good. And though they are abandoned in the forest twice instead of the traditional three times, they find the witch's delicious abode on their third day in the woods.

Setting is critical in science fiction, which relies on a vision of the future. The miracles of technology and the world of scientific invention hold center stage, and characters use out-of-this-world vehicles to transport themselves through space and time. High fantasy has much in common with science fiction in that it creates another world, though it does not usually dwell in "another galaxy far, far away." Instead, the land of high fantasy is accessible in our own time, if we can only find the entrance. Falling down a rabbit's hole to Wonderland, stepping through a wardrobe into Narnia, or even pushing past the barrier of platform nine and three-quarters creates a connection between the real world and the land of high fantasy.

Over the years, literary critics have cast and recast the genre lines because genres are "not permanent classes but . . . families subject to change" (Fowler, 1982, p. v). Figure 2.2 offers a few of the central literary genres in prose divided by reality and fantasy, but keep in mind that the definitions and examples from the various subgenres are changeable. Amidst the seemingly arbitrary categories, there is an important notion for you to communicate to your students: Stories follow patterns, and an understanding of genre will aid their literary engagement.

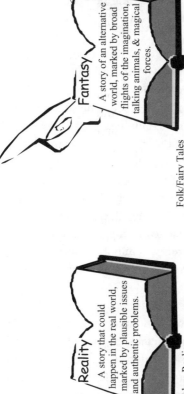

Fantasy

A story of an alternative world, marked by broad flights of the imagination, & magical forces.

Folk/Fairy Tales

Originating in the oral tradition, these tales transform with each generation. They are often marked by "wonder" and contain life lessons.
- *The Hunter* (Cassanova)
- *The Gold Coin* (Ada)
- *Ma'ii and Cousin Horned Toad: A Traditional Navajo Story* (Begay)
- *Ella Enchanted* (Levine)
- *Hansel & Gretel* (Grimm Brothers)
- *The Paper Bag Princess* (Munsch)
- *The True Story of the 3 Little Pigs* (Scieszka)

Fables

Brief stories leading to an explicit moral, usually with two animal characters.
- *Aesop's Fables* (Santore)
- *Aesop's Fox* (Sogabe)
- *Fables* (Lobel)

Tall Tales/Legends

Exaggerated tales of fiction as well as authentic national heroes who become larger than life.
- *John Henry* (Lester)
- *The Seeing Stone: Arthur Trilogy Book One* (Crossley-Holland)
- *The Woman who Outshone the Sun: The Legend of Lucia Zenteno—La Mujer Que Brillaba Aun Más Que El Sol: La Leyenda De Lucia Zenteno* (Martinez, Zubizarreta, Rohmer, & Schecter)

High Fantasy

Stories centered on struggles between good and evil, where entire imaginary worlds are created in rich detail with fully developed characters.
- *Harry Potter and the Sorcerer's Stone* (Rowling)
- *The Lord of the Rings* (Tolkien)
- *The Hero and the Crown* (McKinley)

Myths

Stories of people and their gods which provide guidance, spiritual strength, and explanations of natural phenomenon.
- *Troy* (Geras)
- *A Gift from Zeus* (Steig)
- *In the Beginning: Creation Stories from Around the World* (Hamilton)
- *How the Birds Got Their Colors* (Johnston)

Science Fiction

Stories cast into the future which emphasize alternative, often problematic worlds and the influence of technology.
- *The Ear, the Eye, and the Arm* (Farmer)
- *The Giver* (Lowry)
- *A Wrinkle in Time* (L'Engle)

...and then there's nonfiction.

Reality

A story that could happen in the real world, marked by plausible issues and authentic problems.

Problem Realism

Fiction that deals with specific problems as well as basic truths of human nature.
- *A Step from Heaven* (An Na)
- *The View from Saturday* (Konigsburg)
- *A Chair for my Mother* (Williams)
- *Yang the Youngest and his Terrible Ear* (Namioka)
- *My Very Own Room / Mi Propio Cuartito* (Perez)

Historical Fiction

Fiction that hinges on a setting in the historical past. Language is authentic to the times, and setting is key.
- *The Watsons Go to Birmingham—1963* (Curtis)
- *The Birchbark House* (Erdrich)
- *Esperanza Rising* (Muñoz Ryan)
- *Baseball Saved Us* (Mochizuki)

Mysteries

Fiction that relies on suspense, culminating in a denouement, often revealed by an experienced detective.
- *Mysteries of Harris Burdick* (Van Allsburg)
- *Encyclopedia Brown Takes a Case* (Sobol)
- *The House of Dies Drear* (Hamilton)

Animal Stories

Fiction that hinges on the very real actions of animals, often in connection with humans who love them.
- *King of the Wind* (Henry)
- *Shiloh* (Naylor)
- *Because of Winn-Dixie* (DiCamillo)

FIG. 2.2. Central Genres in Literary Prose: Definitions & Examples.

53

Theme

Theme is the heart of a story—an idea or comment about life that often illuminates the emotional content of the human condition. Bringing meaning to all parts of the tale, authors craft their themes—whether singular or more complex—through the orchestration of the other components. Using several critical lenses, the questions that you and your children might ask are varied. With a transactional lens, a question might be: What are the themes of this narrative and what relationship do they have to my life? Using a formal perspective: Are the themes explicitly stated or implicit and far more subtle? Looking through a text-to-text or a sociocultural perspective: What connections do the themes of this tale have with other texts, experiences, and times?

Simple stories have straightforward and often didactic themes. For example, golden rules and aphorisms abound in the world of the fable, though this is appropriate to the genre. In fairy tales the themes are not so outspoken, but they still come through loud and clear, "intelligence is more important than strength" and "good conquers evil." When children discuss *Hansel and Gretel*, they're often struck by the clear evil of the stepmother and the witch, but the father is more perplexing. Why would he follow his wife's suggestion and abandon his children in the forest? When my daughter was seven years old, we struggled with this idea until Lindsey suggested that if the father didn't comply, "the stepmother might kick *him* out!" Although I fruitlessly struggled for the father to break out of his traditional character, Lindsey knew he could not. The stepmother's power over the children was minor compared to her ability to manipulate their father. For all he knew, he would be the next one left alone in the forest.

By following the trail of *Hansel and Gretel*, children come to realize once again the home-away-home pattern in children's literature, when adults, for whatever reason, must stay out of the way. Two themes are repeated again and again. First, using their wits, children can conquer powerful forces. They can defeat a terrifying witch, though their father is helpless. They can vanquish the wolf at the door when their mother is away. And they can outwit and out-wizard an evil so terrible no one even wants to say its name. Second, children are much closer to the magic in life. They can cram their pockets full of a witch's treasure before making their way home again. They can hear the gift of Santa's Christmas bell, though their parents cannot. And they can fly to the magical shores of Neverland, a place where grown ups can *never land*.

Even though themes are often explicitly stated, more complex stories develop themes on an implicit level through the affect and actions of their characters. In some stories, the themes are revealed on both planes. In *Charlotte's Web*, for example, the theme of the power of friendship to uplift one's life is directly stated, but it is the spider's constant attention and caring actions throughout the story that support that statement. Although simple stories suggest singular themes, more complex stories develop multiple ideas with both primary and secondary themes. The themes are layered and interconnected.

In the story of *The Watsons Go to Birmingham—1963*, the dynamic growth of young Kenny from naiveté to a mature understanding of his social world is supported by themes that emphasize the strength of the African American family and the belief that dignity, persistence, and resistance can effectively confront racism. Curtis's epilogue adds another thematic layer, for in his research on the civil rights movement, he was inspired by the heroism of people trying to make a difference in the world. He wanted his readers to reflect on how understandings of others' lives, situations, and actions can help them to become heroes in their own right:

> Many heroic people died in the struggle for civil rights. Many others were injured or arrested or lost their homes or businesses. It is almost impossible to imagine the courage of the first African American children who walked into segregated schools or the strength of the parents who permitted them to face the hatred and violence that awaited them. They did it in the name of the movement, in the quest for freedom.
>
> These people are the true American heroes. They are the boys and girls, the women and men who have seen that things are wrong and have not been afraid to ask "Why can't we change this?" They are the people who believe that as long as one person is being treated unfairly, we all are. These are our heroes, and they still walk among us today. One of them may be sitting next to you as you read this, or standing in the next room making your dinner, or waiting for you to come outside and play.
>
> One of them may be you. (p. 210)

In literature, children are often portrayed as heroes, but the witches and monsters they face can take on metaphorical meaning. In *The Watsons*, Kenny faces the Wool Pooh twice, dragged down under the water by the monster the first time and then meeting the gray, square-toed horror in the bombed-out church. Even when his brother, Byron, contests the existence of the Wool

Pooh, Kenny knows what he saw, "If he'd ever had his ankle grabbed by it he'd know it was real, . . . if he'd ever seen those horrible toes he'd know the Wool Pooh was as serious as a heart attack" (p. 204).

Children, even very young children, can interpret theme in literature with the aid of capable teachers. They see the messages in life all around them, so the themes in stories are there for the taking and the talking. Children need and deserve opportunities to explore what Faulkner calls the "the human heart in conflict with itself." And then, like Kenny, they can move on to explore the very real magic that exists in the small and larger moments of familial life and love.

Character

Characters are animate beings with emotions, motivations, and intentions. They move in the time and space of a story, interacting with friends and foes, reflecting and taking action. At times, characters' thoughts are made explicit for the reader, but often we observe only the action and must infer the drive behind it. Questions that you and your children can consider are: Who are the characters? Are they flat and unchanging or round and dynamic? How do the characters move, think, and feel? Do they take on primary roles, or do they stand in the background? How do they change during the course of the story? Using transactional criticism, your children can compare and contrast the characters on the page to themselves or to individuals they know in the world. Using a sociocultural lens, they can analyze the accuracy of the portrayal of character.

In the world of children's literature, characters may be human or not. The critical characteristic is that they be animate. Talking, thinking, and feeling animals abound—elephant kings, frogs and toads, runaway bunnies, and velveteen rabbits. Human characteristics are also given to plants, resulting in flowers that talk, trees that give friendship, and vines that ensnare to reveal the pain and imagination of artists like *Frida* (Winter, 2002). Animate characteristics are also ascribed to objects. There are engines that think they can, nutcrackers that come to life under the Christmas tree, and clouds that fly children from the Empire State Building all the way to *Sector 7* (Wiesner, 1999). Although one might assume that animal and object characters are only found in primary texts, they move into intermediate levels as well. No one could doubt the evil intentions of the Wool Pooh, or Lord Voldemort, or even the "peculiar such thing" who returns in the night to retrieve his "tailypo" from the poor fellow who foolishly chopped it off and ate it for supper and then became supper himself (Hamilton, 1985). On the gentler side of story, the motivation of a gentleman mouse to get off *Abel's Island* (Steig, 1976) and find his way home, is even more compelling because Abel is not human. Indeed, the Robinson Crusoe pattern in this story is effective because the hero is a mouse.

Because characters are real, they experience emotion, they are motivated by life's circumstances, and they have purposes and intentions for accomplishing their goals whether it be flying away from slavery or defeating the evil witch. In *Hansel and Gretel*, even young children recognize that the stepmother and the witch are one and the same, for Anthony Browne provides strikingly similar portraits of the two characters. Both women stand in their homes framed by doorways and windows, staring out in disgust at the children. They share the same dark eyes, the same down-turned grimace, and the same mole in the exact same spot. Beyond their visual similarities, they even use the same language, both calling the children "lazybones" as they wake Hansel and Gretel up in the morning, a comparison that led my 7-year-old daughter to exclaim:

> "Do you know what I think? You know how her mother said 'Get up, lazybones'? I think the witch *is* the mother."
>
> She began to flip back and forth between the two pictures, "Now look at the mother and look at the witch." Pointing to the mole on the stepmother's face she exclaimed, "See that black spot?" She then pointed to a matching feature on the witch, "See *that* black spot?" She shuffled back and forth between the pages again, "See the red cheeks and see her frown? See *her* frown?"
>
> "It's the same frown. It's the same mole." I agreed.
>
> "In the same place!" Lindsey compared the stepmother framed by the door of the cottage and the witch framed by the window.

As you read this last vignette, you might think that Lindsey made this comparison because she is my daughter and has been read to since she was an infant. However, if you read this text to other children, including children who have not had the same extensive exposure to books, you would find that similar things happen. Anthony Browne makes the relationship so visually clear, children take note, and they begin to consider the other characteristics the women share, particularly their cruelty towards children.

The more sophisticated the character, the richer the description—the author rounds the character through physical as well as affective insights and details. Some characters remain unchanging, but others are dynamic—maturing through both the action of the story and personal self-reflection. When two characters meet, their emotions, motivations, and intentions intertwine. Charlotte and Wilbur present a classic example. They are motivated by the same desire to save Wilbur's life, but their emotions and intentions differ. Wilbur is a frightened child, who weeps and whines at the very mention of bacon. Charlotte, on the other hand, is teacher and mother wrapped into one; she is calm, commanding, and consistent. While she devises a clever plan for tricking the humans, Wilbur is content to follow her directions, though he matures in the story from "some pig" to increasingly terrific, radiant, and finally, humble. Through the security of constant support and friendship, he learns what it means to be a friend.

In the analysis of character, your children can list and discuss features, compare and contrast characters, and follow them over time. In the case of *The Watsons Go to Birmingham—1963*, Kenny and Byron shift most dramatically in response to the racial events of their times. For example, in the beginning of the novel, Kenny is relatively innocent. He knows about prejudice and has witnessed racial confrontations on TV, but it all still seems relatively distanced. However, when his family drives to Birmingham and into the violence of the Civil Rights era, Kenny learns about the horrific repercussions of people's hatred for one another. At first, he is in a state of shock and withdraws even from his own family. But his long reflection combined with a conversation with his brother, Byron, helps him to figure out how to "keep on steppin" (p. 203).

In following the development of Kenny and Byron in this novel, two teaching strategies come to mind. One is for children to build a matrix of character development based on their literary discussion of the text. Figure 2.3 shows a sample matrix. Here I've created the categories and filled in the cells with quotes from the book, but in reality this is something that you would do in collaboration with your students. While you can create the categories and have ideas about what goes in the cells, your students' own words and selected quotes should fill them.

A second strategy is for students to keep a double entry journal of character development. Students could enter teacher-selected quotes concerning the two characters at the beginning of the novel. On the facing page (or in a second column), they would provide a written response to these quotes—justifying how or why the quotes show particular features of character. For example, to introduce your children to Kenny's character, you could ask them to respond to Kenny's difficulties with his friend Rufus. In the beginning of the novel, Kenny is relatively sweet and naïve. He is strongly supported by the love of his family and knows that when he has a problem, his

Character Development Matrix

The relationship between Kenny & Byron in *The Watsons go to Birmingham—1963*

	Beginning Character	Understandings of Racism	Time & Trial	Ending Character	Understandings of Racism
Kenny	Innocent and sweet, but not always as good friend, such as when he teases Rufus.	Bewildered: "...I didn't really know how these white people could hate some kids so much" (pp. 122-123).	• Byron pushes the family too far and they decide to take him to Grandma's. • Kenny nearly drowns in the whirlpool.	Less innocent and even more reflective. Takes his courage from his family.	Shows courage in the face of horror: "Me and Momma and Dad was all too scared, you was the only one brave enough to go in there" (p. 202).
	The brothers in conflict: "Then he made his eyes go crossed, which was his favorite way of teasing me, but I didn't care, I knew who had won this time" (p. 19).			**The brothers in collaboration:** Momma whispered, "What's going on, By? Why was Kenny crying like that, is he O.K.?" He told her, "Kenny's gonna be cool" (p. 204).	
Byron	A mean-spirited bully—"officially a teenage juvenile delinquent" (p. 2).	Naïve: "He's got to realize the world doesn't have a lot of jokes waiting for him" (p. 123).	• Church bombing in Birmingham. • Kenny enters the Pet Hospital.	Still cocky, but more compassionate and considerate of his family.	More realistic: "Kenny, things ain't ever going to be fair.... But you just gotta understand that that is the way it is and keep on steppin'" (p. 203).

Double Entry Journal

Book Quote

A couple of days later Momma asked me to sit in the kitchen with her for a while.

"How's school?"

"O.K." I knew she was fishing to find what was wrong and hoped it wouldn't take her too long. I wanted to tell her what I'd done.

"Where's Rufus been? I haven't seen him lately."

It was real embarrasing but tears just exploded out of my face and even though I knew she was going to be disappointed in me I told Momma how I'd hurt Rufis's feelings.... (p. 45).

Student Response

When I first read this quote, I thought of how Kenny and I are sort of alike. It's just so hard when you fight with your friends. I liked how Kenny described how the "tears just exploded." That's what it feels like when you don't want to cry but you can't help it.

I also thought it made sense for his character that Kenny would go to his mom for help. Byron would never do that! I'm more like Kenny because my mom often helps me understand what to do.

FIG. 2.3. Character Development Matrix & Double Entry Journal.

mother will be there to help him. Figure 2.3 provides a selected quote and a sample student response from a transactional perspective. After responding to the quotes you select, your students should self-select other quotes that demonstrate how the characters develop sufficient strength and insight over time to support individual acts of heroism. Your children could then bring their journal entries to a literary discussion group, to aid in the conversation as well as in the creation and completion of the character development matrix.

Through opportunities to compare and contrast characters and reflect on critical quotes, your children will come to understand that characters in complex novels develop over time, through the details, as well as in relationship with other characters. They will also realize that even flat, unchanging characters are delivered, if not developed, through stereotypes like the wily fox, the wicked witch, or even the big, bad wolf. Whether the characters are flat, round, static, or dynamic, your children will be able to analyze the connections to other literary elements as you help them explore how characters get the message across, why characters are controlled by the kind of story they're in, what point of view best serves the revelation of character, as well as how the setting can impact character development.

Setting

Setting includes the main features of time, place, and situation. But these features are not to be memorized and recited (e.g., Kansas, early 1900s, cyclone coming), but explored for the features and possible shifts in setting that reflect the general mood of the story and feelings of the characters. Dorothy is a far different person in Kansas than she is in Oz! Questions you and your children can explore include: Is the setting integral to the story or merely a backdrop, where the actual time and place are less important than the situation? How does the setting influence character mood or highlight the conflict? From a sociocultural perspective, what is the significance of the setting? From a formal perspective, how do shifts in setting impact the story?

The simplest settings often serve as a backdrop to the tale. In fables, for example, time and place are unimportant, for the boy who cried wolf could play his joke and receive his comeuppance almost anywhere, at any time. Fairy tale settings are often stereotypical—"Once upon a time a long time ago"—but they retain their power just the same and provide beginning insights into the role of setting as symbol. The "forest" conjures up immediate images of trees that reach out to grab escaping heroines, with wolves and witches hiding therein. A "castle" needs little explanation—the word itself sparks flickering candles that shed light on stone walls and sumptuous banquets attended by fairies, kings, and queens.

Authors use setting shifts to dramatize their characters' predicaments. The setting shifts in *Hansel and Gretel* are highly dramatic. Though the children's lives at home as well as at the witch's house are both frightening, the threat becomes more real in the woods. Even more important, there is a startling difference in the home from the beginning of the story to the end. The house Browne illustrated at the beginning of the story is rather gray and shabby with ugly smudge marks on the door and a black bird perched ominously on its roof. But the home the children triumphantly return to with the witch's jewels in hand, is lighter and cleaner. The smudge marks are replaced by a soft shadow. Most important, at this point in the story both the stepmother and the witch are dead. When I read this story to my daughter, Lindsey noticed the difference in the houses right away:

"Look at their house ... it's all new 'cause they used all the jewels," she exclaimed.

"Do you think that they can make that house new?" I turned back to the illustration at the beginning of the story. "Certainly looks brighter than it did there."

"And that," Lindsey pointed to the door. "Look at the door."

"Oh, yeah. Looks brightly painted." Following up on her earlier suggestion, I added, "Maybe they could turn in some of the jewels."

Lindsey took the book and turned back to the beginning illustration. "Maybe the house was darker 'cause the mother's really dark and mean."

"Oh, yeah," I agreed. "And now that she's gone the house is lighter."

"And newer," Lindsey continued. "Cause she was old and ugly."

Extending her interpretation I asked, "Do you think that people have that ability to make, you know, a whole atmosphere, where they live, sort of dark and somber?"

"Because of them?" Lindsey asked.

"Because of them," I nodded.

"I don't know," Lindsey mused. "But in story tales they definitely could do that!"

The visual features of the house had changed, and Lindsey offered two explanations. The first was logical: jewels were like money, and money could be used for renovation. The second was symbolic: the personality of the stepmother cast a "mean and ugly" light over the house, but with her death the house was new again. In Lindsey's eyes, both home and heart were restored.

In a longer novel like *Bridge to Teribithia* (Paterson, 1977), setting shifts are vital to the growing friendship of Jess and Leslie. In this story there are two main settings: the real one of home and school and the fantasy setting of Teribithia. Each differs in its general description, accessibility, inhabitants, and attraction. At home and school, Jess and Leslie have to face the day-to-day disappointments and challenges of races lost and getting back at rivals. But in Teribithia, they are in control. In more complex stories, such as Paterson's tale, setting has several functions—it sets the mood, reveals character and conflict, and serves as metaphor.

The same is true in *The Watsons Go to Birmingham—1963*. Everything changes when the Watsons leave Flint, Michigan and head south. Byron— who had been dubbed "officially a teenage juvenile delinquent" (p. 2), suddenly becomes more obedient and considerate of his family. In puzzlement, Kenny exclaims, "Who could understand Byron? . . . Something was wrong with him. If he was in Flint and you told him not to do something he'd go right out and do it, but now he was acting real dull and square" (p. 170). Kenny, on the other hand, is more adventurous, and his risk taking leads him to his two confrontations with the Wool Pooh—emblematic of the very real conflict in the novel as Kenny comes face to face with the blatant racism in Birmingham.

When Curtis was writing his novel, he originally decided to have the Watsons travel to Florida. He was an autoworker in Flint, and he had many friends who on short vacations would head to the South, driving without stopping. When Curtis's sister-in-law moved to Florida, the family decided to visit, and his wife meticulously planned the entire trip with stops included. But Curtis had another plan—to drive 24 hours without stopping—a plan he put in his novel. Still, he realized that when the fictional family got to Florida, nothing happened. In an interview with David Weich (2000), Curtis explained, "So I set [the novel] aside for a while, until my son brought home a poem by Dudley Randall called 'Ballad of Birmingham' about the bombing of the 16th Street Baptist Church. As soon as I heard it, I said, 'Ah! The Watsons want to go to Birmingham!' and I wrote the rest of the story." The contrast between his original and his final plan shows how authors depend on setting to make their stories all the more compelling.

Plot

Plot is a sequence of events that moves the narrative from beginning to end. Quite often, the plot begins with a problem for a major character to solve, shows the difficulties of the problem in the middle of the story, and ends with a resolution of that problem. Plot reveals the movement of characters through time, space, and adversity. Questions you and your children might explore include: How is the plot structured? How does the resolution of one event lead to the next episode? What clues does the author offer through foreshadowing? What is the use of time—does it move unerringly forward or are there flashbacks, stories within stories, and dream sequences which bend or suspend time? From a sociocultural perspective, does the plot emphasize conflict or continuity?

The simplest view of plot shows us that stories have beginnings, middles, and endings. In the beginning of Perrault's (1954) *Cinderella*, a young girl is faced with a lifetime of drudgery and derision. Her fairy godmother arrives in the middle of the tale to offer her some sparkling alternatives. Ultimately, Cinderella discovers the old adage "if the shoe fits, wear it" and lives happily ever after with her prince. More sophisticated views of plot show the sequence of time in related episodes. In the African story of *Mufaro's Beautiful Daughters* (Steptoe, 1987), for example, the polarity of the actions and reactions of two sisters lead them into very different futures. The gentle and generous Nyasha meets and marries her king, while the bad-tempered Manyara is left to be a servant in her sister's household. Steptoe foreshadows the ultimate events through Manyara's dire, though misguided, predictions and the early appearance of the young king in a variety of symbolic guises. Because they're fairy tales, both stories are marked by the rule of three. Cinderella attends the ball three nights before her prince discovers her identity, while Nyasha must face three trials before she and her king are married.

In the classroom, children often analyze and comment on the effectiveness of plot. They ponder what works and what doesn't. For example, I've heard 6-year-olds debating Hansel's use of bread instead of stones on the second day the children are led into the forest. "Why didn't they just follow the stones from the day before?" asks one. Another counters, "Maybe their parents took them in a different direction!" They debate the death of the witch and wonder what they might have done in Gretel's place. And they love to discuss the stepmother's death at the end of the book. While the text says little, children conjure up all sorts of reasons for her demise, and often return to the associations between the stepmother and the witch.

I've also seen children graph plots to show the interplay of a story's action with the emotions of the characters. Figure 2.4 offers three possibilities. With my own primary children, I drew a plot line of *Where the Wild Things Are* (Sendak, 1963) to demonstrate the rising action of plot till the climax of the

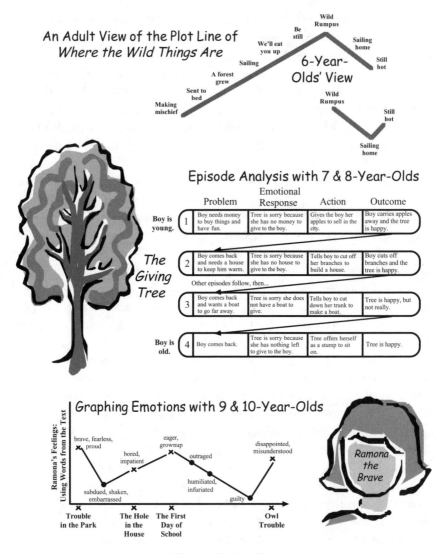

FIG. 2.4.   Graphing Plot.

wild rumpus and then the falling action as Max makes his way back home again. But my class of 6-year-olds told me I was wrong. Instead, they drew a slight rise in the action when Max is finally home with his supper, explaining, "Getting home is the best feeling of all."

I've seen 7- and 8-year olds graph *The Giving Tree* (Silverstein, 1964) following the repeated pattern of problem, emotional response, action, and outcome—with each episodic pattern leading to the next episode. In one classroom of 9- and 10-year-olds, I observed the children graph the emotional responses of *Ramona the Brave* (Cleary, 1975) to the events she encounters. As their teacher explained, "The action of the plot is very ordinary, with typical everyday situations. But it is Ramona's emotional responses that make the story come alive." The timeline in Fig. 2.4 follows Ramona's feelings through the initial episodes. The Xs represent episodes, and the dots show mood changes within the episodes.

Even a novel as complex as *The Watsons Go to Birmingham—1963*, can be graphed. But it might be even more effective to compare the plot of the novel with the plot of the real historical events. Four little girls—Denise McNair, Cynthia Wesley, Addie Mae Collins, and Carole Robertson—died in the bombing of the Sixteenth Street Baptist Church on September 15th, 1963. This day was followed by a series of dates over a period of nearly forty years—dates which demonstrate the delays, the misdirection, and finally the determination of a few to bring the perpetrators to trial. Older children and young adolescents could get a stronger sense of the history through the film *Four Little Girls* by Spike Lee or by studying the proceedings online at sites such as: http://www.4littlegirls.com. Examining the actual events could enhance their understanding of the horror that Kenny met in the church.

This horror brings us to one of the most powerful shifts in plot and setting in the novel, for when Kenny returns home he seems to disappear from his family, hiding behind the couch and waiting to get better. He explains:

> I had been disappearing, but Momma really didn't need to worry, I wasn't going anywhere. I'd just been going behind the couch for a little while every day. There was a big enough space between the couch and the wall for me to squeeze in back there and just sit in a little ball. It was quiet and dark and still back there.
>
> Byron called this little area the World-Famous Watson Pet Hospital and he made me and Joey believe that magic powers, genies and angels all lived back there. I was waiting to see if that was true.
>
> He started calling it the World-Famous Watson Pet Hospital after we noticed that if something bad happened to one of our dogs or cats they just automatically knew they had to crawl in that space and wait to see if they were going to get better. (p. 193)

The image of Kenny wrapped up tight in his pain, waiting for the magic powers to come and make him get better is one of the most poignant portrayals of childhood depression in all of children's literature. He has noticed that the family dogs that go behind the couch often come out for the better, if they come out at all, but the cats are almost always meaner.

What, he wonders, will be his fate? "I was waiting to see if the magic powers were going to treat me like a dog or a cat, or if when Byron or Joey woke up one morning they'd find a crumpled-up yellow towel where I was supposed to be" (p. 195). The hatred he has witnessed is made clear in the image of the "crumpled-up yellow towel," and like Kenny, readers can only hope for the best. Plot hinges on emotion, and in this scene all the literary elements work in collaboration to offer us a view, through Kenny's eyes, of his pain. Through literary analysis and discussion, your children will learn how authors structure plots, how they foreshadow events to come, and how they link episodes toward conflict as well as final resolution.

Point of View

Through choices in point of view, the author decides what the reader will see and know. The view can be limited to the actions of characters or spread to their innermost thoughts and feelings. The view can offer insight into a single character or expand to everyone involved in the story. Point of view is the outlook on the action that the reader will follow. Questions for you and your children include: What is the chosen point of view? Does the choice provide you with adequate information or would the story be better served by an alternative? From a formal perspective, how does the point of view work to reveal character motivation and intention? Using a sociocultural lens, how authentic is the voice?

In the *objective* point of view, the action speaks for itself. The innermost feelings of characters are not revealed, and readers must infer intention and motivation only from what characters say and do. Although this choice is typical of drama, it is rare in the world of children's literature. Much more common is the *first-person* point of view, where the "I" is both character and narrator. The story of *The Watsons Go to Birmingham*—1963 is told from Kenny's point of view. He tells of his fears and futile attempts to understand racism in the world. For example, when Byron finally persuades him to come out of the World-Famous Watson Pet Hospital, Kenny breaks down and cries all the tears he'd been holding inside:

> Byron sat next to me on the floor and put my head in his lap. I still couldn't stop, even though I was soaking him worse than Joey ever drooled on anybody.

It was real embarrassing. "I'm sorry, By."

"Shut up and cry if you want."

That sounded like a real good idea so I did. I think I cried for about two hundred hours.

"Why would they do that, Byron?" I was sounding real bad. My throat was jumping around in my neck and making a bunch of weird noises. "Why would they hurt some little kids like that?" (p. 199)

It is Kenny who describes the number of tears, the amount of drool, the jump of his throat, and the sense of embarrassment. Through Kenny we hear Byron's words, and though they sound harsh, Kenny tells us that they "sounded like a real good idea," and we know from the fact that Byron put Kenny's head in his lap, his intentions are good. But in this first-person point of view, we aren't allowed into Byron's head, for Kenny states the action and delivers the interpretation.

Even in much lighter scenes, it's Kenny who tells us about Byron and the other members of his family—the Weird Watsons. Earlier in the book, when Momma gets fed up with Byron's antics, especially his propensity for playing with fire, she decides:

"I'm just going to burn his fingers enough so he won't be tempted by fire ever again."

Those were like magic words; they snapped Byron right out of the spell Momma put on him. It was like his hands said, "Fingers? Did she say she was gonna burn someone's fingers?" Because when they found out it was them that were going to get burned they let go of Byron's throat and joined the rest of his body in deciding to wait at Buphead's until Dad got home. (pp. 72–73)

It's easy to see from this passage that the first-person point of view is not as limited as one might expect, for Kenny not only interprets Bryon's thinking, he even personifies Bryon's hands which take quick action when its fingers are at stake!

In other stories, authors provide an omniscient point of view, allowing us to hear and understand the thoughts and feelings of multiple characters. E. B. White made this choice in *Charlotte's Web*, and the text is marked by the third person (i.e., she, he, they) to provide us with an interpretive take on all the characters' talk and actions. The Grimm Brothers made the same choice in *Hansel and Gretel*, though the omniscient view is more *limited* to align with the children and their father. We are told less about the motivations of the stepmother and even the witch. Their actions are stronger than insights into their feelings. For example, when the children are first led out into the forest, they follow a trail of stones back home:

> The children walked all through the night and at daybreak reached home. They knocked at the door, and when the stepmother looked out and saw who it was, she said, "You wicked children! Why did you sleep so long in the forest? We thought you were never coming home."
>
> But their father was glad, for it had broken his heart to leave them behind all alone.

Thus, while we can only infer the stepmother's rage and disappointment that her dastardly plan had failed, the authors allow us to feel the father's broken heart.

The connection between point of view and character is particularly strong, for the viewpoint focuses our attention, and often our sympathy and empathy, towards particular characters and away from others. Recently, children's literature has followed less traditional trails, shifting the point of view away from the likely hero. Later in this chapter, there is a poem by Gwen Strauss (1990) that tells the tale of *Hansel and Gretel* entirely from the father's point of view. Shifts in point of view are becoming increasingly popular in the world of the fairy tale. One example is Scieszka's (1989) *The True Story of the 3 Little Pigs!*, but there are many others.

Shifts in point of view within a story are occurring more frequently as well. For example, Wolff's (1997) *Bat 6* tells the story of a girls' softball game, and more than 20 narrators step up to the plate to provide their take on a second "date which will live in infamy" in our nation's history—the beginning of the internment of Japanese American citizens. While some feel that a batting order of so many narrators will confuse children, in the hands of a capable teacher these difficulties are easily surmounted. I've seen teachers and children create a roster of the details of each character on butcher paper as they read the story. One teacher had his children construct baseball cards, giving the "stats" of each character, including their position on the field as well as their position on the central conflict. I've seen other teachers and children place more emphasis on the community rather than the individual characters, focusing on what's being said, rather than who said it. Either choice reflects point of view, for this literary element helps you and your children to take a stance on story, aligning yourselves with some characters and staying at a distance from others.

Style

Mark Twain wrote that "the difference between the *almost right* word and the *right* word is really a large matter—'tis the difference between the lightning bug and the lightning" (Neider, 1961, p. 228). When we talk about word choice and the pairing and placement of words into prose, we are talking about style. Authors make stylistic choices to set the mood of their tales, reveal character, and give voice to their individual personalities. With regard to style, you and your children could ask: What are some of the stylistic choices made by the author? With a text-to-text lens, how do the stylistic choices in one story compare and/or contrast to other tales? From a genetic perspective, why is the author's style so recognizable? Using formal criticism, how do specific choices expand or diminish the tale? Does the author make use of a wide variety of stylistic devices or limit the selection to only a few? From a sociocultural perspective, does the style reflect particular ways with words?

In simple stories, style is often more subdued. Fables lay out the scene in short, succinct sentences. Folk and fairy tales make generous use of simile— "hair as beautiful as beaten gold" or the witch in *Hansel and Gretel*, who is described as having "a keen sense of smell, like an animal." Symbols are simple words that stand for much larger issues. Indeed, the words "witch" and "stepmother" conjure up complicated images of evil and envy, and little more needs to be said than "into the woods" and we know where the danger lies. On the other hand, tall tales are known for their hyperbole—a literary term for exaggeration. For example, when *John Henry* (Lester, 1994) is born the sun is so thrilled he forgets to call it a night, and the grown-up hero can swing his hammer so fast a rainbow hugs his shoulders.

At the simplest level, science fiction is often marked by technical vocabu-lary. In *The Ear, the Eye, and the Arm* (Farmer, 1994), Tendai's home in futur-istic Zimbabwe is tended by robot gardeners, message-bearing holophones, and an automatic Doberman, but the complexity of issues raised in the novel extends far beyond the technicalities. And in her latest National Book Award winner, *The House of the Scorpion*, Farmer (2002) takes us even further to question computer chips that ensure docility in humans as well as consider the fate of human clones, who are harvested for organs to prolong the life of the rich and powerful.

As tales increase in complexity, the range of stylistic devices expands. Imagery appeals to the senses, allowing us to see, hear, feel, and even smell the world the author is creating. The use of figurative language expands the denotative or dictionary definition of words and phrases into unique images using personification, simile, and metaphor. Listen and feel a passage from *Charlotte's Web* that describes the shifting seasons:

> The crickets sang in the grasses. They sang the song of summer's ending, a sad, monotonous song. "Summer is over and gone," they sang. "Over and gone, over and gone. Summer is dying, dying.
>
> The crickets felt it was their duty to warn everybody that summertime cannot last forever. Even on the most beautiful days in the whole year—the days when summer is changing into fall—the crickets spread the rumor of sadness and change. . . .
>
> The sheep heard the crickets, and they felt so uneasy they broke a hole in the pasture fence and wandered up into the field across the road. The gander discovered the hole and led his family through, and they walked to the orchard and ate the apples that were lying on the ground. A little maple tree in the swamp heard the cricket song and turned bright red with anxiety. (pp. 113–114)

While the imagery and figurative language in the passage help you to feel the "rumor of sadness and change," the effect is enhanced by the actual sound of the words. Indeed, in any well-crafted tale, consonance (a clicking collective of consonants), assonance (echoing vowel sounds), and alliteration (first letters repeating in a lyrical list) help to establish rhythm as well as set mood.

Authors select and blend stylistic devices in their stories. For example, Mildred Taylor (1976) makes extensive use of a variety of stylistic devices in *Roll of Thunder, Hear My Cry*—rhythm, rhyme, and the overarching metaphor of the African American spiritual from which the book's name is derived; the use of African American English, especially the discourse patterns, to reflect the characters' lives; and personification as the school bus careening down the road takes on a life of its own.

In *The Watson's Go to Birmingham—1963*, Curtis weaves his own cloth of stylistic threads, and the resulting blend of color and craft shimmers off the page. Consider the following passage, when Kenny enters the church looking for his sister, Joey, and finds what he thinks is her shoe under the rubble:

> I bent down to pull the shoe from under the concrete and tugged and pulled at it but it felt like something was pulling it back.
>
> All the hair on my head jumped up to attention. The light flickered back on and the smoke cleared and I could see that hanging on to the other end of the shoe was a giant gray hand with cold, hard square fingers.

> Oh-oh. I looked up and saw a familiar guy and before he got covered with smoke he looked at me and I saw he had big square shoulders and nothing where his face should have been. The Wool Pooh.
>
> Oh, man. I gave the shoe one more hard tug and it popped loose from a frilly white sock. I got real scared. I walked as slowly and as quietly as I could out of the church. Maybe if I moved quietly he wouldn't come for me. Maybe if I walked and didn't look back he'd leave me alone. I walked past where the adults were still screaming and pointing, I walked past where that guy had set the little girl in blue, right next to where someone else had set a little girl in red. I knew if Joey sat down next to those two their dresses would make the red, white and blue of the American flag. Grown-ups were kneeling down by them and the adults' hands fluttered down toward the little girls, then before they touched anything, fluttered back up, over and over. Their hands looked like a little flock of brown sparrows that were too nervous to land. (pp. 185-186)

It's hard to know where to begin with a passage of such aching beauty, but let's first consider the pull of the shoe, that literally pulls us into the scene with Kenny. When he feels the resistant tug, Kenny knows immediately who it is, and his fear is personified as "all the hair on [his] head jumped to attention." The Wool Pooh is personification as well—a symbol, a metaphor for the gray and faceless, cold, hard body of racism that would drag a little girl to her death. Indeed, the monster is so menacing he doesn't even need a complete sentence. He stands alone as "The Wool Pooh."

Kenny's "Oh-oh" and "Oh, man" seem like such simple statements, but their simplicity tells us much more than an elaborate explanation would. And you can hear the sound of the shoe as "it popped loose from a frilly white sock"—with the assonance of "popped" and "sock" adding rhythm to the painful reality. The repeated use of "walked" is what Ray (1999) calls a "close echo" (p. 31), a word that doesn't need to be repeated, but its consistency sends a vital message. The repetition conveys the feeling of Kenny moving in a dream world, trying to walk past the chaos, but still inescapably a part of its reality.

The images to follow are the most direct, as Kenny sees the red and blue dresses of two little girls "set" down by adults, and he knows that "if" his sister "sat down" with them, "their dresses would make the red, white and blue of the American flag." The difference between the more passive "set" and Joey's more active "sat" gives us hope that she is alive, as does the crucial use of the hypothetical "if." But we know there is no hope for the two "set" down. The irony of the image of the flag reminds us that life, liberty, and the pursuit of happiness will not be granted to these children. Finally, the helplessness of the adults is symbolized in the simile of their hands "like a little flock of brown sparrows that were too nervous to land." The close echoes in "fluttered down" and "fluttered back up, over and over" reiterate the shock of the scene.

This brief analysis demonstrates what you and your children can do when you pay close attention to style. What's critical to remember is that this kind of formal criticism does not diminish the emotional weight of the text. Instead, it enhances it, allowing us to see the care with which Curtis crafted his message, helping us to care more deeply about Kenny in his confrontation with the Wool Pooh.

Tone

Tone is an expression of the author's attitude toward his or her subject. Integrally linked to style, tone not only reveals character, setting, plot, and theme, but it unveils the author's feelings about how these literary elements should play out. Tone can be humorous, serious, affectionate, warm, cool, condescending, or even sarcastic. When you and your children discuss tone you might ask: What is the tone used in this particular passage or about this particular character? From a genetic perspective, what does the tone reveal about the author and her or his life experiences? Is a similar tone maintained throughout the story or does it shift depending on the scene or the character? From a formal perspective, how is tone reflected in stylistic choices?

Simple stories often have a uniform and straightforward tone. Fables call for consistency. Tall tales thrive on the humor of hyperbole. Folk and fairy tales, known as *zaubermärchen* in Germany and *contes merveilleux* in France are marked by an overarching tone of wonder (Zipes, 1991). Still, these oral wonder tales shift underlying tone for different characters—no one can doubt the author's alternating attitudes toward the wicked stepmother and the young *Hansel and Gretel*. Even when the words are minimal, Anthony Browne's illustrations make up for what the words do not say.

Although the stepmother has been complaining that they have no money, her bedroom dresser is covered with luxurious items—powders, polishes, even Oil of Olay. As she leads the poorly dressed children off into the forest, she sports a leopard skin coat with tall black boots and a cigarette dangling from her blood-red lips. While the children's and father's clothes are smudged with dirt, the stepmother's coat looks like it just came back from the dry cleaners. Although we cannot directly hear illustrators' explanations of how they feel about characters or events, we can see and feel their meanings in the stylistic choices they make.

As stories become increasingly complex, shifts in tone are common. For example, towards the end of *The Circuit* (Jiménez, 1997), we have a sense of hope for Francisco and his migrant family. His brother, Roberto, has just gotten a year-round job and through sheer determination, Francisco is learning English. He's even memorized a section of the Declaration of Independence to recite to his teacher, but before he can present the "inalienable rights . . . of life, liberty, and the pursuit of happiness," the Border Patrol appears and takes him away in his car. In this poignant scene, the tone shifts from hope to despair, like a candle being snuffed out.

In *Matilda*, Roald Dahl (1988) provided a dramatic shift in tone as he moved from character to character—innocent, intelligent Matilda, the caring Miss Honey, and the towering inferno of the headmistress Miss Trunchbull. Even the character names hint at the tone, and anyone familiar with Dahl's own experiences with boarding school knows his intense dislike of the many adults placed in charge of children's minds. Thus, a rose by any other name may not smell as sweet. Consider the differences in the names and descriptions of characters in *Harry Potter and the Sorcerer's Stone* (Rowling, 1998): Draco Malfoy in contrast to Harry Potter, Snape as opposed to Dumbledore, and lest we forget, Voldemort, with the Latin root of death (mort) lurking in his name. In this popular fantasy, the names point to the conflict between good and evil as well as reveal Rowling's attitudes toward the characters.

In *The Watsons Go to Birmingham—1963*, Curtis's feelings about the "Wool Pooh" are equally clear. At first, it's evident that the children have confused the term with a "whirlpool" in a nearby swimming hole that their grandmother has warned them against. Their mispronunciation takes on an even funnier tone when Byron tells Kenny and Joey "the Wool Pooh is Winnie's evil twin brother. . . . What he does is hide underwater and snatch stupid kids down with him" (p. 170). But from the moment Kenny goes swimming by himself and the Wool Pooh appears, the tone shifts dramatically:

> That's when he came swimming real slow out of the deep, and even though my head was underneath the dark water I could see him coming right at me. He didn't look like he was related to Winnie-the-Pooh at all, he was big and gray with hard square-looking fingers. Where he should have had a face there was nothing but dark gray. Where he should have had eyes there was nothing but a darker cooler-looking color. He grabbed my leg and started pulling me down. (p. 176)

Though Byron saves Kenny from the Wool Pooh's clutches this time, the second time Kenny meets him in the church, he faces his fate alone, and the tone is much more menacing.

One of the reasons the Wool Pooh is so threatening in his second scene is because the event takes on broader significance. In the first scene, Kenny almost meets death because he's swimming where he shouldn't, and he escapes because Byron rescues him. However, in the second scene, he witnesses the church bombing and the death of little Sunday school girls, and even the love of his family cannot help him escape from racism. Thus, shifts in tone do not always hinge on characters, but on the events of the story as well. The beginning of Curtis's story is one of marvelous humor, with hysterical as well as affectionate scenes of the Weird Watsons in action. But once the family heads south to Birmingham, the tone shifts from hilariously funny to as "serious as a heart attack" (p. 204).

Kenny's stay in the World-Famous Watson Pet Hospital is marked by Curtis's pain that a world like this exists and that children have to face it. We hear his concern through Kenny's parents as they sit on the couch and try to think how they can explain the bombing of a church to their children, "Some of the time they were mad, some of the time they were calm and some of the time they just sat on the couch and cried" (p. 191–192). Although the children have denied it, they think that Kenny might have gone into the church, and Kenny's mother painfully cries, "Lord, who knows what that poor baby saw" (p. 192). In his moving epilogue for the story, we also hear Curtis's awe and respect for the "many heroic people [who] died in the struggle for civil rights" (p. 210). His tone offers both challenge and support for the heroism that potentially exits in us all. Thus, tone in a novel as complex as *The Watson's Go to Birmingham—1963* shifts dramatically depending on character and situation, revealing the authors' feelings, attitudes, and even hope against hope for a better world.

Poetry

From prose we now turn to poetry, a much older art form, and a genre known for rhythm, rhyme, structured sound patterns, figurative language, and even shapes that deliver evocative images and emotional intensity in a highly compact form. Figure 2.5 offers brief definitions of these central features as well as a list of some of my favorite books of poetry.

As Eleanor Farjeon explains, poetry is "not a rose, but the scent of the rose . . . Not the sea, but the sound of the sea" (Huck, Hepler, Hickman, &

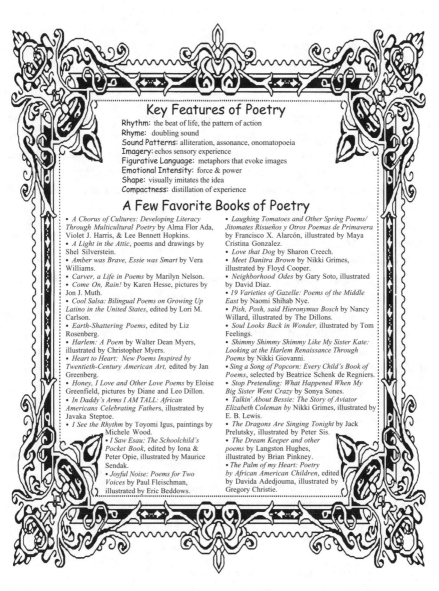

Key Features of Poetry

Rhythm: the beat of life, the pattern of action
Rhyme: doubling sound
Sound Patterns: alliteration, assonance, onomatopoeia
Imagery: echos sensory experience
Figurative Language: metaphors that evoke images
Emotional Intensity: force & power
Shape: visually imitates the idea
Compactness: distillation of experience

A Few Favorite Books of Poetry

- *A Chorus of Cultures: Developing Literacy Through Multicultural Poetry* by Alma Flor Ada, Violet J. Harris, & Lee Bennett Hopkins.
- *A Light in the Attic*, poems and drawings by Shel Silverstein.
- *Amber was Brave, Essie was Smart* by Vera Williams.
- *Carver, a Life in Poems* by Marilyn Nelson.
- *Come On, Rain!* by Karen Hesse, pictures by Jon J. Muth.
- *Cool Salsa: Bilingual Poems on Growing Up Latino in the United States*, edited by Lori M. Carlson.
- *Earth-Shattering Poems*, edited by Liz Rosenberg.
- *Harlem: A Poem* by Walter Dean Myers, illustrated by Christopher Myers.
- *Heart to Heart: New Poems Inspired by Twentieth-Century American Art*, edited by Jan Greenberg.
- *Honey, I Love and Other Love Poems* by Eloise Greenfield, pictures by Diane and Leo Dillon.
- *In Daddy's Arms I AM TALL: African Americans Celebrating Fathers*, illustrated by Javaka Steptoe.
- *I See the Rhythm* by Toyomi Igus, paintings by Michele Wood.
- *I Saw Esau: The Schoolchild's Pocket Book*, edited by Iona & Peter Opie, illustrated by Maurice Sendak.
- *Joyful Noise: Poems for Two Voices* by Paul Fleischman, illustrated by Eric Beddows.
- *Laughing Tomatoes and Other Spring Poems/ Jitomates Risueños y Otros Poemas de Primavera* by Francisco X. Alarcón, illustrated by Maya Cristina Gonzalez.
- *Love that Dog* by Sharon Creech.
- *Meet Danitra Brown* by Nikki Grimes, illustrated by Floyd Cooper.
- *Neighborhood Odes* by Gary Soto, illustrated by David Diaz.
- *19 Varieties of Gazelle: Poems of the Middle East* by Naomi Shihab Nye.
- *Pish, Posh, said Hieronymus Bosch* by Nancy Willard, illustrated by The Dillons.
- *Soul Looks Back in Wonder*, illustrated by Tom Feelings.
- *Shimmy Shimmy Shimmy Like My Sister Kate: Looking at the Harlem Renaissance Through Poems* by Nikki Giovanni.
- *Sing a Song of Popcorn: Every Child's Book of Poems*, selected by Beatrice Schenk de Regniers.
- *Stop Pretending: What Happened When My Big Sister Went Crazy* by Sonya Sones.
- *Talkin' About Bessie: The Story of Aviator Elizabeth Coleman* by Nikki Grimes, illustrated by E. B. Lewis.
- *The Dragons Are Singing Tonight* by Jack Prelutsky, illustrated by Peter Sis.
- *The Dream Keeper and other poems* by Langston Hughes, illustrated by Brian Pinkney.
- *The Palm of my Heart: Poetry by African American Children*, edited by Davida Adedjouma, illustrated by Gregory Christie.

FIG. 2.5.   Key Features & Favorite Books of Poetry.

Kiefer, 1997, p. 390). Indeed, poetry seems to demand poetic explanations. Emily Dickinson said, "If I read a book and it makes my whole body so cold no fire can ever warm me, I know that is poetry. If I feel physically as if the top of my head were taken off, I know that is poetry" (cited in Lukens, 2003, p. 241). And Dickinson was dismissive of prose, "They shut me up in Prose— / As when a little Girl / They put me in the Closet — / Because they liked me 'still' — / Still!" (Franklin, 1999, p. 206).

Robert Pinsky (1998), the Poet Laureate of the United States, used yet another poet's comment to separate prose from poetry, "Ezra Pound wrote that poetry is a centaur. That is, in prose, one aims an arrow at a target. In a poem, one does the same thing, while also riding a horse. The horse I take to be the human body. Poetry calls upon both intellectual and bodily skills" (p. 8). Thus, poetry, at its best, hits the target of image and emotion, while hanging on tight to the rhythm of the movement and the sound of the hoof beat.

To demonstrate some of the features of poetry, I've selected several poems that have close ties to the touchstone texts for this chapter: *The Watsons Go to Birmingham—1963* and *Hansel and Gretel*. As Dickinson, Pinsky, and Pound suggest, poetry *is* different from prose. Yet, teachers of literature must teach both, and although it's important to understand their unique qualities, children might see their distinctions best in combination as well as in contrast. Thus, the text-to-text and formal criticism I use to analyze the upcoming poetry is designed to not only emphasize the differences in structure and sound, but to underline the similarities in theme and emotion. Let's begin with the fairy tale.

Text-to-Text Poetry for Hansel and Gretel

One place to start is quite obvious, for there are three small poems inserted into the prose text of *Hansel and Gretel*. The first poem is in the form of two couplets as the children begin to feast upon the witch's house:

Then a low voice called from inside the house:
  "Nibble, nibble, little mouse,
  Who is gnawing at my house?"
The children answered:
  "Only the wind,
  The heaven-sent wind."

The couplet is a very old rhyming form, and consists of two rhyming lines that are often the same length. Although a couplet can be a poem in itself, these couplets form a conversation.

The first couplet contains an end rhyme as well as the repetition of the word "nibble." We know from the story that the witch has created her house as a trap for children, but her words "little mouse" make her sound like a mother crooning to her own children, instead of luring them into her house and later, her oven. The fact that the witch's couplet has the same number of syllables and rhythm gives her call a singsong quality and makes it all the more inviting. The second couplet rhymes as well, but the line length is uneven and the same word creates the rhyme which makes the children's response seem more open and free like the word "wind" itself. Perhaps it foreshadows that the witch will not be able to confine them for long.

The second poem in *Hansel and Gretel* occurs when the children have defeated the witch and are on their way home. They come to "a great stretch of water" and without a boat or a bridge in sight, Gretel calls out to a duck for help

> *"Little duck, little duck,*
> *Here stand Hansel and Gretel.*
> *There is no bridge upon our track,*
> *Take us over on your white back."*

This is a quatrain, which consists of four lines, though the rhyming pattern can vary. Still, the quatrain in *Hansel and Gretel* is unusual. The repetition of the "ck" sound makes a clear end rhyme in lines three and four, but also brings an echoing rhyme with similar sounds in line one. The second line is the most distinct, *"Here stand Hansel and Gretel,"* and without a hint of a rhyme with the other lines, it makes the children's independent stance all the more prominent.

The final poem is a couplet that appears at the very end of the tale:

> *My tale is done; see the mouse run;*
> *Catch it if you would, to make a fur hood.*

This couplet has an internal rhyme in both lines. Livingston (1991) told us, "When one couplet makes a complete poem, it is called a *closed couplet*"

(p. 38), and this makes a fitting closing to the tale as well, bringing us away from the dream world of story and back to reality.

Indeed, the placement of the three poems in *Hansel and Gretel* seem to mark special places in the prose that show us when we are passing from one world to the next. The first appears when the children truly leave reality and enter into the fantasy world of the witch's house. Maria Tatar (1987) explained:

> Parental abandonment of children is no routine, everyday event, but it remains within the confines of plausibility. Not so with the incidents that follow hard upon the desertion of the children. Here, fairy tales and facts part company. Once Hansel and Gretel enter the forest, they find themselves in a world that not only admits the supernatural, but also takes it completely for granted. Here houses can be made of bread, roofs of cake, and windows of sugar; witches with red eyes lie eagerly in wait for young innocents; and ducks routinely offer children ferry service. (pp. 50-51)

The duck provides a second service as well, for it literally ferries the children out of the fantasy part of the tale and helps them home. The final poem offers a significant shift as well. First, it alters the point of view from a more omniscient voice, to that of the storyteller as indicated by "*My tale is done.*" It's almost as if we are so entranced with the dream world of the tale that we forget the real world around us as we listen. The break occurs in the recognition of a mouse running across the floor, and the storyteller's words awaken us to action. Thus, you might think of the poetic interludes in the predominately prose text of *Hansel and Gretel* as a dream within a dream. The children's entry into the forest and escape from the witch is the central dream, but it is surrounded by your own entrée and exit from the world of story.

The image of a mouse leads us to our second text-to-text connection with *Hansel and Gretel*—a poem by Ruth Whitman (1968) entitled "Listening to Grownups Quarrelling":

> standing in the hall against the
> wall with my little brother, blown
> like leaves against the wall by their
> voices, my head like a pingpong ball
> between the paddles of their anger;
> I knew what it meant

to tremble like a leaf.
Cold with their wrath, I heard
the claws of the rain
pounce. Floods
Poured through the city,
skies clapped over me,
and I was shaken, shaken,
Like a mouse
between their jaws. (p. 9)

This poem has clear links to the prose text of *Hansel and Gretel*, when the children overhear their parents arguing about what to do with them. Indeed, the poem allows us to expand on the emotions in this scene. In prose, the text tells us "Hunger had kept the children awake, too, and they heard what their stepmother said to their father. Gretel cried bitterly and said to Hansel, 'It's all over for us now.'" But the poem helps us feel the children's helpless terror even more.

Although Whitman's poem is free verse, there is internal rhyme in "hall," "wall," and "ball." There's also a fair amount of repetition in well-chosen words, particularly "leaves / leaf" and "shaken, shaken." These choices double the impact of the central similes—images that painfully describe parental fury. The children are blown up against the wall "like leaves." They are shuttled back and forth "like a pingpong ball between the paddles of their anger." And the eldest child feels "like a mouse" at the mercy of the "pounce" of the cat-like storm, accentuated by a final rhyme of "claws" and "jaws." These two words are "clapped" over the heads of the children as the claws come down followed quickly by the jaws.

The children in Whitman's poem are at the mercy of their parents' tempest, but the tale of *Hansel and Gretel* shows how they emerge from the storm and conquer the forces therein. While Gretel is pictured in prose as crying bitterly over her fate, she is the one who defeats the witch as well as poetically negotiates with the duck for their passage home. Her growing independence leads us to our third text-to-text poem, and this poem is linked in several ways. It comes from Gwen Strauss's (1990) *Trail of Stones*, and, like *Hansel and Gretel*, it is illustrated by Anthony Browne. The poetry in this book takes altering points of view on traditional fairy tales, and the one linked to *Hansel and Gretel* is told from the point of view of "Their Father." The second half of the poem shows his anguish at the loss of his children, his wife's

increasing anger and ultimate death, and the shift in his relationship with
Gretel when she returns home:

> The time they were away is silent
> but for the sawing of inward anger.
> I dreamed of birds,
> swooping down on their trail.
> My wife ate and ate
> but grew thin in front of me.
>
> I did nothing. When she died
> I drew inside the cottage,
> shutters closed, a cage.
> I lived in the smallest gestures:
> sweeping, building a fire.
> I moved as little as possible.
>
> If I had the courage
> I would enter the woods,
> but I clung to cupboard habits.
>
> Gretel, with her apron full of pearls,
> has bought us a flock of geese.
> Each morning I scatter crumbs for them;
> Gretel likes it when I help:
> either that, she says, or when I stay
> out of her way. (Strauss, 1990, pp. 2-4)

The illustration that accompanies this poem shows their father staring blankly
out to us. He sits in a shuttered room, and on the wall behind him is a
painting of "The Scream" by Edvard Munch—an infamous portrait of despair.
The peeling wallpaper mirrors the father's dream of birds that begin with
dark images of bats, but as they climb higher on the wall they emerge into
lighter birds in flight. His forearm bears a heart-shaped tattoo pierced by an
arrow.

The images in the words of the poem are equally revealing. While the stepmother wastes away in anger, he is trapped by immobility, both literally and
figuratively. The opening sentence in the second stanza—"I did nothing"—
speaks volumes. Even when he speaks of courage it is tenuous and short
lived, just as this stanza is shorter than the others. Furthermore, the images

of confinement are marked with alliteration in "cottage," "closed," "cage," "clung," and "cupboard habits." Of course, the jolt in the poem comes with the ironic last stanza. Now it is Gretel who is in charge of the house, and the father's tasks are either simple or he must simply "stay / out of her way." The end rhyme in this final set of lines reiterates how isolated and inept he has become. Like the geese he feeds, Gretel feeds him only the smallest of crumbs.

The negligence of fairy tale fathers is well known, yet they usually manage to avoid punishment. As Tatar (1987) explained, "they remain benevolent personages largely because benign neglect contrasts favorably with the monstrous deeds of their wives" (p. 149). Not so in this poem. Instead, the father must pay the price of passivity. While Gretel doesn't browbeat him as his wife did, she is well aware of his complicity and cowardice, and keeps him to his "cupboard habits," especially those that can keep him at a distance. She has laid down her own trail of stones, and she doesn't need her father to accompany her on her path.

Making links between prose and poetry as well as looking for places where paths cross and double back, is not simply the work of literary critics. Your children, too, can actively engage in this kind of analysis, especially if you choose links that will help them lift their own meanings off the page. What child hasn't entered into imaginary worlds, defeated a witch, and dreamed of riding home with pearls in her pocket? What child hasn't heard adults argue and wondered about his fate? What child hasn't dreamed of being in charge, with the adults in her life in the background? Thus, the compression of sound and image in poetry works well to expand the prose. And the opposite is true as well, for we would never understand the poem of "Their Father" if we hadn't read the prose version of *Hansel and Gretel* first. Thus, the analytic combination of prose and poetry can further amplify your children's literary engagement.

Text-to-Text Poetry for The Watsons

We start here with the poem that inspired Christopher Paul Curtis. Recall that in an interview, Curtis explained how the Watsons were originally on their way to Florida when his son brought home the "Ballad of Birmingham" by Dudley Randall (Danner & Randall, 1969). The poem provided Curtis with a new destination for the Watsons as well as for the novel itself:

"Mother dear, may I go downtown
Instead of out to play,

And march the streets of Birmingham
In a Freedom March today?"

"No, baby, no, you may not go,
For the dogs are fierce and wild,
And clubs and hoses, guns and jails
Aren't good for a little child."

"But, mother, I won't be alone.
Other children will go with me,
And march the streets of Birmingham
To make our country free."

"No, baby, no, you may not go,
For I fear those guns will fire.
But you may go to church instead
And sing in the children's choir."

She has combed and brushed her night-dark hair,
And bathed rose petal sweet,
And drawn white gloves on her small brown hands,
And white shoes on her feet.

The mother smiled to know that her child
Was in the sacred place,
But that smile was the last smile
To come upon her face.

For when she heard the explosion,
Her eyes grew wet and wild.
She raced through the streets of Birmingham
Calling for her child.

She clawed through bits of glass and brick,
Then lifted out a shoe.
"O, here's the shoe my baby wore,
But, baby, where are you?" (p. 4)

Quatrains typically rhyme in the second and fourth lines, and this pattern holds in the "Ballad of Birmingham." The poem was originally published in a broadside that appeared as a folded card with an illustrated cover, the poem inside, and publication information on the back. Broadside ballads were typical in 16th and 17th century England, but Randall used this traditional form to address his own political times. He sold this first broadside publication in 1965 for 35 cents. Sullivan (1997) explained:

> Randall's broadside reminds the audience of what is at stake in the struggle for civil rights—no sanctuary, no respect for innocence, the potential for violent resistance not just to social change, but even to the presence, new or continued, of blacks in community with whites. There is no such thing as staying out of the struggle in order to avoid trouble. The violence touches even this woman who would keep her family out of the danger of active political protests like the Freedom March. To read, buy, have, or give the card is to participate in the struggle she could not stay out of.

The poem begins with a conversation between a child and her mother. The child is calling for political participation in "Mother, dear, may I go downtown." But the mother, who knows the cruelty of the world, refuses the call—"No, baby, no, you may not go." The repetition in the word "may" hints at the repetition often seen in call-and-response patterns in African American English, but the refusal seems contrary to a pattern that is often marked by encouragement. However, the back-and-forth nature of their conversation breaks at the mid-point of the poem, and the point of view shifts to a limited omniscient view focused on the mother. The shift in view foreshadows the loss of her daughter, for the mother will be alone with her thoughts from now on. Her conversation with her daughter is finished.

Repetition with a slight alteration alerts us to the danger. The internal rhyme of "smiled" and "child" reflects the sense of safety the mother feels about church as "a sacred place,/But that smile was the last smile/to come upon her face." The sense of contentment is shattered with the word "explosion," and the pace of the poem picks up as the mother "raced through the streets of Birmingham" (p. 102). The image of the mother's race has strong parallels to Kenny's description in *The Watsons*, for after he hears the explosion and sees his brother Bryon take off in the direction of the church, he says, "It looked like someone had set off a people magnet, it seemed like everyone in Birmingham was running down the street, it looked like a river of scared brown bodies was being jerked in the same direction that By had gone, so I followed" (pp. 183–184).

The final stanza of the "Ballad of Birmingham" has the closest connections, not only to the novel, but also to the reality. The mother of Carole Robertson, one of the children who died in the explosion, talked about the shoes her daughter wore to Sunday school that day:

> She and I had gone shopping and we found the shoes, which were shiny black ones. . . . And on that Sunday morning she wore the new shoes and her necklace. After the bombing, I think some weeks after, Mrs. Lillian S. Moore of the Davenport and Harris Funeral Home, came and brought me the shoes. There wasn't a scratch on them. Not one mark. I kept them for years and years . . . (Sikora, 1991, p. 17)

Like the mother in the "Ballad of Birmingham," when Kenny enters the church he, too, discovers a shoe in the midst of the destruction, but he can't find his sister.

In the poem, the child is "combed and brushed" and "bathed," and has gloves and shoes "drawn" on. These verbs provide a vision of her peaceful preparation for church. Yet, the words stand in stark contrast to the mother's "wet and wild" run through the city and how she "clawed" her way through what she thought was "a sacred place." Even more emblematic, the point of view shifts again in the final two lines, and the mother's lament is her own, though this time, the call will yield no response.

Still, calling out to voice hope for a better world is a central theme in *The Watsons Go To Birmingham—1963*, and this call leads us to our last poem. Part of a collection of African American poetry in Tom Feelings' (1993) astonishing Caldecott winner *Soul Looks Back in Wonder*, the poem is entitled "To You" and was written by Langston Hughes:

> To sit and dream, to sit and read,
> To sit and learn about the world
> Outside our world of here and now—
> Our problem world—
> To dream of vast horizons of the soul
> Through dreams made whole,
> Unfettered, free—help me!
> All you who are dreamers too,
> Help me to make
> Our world anew.
> I reach out my dreams to you.

Langston Hughes composed this poem "to accompany Tom Feelings's art on a poster for the Congress of Racial Equality in 1962." Though it was published for the first time in *Soul Looks Back in Wonder*, the central image of a dream occurs in many of Hughes's poems. He wrote "Harlem" with its famous opening line about "a dream deferred," as well as "Dream Boogie" and "Dream Variations." As Nikki Giovanni (1996) explained, "I like Langston because he picked at things. He knew not just that he had a wonderful line, but he had a wonderful concept.... But it's not just a dream, it's a right" (p. 52).

It was a right that Langston Hughes believed in—even when he saw it deferred and denied time and time again. He so believed in the dream that in a short poem of only eleven lines, he used variations on the word five times. And the long *e* in dream echoes in the assonance of the poem—re<u>a</u>d," fr<u>ee</u>," "m<u>e</u>," and "r<u>ea</u>ch." The poem also pivots on a shift in voice—it begins with the infinitive—a basic verb form that names the action without naming the subject, "To sit and dream, to sit and read." But by the end of the poem, the verb becomes an imperative, a plea, a command, a repeated cry: "Help me!" The subject becomes clear in "All of you who are dreamers too, / ...I reach out my dream to you." The direct address in the poem calls for action.

This is true of the epilogue of *The Watsons* as well. Here Curtis explains the history of civil rights with a more distanced voice. He provides dates and facts and places and events. He names the children who were murdered in the church. Yet, after naming the girls to whom he dedicated his novel, he shifts his voice to speak openly with the reader, "Although these may be nothing more than names in a book to you now, you must remember that these children were just as precious to their families as Joetta was to the Watsons or as your brothers and sisters are to you" (p. 209). Following this connection with his audience, he shifts back to describe the heroes of the Civil Rights movement. Still, as he nears the end of his exposition, he switches again from "they" and "many heroic people" to direct address: "One of them may be you." Thus, both Curtis and Hughes call out to their readers for heroic action, "Help me to make / Our world anew." And it's clear they expect a response.

Summary

In truth, all prose and poetry call for a response. They call out for interpretation, inviting readers to enter into textual worlds and to construct meaning in powerful ways. Still, I believe children's personal transaction with literature is enhanced when they use a variety of critical lenses. In this chapter, I emphasize formal criticism to showcase the features of both prose and poetry. Using *Hansel and Gretel* and *The Watsons Go to Birmingham—1963* (among other examples), I offer an overview of the eight components: genre, theme, character, setting, plot, point of view, style, and tone. For each component, I provide a definition, discuss associated literary terms, and show how you can effectively explore these features with children. As Peterson and Eeds (1990) argued, "a gradual increase in awareness of how various authors use these elements in particular stories enables us to enter ever further into story worlds and see and understand them so much more. It is the interaction of the elements of literature that brings story into existence" (p. 25).

From prose, I turn to poetry, selecting poems with clear connections to the touchstone texts. I then analyze these poems using formal criticism. Livingston (1991) suggested, "We don't ask the question *What* does a poem mean? for if the poet has written well, we seem to know inside of ourselves what it means to us. It is better to ask, as John Ciardi has said, *How* does a poem mean?" (pp. ix–x). Analyzing the *how* often comes with close attention to rhythm, rhyme, figurative language, and sound patterns, emphasizing a poem's compact and highly connotative ways of communicating feeling. I also apply text-to-text criticism to show how the selected poems compared and contrasted with the touchstone texts.

Throughout the chapter, I try to provide some examples of ways that you could teach these texts. I mention using double entry journals to analyze character and graphing plot. But I purposefully downplay the pedagogical examples, in order to emphasize how prose and poetry work. Like the Livingston quote above, I believe that if you know *how* a story or verse makes meaning, you will be better equipped to know *what* to do with a piece of prose or poetry to help your students make meaning as well.

In the opening of this chapter, I emphasize the predominant "home-away-home" pattern in children's literature. The central idea is that in order to mature, children must do it by themselves. I showcase example after example where children fell down a rabbit hole, sailed away to rumpus with wild things, swirled from Kansas to Oz in the eye of a storm, and entered the woods on their own. Even in less fantastic fiction, children must often face their fates alone. But this pattern is not the case in teaching children's literature. Children need capable teachers to guide them, and the more knowledge about prose and poetry you have, the more opportunities your children will have for literary engagement. As Perry Nodelman (1996) clearly suggested:

> The ability to respond to literature with an understanding of its subtleties, and with a flexible attitude to the possibilities of meanings it might convey and emotions it might arouse—in other words, the ability to enjoy literature—is a learned skill. Those of us who enjoy reading may have developed our own skills

for enjoying literature unconsciously, simply by reading a lot. But many people who have read less can be encouraged by sensitive teachers to learn the skills of literary enjoyment. Children in particular can learn to become more perceptive readers of literature—and greatly increase their pleasure in the act of reading as a result of it. (p. 23)

I'd even argue that "those of us who enjoy reading" probably got to that point not "just by reading," but by reading *with* someone we cared for and admired, someone who opened the doors to literary worlds and ushered us in, someone who stopped to say, "Did you see this?" and "What did you think about that?" and "Doesn't this poem remind you of that piece of prose?" and, of course, *"How does a poem or a piece of prose mean?"*

As teachers of literature, it would be a poor choice to send children into the forest of criticism alone, no matter how lovely, dark, and deep the woods may be. Literary engagement is a *learned skill*. More important, it's a *social experience*. Thus, if we truly want children to follow the trail of stones put down by prose and poetry and find their way home again—safe, but altered— we need to help them see some of the patterns in the path. And they will, no doubt, help us to see others.

BOOKS FOR THE PROFESSIONAL

Huck, C. S., Hepler, S., Hickman, J., and Kiefer, B. Z. (1997). *Children's literature in the elementary school* (Sixth edition). Dubuque, IA: Brown & Benchmark. This tome is one of the best of the comprehensive textbooks available, and written by four of our leading scholars in children's literature: Charlotte Huck, Susan Hepler, Janet Hickman, and Barbara Kiefer. Filled with examples (over 4,000!) from children's prose and poetry, the text chapters range from a history of children's literature to how contemporary teachers plan their literature programs. The chapter on poetry is particularly informative.

Livingston, M. C. (1991). *Poem-making: Ways to begin writing poetry.* New York: HarperCollins. Myra Cohn Livingston is a poet, anthologist, and teacher of note. Here she provides a wonderful handbook, with clear and concise chapters on the features of poetry and how they work in individual poetic forms.

Lukens, R. (2003). *A critical handbook of children's literature.* New York: HarperCollins. This handbook is a must have for teachers who want to know even more about the components of narrative. Rebecca

Lukens provides chapters on genre, character, setting, plot, theme, style, point of view, and tone that are packed with examples. She also has informative chapters on poetry, picture books, and nonfiction.

Dresang, E. T. (1999). *Radical change: Books for youth in a digital age.* New York: H. W. Wilson. In this beautifully designed book, Eliza Dresang introduces us to *radical change*, suggesting that books for youth today are changing forms and formats, changing perspectives, and changing boundaries, making ample room for all children's voices, altered forms, and topics and themes that will draw children in rather than shut them out.

Chapter Touchstone Texts

Curtis, Christopher Paul. (1995). *The Watsons go to Birmingham— 1963.* New York: Delacorte. A winner of both Newbery and Coretta Scott King Honor Awards as well as an Honor book for the Jane Addams Book Award, Curtis tells the tale of a family of immense humor and greater courage who leave their home in Michigan to travel south towards "one of the darkest moments in America's history." This "new classic" demonstrates the deft integration of the narrative components from a gifted writer.

Grimm Brothers. (1981). *Hansel and Gretel*, illustrated by Anthony Browne. New York: Alfred A. Knopf. An old classic takes on new dimensions through the talents of a winner of the Hans Christian Andersen Award—an international children's book award for an author or illustrator's body of work. Browne's symbolic images, especially the visual link between the stepmother and the witch, make the plight of the children all the more frightening.

Recommended Tradebooks for Prose & Poetry

Ada, Alma Flor. (1991). *The gold coin*, illustrated by Neil Waldman. New York: Atheneum. In this new folktale, a thief named Juan follows Doña Josefa from place to place in an attempt to steal her gold. As he travels, he notes her kindness and finds himself in the unusual position of helping others as well. When he finally meets up with Doña Josefa and demands her coin, she gives it to him, recognizing his need. As a sign of his growing moral understanding, he too passes the coin on to another. The story's theme is one that children love to discuss. One teacher I know gave a young child a packet of chocolate gold coins, which he eagerly accepted at the start of the story. Yet, at the end of their story discussion, he quietly returned them, explaining that perhaps someone else needed them more.

Dorris, Michael. (1994). *Guests.* New York: Hyperion. This is the story of the first Thanksgiving, told from the Native American point of view. Exasperated with the coming of unwanted company, Moss enters the forest alone to find himself. Ultimately he discovers that you are who you are, especially if friends and family support you. This novel is marked by stories within stories, which makes the analysis of plot and theme all the more intriguing. Dorris also wrote *Morning Girl* (1992) a story that alternates point of view, as Morning Girl and her brother Star Boy—both Taino Indians—take turns telling about the arrival of the first Europeans in 1492.

Feelings, Tom. (1993). *Soul looks back in wonder.* New York: Dial. This Caldecott Award winning collection of African American poetry is gloriously illustrated by Tom Feelings. With poems by Eugene B. Redmond, Langston Hughes, and Askia Toure among others, the book is a celebration of African American creativity. One of my favorite poems is entitled "I Love the Look of Words" by Maya Angelou, which demonstrates the delicious quality of language as it moves into a child's life. Much influenced by the prose and poetry read to her by a friend of her grandmother's, Angelou writes, "Most of the things I do now come out of what that understanding woman read to me and got me to reading as a child."

Myers, Walter Dean. (1997). *Harlem: A poem*, illustrated by Christopher Myers. New York: Scholastic Press. What a book! An award-winning author for both his prose and poetry, Walter Dean Myers joins with his award-winning son for a poem that captures the promise of Harlem. The sounds of Harlem's history and its living, breathing present are made all the more glorious by the sights that Christopher Myers provides in mixed-media collage. The book won a triple crown of prestigious Honor designations from the Boston Globe/Horn Book Award, the Coretta Scott King Award, and the Randolph Caldecott Award.

II

Ways of Taking From Literature

3

Talking About Literature

In Polly Horvath's (1999) wonderful book, *The Trolls*, Aunt Sally comes to care for Amanda, Melissa, and Pee Wee while their parents are on vacation. She's a storyteller extraordinaire, and one of her many tales is about a mysterious man who appeared one day on the beach path near her home. As a child, Sally saw that her own Aunt Hattie was infatuated with the gentleman:

> "I knew there was something different about his clothes. They weren't like the pants men in town wore, or like the ones my father wore to the mill. Those khakis, I realize now, were expensive and beautifully cut. I sensed this then and that made it all the more exciting to see them being worn so carelessly through the sand."
>
> "What are khakis?" asked Amanda.
>
> "You know, a kind of brown pants," said Melissa.
>
> "What's beautiful about brown pants?" asked Pee Wee. "I wear brown pants all the time."
>
> "You don't wear beautifully cut brown pants," said Melissa.
>
> "If I ever cut my pants, Mom would be mad," said Pee Wee.
>
> "No, beautifully cut means that they were, well, shaped nicely," said Aunt Sally.
>
> "I don't think that's anything to get so excited about," said Pee Wee.
>
> "If they want to get excited over some nicely shaped brown pants, they can," said Amanda. "This is your great-aunt we're talking about. Show a little respect."
>
> "I am," said Pee Wee. "I just said that I think it's stupid getting all excited over a certain kind of pants. So what if he had brown pants?"
>
> "Will you please ignore him and go on?" said Melissa.
>
> "I'm always happy to get Frank's take on things. Do you have anything else you'd like to share on the subject, Frank?" [Aunt Sally asked, using Pee Wee's real name.]

> Frank shook his head regally. It wasn't often his opinion was valued. He
> gestured silently that she should continue the story. (pp. 77–78)

Aunt Sally's stories draw the children in, inviting their questions about the
meaning of words and character motivation, allowing them to voice where
they agree and disagree. Rather than see their comments and questions as
interruptions, she knows they are opportunities for further reflection. Even
though the two older girls would prefer to ignore their little brother, Aunt
Sally never does. Instead, she makes ample room for Frank's voice—refusing
to address him by his diminutive, Pee Wee, as well as declining to discount his
opinion. While she is telling a story and not reading from literature, her stance
is that of the best of teachers who want to encourage literary engagement,
primarily because she places so much value on children's talk.

Talk: The "Tool of Tools"

Cultural and cognitive psychologists consider language to be key. As Vygotsky
(1986) suggested: "thought does not express itself in words, but rather realizes
itself in them" (p. 251). Michael Cole (1996) called language the "tool of tools"
and used a quote from Luria to explicate this view:

> In the absence of words, human beings would have to deal only with those
> things which they could perceive and manipulate directly. With the help of
> language, they can deal with things that they have not perceived even indirectly
> and with things which were part of the experience of earlier generations. Thus,
> the word adds another dimension to the world of humans. . . . Animals have only
> one world, the world of objects and situations. Humans have a double world.
> (p. 120)

This double world is particularly vital in interpreting literature. An author in
some time, place, and situation communicates his or her vision of the world
through language, and we receive and perceive it in our own world, which
is far distant from that of the author. Our talk with others about text extends
the world building even further as we fold in our own experiences and those
of our fellow readers, interpreting text together. One reader's interpretation
alters our view and when we add our opinions the view is altered again.

Let me elaborate on this point by having you listen in on a group of 10-
year-olds as they discuss the passage from *The Trolls* with which I opened
this chapter:

Alicia: I feel *sorry* for Pee Wee. Why do they even call him that? His name is Frank.

Charlie: It happens to me all the time. My mom calls me a bunch of stupid names!

Alicia: Like what?

Charlie: Oh, you know—baby names. Stuff she's called me since I was a little kid.

Alicia: And you hate it?

Charlie: Yeah, 'cause it makes me feel— You know. Little.

Nate: Yeah, I can understand that. But what's worse is how Pee Wee's sisters— Uh. I mean *Frank's* sisters never listen to him.

Alicia: Yeah! Reminds me of my big brother. He *never* listens.

Joe: But you know how Aunt Sally listens? She really listens. I bet Frank likes that. Like look where it says, *"Frank shook his head regally. It wasn't often his opinion was valued."*

Charlie: What's "regally"?

Joe: It's like a king. Aunt Sally listened, and it made him feel like a king.

Children feel valued when they are heard, when their opinions matter, when their connections count. Notice in the discussion above how Charlie relates to Frank's dilemma because of his own experiences with his mother. Nate empathizes with his peer, but then ups the ante on the discussion by saying that it's not just the diminutive (Pee Wee), but also the unwillingness of Frank's sisters to pay attention to their brother. The fact that Nate begins his comment using "Pee Wee" but then quickly converts it to "Frank" shows that he has paid attention to his peers' comments about how annoying nicknames can be.

Nate's comment brings about another personal connection as Alicia compares the action of the siblings in the book to her own brother's actions. Her idea of not listening causes Joe to think about who does listen in the story, and he points out how Aunt Sally's reversal of the typical trend must be something that Frank appreciates. Joe goes straight to the text to justify his idea, quoting the section on Frank's royal head shake and the fact that "it wasn't often his opinion was valued." Charlie asks for a definition of "regally," and Joe provides the crowning touch, commenting on how Frank must feel "like a king" in the glow of his Aunt's attention.

The children in this group are fully engaged in literature. They use transactional criticism as they bring in their own personal experiences as well as formal criticism as they do a close reading of the text to justify their ideas about character interpretation. They touch on sociocultural criticism as they analyze how unusual it is for an adult to listen to and value a child's opinion. They are learning new vocabulary, enhancing their comprehension through collaborative meaning making, and learning a thing or two about listening to peers as well. And though their teacher is not present during this discussion, you can bet that she has been there—modeling critical questioning, inviting intriguing connections, and reminding children of the importance of justifying their ideas with textual evidence.

Talk about literature is vital, because children who do not have opportunities to extensively explore interpretive possibilities are missing basic skills that are essential to being literate. On the contrary, you want to give your children ample opportunities to express their conclusions, their conjectures, and even their confusions in collaboration with their peers. Sloan (1991) explained it well:

> Talking is a major way in which students express their responses to literature and—through the process—amplify, clarify, and extend those responses, while at the same time working their way into deeper understanding both of a particular work and of general literary principles. Time for purposeful talk after the experience of literature is analogous to the lab after a presentation in science. It is time for experimenting with ideas, exploring concepts, making observations, and drawing conclusions. . . . From their first encounter with a new class, teachers need to work to establish a climate of mutual respect where ideas and opinions are heard and valued. This is particularly important in literary studies where . . . the discussion is in response to questions that require genuine reflection and critical thinking. . . . (pp. 132–133)

But if a teacher needs to begin from his or her "first encounter with a new class," where are the spaces and places for such talk, and what does it sound like? In the sections to follow, I show critical opportunities for interpreting literature in three curricular areas: (a) the read-aloud, (b) independent reading, and (c) literature discussion.

The Read-Aloud: A Focus on the Unexpected

When Aunt Sally tells a story in *The Trolls*, Amanda, Melissa, and Pee Wee sit up and listen. Although she tells a number of stories within the book, the central tale is about how she once abandoned her little brother, Robbie, on the beach one dark and dreary Halloween night with the hint that trolls would soon kidnap him. She was fed up with his self-centered and annoying ways and wanted to give him a good scare. And she succeeded.

But Aunt Sally's story is not notable for her success as much as for how she leads up to the ultimate outcome with a focus on the unexpected. For example, early in the book she's humming along with a story of how her brother John once stuck his finger in a clam to avoid a violin exam with the Royal Academy, when Pee Wee makes a comment that turns the tone of her story from hilarity to something more menacing:

> "I'd never stick my finger in any clam's mouth, that's for sure," scoffed Pee Wee.
> "Never say you'd never do something. You have no idea the things you are capable of doing. Always, always keep that in mind," said Aunt Sally.
> A sudden chill went inexplicably through the girls, the way a sudden breeze makes ripples on a lake, and then it was gone. (p. 19)

In the first chapter, I talked about the qualities of story, relying on the triad of sound, metaphor, and structure. But literature also relies on the unexpected. Burke called it Trouble with a capital T: "a story (fictional or actual) requires an Agent who performs an Action to achieve a Goal in a recognizable Setting by the use of certain Means—his dramatistic Pentad.... What drives a story is a misfit between the elements of the Pentad: Trouble" (Bruner, 2002, p. 34).

In Aunt Sally's story, Trouble with a capital T appears in the guise of the trolls, "'There are no locks to keep out the trolls,' said Aunt Sally. 'But don't worry, the trolls don't come to you. It's your own darkness that leads you to the trolls' " (p. 57). And stories lead us to unexpected possibilities. As Bruner further explained:

> ... storytelling and story sharing make us deft in imagining what might happen if.... We humans are enormously specialized to adapt to the ordinary state of things around us—which psychologists have long called our "adaptation level," when we stop attending and go on automatic pilot. We go flat in response to monotony. But a century of brilliant neurophysiology has made it plain that human attention is also specialized to keep us vigilant about departures from the routine. An unexpected signal alerts us as nothing else does.... Stories reassert a kind of conventional wisdom about what can be expected, even (or especially) what can be expected to go wrong and what might be done to restore or cope with the situation.
>
> Narrative achieves these prodigies not only because of its structure per se but because of its flexibility or malleability. Not only are stories products of language,

so remarkable for its sheer generativeness, permitting so many different versions to be told, but telling stories soon becomes crucial to our social interactions. How early the young child learns just the right tale for the occasion! Storytelling becomes entwined with, even at times constitutive of, cultural life. (pp. 30–31)

Beyond the myriad versions of storytelling and story sharing that occur in children's homes, the classroom is a perfect location for how children learn just the right tales for every occasion, especially if you use the read-aloud as an opportunity to focus on the unexpected. Still, there are certain expectations for excellent read-alouds, and I believe there are at least five features you should carefully consider. I explore these ideas in the upcoming sections.

Read Aloud Everyday. First and foremost, read aloud everyday—typically for 20 minutes to a half hour. You might open the day with a short passage and then read for a longer period later in the day. While the read-aloud is a stalwart in most primary classrooms, its application should actually extend across the grades from kindergarten through eighth grade. Fourteen-year-olds enjoy hearing and discussing stories as much as 5-year-olds. Without a read-aloud, students might be limited to texts they can decode on their own, and if they have troubles with decoding they are given simplified texts that have little connection to fine literature. Leveled books are perfect for learning to read, but offer less opportunity for reading to learn because what a child can't decode has little to do with what a child can talk about. A bilingual teacher I know, Sandra Vazquez, told me that when her 8-year-old struggling students read leveled texts in the literacy lab, they often complained of being bored and tired. They didn't know what to do or say in response to the limited prose offered. However, once she began reading them more complex literature aloud, modeling her own interest, curiosity, and surprise in the literature, they woke up and began to participate.

Create a Community Atmosphere. Try to create a special atmosphere for the read-aloud—designating a specific place in the classroom where your children and young adolescents will gather to listen while you share a picture or chapter book. The close proximity of the group to the book is particularly important in sharing picture books—for while you are reading the words, your children are reading the illustrations.

Crafting an ambiance for read-aloud time is critical. One teacher I know lights a candle to call his children to the woven rug where read-alouds are held. Another calls her children to a pair of hand-me-down sofas while she sits in a rocking chair and shares a story. In my own classes—unusual as it may sound—I ask my university students to join me on the rug, and I throw down a large stuffed sheepdog I named Nana after the children's guardian in *Peter Pan* (Barrie, 1988). At first a bit taken aback by being asked to sit at the feet of their professor along with a stuffed animal, they are scrambling for a spot next to Nana within a couple of classes. They quickly realize that sitting on the floor while I'm in a chair doesn't constitute a demeaning posture, but allows them to better hear and see the story. Even more important, the atmosphere of the read-aloud calls for attention. As Lucy Calkins (2001) explained:

> How important is reading aloud? Critically important. "Don't you ever want kids to just lie back and let the words flow over them . . . to just listen?" people sometimes ask about the read-aloud. But I have to admit that I don't really see the read-aloud in this dreamy, sleepy sort of way. Too often children consider the read-aloud as a time to doze, dream, fiddle, and snack. I see the read-aloud as the heart of our reading instruction time, and I want kids' full attention to be on what we do together. (p. 63)

Thus, creating an atmosphere is more than lighting candles and arranging furniture and stuffed animals. It's about creating a community with clear attention to the topic at hand.

In Cynthia Lewis's (2001) lovely ethnography of an exemplary fifth / sixth-grade teacher, the importance of community in their read-aloud is clear:

> Once, in a section Julia read from a book about the American Revolution, the author wrote that a man's head bounced off his body. The children laughed and whooped. Julia stared at them in silence, then spoke softly. This was not Wiley Coyote, she told them, but human life. Forming a community was important to her, but it had to be the kind of community in which she would want to live. (p. 63)

Creating community in read-alouds means a place where children want to live as well—where they'll feel heard and respected, and where they'll want to spend time everyday.

Read With Panache. Getting and keeping children's attention as well as helping them hear the serious in contrast to the hilarious is easier if you read with panache. The exemplary teachers I've watched over the years all read with expression—their children *hear* the story through their choices in intonation, accent, and vocal characterization. While they're not hams, and they're rarely melodramatic, they take the opportunity of the read-aloud to help children hear how the language of literature sounds.

Remember Bruner's admonition about what happens "when we stop attending and go on automatic pilot. We go flat in response to monotony"? The read-aloud should never be flat, for monotony can kill a story. In its funereal wake, children will nod off quickly or find something far more entertaining to do! As Cynthia Rylant extolled, "Take their breath away. Read with the same feeling in your throat as when you first see the ocean after driving hours and hours to get there. Close the final page of the book with the same reverence you feel when you kiss your sleeping child at night.... Teach your children to be moved" (Calkins, 2001, p. 53).

I've been reading stories aloud for years—to children and adults—and I'm still learning how to move my audience. I take my first lessons from the words of the story and how they move me. I test out accents and character voices, noting where I can take a risk, raise or lower my voice, or even sing a song. When should I let the quiet of the text slow me down? When should I speed it up to capture a breathless pace? How might I communicate the accusation, the denial, the hesitation, the humor, and the sheer joy in a story?

In addition, I study the masters. Famous actors are often creating audio and videotapes of well-known stories. For example, once you hear Adrian Vargas read *The Circuit: Stories from the Life of a Migrant Child* (Jiménez, 1997), or Jina Oh deliver *A Step from Heaven* (Na, 2001), or Jim Dale read *Harry Potter and the Sorcerer's Stone* (Rowling, 1998), you will never hear these stories in quite the same way again. The same is true when you listen to Meryl Streep read Beatrix Potter's (1903) *The Tailor of Gloucester* in a Rabbit Ears production. Through the lilt of lyrics and a variety of accents, these performers know well not only how to perk up the reader's ears, but how to engage the listener's heart.

Encourage Literary Engagement.   Still, even a fine vocal interpretation of a story could disengage children if they never get a chance to talk. Thus, the read-aloud should be a place for dialogue, not monologue, no matter how effectively rendered. When Aunt Sally explains that she first tried to enlist her other brothers' help in leaving Robbie for the trolls on the beach, Melissa and Amanda have a lot to say, especially since Robbie is their father:

"You didn't give Daddy to the trolls, though," said Melissa. "Did you?"

"Because he's here now. So you must have decided not to," said Amanda.

"Or there's no such thing as trolls!" said Melissa suddenly with relief.

"Yes, that's it! The whole thing was made up," said Amanda.

Both girls had the covers pulled up to their chins. (pp. 65–66)

Both the pull of the covers and the girls' problem solving signal their engagement, but what is driving their questions and comments is the unexpected idea of their Aunt abandoning their father to the trolls. What was she thinking? No matter how annoying their father's habits were as a child, can Aunt Sally's decision be justified? And, most important, are the trolls real or a metaphor for what happens when siblings drift apart?

Teachers who want to encourage literary engagement in children know how to model just these kinds of questions and comments. Rather than constantly appear as the experts, they demonstrate surprise in the workings of story. For example, they ask:

- Wait a minute. I'm confused. What do you think is going on?
- When I was growing up my little brother was a pest, but leaving him on the beach? I don't think I could. Could you?
- The idea of the trolls makes me nervous. Do you think they're real?
- Will Aunt Sally really abandon Robbie? Will her other brothers help?
- I wonder how much sleep Melissa and Amanda will get tonight. Will they have troll nightmares?

In using questions and comments akin to those above, you have a chance to model ambiguity, showing your own hesitations, doubts, and wonderings. Because children are typically asked to retrace well-worn paths of known-information questions, they can initially be suspicious of questions that ask them to explore the unknown territory of interpretation. Still, if you persist in demonstrating the unexpected, you will make room for your children to try on and test out ideas without apprehension about "right" and "wrong" answers. By emphasizing the uncertainty of your own literary interpretations, you will provide more space for your children to take risks in articulating their own opinions.

Comment on Craft. However, there are places for you to be more certain, especially when you point out aspects of fine writing. Although I explore this issue in more depth in chapter 6, it's important to mention it now, for the read-aloud is a perfect place for discussing how authors craft language for particular effects. In truth, this is just one of many ways to encourage literary uptake, but this form is most closely linked to formal criticism and its hopeful connection to children's own writing. As you name and explore stylistic devices, you encourage your children to pay attention to the qualities of sound, metaphor, and structure in story. It helps children recognize how Trouble with a capital T is crafted.

Listen to the following passage from *The Trolls* to learn how trouble begins and grows. At this point, Aunt Sally is telling the girls how she always won the annual art contest at her school, but one year, much to her surprise, her brother Robbie won, and when he did Aunt Sally felt that a "stone began to rattle around in [her] stomach":

> "I went to the principal and asked her if perhaps they had meant to name me the winner and gotten my little brother by mistake. She said no. The stone turned into a boulder.
>
> "I waited for Robbie to say something to me like 'And you said I couldn't possibly win.' But he never did. He just smiled a particularly annoying, smug little smile. This made the situation even more insufferable. And, as far as I could tell, no one, *no one*, gave one moment's thought to how bad I might be feeling for losing.
>
> "Grandpa Willie did the usual ice-cream thing, with Robbie gloating the whole evening, and that night Great-uncle Louis gave him a complete drawing set with colored pencils and everything. Naturally, when I had won the contest in years past, he had given me zip. That's when I began to wonder about the trolls. (pp. 62–63)

Because the trolls have been described as having "faces of stone" and hard to see since they often "lean against shale ledges" (p. 51), the image of the stone rattling around in Aunt Sally's stomach that later turns into a boulder is a particularly fine metaphor and one that deserves discussion. In addition, you might point out the alliteration in the description of Robbie's "smug little smile . . . [that] made the situation even more insufferable." On the other hand, you might comment on the effective use of repetition of the word "one" in "no one, *no one*, gave one moment's thought" to Aunt Sally's feelings. You could also point out the difference between "a complete drawing set with colored pencils and everything" and "zip," for the contrast between elaborate description and a single word with punch.

FIG. 3.1.   The Read-Aloud.

Figure 3.1 summarizes the five attributes that you can model in your read-alouds. The door to literature is open to children when you: (a) read aloud everyday, (b) create a community atmosphere, (c) read with panache, (d) encourage literary engagement, and (e) comment on craft. And through fine modeling, your children will learn to do the same. Still, the read-aloud is only one place where talk is key. A second is in independent reading—where self talk and the sharing of crystallized insights with teachers and peers is strongest.

Independent Reading: From Self-Talk to Sharing

One of the basic tenets of this book recognizes talk as the "tool of tools" and stresses the critical importance of collaborative talk among teachers and children. However, most of us who are readers as adults spend quite a bit more time reading independently than reading and discussing literature with peers. We may belong to a book club either directly or indirectly (through Oprah!), and we may talk over our latest favorites with friends and family, but for the most part these interactions take up far less time than what we do on our own.

Just this week, I finished reading Louise Erdrich's (2001) *The Last Report on the Miracles at Little No Horse*—an astonishing tale of a woman living among and learning from the Ojibwa as a priest. I read "Book the Fourth"— *The Miserable Mill*—in Lemony Snicket's (2000) darkly amusing *Series of Unfortunate Events*. For my professional reading and to help me think about this chapter, this month I read or reread several academic texts on teaching literature. Although all this sounds like something I did totally on my own, Calkins (2001) argued:

> The books that matter in our lives are the books we have discussed. "It takes two to read a book," Alan Purves has said, and it is true in my life that the books I remember most are those I have shared. If I simply ask people, "What are you reading in your independent reading life today?" and then, "Is there something social behind this book? Was it recommended by someone? Is it part of a conversation with someone?," it soon becomes clear that our so-called "independent" reading lives are not independent after all. (p. 74)

As usual, Calkins makes an excellent point. I know that I briefly discussed the Erdrich book with my husband and recommended that he read it. My daughter Ash and I laughed over the Snicket series; she's further along than I am and has finished Book the Fifth. We discussed our favorite parts—especially Snicket's erudite and entertaining vocabulary explanations.

On the professional side, the academic texts I read also exist in a swirl of conversation—recommendations from colleagues and books I've taught or shared with students. I also read the newspaper this week—the local daily and the Sunday *New York Times*—and I discussed a few of the stories with my family. My husband pointed out an article I'd missed on how standardized tests often modify literary excerpts to be sure that offensive language of any kind does not appear in their passages. We both chuckled over the article's title: "The Elderly Man and the Sea? Test Sanitizes Literary Texts" (Kleinfield, 2002). But the time spent reading all these texts and thinking about them far exceeded time spent talking with others. Although the words of these books and articles exist in a web of social interactions, through self-talk I weave new words and insights from my reading, and then think about how to share them with you.

Bakhtin (1981), a Russian literary theorist, believed that words are only half one's own. It is only when a speaker takes a word and "populates it with his own intention" (p. 293) that he or she can take part ownership. When prose authors use words, they do not empty out past intentions. Rather, an author welcomes words "that are already populated with the social intentions of others and compels them to serve [her or his] own new intentions, to serve a second master" (p. 300). To extend on Bakhtin's idea, this is, in turn, what happens to the reader. The reader becomes the third master, using part of the intention of the author, but creating his or her own reshapings of text. The active and individual mind constantly contributes to meaning construction.

Because of the potential for meaningful interpretation, make ample room for independent reading in your classroom. The models you provide in your read-alouds will serve as inspiration for how your children might deeply engage in literature. And just as with read-alouds, there are critical features that you can instantiate as a part of your reading instruction. In this case, I believe there are four essential attributes.

Devote Time for Daily Independent Reading. As essential as a teacher's decision to read aloud everyday, children need time for daily independent reading. If they are going to become life-long readers, they must see reading as desirable and they need to build the necessary stamina to pursue it. Santman (2002) explained:

> Reading requires stamina. It has the power to captivate our minds, but only if we can manage to live inside a story long enough to get hooked. Too many kids in our classrooms have no stamina. They are only able to sustain reading for ten or fifteen minutes. How can they keep a story alive at five pages a day? (p. 205)

Very young children often spend more time studying illustrations than decoding or they approximate texts they know well, but this is nonetheless reading as decades of research on emergent literacy have proved. Still, to build stamina to the lengths we would expect older readers to be able to maintain, we have to provide stretches of time for children and young adolescents to build their textual staying power.

Combine Choice With Recommendations. The time to read would mean little if children were not intrigued with what they were reading, and this often means that children are able to choose what they want to read as well where they want to read. Some children prefer a good mystery novel laid flat on the top of their desk; others prefer a fantasy while occupying a corner of the classroom library. Still others might like reading next to a buddy or even reading the same text in quiet pairs, and this option often occurs in primary classrooms. When choice is offered, children often read popular texts—even those books that a classroom teacher might typically avoid. Lewis (2002) argued that this kind of reading offers children "subcultural capital...the status one gains from being 'in the know' about popular culture" (pp. 160–161). In an interview with one student in Julia's class, Lewis discovered that the child had read at least 20 books by R. L. Stein and 10 by Christopher Pike. The child was very clear on the differences among these books and the ones Julia typically read: "Well, the ones that she picks usually have a meaning that you could learn something from, but R. L. Stine books don't really have anything that you would learn.... You're in school, but you don't have to be learning something all of the time" (pp. 161–162).

Fair enough. We've all read books we know aren't of the highest literary quality. Still, teachers like Julia nudge children towards better literature through recommendations, routinely promoting intriguing books based on what they know about students' gifts and needs:

- To a 6-year-old: The other day you wrote in your journal that you wanted to know more "big words." I was thinking about that, and I have a book I think you'll like. It's called *Martin's BIG Words* (Rappaport, 2001), and it's about Martin Luther King, Jr. When he was a little boy, he thought he could make a difference in the world with his words, and he did. Maybe that's what your big words can do someday. By the way, when you're reading this book, you might want to really study the art. It's fabulous.
- To an 8-year-old: I've been laughing over the new Lemony Snicket (e.g., 2000) series. I know how much you liked Raold Dahl's (1982) *The Twits* when I read it to the class. I think you'd really like this series. Snicket's writing has that quality of the ridiculous that I know you enjoy.
- To an 11-year-old: Next year you're off to middle school, and I'll bet you've been thinking about that. I know you typically like fantasy, but I think you might like to try some realistic fiction. Some of the middle-school kids I've known have liked the short stories in *Baseball in April* by Gary Soto (1990). There's a tough reality in Soto's stories that's very appealing. I also just finished reading *The Jumping Tree* (Saldaña, 2001), and it has a similar writing style. Do you want to give one of these a try?
- To a 14-year-old: I know how much you liked *Harry Potter.* You're probably dying for that next book to come out. But, you know, you're such a good reader you might want to try Philip Pullman's (e.g., 1996) series

on "His Dark Materials." The first book in the trilogy is *The Golden Compass*. I loved it. A couple of months ago I read an article in *The New York Times Book Review* that called this series "Harry Potter for grown-ups" (Jefferson, 2002). I think you ought to try it.

It takes a lot of reading and a lot of kid watching to know how to match a student with a book, but if you consider your class context, your children's particular interests, and what they might need for a bit of an added push into another genre or more challenging reading, you'll be able to make fine recommendations. Still, just because a book is extraordinary in its own right doesn't mean it will appeal to every child. Even if you love it, there's no guarantee a child will. But I'm sure you'll know enough about your students to make more matches than mismatches.

Create an Enticing Classroom Library.   When you're just beginning your teaching career, creating a classroom library seems a daunting task. Visiting the classrooms of experienced teachers only seems to make it worse. A young preservice teacher I worked with visited a bilingual classroom and wrote: "The classroom has so many books in Spanish and English, that it almost made my eyes pop out. . . . I hope to have a classroom with wall-to-wall bookshelves like that someday" (Wolf, Ballentine, & Hill, 2000, p. 560). But the funds needed for this kind of library as well as the expertise for selecting the best texts are harder to come by.

Most young teachers begin with their school library, and make a weekly visit to check out books. I know I did. In my first year of teaching first grade, I spent every Friday afternoon in the school library quizzing the librarian about the newest texts as well as her old favorites. I hauled a huge stack back to the class and sorted them into plastic bins based on genre or topic. I then selected about a dozen (predominately picture books and a couple of chapter books) to take home for weekend reading. I used these books to prepare for my Monday "Book Talks" in which I introduced some of the most captivating new books to my children. When they expressed keen interest in a text, I added it to my planning for our upcoming read-alouds.

Then I did what many teachers do—I hunted for books in garage sales and used bookstores, knowing that the wear and tear of used books was only a signal that the books were once loved. I went to library sales and wrote small grants for funding. I joined several publishers' book clubs and encouraged my children to do the same so I could save the points towards more and more books. When I had parents who could make donations, I asked them for books, but more often I hounded some of the local businesses, particularly bookstores.

To be discerning in my choices, I read *The Horn Book Magazine* (a premier children's literature journal) and studied lists of Caldecott and Newbery winners, but for today's classroom teacher, reading reviews of books does not take hours in the local library. You can go online for review articles from *The Horn Book* at http://www.hbook.com/index.shtml. You can also easily locate many of these reviews and others from *Kirkus Reviews, Booklist*, and *School Library Journal* on barnesandnoble.com, amazon.com, or a resource like the Children's Literature Comprehensive Database (CLCD) at http://clcd.odyssi.com. In addition, you can go on line with the Cooperative Children's Book Center (CCBC) at http://www.education.wisc.edu/ccbc to read about their Book of the Week. You can also join the CCBC's electronic conversations for focused and highly informative discussions on children's literature.

In terms of technology, today's classroom libraries should include access to the Internet and CD-ROM books. Chambliss and McKillop (2000) suggested:

> Daily the WWW has new entries of beautiful, easy-to-read sites for children's reading and research needs. Sites of particular interest to help motivate student reading include children's author home pages where students can e-mail the authors of some of their favorite books and book report/review sites written by children for children. Over the past decade a growing market for CD-ROM books has developed. With superior sound quality, enticing graphics, and video capabilities, these books have quickly found an audience. (p. 112)

What used to take on a sense of hopeless letter writing out into the void, can now take minutes on the World Wide Web, as children come into virtual contact with authors and other children who share their interests in particular books, topics, and themes. In their home pages, authors often discuss their motivation for writing particular stories and provide insights into their texts that offer much in terms of genetic criticism. CD-ROM books are often visually delightful and offer opportunities for interaction with text. The downside of these books, however, is often in the comprehension "quizzes" that follow, and rare is the electronic book that asks children to think about character development, significance of setting, or the stylistic features of the writing. Still, these texts can help entice children into reading.

In addition to computer access, it's often helpful to place a listening center in your classroom library. Books on tape from Westin Woods and Rabbit Ears (two of the most famous) are wonderfully rendered by well-known actors and accompanied by music and sound effects that add to the attraction. A tape recorder and attachments for four to six headsets are usually available from school libraries or district headquarters. Multiple copies of books with the audiotape allow children to track as well as think about text in inviting ways.

No matter how small your classroom, it's critical to try and create a space for the library. It should be an enticing space, lovingly designed. Regie Routman (2000) purposefully used the word "design ... because how the classroom library looks and feels—its design—impacts its use. Make your library space as comfortable and attractive as possible. Comfortable seating and colorful displays of books promote reading by inviting easy, relaxed participation" (p. 86). Still, the notion of "easy" and "relaxed" should be balanced with reflective record keeping, the culminating component of independent reading that I turn to in the next section.

Review Reflective Record Keeping.   Most teachers are busy people, especially if they're keeping track of 22 six-year-olds, 28 ten-year-olds, or 128 fourteen-year-olds. And if they're expected to make targeted book recommendations as well as monitor children's self-selections, they need to follow what students are reading in efficient ways. Ms. Olinski, a 4th grade teacher that I came to know well, provided each of her children with a reading folder. After her daily read-aloud, the children moved into their own reading—each in their own paperback books. One of her students explained his book to me, "It's realistic fiction and I like that." He demonstrated how his reading folder worked as the students noted the date, book title, author, and number of pages read each day. They also had a set of sheets in the front covers of their folders that provided squares for listing their reading under "Realistic Fiction, Historical Fiction, Fantasy, Mystery, and Science Fiction" among other genres, which made it easy for Ms. Olinski to see the children's genre preferences and avoidances at a glance.

In addition to generalized lists, children should write their reflections about a book, noting brief insights and quotes they might want to remember. They needn't write elaborate essays or book reports of each, but they should make some notes about the outstanding features of the text as well as their questions and curiosities. These notes can then be a jumping off point for short interviews with their teacher about how their reading is progressing. Many of the teachers I've observed began their initial forays into independent reading time by reading along with their children—hoping to model their own interest in reading. But they found that it was more important to demonstrate their love of reading in other ways—though read-alouds and recommendations— and use their students' independent reading time as an opportunity to circulate and review their young readers' records in short interviews. These conversations allow children to share some of their self-talk about texts.

In her conferences with children, Ms. Olinski stressed that she was trying to get kids to "move away from literal recall and into thinking about what the book is teaching them." For example, in a conference with Angelica, Ms. Olinski helped the 9-year-old articulate a more specific response, "You tell me that the book was awesome, but why was that?" She listened to Angelica talk from her notes and then asked her what else she liked about her book. Angelica responded that she loved the part in her text where the dog got gum all over his fur. Ms. Olinski encouraged her to note this aspect of the story because it added "to the richness of the response." At the end of her conferences for the day, Ms. Olinski took the time to make notes in her own anecdotal record, writing the date along with succinct insights into each child's progress.

Figure 3.2 summarizes the four attributes that you can highlight in promoting independent reading: (a) devote time for daily independent reading, (b) combine choice with recommendations, (c) create an enticing classroom library, and (d) review reflective record keeping. The fact that a child is reading independently does not mean that his or her thoughts about text are totally private. Instead, in a comfortable as well as stimulating atmosphere children learn to share their textual thoughts with teachers and peers in multiple ways. Furthermore, moving from self-talk to sharing helps prepare them for the third curricular essential: literature discussion groups.

Literature Discussion: Upping the Ante on Talk

Fine literature moves us. That's such a simple statement, but its elemental nature can't hide the deeply complex reactions we have when reading calls out to us. In *The Trolls*, Aunt Sally continues to unveil the story of her relationship with her brother Robbie. On the last night of her visit, she finishes the tale explaining how she and her other brothers did leave Robbie on the

To promote independent reading, you need to:

Devote time for daily independent reading

Combine choice with recommendations

Create an enticing classroom library

Review reflective record keeping

FIG. 3.2. Independent Reading.

beach for the trolls. After they let him stew for a while, they went back to get him, but he was gone. Search parties of Royal Canadian Mounted Police were organized, but it was the children's Great-uncle Louis that finally found him and brought Robbie home. He claimed that he had rescued Robbie from the trolls, but no one believed him. Though Sally and her brothers waited nervously for their little brother to tell on them, he remained completely silent on the subject. Even when they apologized, Robbie kept quiet and distant:

> John and Edward and I tried explaining to Robbie that it was only a Halloween joke. That we would never let the trolls get him. Robbie seemed to accept our apology, but I guess knowing that your own trusted family could give you away, even in jest, well, it changes things. It changes things forever. If we wanted to cure him of his self-centered ways, we certainly had. He was never boastful or mean with us again. He wasn't, in the end, ever with us again.
>
> "But were there trolls? Did he tell you that the trolls took him, like Great-uncle Louis said?" asked Amanda.
>
> "Yeah, what did Daddy say happened?" asked Melissa.
>
> "He didn't tell us anything," said Aunt Sally.

"But it couldn't have been trolls," said Melissa. "Because Great-uncle Louis said that once you give something to the trolls you can never ever have it back."

"But we never did get Robbie back. Or Lyla. Or Great-uncle Louis. We thought we would be well rid of him, but a lot of life was gone from the dinner table after he left. We all drifted apart, until finally we grew up and John went to Alaska, Lyla and Robbie went to college in Ohio and settled here and we rarely saw them, Edward drowned at sea, and Grandma and Grandpa died. Now there's just me on the island and there is no more family. So either Great-uncle Louis was right and the trolls never do give back what they take, or some acts alter everything forever, but that's how it was on the island. And when I pass our old clapboard house that I loved so much, I am a stranger. Now listen, it's very late. That's the end of my stories. I'll see you in the morning." Aunt Sally stood up and walked quietly out, closing the door behind her.

"Wow," said Melissa softly.

"It wasn't frightening like I thought it would be," said Amanda.

"No," said Melissa. It was just sad." (pp. 131–132)

Stories that we love pull on the heart, and in that long pull we have multiple questions and comments. Individual plot lines and character motivations intrigue us and make us want to know more. When we read independently, we sometimes stop and ponder the direction of a tale and the decisions characters are making. But even when our self-talk is relatively pensive, we often proceed rather quickly, hoping the next passage will deliver the answer.

On the other hand, in literature discussions we stop and dwell in the text for longer periods, and we talk in more extended ways, expressing our comments and queries as well as listening to and responding to others' ideas. Teachers who have stories to share, rather than simply deliver, do everything they can to up the ante on talk, because they know that through language—the "tool of tools"—children come to express and expand their thinking.

The design of a literature discussion group is relatively straightforward, though there are many variations described in the research literature. Judith Langer (1995) discussed opportunities for "envisionment building" and described the "stances" readers take on as they try to make sense of words and worlds. Peterson and Eeds (1990) called their groups "grand conversations" where children rely on intensive reading to enter into dialogue about books. Short and Pierce (1990) called these kinds of conversations "literature circles," and Daniels (1994) took this term even further by assigning specific roles such as the "Discussion Director" and the "Illustrator" to help children focus their conversations. Raphael and McMahon (1994) called for a "Book Club" that is marked by ongoing teacher instruction as well as children's written insights, group discussion, and time to share their ideas with the larger classroom community.

No matter the terms, children and adolescents meet in a small group (usually four to six members) to discuss a text they've all read. With older children reading longer books, they agree upon how many chapters they will read in advance of the discussion, and they typically come prepared with written comments and questions that they want to offer for group consideration. It is critical that children meet in heterogeneous groups in terms of gender, ethnicity, personality, and, most important, ability. As I've pointed out, how a child can think about literature is not dependent on decoding skills. Children with difficulties in decoding can listen to the text on tape or have an oral reading pal, a teacher's aide, or a parent read the story to them.

Literature discussion groups do not usually meet every day; twice a week is a more reasonable goal because most teachers must balance literature discussion with myriad other aspects of their literacy curriculum—guided reading groups, independent reading time, read-alouds, literature extension activities, etc. While most groups are teacher-led, or more important teacher facilitated, some groups are peer-led depending on the maturity of the children.

Oftentimes, you will choose the text to fit within a larger curricular plan. For example, you might assign *The Watsons Go to Birmingham—1963* as part of a larger unit on African American heroism. You could jump start the conversation by using the opening chapter as a read-aloud—for it is a wildly funny introduction to the "Weird Watsons" that I've never seen fail to entrance children and make them want to devour the book. On the other hand, you might choose to continue reading *The Watsons* as the classroom read-aloud and then offer choice for literature discussion groups. One group might read *Roll of Thunder, Hear My Cry*, while another reads *Through My Eyes*, and still another reads a set of thematically related picture books.

I believe there are five essentials for teachers in facilitating literature discussion groups. As Fig. 3.3 indicates, you need to (a) lead as well as follow, (b) highlight criticism, (c) encourage coding of comments and questions, (d) emphasize multiple modes of response, and (e) extend the conversation to the community. Let's look at each of these characteristics in turn.

To facilitate literature discussion, you need to:

- Lead as well as follow
- Highlight criticism
- Encourage coding of comments & questions
- Emphasize multiple modes of response
- Extend the conversation to the community

FIG. 3.3.   Literature Discussion.

Lead as Well as Follow.   In the past few years, there has been a lot of emphasis placed on offering children multiple opportunities for independence. In terms of literary conversation, the ideal portrays children involved in deep discussion without the need for much teacher direction. For example, listen in on the following discussion in a 4th grade classroom of children discussing *James and the Giant Peach* (Dahl, 1996):

Mary: Why didn't he [James] just leave? He didn't have to wait for the giant peach or anything. I think he was pretty stupid.

Teacher: But I think . . .

Amanda: Maybe he didn't know where to go . . . or he could have been scared.

Wes: He could have called somebody and reported child abuse, and the police would come and, you know, got him.

Mary: And put him in, what do you call it . . .

Amanda: A foster home.

Teacher: But I think . . .

Mary: I wonder if his parents made his aunts his guardians. I mean, do you think they had a will?

Wes: Yeah, if my parents die, I know who I'll go to.

Bridgett: Maybe they didn't know the aunts were so mean.

Sudi: Yeah, maybe they just put on a show in front of the parents.

Wes: So James could do all their work for them.

Teacher: But I think . . .

Bridgett: [grinning broadly] I think the teacher has something to say. (Villaume, Worden, Williams, Hopkins, & Rosenblatt, 1994, p. 480)

Bridgett's grin is a broad indication of children's burgeoning dominance in literature discussion. And it's true that if teachers would step out of the way more often, they would find their children quite capable of conducting rich conversations.

On the other hand, we know from research that not all conversations are "grand" (Roller & Beed, 1994) and can even get out of hand if there is gender inequity or just a bossy group member. Karen Evans (2002) carefully explored the "intersection of gender and bossiness, and the possible connections between bossiness, gender, and race" (p. 66). In looking at some of the ineffective qualities of peer-led discussion groups, she wrote:

My best guess is that some of [the students'] experiences resulted in very little learning about things such as character development, vocabulary, or theme. Furthermore, what likely was learned about issues of power relationships, gender, and teacher authority makes me feel, at best, uncomfortable and, at worst, wondering if some of these experiences may have been miseducative for some students. (p. 66)

Her warnings are reminiscent of Sally and her brothers leaving Robbie for the trolls. When children are completely left to their own devices, how will their decisions impact all members of the group? Will they get along, sharing a discussion marked by respect, or might somebody get left behind? As Aunt Sally suggested, "some acts alter everything forever," and if a child is silenced by peers, it makes sense that the possibility for engagement would be limited as well.

Teachers often struggle with the balance between leading and following, especially when the ideal of peer-led groups suggests that children will live "happily ever after" without guidance from the teacher. Cynthia Lewis (2001) described Julia's dilemma well:

> Julia felt strongly about her role as an active member of literature discussion groups and defined these groups as teacher led despite reservations about her degree of involvement. Although she believed that children need time to construct knowledge together without the interference and control adults often impose, she also felt strongly that, as adults, teachers must offer children their knowledge and guidance. This view of the teacher's role stood in opposition to some of what she had learned in university classes, in educational journals, and from district philosophy. Often, she felt, these sources promoted a "hands-off" approach that did not make sense to her. (p. 120)

It doesn't make sense to me either. The teachers I've observed work to create a balance between leading and following, trying hard not to tip over into too much control or too little guidance. Even when they sit on the periphery of the group or move among several peer-led groups, they are present—stopping to offer a suggestion, asking a group to summarize their accomplishments, kid watching to see who's talking and who's listening, and making notes (both mental and written) about participation as well as the quality of children's contributions.

Highlight Criticism. In their leadership capacity, one of the central characteristics of accomplished teachers is that they highlight criticism. In chapter 1, I discuss five kinds of criticism: (a) *genetic criticism* with an emphasis on the author, (b) *formal criticism* with attention to the text itself, especially the language of the story, (c) *text-to-text criticism* with an eye on comparing the text with other written and media texts, (d) *transactional criticism* with a concentration on the interaction of the reader with the text, and

(e) *sociocultural criticism* with an emphasis on cultural, political, and social-historical perspectives. Working with a blend of critical perspectives, you can reveal insights about the book's author, analyze the narrative components, highlight themes in similar and/or dissimilar books, make comparisons among textual actions and character traits with events and people you know, and emphasize the sociopolitical dimensions of stories. And you can ask your children to do the same.

Teachers tend to lead more directly when they're helping children get used to the idea of discussion. For example, one teacher I worked with, Sandy Quezada, was trying to refine her role in literary discussion groups, and she was intrigued with a study by Almasi, O'Flahavan, and Arya (2001) as they compared more and less proficient literature discussions. She summarized some of the researchers' suggestions: "In their comparison of what works and what doesn't they highlight . . . the role of the teacher and the importance of timely and appropriate scaffolding as well as the need for sufficient time to meet and allow the group to 'gel'. In addition, students must learn how to monitor their own discussion."

Sandy taught a group of sixth graders who all "participated in literacy lab to accelerate their reading." Because many of the children came to her for additional reading support, she decided to have them read *Joey Pigza Loses Control* (Gantos, 2000), a Newbery honor book about a kid who is diagnosed with Attention-Deficit Hyperactivity Disorder (ADHD). Sandy's 11-year-olds had all read the opening chapter about Joey's mom driving him to spend the summer with his dad—a worrisome situation, exacerbated by the father's alcoholism and erratic behavior. As Sandy opened the conversation, she "modeled summarizing for the students and then made a few personal connections to the text." In the following transcript, I note Sandy as Ms. Quezada so it's easy for you to see when the teacher is talking and when the children come in:

Ms. Quezada: This part where Joey's on his way to visit his dad reminds me of a time when I was about Joey's age and my mother and my brother and I were on our way to visit my dad. I remember being excited and scared at the same time. I also remember my mother being *stressed*, just like Joey's mom. I remember wondering why she was so grumpy. This part on page 10 where it says, "Her voice sounded like she had a long list of other things to say, but didn't." I wonder what it is she wants to say, but doesn't?

Maria: I thought about this. She didn't say anything else because it might be all bad things, like the dad's mean and stuff? And Joey might be afraid of him and be scared and not want to go, but he has to. So she doesn't want to scare him.

Ms. Quezada: That's an interesting point. Does anyone want to add on to that? [pause, no response] Does anyone have something different they want to say? [pause, no response] Okay. If you had to describe Joey right now, how would you describe him? What do you *think* about Joey?

Angel: Ummm. [pause] He's very curious?

Angela: He's ner—He's nervous.

Ms. Quezada: Curious, really nervous. Anxious, maybe? Stefanie, what do you think?

Stefanie: He's basically like a normal kid, you know? But sometimes I think that [pause] like maybe he doesn't know what's going to happen next? So he just wants to be sure about his dad. He wants to find out more about him.

Maria: If I had to describe Joey, I'd say he's really *anxious* to meet his dad. I think he's sort of nervous because he hasn't seen him for a while, and he doesn't know what he's like. And he's probably going to miss his mom. But, I also think he's a wild kid? [pause] Because of the way he's on the picture, see. [She holds up the cover of the book.] He's all upside down. [She refers back to the scene where Joey throws a dart and hits his dog in the ear.] Then when he starts, like, doing bad stuff, and his mom tells him "No." Like he just throws darts and messes up the house. He's just wild.

For a group of children who normally weren't engaged in literature and literary discussions, Sandy's opening remarks as well as her extensions up the ante on their willingness to talk. She begins with transactional criticism, making a personal connection from her own childhood experiences, and then moves into formal criticism, asking for character analysis of Joey. While there are a number of pauses, Sandy is patient. She asks the children to add on to Maria's point, but when the pauses persist, she shifts gears slightly asking them what they "think about Joey."

Her request really opens up the conversation, as the children move from one-word characterizations ("curious," "nervous") to longer conjectures. They even begin to build on one another's comments. For example, when Stefanie describes Joey as a "normal kid . . . [who] doesn't know what's going to happen next?" she's hedging her comment with a questioning lilt. Maria does the same when she suggests a potential contrast—that Joey is "a wild kid?" But as she looks to the cover illustration as well as the scene where Joey nails his dog with a dart, she uses textual support to gain confidence in her characterization. While Sandy's emphasis on criticism is not yet marked by the technical vocabulary often associated with character ("static," "dynamic," "flat," "round"), she's leading them straight to character motivation, for what drives characters to say what they say and do what they do is essential interpretive work in formal criticism. Most important, she stresses children's thinking, and this emphasis always pays off.

Encourage Coding of Comments & Questions. Sandy's willingness to lead and follow as well as her emphasis on criticism and critical thinking, bring us to the third characteristic of encouraging comments and questions. As I suggested in the last section, the balance is tipped towards stronger guidance from teachers in the beginning, but they must learn to "gradually release responsibility" (Pearson & Fielding, 1991, p. 818) to their students. Still, this release is marked by two related requirements: (a) students code or take notes on the text with Post-its or response journals, and (b) students are challenged to substantiate their claims as well as ground their questions with textual support. Harvey and Goudvis (2000) suggested:

> In the same way as animals leave tracks of their presence, we want readers to "leave tracks of their thinking". . . so they can remember later what they were thinking as they read. Kids love the idea of making tracks in the margins, tracks on sticky notes, tracks in their journals. These written tracks help the reader monitor comprehension and enhance understanding. They also provide clues to the teacher about a reader's thinking, evidence that is difficult to ascertain without some form of oral or written response. (p. 19)

In writing about her group's first discussion, Sandy said: "Thus far, only Maria has referred back to the text to support her connections, comments, and questions. I noticed this and explicitly discussed the importance of using the text to explain our individual interpretations."

She showed them how to code their books, marking pages with Post-its and abbreviated comments to help translate their self-talk into group conversation. By the time they reached chapter 10 of *Joey Pigza Loses Control*, the children were proficient at referring to their Post-it notes to analyze characters and events. At this point in the novel, Joey's frenetic father has convinced him that he doesn't need his ADHD medication and has thrown Joey's patches away. When his mother calls to check on him, Joey lies. The following conversation ensued:

> **Ms. Quezada:**   Who wants to start today?
>
> **Maria:**   I can. If ya look on pages 119 and 120, where Joey is at first trying to change the subject? Well, next, he just flat out lies to his mom. This makes me think Joey is becoming more like his dad.
>
> **Angel:**   [Shakes head] I don't agree completely with Maria. I don't think Joey is becoming like his dad. [Pause] I think Joey loves his dad and wants to give him another chance. But he *knows* if he tells his mom the truth, she'll come and get him and won't let him see his dad, and he doesn't want that.
>
> **Ms. Quezada:**   These are both very valid ways to understand the story. One of the best things about being in a book club is that you get to hear what other people think about the story. And it's okay if they think differently than you do. In fact, it's even better because then it helps you to see a bigger picture . . .
>
> **LeAnn:**   Or from another person's perspective.
>
> **Angel:**   I wanna talk about . . . [pauses, turns to another Post-it] On page 129 it says, "I wanted to tell her my secret." This connects to me because if something bad happens, I want to tell my parents. But then I think, "What will happen if I tell?" That's hard.
>
> **LeAnn:**   I think I'd like to add onto what Angel said. Yeah, sometimes it's like hard to know if you want to choose to tell them or not because—
>
> **Maria:**   Of the consequences.
>
> **LeAnn:**   Yeah, so sometimes it's kinda hard to decide *if* you want to tell them. So you have to think what might happen. If you know your parents well enough, you'll know how they might react.

As Sandy explained in her written commentary on this interaction, "Clearly, students are beginning to participate more than before. They are beginning to refer back to the text to support their connections, and they are extending their connections to the world at large." Yet, she was cautious in her enthusiasm, for she knew there was still much the group could accomplish. Indeed, she wanted to balance the groups' personal responses with even more textual reference. For my own part, I think a comment from her about Joey's mother might serve to bring the children back to the book through their personal

- *Grandfather's Journey* (Say, 1993) is about the author's maternal grandfather's immigration from Japan to America and how he loves two countries at the same time. **Questions:** How did your family come to America? If your family is Native American or Mexican American and has lived in the United States for generations: What do you know about the history of your family in America?

The use of well-crafted questions combined with the opportunity to discuss important issues with family members, heightens children's uptake of literary text. As Jill watched her first graders respond to more specific questions she noted, "It seemed as though the thoughts students recorded on their Post-it notes became more specific as well. They began to include more predictions and reactions from the text. Even their parents began to make connections to the text and encourage their children to write down how the book made them feel or think."

Although "book bags" are just one way to extend the conversation out into the community, it is a critical link. Unless a family situation is highly unusual, parents—all parents—want their children to succeed in school. And if you give them specific ways they can help and supply the materials, their contributions can be invaluable. This is especially true if you "involve [your] students actively in their own learning and . . . build directly on knowledge or practices found in local homes" (Moll, 2000, p. 260). A plastic bag with a book, a pencil, Post-its, and a question certainly seem like simple materials, but if your emphasis is on the quality of the interaction, you can be sure that you will up the ante on talk about literature, allowing children and their families to take up text in vibrant and vital ways.

Summary

In this chapter, I focus on literary interpretation through language—the "tool of tools"—suggesting that engagement in literature is critically dependent on talk. All too often, children are denied opportunities to express their thinking, particularly if teachers believe it is their job to deliver correct interpretations of literature rather than help children construct meaning. But expert teachers do everything they can to extend talk through a triad of literature-based activities—their read alouds as well as opportunities for independent reading and literary discussion.

To deepen some of the ideas presented in this chapter, I lean on *The Trolls*, a wonderful tale of Aunt Sally's visit with her estranged brother's children and how her skilled storytelling is only surpassed by her willingness to encourage children's questions and comments. When I've taught this text to teachers in the past, I've used a text-to-text related book—*The Troll with No Heart in His Body*—by another storyteller extraordinaire, Lise Lunge-Larsen (1999). In her author's note, she explained that as a child growing up in Norway, stories of trolls were legion, and as an adult she tells troll stories to children "because children *need* stories like them" (p. 7).

The insight into children's need for stories that speak to them was made clear for me when I taught *Joey Pigza Loses Control* to teachers one spring. At the end of the semester I asked the teachers to vote for their favorites of the books we'd read together, and *Joey* was a clear loser. When I asked the teachers "Why?", they said it was just too exhausting to read. As an ADHD kid, Joey's voice was too frenetic, too intense. And then, of course, there was the problem of his alcoholic father and chain-smoking, hard-talking grandmother. One of the teachers in the group, Lorynda Sampson, disagreed and tried to explain why a book like *Joey* was essential not only to teachers but to children, especially children with ADHD or those from complex families. The next day she told her class of 9- and 10-year-olds about the vote, and they were irate. Lorynda emailed our class:

I just had to put my final "two cents" in for *Joey Pigza*. Although it's a tough book in a lot of ways, and it may be exhausting for many to read, I think it's an important piece of literature for teachers. It gives us a peek, fiction or not, into the lives of so many of the students we have in our classrooms today. Unless we can experience, even vicariously through great literature, what those ADHD or dysfunctional families are like, it's incredibly hard to reach them in the classroom.

Now with that said, and having taken more than "two cents" worth of your time, I have to tell you how angry, indignant and shocked my students were when I told them about the "voting verdict" last night and the comments made about the book during our *Pigza* discussion night. My students were ready to give our class the "what for." They couldn't believe that (1) some folks just didn't like the book, (2) didn't feel comfortable or think it quite appropriate for kids, and (3) couldn't see how valuable the book is. They were incredulous!

\

Children have questions and comments, not only about the lives on the page, but the experience of living in the real world, and if we deny them access to stories, or even more harmful, deny them opportunities to talk about story, how will they come to build the strength they need to live their lives? Lise Lunge-Larsen (1999) addressed this point eloquently:

> As a society we have come to think of folktales as amusing entertainment, quaint relics of the past. We certainly do not view them as vehicles for understanding. Yet folktales explore issues as complex as the nature of good and evil, and the triumph of kindness and patience over bullying and anger. Folktales reveal universal truths. Take the story of "Butterball," a perennial favorite in my storytelling sessions. In this story a troll hag, carrying her head under her armpit, captures a silly, butter-loving boy because he ignores his mother's advice. The troll hag orders her daughter to cook stew out of Butterball while she fetches her husband, the troll. In the end, this seemingly silly boy outwits the daughter and gets rid of the entire troll pack. This story is the most frequently requested story in my repertoire. I had always thought its principal attraction was the hideous troll herself, who carried her head under her armpit, until one day a child blurted out, "How come Butterball is so stupid while he is at home with his mom, but when he is on his own he manages just fine?" After years of telling this story the compelling element, immediately spotted by a child, had completely escaped me: your family, your community can help, but ultimately you have what you need to succeed inside yourself. Strength comes from within. (pp. 7–8)

Still, strength can be enhanced if children are encouraged to talk about text in the classroom and in their community—exploring the nuances of language, the motivation behind characters' actions, and the subtle and not-so-subtle messages in stories both on and off the page.

At the end of *The Trolls*, Aunt Sally tells another story from the pencil sketch of family characters she's drawn. The children are pouring over the picture, hoping to stretch out their aunt's stories just a bit farther by asking their final questions. She tells them to "ask your parents all these questions before it's too late, and what they won't tell you about your family, I will" (p. 113). As Aunt Sally looks at the picture, she sighs, and I believe her words are a powerful metaphor for the need for literature teachers to up the ante on talk:

> "I ought to do you a nicer one than this pencil sketch. I'll get my paints out when I get home and do another one and send it to you for Christmas."

"But you won't leave anyone out, will you?" asked Amanda, studying the picture.

"No," said Aunt Sally, "I won't leave anyone out." (p. 123)

BOOKS FOR THE PROFESSIONAL

Bruner, J. (2002). *Making stories: Law, literature, life.* New York: Farrar, Straus and Giroux. A prominent psychologist and eminent educator, Jerome Bruner is a critical voice in understanding narrative. In a landmark volume—*Actual Minds, Possible Worlds* (1986)—he explored how actions in the real world co-exist with mental processes that help interpret their meaning. This later volume explores the pivotal role of stories in the laws we live by and the lives we lead, marked by predictable patterns and, even more important, unexpected events.

Calkins, L. M. (2001). *The art of teaching reading.* New York: Longman. This beautifully written book explores the teaching of literature with a comprehensive perspective—ranging from guided reading and phonics to talking about literature as well as nonfiction. As a master teacher, Lucy Calkins brings her considerable knowledge to the literary table and delivers a persuasive message about the power of children's interactions with text.

Lewis, C. (2001). *Literary practices as social acts: Power, status, and cultural norms in the classroom.* Mahwah, NJ: Lawrence Erlbaum. In a year-long ethnography of a fifth-sixth-grade classroom, Cynthia Lewis provides an enlightening view of the highly social nature of literary interpretation through four classroom practices—read-alouds, peer-led as well as teacher-led literature discussions, and independent reading.

Peterson, R., & Eeds, M. (1990). *Grand conversations: Literature groups in action.* New York: Scholastic. Though this book is small in size, the scope is indeed "grand" as the authors explore children's meaning making potential through rich dialogue about story.

Routman, R. (2000). *Conversations: Strategies for teaching, learning, and evaluating.* Portsmouth, NH: Heinemann. Packed with myriad ideas, strategies, and examples, Regie Routman's text provides a comprehensive look at fine literary teaching.

Chapter Touchstone Texts

Horvath, Polly. (1999). *The trolls.* New York: Farrar Straus Giroux. "Don't worry, the trolls don't come to you. It's your own darkness that leads you to the trolls." So says Aunt Sally, a gifted and hilarious raconteur, whose stories raise more than a few intriguing questions and offer some serious answers. This book won honors from both the National Book Award and the Boston Globe/Horn Book Award.

Gantos, Jack. (2000). *Joey Pigza loses control.* New York: Farrar, Straus and Giroux. Before Joey went to special education classes and received helpful medication for ADHD, he just couldn't sit still. But now his dad wants to take his meds away! In this 2001 Newbery Honor, view-altering novel, Jack Gantos provides a picture into Joey's *wired* world where humor, compassion, and alternative pedagogy are essential for kids in school. This novel is the second in the Joey series, which is book ended by *Joey Pigza Swallowed the Key* (1998) and *What Would Joey Do?* (2002).

Recommended Tradebooks for Talk

Alvarez, Julia. (2002). *Before we were free.* New York: Alfred A. Knopf. From an award-winning author famous for her adult literature, this tale details the life of 12-year-old Anita, whose family stays behind in the Dominican Republic while her cousins flee to America. What can be talked about and what can't while living in a dictatorship are at the heart of this compelling novel, for as one character suggests: "No flies fly into a closed mouth." Still, secrets and silence can't always protect those who are willing to sacrifice their lives for freedom. This novel is a "testimonial" for those who chose to speak out.

Konigsburg, E. L. (1996). *The view from Saturday.* New York: Atheneum. This is a tale of Noah, Ethan, Julian, and Nadia—four 6th graders whose stories overlap in surprising ways. They come together as friends, and learn to ask questions in ways they've never done before. They also join as an academic team under the tutelage of their wise teacher, Mrs. Olinski, and they learn to answer quite a few questions as well. E. L. Konigsburg won the Newbery for this extraordinary novel, and she is known for novels that get kids talking. One of her latest, *Silent to the Bone* (2000), also stresses the power of talk as one friend works to break the mystery of another's silence.

Martin, Ann M. (2002). *A corner of the universe.* New York: Scholastic. Winner of a Newbery Honor, this is a moving tale of 12-year-old Hattie Owens, whose mentally disabled uncle Adam returns from his boarding school to live once again with Hattie's grandparents. What makes this novel so perfect for talk is the fact that the adults don't really want to talk about Adam's disability. Indeed, they've managed to deny his existence for years, and the silence and rejection are overwhelming for a childlike man who only wants someone to lift a corner of the universe and see him, talk with him, listen to him. Adam's tragic death at the end of the novel makes Hattie well aware of the need to speak about things that all too often remain unspoken.

Sachar, Louis. (1998). *Holes.* New York: Farrar, Straus, & Giroux. Winner of the National Book Award and the Newbery, *Holes* is an imaginative tale of Stanley Yelnats (whose name is a palindrome that works both ways). He's told that digging holes will build his character, though the warden of his detention camp really just wants to fill her own pockets with treasure. Still, there's something deeper than these surface features, for while Stanley is literally digging holes in the desert, he's metaphorically filling in holes from his own complicated past. The holes are not really empty spaces; instead they link places in his past and present to make for a more satisfying future.

4

Culture & Class
in Children's Literature

In *Esperanza Rising* by Pam Muñoz Ryan (2000), the title character remembers that when she was little she thought she would grow up to marry Miguel. Her mother explained that she might think about this choice differently with age, yet Esperanza was determined.

> But now that she was a young woman, she understood that Miguel was the housekeeper's son and she was the ranch owner's daughter and between them ran a deep river. Esperanza stood on one side and Miguel stood on the other and the river could never be crossed. In a moment of self-importance, Esperanza had told all of this to Miguel. Since then, he had spoken only a few words to her. When their paths crossed, he nodded and said politely, "*Mi reina*, my queen," but nothing more. There was no teasing or laughing or talking about every little thing. Esperanza pretended not to care, though she secretly wished she had never told Miguel about the river. (p. 18)

In 2002, *Esperanza Rising* won the Pura Belpré award for "the Latino/Latina writer . . . whose work best portrays, affirms, and celebrates the Latino cultural experience in an outstanding work of literature for children and youth" (http://www.ala.org/alsc/belpre.html). Established in 1996, this award is given every two years by cooperating divisions and affiliates of the American Library Association. The award is named after Pura Belpré who was America's first Latina librarian in the New York Public Library. In addition, the book won the Jane Addams Children's Book Award in 2001, an award given to a book "that most effectively promotes the cause of peace, social justice and world community" (www.education.wisc.edu/ccbc/public/jaddams.htm).

131

A tale of transformation for a 12-year-old girl, Esperanza must move from a sheltered and privileged life in Mexico to one of labor, economic hardship, and racial prejudice in California during the Great Depression of the 1930s. Culture and class play prominent roles in the story—and the river that Esperanza must eventually cross is a metaphor for the rifts that exist among people whose race, ethnicity, and socioeconomic status differ widely.

In the world of children's literature, issues of culture and class are critical, but this has not always been the case. Indeed, in early years Nancy Larrick (1972) called it "the all white world" of children's book publishing. While changes have been made, and authors and illustrators of color are being published, the progress is still far too slow in the face of a rapidly widening gap between teachers and their children. The statistics indicate that while teachers are predominately European American, female, and middle class, the population of children is far more diverse. Numbers from the National Education Association predicted that by the year 2000, less than 5% of the teaching force would be teachers of color, while students of color would make up 45% of the student population—a comparison that makes one "appreciate the alarming nature of the trend" (Weil, 1998, p. 163). What isn't revealed in these statistics, but is equally clear, is the gap between predominately middle class teachers and children who live below the poverty line. How then do teachers cross the river of such statistics to meet the needs of their students?

At this point, you might stop to wonder why I am creating a separate chapter to focus on issues of culture and class. Does this signify a "separate but equal" orientation? Might it indicate a "less than" attitude towards diversity and multicultural literature, relegating it to its own space, rather than integrating it into the whole? No. On the contrary, I placed this chapter specifically after the work on talk to highlight the fact that literary interpretation is critically dependent on who you are and who your students are. How do you select books for your students? What do you make of the fact that some children seem eager for interpretive questions and others remain silent or choose other modes of response? How do you analyze multicultural literature in terms of its authenticity as well as its aesthetic qualities? Are you growing in your understanding of cultures other than your own, or are you daunted by just how much there is to know? For far too long, research that focuses on teachers' knowledge and beliefs has "ignored contextual variables such as the students' cultural background or the degree to which changes in the curriculum influence their thinking" (Ríos, 1996, p. 8). In contrast, my purpose in this chapter is to move cultural contexts to the foreground of your thinking.

Toni Morrison (1992) suggested that we live "in a highly and historically racialized society" (p. 4), and a failure to take this into serious account might blind you to aspects of literature, and more important, aspects of your children that are struggling to be seen. Who you are and how you think about teaching is the product of your experiences, and if your experiences are fundamentally at odds with those of your students—in terms of race, ethnicity, culture, class, and gender—you might make assumptions that will lead you away from your children rather than toward them. You might think of them more in terms of what they can't do than what they can. We know from research that children of color are far more likely to be sorted for special education, grade retention, and slowed instruction (Shepard, 1991). And such sorting and segregation inevitably leads children away from literature and toward leveled books that have a stronger focus on learning to read than reading to learn. However, the idea that children who have difficulty with decoding should be held back from rich literary interpretation is nothing but a myth. As Flores, Tefft Cousin, and Díaz (1998) extolled:

> The myths about children of color, children from low socioeconomic back-grounds, and children identified as learning disabled need to be exposed and discarded from our beliefs, our expectations, and from our everyday prac-tices. Debilitating myths imprison the mind and render people voiceless and therefore powerless. This voicelessness and powerlessness perpetuates the cy-cle of oppression, the cycle of inadequacy, the cycle of failure. We can no longer believe in these myths; we can no longer tolerate their intellectual pres-ence; we must begin to *transform* ourselves by not participating in their daily use. (p. 36)

But how can we continue on this path of transformation once we have begun? In this chapter, I provide some answers to this question by exploring two es-sentials of literary engagement in terms of culture and class: (a) the right to write and (b) the need to talk with children about critical sociocultural issues. While earlier chapters focused more heavily on formal and transactional crit-icism, this chapter emphasizes genetic and sociocultural views. Still, formal criticism plays a strong role in helping you determine how the nuances of language deliver or fail to deliver an authentic view of a particular group, time, place, and situation as well as the themes of a story. Transactional criticism will still be strong in determining how to link children to books that speak not simply about them, but to and for them (Sims [Bishop], 1982).

The Right to Write

When I first began teaching elementary school in 1977, multicultural literature was as rare as hen's teeth. I begin with that distant date as well as an even more antiquated phrase (one used often by my grandmother) to establish the fact that just a quarter of a century ago children's books that celebrated diversity by authors and illustrators of color were nearly impossible to find. Although that was on the cusp of change, another old phrase suggests caution, "The more things change, the more they stay the same."

In that same year, Mildred Taylor (1976) won the Newbery award for *Roll of Thunder, Hear My Cry*. The John Newbery Medal is the most coveted award in children's literature, and it is given annually to "the author of the most distinguished contribution to American literature for children" (http://www.ala.org/alsc/newbery.html). Ms. Taylor (1986) was motivated by the difference between the stories her father told her of her African American heritage and the stories she read in school. In her Newbery acceptance speech, she wrote:

> Those stories about the small and often dangerous triumphs of Black people, those stories about human pride and survival in a cruelly racist society were like nothing I read in the history books or the books I devoured at the local library. There were no Black heroes or heroines in those books; no beautiful Black ladies, no handsome Black men; no people filled with pride, strength, or endurance. There was, of course, always mention of Booker T. Washington and George Washington Carver; Marian Anderson and occasionally even Dr. Ralph Bunche. But that hardly compensated for the lackluster history of Black people painted by those books, a history of a docile, subservient people happy with their fate who did little or nothing to shatter the chains that bound them, both before and after slavery. There was obviously a terrible contradiction between what the books said and what I had learned from my family, and at no time did I feel the contradiction more than when I had to sit in a class which, without me, would have been all white, and relive that prideless history year after year. (p. 25)

Ms. Taylor was the second African American author to win the Newbery gold medal. Virginia Hamilton (1974) was the first when she won the award for *M. C. Higgins, the Great* in 1975. And it should not be forgotten that Arna Bontemps (1948) was the first African American to win a silver "Honor Book" medal in 1949 for *Story of the Negro*. In the late '60s and early '70s, several authors—Julius Lester (1968), Sharon Bell Mathis (1975), and Virginia Hamilton (1971) herself—won silver medals as well. The '80s and '90s would bring more silver to African Americans, including two more medals for Hamilton (1983; 1988). Both Patricia McKissack (1992) and Walter Dean Myers (1992) won silver in 1993. Still, the sheer excitement and hope represented by these awards should not belie the fact that from Hamilton's win in 1975 and Taylor's in 1977, more than twenty years would pass before another African American would win the gold. In 2000, Christoper Paul Curtis (1999) won the award for *Bud, Not Buddy*.

These milestones are critical, because African Americans have led the way toward balance in children's literature. But the road has been hard, and it is harder still for other cultural groups. Just recently, Linda Sue Park (2001) became the first Korean American to win the Newbery for *A Single Shard*. Only two other Asian Pacific Americans have won. In 1928, Dhan Gopal Mukerji (1927), an author of Indian descent, won for *Gayneck, the Story of a Pigeon*, and Lawrence Yep (1975; 1993) won a silver award in 1976 for *Dragonwings* and another in 1994 for *Dragon's Gate*. Thus far, neither a Native American nor an individual of Latino heritage has won the gold.

The Randolph Caldecott Medal, awarded annually for "the artist of the most distinguished American picture book for children" (http://www.ala. org/alsc/caldecott.html), follows a similar pattern. Leo and Diane Dillon won the gold medal twice in the mid-'70s for *Why Mosquitoes Buzz in People's Ears* (Aardema, 1975) and *Ashanti to Zulu: African Traditions* (1976). Leo Dillon was the first African American to win this award; his wife, Diane, is European American. While there have been several silver medals awarded to African Americans over the years including John Steptoe, Christopher Myers, Jerry Pinkney (who has five silver medals), and his son Brian Pinkney (who has won two), as of 2003, with the exception of Leo Dillon, the gold has remained out of reach. The gold Caldecott medal for Asian Pacific Americans is also rare. Ed Young (1989) was the first to win for *Lon Po Po: A Red-Riding Hood Story from China* in 1990, followed by Allen Say's (1993) win for *Grandfather's Journey* in 1994. David Diaz is the only Latino American to have won the award for *Smoky Night* (Bunting, 1994). Native Americans have yet to win the gold medal.

Don't be fooled into thinking that the rarity of gold medals for authors and illustrators of color means that their work is not of the quality that these awards demand. On the contrary, think of it in terms of unequal access to the gold—for authors and illustrators of color are overwhelmed by the numbers of European American artists who can expect to be published. Indeed, the perceptions by publishers of what will sell and what won't often drive the system. As Lisa Holton (2001) explained:

> As a white person in publishing, I hear other white people say things they wouldn't dare say to a black person. Over the years, I have been told that blacks don't buy books, that there is a dearth of black and Hispanic talent, and that black illustrators just aren't up to "mainstream" standards. I asked Andrea Pinkney to join me in starting Jump at the Sun, an imprint celebrating African-American culture, because I was tired of hearing things I knew weren't true. Building the imprint has been one of the greatest joys of my professional life, but it has also been an eye-opener.
>
> Children of all colors are fascinated by themselves and each other—they care deeply about what makes them alike and what makes them different. But many adults in charge of selecting which books go on the shelves—whether it's in the supermarket or in the classroom—still seem to believe that white children aren't interested in black children's culture (implicit in this belief, however, is the assumption that black children are fascinated by white culture). (pp. 503–504)

As a result, awards specifically designated for various groups have been growing in order to recognize what is all too often unrecognized excellence. The Coretta Scott King Award, established in 1970 and affiliated with the American Library Association in the early '80s, is for "authors and illustrators of African descent whose distinguished books promote an understanding and appreciation of the 'American Dream'" (http://www.ala.org/srrt/csking). The Pura Belpré Award began its ALA affiliation in 1996. In 2001, a new ALA award for Asian Pacific American children's literature began. Figure 4.1 offers a summary of the major multicultural awards and web sites.

However, there has been criticism of these awards. For example, Marc Aronson (2001) challenged the proliferation of prizes that are "identity-based." He argued that such awards might actually persuade Caldecott and Newbery committees to ignore books by authors and illustrators of color because they now have their own awards. He suggested that ideally these committees should be challenged to open up their view to more diverse literature. But his own argument was challenged on several levels. A number of scholars and award committee members, especially those who were involved with the Pura Belpré and Coretta Scott King Awards, reminded him that their aesthetic criteria for evaluating books were just as high as for any outstanding

Native American Literature

Oyate

There is currently no award for Native American children's literature. However, Oyate is a "Native organization working to see that our lives and histories are portrayed honestly, and so that all people will know our stories belong to us." In addition to detailed reviews of children's literature, Oyate provides helpful materials for "Teaching Respect for Native Peoples." **http://www.oyate.org**

Latino/a Literature

The Pura Belpré Award

Presented biennially for the "Latino/Latina writer and illustrator whose work best portrays, affirms, and celebrates the Latino cultural experience in an outstanding work of literature for children and youth."
http://www.ala.org/alsc/belpre.html

Américas Award

This award is "given in recognition of U. S. works of fiction, poetry, folklore, or selected non-fiction (from picture books to works for young adults) published in the previous year in English or Spanish that authentically and engagingly portray Latin America, the Caribbean, or Latinos in the United States."
http://www.uwm.edu/Dept/CLACS/outreach_americas.html

African American Literature

Coretta Scott King Award

Presented annually for "authors and illustrators of African descent whose distinguished books promote an understanding and appreciation of the 'American Dream.'"
http://www.ala.org/srrt/csking

This committee also chooses winners for the:

John Steptoe Award for New Talent

Presented annually to "a black author and to a black illustrator for an outstanding book" this award "is designed to bring visibility to a writer or artist at the beginning of his/her career as a published book creator."
http://www.ala.org/srrt/csking/new_talent.html

Asian Pacific American Literature

Asian Pacific American Award for Literature

Presented biennially for Asian Pacific writers of young adult and children's literature. Authors and illustrators are jointly eligible for their picture books.
http://www.uic.edu/depts/lib/projects/resources/apala/laward

Multicultural Awards & Web Sites

FIG. 4.1.   Major Multicultural Awards and Web Sites.

book award. Andrea Pinkney (2001) also reminded Aronson, "The truth is, we don't live in an ideal world. To my way of thinking, three Newberys (and a handful of Newbery honors) in seventy-nine years does not mark significant progress" (p. 536).

In terms of my own progress in thinking about these issues, I distinctly remember in the spring of my second year of teaching—standing in a bookstore and holding the new Caldecott winner in my hand, debating its purchase. My teacher's salary was so low, any book purchase was one not lightly made (though that is, no doubt, still the case for most teachers today). But *The Girl Who Loved Wild Horses* was a book about Native Americans, and even then I understood its rarity. However, what I did not well understand at the time was the significance that its author/illustrator, Paul Goble (1978), was a British citizen who had been fascinated with Native American culture since childhood. Since that time, I have come to spend long hours of reading as well as discussion and debate with preservice and practicing teachers around the "right to write," a term two of my teacher colleagues—Darcy Ballentine and Lisa Hill—and I used to explore whether an author can authentically represent a group of which she or he is not a part:

> Some advocates believe that "insiders" are better able to write stories that capture the themes, languages, and tropes—essentially the social worlds—that groups claim as their own. Rather than an issue of "political correctness," it is one of political consciousness, especially in light of social inequities that are reflected not only in historical racism, but in a modern publishing industry more interested in producing a book that will *sell* than a book that *celebrates* voices rarely heard in the canon of literature. In opposition, others argue that what matters is not a question of perfect parallels between author and the represented characters, but what Henry James called the "aesthetic heat" of the creator—the power of the author and/or illustrator to shape language and art to engage the reader's mind and heart. As Lasky (1996) explained, "A writer can have all the right credentials in terms of ethnic background and culture but can still fail if he or she does not have the aesthetic heat. Such a heat is not the product of ethnicity. It transcends ethnicity. It is within the realm of the artist." (Wolf, Ballentine, & Hill, 1999, p. 7)

Although these controversies have received heated debate among academics, especially in the last decade, the issues were quite new to me as a young teacher, and I find them still new to the teachers I meet in my classes today.

However, once they look at the surveys conducted by children's literature scholars—especially the numbers and images portrayed—they start to more carefully analyze authenticity and aesthetic heat in the literature they select.

Surveying the Numbers, Studying the Images

My own exploration was initially inspired by the work of Rudine Sims [Bishop] (1982). In her seminal study of children's literature, she conducted a survey and analysis of 150 children's books about African Americans between 1965 and 1979. The books she studied fell into three categories. She called the first category the "social conscience" literature. Zero percent of the books were written by African Americans. The purpose of these books was to help non-African Americans develop an understanding of and responsibility for the civil rights of all. Sims [Bishop] used the metaphor of "Guess who's coming to dinner?" for only one type of book, but the idea ran throughout the entire category—an overly simplified Hollywood version where Black and White interact with ease. Although the social conscience books had the potential to be a small step forward, they ultimately created more subtle and often more damaging stereotypes.

Sims [Bishop] labeled the second category "melting pot" literature. Of these books, only $12\frac{1}{2}$ percent were written by people of African descent. The metaphor for these books was "people are people are people" (p. 33), and it placed emphasis on the universality of all people. Typically, the only way to recognize that the characters were African American was by the skin color in the illustrations. While many of the patronizing stereotypes of the "social conscience" books were diminished, this literature still lacked an understanding of the details and texture of African American culture.

These first two categories of books were more than likely the kinds of books that Mildred Taylor (1986) read as a child. Her response to them was telling:

> As I grew, and the writers of books and their publishers grew, I noticed a brave attempt to portray Black people with a white sense of dignity and pride. But even those books disturbed me, for the Black people shown were still subservient. Most often the Black characters were housekeepers, and though a source of love and strength to the white child whose story it was, they remained one-dimensional because the view of them was a white one. Books about Black families by white writers also left me feeling empty, not because a white person had attempted to write about a Black family, but because the writer had not, in

my opinion, captured the warmth or love of the Black world and had failed to understand the principles upon which Black parents brought up their children and taught them survival. It was not that these writers intentionally omitted such essential elements; it was simply that by not having lived the Black experience, they did not know it. But I did know it. (pp. 25–26)

Not only did Taylor know it, she began to write it. And her writing exists within the third category that Sims [Bishop] calls "culturally conscious" literature. Predominantly written and illustrated by African Americans, the metaphor for these books was to help children understand "how we got over," emphasizing "survival, both in a spiritual and a material sense" (p. 49). These books spoke *to* and *for*, not *about*, African American children, and they celebrated the uniqueness of growing up Black and American. They are noted for accurate portrayals of African American English communicative styles, close extended family relationships, positive descriptions of skin color, and an emphasis on historical and cultural traditions.

Since her seminal dissertation research, Bishop has gone on to write extensively about multicultural literature, and she is not alone. Numerous scholars—especially children's literature scholars of color—have conducted their own surveys and analyzed the books concerning particular cultural groups. For example, Barrera and Garza de Cortes (1997) studied children's books with Mexican American themes published in the '90s and compared their findings to an earlier survey conducted in 1975. Although the average number of Mexican American children's books published annually rose from 6 in the earlier years to 19 in the '90s, the numbers are "still depressingly low in light of the increased production of multicultural children's literature, . . . not to mention the marked growth of the Mexican American population in recent years, particularly in schools" (p. 130). In the earlier survey from the '70s, almost all the books were written by European Americans, but in the later survey, approximately "a third . . . were written by individuals of Mexican American descent. However, of this sub-total, almost half . . . are by *one* Mexican American writer, Gary Soto" (p. 131).

The statistics for Asian Pacific American children's literature are worse. Yamate (1997) explained, "In any given year, while four to five thousand new children's books are published, fewer than ten are by or about Asian Pacific Americans" (p. 97). And one can easily imagine that certain well-published authors like Allen Say, Yoshiko Uchida, and Lawrence Yep take up a good percentage of this slim number. This is not to say that successful authors of color should not be published. However, it does make me wonder if their success allows publishers to point with false pride to their lists and consequently avoid seeking out new voices.

The most tragic numbers are reserved for Native American children's literature. Statistics offered by Reese and Caldwell-Wood (1997) indicated that it is a rare book that clearly identifies a specific Indian nation. Even more disturbing was the fact that "in 1995, 98½ percent of the books written about Native Americans published by mainstream publishers were written by non-Native authors" (p. 158). Indeed, they decry the fact that "throughout the history of children's literature about Native Americans, most of the writers who have gained profit by writing Indian stories have been non-Native" (p. 162).

Within these dismal numbers, the images are even more depressing. Barrera and Garza de Cortes (1997) explained that while the most blatant stereotypes have diminished, others endure:

> One cumulative message is that Mexican Americans are a simple, fun-loving group of people, perpetually having fiestas and breaking piñatas. Another is that Mexican Americans are tied to the traditional past, in a form of arrested cultural development. Just as counterproductive are the messages given when Mexican Americans are repeatedly depicted in only one or two roles, namely, as migrants and immigrants. For the most part, the larger proportion of this population, which is neither migrant nor immigrant, is ignored and rendered invisible, keeping the literature from serving as a mirror for Mexican American children and a window for other children. (p. 136)

Stressing the importance of family in Puerto Rican life, Nieto (1997) sent a similar message, "Although the Puerto Rican family and family traditions are more salient in newer books than ever before, a few books, primarily but not exclusively those written by non-Latinos, continue to demean or exclude the family and to repeat worn stereotypes" (p. 69).

Yamate (1997) explained that in some cases, the worn stereotypes are often preposterously positive, "Asian Pacific American homes and families are neither odd nor unnatural.... Nor do Asian Pacific Americans all excel in mathematics; indeed, such 'positive' stereotypes are just as damaging as negative ones" (p. 99). And both positive and negative stereotypes continue to prevail in Native American children's literature. As Michael Dorris (1992) observed:

> In the never-never land of glib stereotypes and caricature, the rich histories, cultures, and the contemporary complexities of the diverse indigenous peoples of the Western Hemisphere are obscure, misrepresented, and rendered trivial. Native Americans appear not as human beings but as whooping, silly, one-dimensional cartoons. On occasion they are presented as marauding, blood-thirsty savages.... At other times they seem veritable angels, pure of heart, mindlessly ecological.... And worst of all, they are often merely cute, the special property of small children. (p. 27)

Because small and larger children are the direct recipients of these images, it is critical for you to evaluate the texts you teach.

Analyzing Authenticity & Aesthetic Heat

One of my central goals as a teacher of children's literature is to help my preservice and practicing teachers select multicultural literature with care. With that in mind, I ask them to consider the cogent criteria offered by experts in multicultural literature. For example, two volumes edited by Violet Harris (1993; 1997), an eminent African American scholar, offer specific suggestions for what to look for in terms of authenticity and aesthetic heat. The chapter authors do not suggest that only writers of parallel cultures can write authentic literature. Still, while they work to avoid "cultural pigeonholes" (Barrera, Liguori, & Salas, 1993, p. 213), they make clear that writing outside of one's cultural experience rarely offers more than limited flight.

They also do not imply that authors of color are uniformly successful in creating aesthetically fine literature. As Bishop (1997) explained, "It is well to remember that reading literature, especially fiction, no matter what culture it reflects, ought to be an aesthetic experience. In our search for social significance and our desire for social change, we dare not forget that a well-written piece of literature is a work of art" (p. 6).

Toward this end, when analyzing the aesthetic qualities of multicultural literature, you can lean on all of the aspects of narrative—genre, character, setting, plot, theme, point of view, style, and tone—components we explored in chapter 2. How carefully are the characters crafted? Does the plot move us clearly towards an ultimate resolution, or perhaps dissolution in a clever way? In other words, what's the Trouble with a capital T, and does it untangle or intriguingly retie? Are the metaphors fresh and revealing? Most important, does the story reach out and speak to us as readers, connecting with mind and heart?

Rather than see authenticity and aesthetic heat as opposites, it's critical to see them in relationship. While it's true that heat often rises in the authenticity, or in the "subtle nuances of culture," there is no guarantee that heat has to come in chemical combination with an author of a parallel culture. However, I still believe that combustion often occurs when the light of authenticity and heat of aesthetic endeavor combine.

I can best explain this by taking a closer look at *Esperanza Rising*. First of all, the author, Pam Muñoz Ryan, wrote the story based on the life of her maternal grandmother. In her informative author's note, she provides details of how her grandmother's life parallels that of the novel's protagonist, Esperanza, who was also named after her grandmother. In addition, she relates facts about the difficulties Mexicans endured in trying to find and keep jobs in the U.S. She also describes the Deportation Act that America passed to send huge numbers of Mexicans back to their homeland and thus ease the terrible unemployment of the Great Depression. The plan didn't work, and even worse, many of the "Mexicans" were citizens of the United States who had lived in America for their entire lives and had never even been to Mexico. Flatly stating that many of the "repatriates" were children born in the United States, Takaki (1993) explained that "Repatriation was an employment program for whites—a way to remove a surplus Mexican laboring population and preserve the few remaining jobs for white workers" (p. 334).

Still, the fact that *Esperanza Rising* is based not only on Muñoz Ryan's grandmother's life but also on historical accuracies, only gives us a stripped down reason for the success of the story. We must go deeper to locate the aesthetic heat. In their analysis of commended books or winners of the Américas Award (which can be accessed online at http://www.uwm.edu/Dept/CLACS/outreach_americas.html), Carmen Medina and Patricia Enciso (2002) found four sociopolitical themes in Latino/a literature for children: "1) Border crossing, 2) Coming home, 3) Healing, community, and spirituality, and 4) Shaping language and being shaped by language" (pp. 36–37).

In my own reading of *Esperanza*, their themes echo throughout the novel, especially in the features that demonstrate the relationship between aesthetic heat and authenticity:

The Use of Metaphor. *Esperanza Rising* uses metaphor in ways that are both fresh and focused on cultural issues. The chapters are titled after fruits and vegetables that follow the harvest. Even more important, the titles travel a metaphorical route from the plentiful life Esperanza lived at the beginning of the story ("Las Uvas/Grapes") to the bitterness of Esperanza's first encounter with hard work ("Las Cebollas/Onions"). They also move from her attempts to keep some of the marks of her high social status by rubbing her calloused hands with "Las Aguacates/Avocados" to her burgeoning political understanding of social inequities. The story comes to full fruition in the final chapter, again entitled "Las Uvas/Grapes," as Esperanza is reunited with her mother and grandmother. Although her father can never return, she has learned from his wisdom. Indeed, as her family's wisdom supports her, her story becomes intertwined with her grandmother's tale of the phoenix. In Spanish *Esperanza* means hope, and as the title of the story suggests Esperanza Rises from the ashes of her earlier life.

The View of Sociopolitical Realities. As a privileged child in Mexico, Esperanza had only a naïve understanding of her place in the world. When Miguel tells her that the Mexican saying "full bellies and Spanish blood go hand in hand" means that "those with Spanish blood, who have the fairest complexions in the land, are the wealthiest," Esperanza shrugs and says, "It is just something that old wives say." But Miguel is insistent. "No. . . . It is something the poor say" (pp. 79–80). Once in the U.S., Esperanza begins to learn the hard facts of race, culture, and class. In one poignant scene, she notices that her friend has been praying nightly at a statue of Our Lady of Guadalupe. When she questions her, Isabel explains that she is hoping that she will win the "Queen of the May" at school. Even though the award is based on grades and Isabel has straight As, a classmate has told her the award is typically won by English speakers who also have better clothes. When Isabel doesn't win, Esperanza is outraged, and she begins to question the other inequities in the lives of Mexican Americans.

In even more serious scenes in the novel, Miguel loses a railroad job for which he was well qualified to white men from Oklahoma who agreed to work for lower wages. He takes a job digging ditches in order to put food on the table. The camp for the "Okies" has much better amenities, including a swimming pool that the Mexican Americans are only allowed to swim in on the day before it is cleaned. And Esperanza and her family are faced with hard choices about whether to support workers striking for better conditions, especially in the face of starvation and repatriation.

The Use of Spanish. The fact that Isabel is saying *novenas* at the statue of Guadalupe because she wants to be *la reina* (or queen) like Esperanza makes the skillful use of Spanish clear. Medina and Enciso (2002) explained that "Latino/a authors writing for children use language as a theme and poetic representation in their works, focusing on the relationship between language and identity, language and politics, and language and power" (p. 43). When Esperanza looks back on her earlier life she sees it as *un cuento de hadas*—a fairy tale. Now she must take responsibility as *la patrona*, learning to work hard even when the threat of the immigration police, *La Migra*, threaten her family's very livelihood.

The Focus on Family. While Eurocentric stories often emphasize the home-away-home aspects of children's lives, where they are either forced out or want to escape the boredom of home life, *Esperanza Rising* shows the strength of family relationships. Of all the hardships in Esperanza's life— the hard work of the fields, the early hours, the low pay, the threat of repatriation—nothing is as bitter as being separated from her grandmother who is still in Mexico and her mother who has fallen ill and is hospitalized. Her pain is physical as she curls into a tight ball in her bed each night.

At the beginning of the novel, Esperanza is told by her grandmother that she must not be afraid to begin life again after tragedy has struck. This scene is repeated, yet altered in the novel's lovely conclusion. Now joyfully reunited with mother and Abuelita, Esperanza and her grandmother begin to teach Isabel how to crochet the zigzag pattern that replicates the hills and valleys of life. At first, Isabel's crochet work is crooked, but Esperanza carefully pulls out the uneven stitches reminding Isabel gently, "Do not ever be afraid to start over" (p. 253).

I believe Esperanza's words can be a metaphor for the work you need to do in analyzing multicultural literature for authenticity and aesthetic heat. Even if you are quite familiar with quality literature, you should not be afraid to start over when it comes to learning about stories of other cultures and classes. This is not to diminish your dread. Indeed, your fear in the face of making mistakes is born out in the fact that children are harmed by stories that misrepresent them, or worse, ignore the realities of their lives. But the information about authenticity that was so long hidden from view is increasingly available. The surveys that I've summarized here from research articles and book chapters are devoted to judging the quality of books. There are on-line sources that debate the merits of particular texts. And there are author web sites that provide insights into the parallel or nonparallel status of authors and illustrators.

In addition, children's literature textbooks address these issues quite directly, listing criteria as well as eliciting the opinions of famous authors. For example, children's literature experts asked Alma Flor Ada if she felt an author had to be of the culture to write about it. Ada (1998) is a noted Latina author and the recent winner of the Pura Belpré award for her autobiographical novel, *Under the Royal Palms: A Childhood in Cuba*. While Ada's (2002, cited in Temple, Martinez, Yokota, & Naylor, 2002) first response was "not necessarily," because of the restrictions that would result if only insiders were allowed to write about particular cultures, she stressed the need for responsibility, because "children always deserve the truth at its best. (p. 93). Indeed, children and their teachers deserve "truth at its best," and teachers need access to facts about authenticity and aesthetic heat as they take responsibility for the books they select.

The Need for Authentic Native American Texts.   Two texts written about Native Americans in 1999 will demonstrate the need for accurate information. The first book is *My Heart Is On the Ground: The Diary of Nannie Little Rose, a Sioux Girl. Carlisle Indian School, Pennsylvania, 1880* by Ann Rinaldi (1999). It is the story of a young child's experience at the Carlisle Indian Industrial School, a notorious place founded by Captain Richard Henry Pratt whose infamous motto was "Kill the Indian and save the man." The historical facts indicate shocking hardships for the school's pupils. Children were, for the most part, sent to the school against their parents' will. Children who spoke their Native language were punished, often harshly. The statistics associated with the school indicate high rates of runaways and low rates of graduation. Notwithstanding these facts, in the novel Nannie Little Rose makes a relatively smooth transition to life in this school and quickly comes to appreciate the features of the white world, often to the point of criticizing and even rejecting her Native heritage.

No sooner was the book published than strong criticism began to emerge. Debbie Reese, a Native American (Nambé Pueblo) children's literature scholar, was then a doctoral student concerned with the images of Native peoples in children's literature. She communicated with a group of women with similar concerns (Atleo, Caldwell, Landis, Mendoza, Miranda, Reese, Rose, Slapin, & Smith, 1999), and together they wrote a critical review on line for the Oyate website (http://www.oyate.org), a Native organization devoted to an honest portrayal of the lives and histories of Native peoples. The review is both detailed and devastating in its exposure of the myriad errors and cultural insensitivities within the text.

In May of 1999, Reese posted the review on the CCBC-Net, an electronic forum devoted to discussion of children's literature. Five months later, they took up the challenge of this review and began a discussion of the Rinaldi book in contrast to a National Book Award Honor book: Louise Erdrich's (1999) *The Birchbark House*, a moving tale of an Ojibwa family's life in the face of relentless change and the specter of smallpox. The discussion also included other highly authentic and aesthetically crafted texts, including Joseph Bruchac's (1998) *The Heart of a Chief*. The resulting conversation was heated, even combative, but continually instructive in its exploration of the many serious issues that swirl around multicultural children's literature, especially in evaluating children's books by and about American Indians.

You can access this conversation in the CCBC archives (http://ccbc. education.wisc.edu/ccbc-net), but even if you were to look at the two books side by side, you would be struck by their obvious differences. The Rinaldi book is part of the *Dear America Series*, and these books are designed to look like children's original diaries. Information about the real authors of these texts is typically relegated to the back pages. Indeed, Rinaldi's name doesn't even appear on the cover or binding of the book, though it does appear on the cover page. In contrast, Louise Erdrich's name is listed on both the binding and the cover of *The Birchbark House*, and information about her life and Native American heritage as well as deep connections to her topic are directly stated. As a member of the Turtle Mountain band of Ojibwa, she wrote the text while researching her own family's history with her mother and sister.

The cover of *My Heart is on the Ground* adds to the illusion of the book— a Native American girl, her dark hair adorned with two eagle feathers, is portrayed with her eyes cast down. The picture is not Nannie Little Rose. As Reese and colleagues revealed: "The portrait of the child on the cover..., originally entitled 'Cree Indian Girl, Little Star,' is listed on the permissions page as 'Indian Girl, Little Star.' It was done by James Bama, a painter of romantic western and Indian subjects." Thus a Cree child is portrayed as Sioux, and as Reese and her colleagues pointed out, "A Lakota child in 1880 would not have referred to herself as 'Sioux'. . . . And she would certainly not have referred to Indian men as 'braves.'"

In contrast, Omakayas—the protagonist of *The Birchbark House*—looks out towards her reader from the cover of the book, and Louise Erdrich herself did the art. The words spoken by Omakayas and her family are carefully researched. In both an "Author's Note on the Ojibwa Language" and a "Glossary and Pronunciation Guide of Ojibwa Terms," Erdrich carefully provides definitions for words and delineates the difficulties of capturing the "often idiosyncratic" spellings of a language that was originally "spoken, not written" (p. 240). And throughout the text, Erdrich calls the people Anishinabe (pronounced AH-nish-in-AH-bay) which was the "the original name for the Ojibwa or Chippewa people, a Native American group who originated in and live mainly in the northern North American woodlands" (p. 241).

One has to look a little deeper for the most disturbing contrasts between the two books. Rinaldi took several names of children who had died at Carlisle from tombstones in the school's graveyard to use for characters in her book. She was moved by the names and wanted to honor them, but Reese and her colleagues reviled her choice in their review. Turning to *The Birchbark House*, on her "Thanks and Acknowledgments" page Erdrich told us, "The name Omakayas appears on a Turtle Mountain census. I am using it in the original translation because I've been told those old names should be given life. The name is pronounced Oh-MAH-kay-ahs. Dear reader, when you speak this name out loud you will be honoring the life of an Ojibwa girl who lived long ago." While the decisions of the two authors seem somewhat similar, they are not. As Beverly Slapin of Oyate explained in a CCBC-Net email on October 4th, 1999:

> Louise Erdrich, who is Ojibwa, has used the Ojibwa name of an Ojibwa child in a story that honors and respects Ojibwa children. When Louise says that she's "been told those old names should be given life," that means she has probably consulted with her elders in the telling of this story, and she tells this story from her heart, her spirit, and her life.
>
> For Ann Rinaldi to copy the names of dead Indian children from the gravestones at the Carlisle Indian cemetery and use them as characters in her book dishonors and disrespects the children who died there. It is the coldest kind of appropriation I can think of, and epitomizes the utter lack of sensitivity and respect that characterizes the vast majority of children's books about Native peoples. I don't know and don't care about her intentions; her words speak for themselves.

Indeed, in an interview for *The New Advocate* (Bush, 2001), Rinaldi was questioned about the controversy surrounding her book. Her words speak for themselves:

> Now that was political. A lot of that was political correctness. A Native American woman, very intelligent, very educated, I believe, started it, and objected to a lot of things. . . . They objected to the fact that I used the names of the children in the graveyard, whose names I found on the tombstones, who had died while at the school. Well, I was so moved; the names were so beautiful, and I wanted it to have a taste of reality. And I thought I was honoring these children, but it was taken wrong. Oh, there was a whole list of things! But I understand that the Mohawk Indian Tribe up in New York State loved the book, whereas the Sioux, those who said they were representing the Sioux, hated it. So now, go figure! I did not know that as a white person, you're really asking for it, doing a book on Native Americans. I did not know that! But it's a touchy thing. And I grant them all their feelings, I think that they have justified complaints, more than anybody else, any other minority group that I know. I mean, I acknowledge that we treated the Native Americans terribly! But my book, I didn't intend to do anything but enhance them and honor them. But it was taken the wrong way by this group of people on the Internet. But I have to tell you, that book is selling like crazy, not because of the controversy. . . . That book was my biggest wage earner. (p. 319)

Rinaldi's words are so revealing, I'm tempted to let them stand. But let me add just a few words of my own. Discussions of the "Right to Write" are not about "political correctness," but political consciousness. The term "PC" means that you are only skating on the surface, but being politically conscious implies your deep awareness of the world around you.

As a teacher of literature, you want to select the pieces you teach based on careful analysis, and if you're unsure or even frightened of making a mistake there are now readily available sources where you can research the level of authenticity and the quality of aesthetic heat. Indeed, there is increasing demand for authors to include detailed source notes regarding the origins of their tales, including the cultural context as well as an explanation of how and why they've altered the tale to fit their own aesthetic views (Hearn, 1993). No teacher worth his or her salt would pick a book because it offers a "taste of reality" or because it's selling well. Instead, fine teachers of literature seek out books that celebrate accurate, honest, diverse, and powerful portrayals of human life. And they do it because they honor the lives of the children they teach.

Talking About Culture & Class With Children

In *Esperanza Rising*, the tragedy of her father's death and the double-dealing of two greedy uncles force Esperanza and her mother to flee to America. They travel with Hortensia, Alfonso, and their son Miguel, who had been servants in their household, but would now be their benefactors and protectors as they learn to make new lives in the California labor camps. While on the train heading North, Esperanza is shocked that for the first time in her life she is not riding in first class, but is instead seated in a crowded car with peasants. When a child approaches her to touch Esperanza's beloved porcelain doll, she jerks it away and quickly puts it back into her case. Her mother looks at Esperanza with disapproval and apologizes to the child's mother. In surprise, Esperanza asks her mother why she should allow a child who is poor and dirty to touch her doll. Her mother explained, "When you scorn these people, you scorn Miguel, Hortensia, and Alfonso. And you embarrass me and yourself. As difficult as it is to accept, our lives are different now" (p. 70).

Later Carmen, a peasant woman on the train traveling with her chickens, offers Esperanza some candy, and her mother encourages her to take one. Esperanza can't get over the change in her mother, for she would never have allowed her to accept candy from a stranger before. Even more surprising, her mother falls into easy conversation with Carmen, who sells eggs for a living though she emphasizes the riches of her rose garden, her faith, and the love of her family.

> Mama had always been so proper and concerned about what was said and not said. In Aguascalientes, she would have thought it was "inappropriate" to tell an egg woman their problems, yet now she didn't hesitate.
>
> "Mama," whispered Esperanza, taking on a tone she had heard Mama use many times. "Do you think it is *wise* to tell a peasant our personal business?"
>
> Mama tried not to smile. She whispered back, "It is all right, Esperanza, because now we are peasants, too."
>
> Esperanza ignored Mama's comment. What was wrong with her? Had all of Mama's rules changed since they had boarded this train? (p. 77)

The rules of talking with children about text have changed as well, for issues of culture and class can no longer be ignored in classrooms, especially if we want to encourage children's uptake of literature. *Esperanza Rising* is the tale of a child's transition from one culture and class to another, and it's clear from her questions and comments that the shift is not an easy one. Nor is it easy to talk with children about social issues, but if we select fine literature and let children's questions and comments guide us, our discussions will, no doubt, prove rich rather than poor.

Talking about Esperanza Rising with 11- & 12-year-olds

In the spring of 2002, I had a teacher in my class—Jessica Levitt Knorr—who wanted to improve the quality of her sixth grade children's book discussions. As a literacy resource teacher, Jessica worked with students who were disengaged with reading in their regular classrooms, and they often read well below grade level. She was fascinated by one of the articles I assigned—a National Reading Research Center Report by Commeyras and Sumner (1995). In this provocative piece, the authors explore what happens when students' questions become the nucleus of literature discussions. They realized that given the opportunity, students pose excellent questions and listen carefully to one another in constructing their responses. Jessica was also intrigued with *Esperanza Rising*. Because the majority of her students were Mexican American, she felt there would be many "opportunities for deep personal connections." She also believed that the author's use of "Spanish proverbs and words within the text make this group feel more at home." Of one student Jessica wrote:

> I chose Angel to be in the group to give him an opportunity to express and expand his conceptual and abstract ideas beyond what he has been expected and allowed to do. He tends to get "lost" in the regular classroom and shies away from participation, sometimes substituting it with misbehavior. He claims that he doesn't want to have to "think," yet when given the chance to express his ideas, has absolutely astonished me with his deep insights and interpretive responses. It is my hope that with a small and intimate group, Angel will feel safe enough to allow others to see how smart he really is and feel like his connections, questions, and thoughts are relevant and valued.

Another child in the group was shy and tended to hover on the edges of whole class discussions. Jessica felt that a small group might encourage her to speak out as well. She wrote, "I chose Cristina because she is reading below grade-level and rarely participates in class, resulting in isolation and confusion. She has the ability to ask literal questions, but I want her to move beyond to questions that are more inferentially based and open-ended." In addition,

Cristina loved *Esperanza Rising* from the first chapter because "they speak Spanish, are from Mexico, and it is interesting." She went to the library and checked out her own copy of the book so she could reread what the group read at each meeting. When she promised that she "wouldn't go ahead," Jessica encouraged her to do so if she liked.

Jessica's group sessions lasted for 70 minutes, two days a week, and followed a particular pattern of instruction. She explained:

> First, we reviewed the story and any ideas, questions, and comments the students had from the previous session. Next, I read a chapter aloud to the group. During this time, I would pause at appropriate intervals and ask the students to write down questions they had so far. Sometimes I would ask for a specific number of questions to be written down, and eventually I was able to allow them to make that decision independently, based strictly on what they authentically found curious. I believed it was necessary, however, to initially provide an expectation so they would have practice in developing their own questions, and that any excuses claiming, "I don't have any!" would be a non-negotiable. I also modeled the difference between a literal and text-based question versus a more highly interpretive and abstract question. We called these *skinny* and *fat* questions.
>
> The students eventually began writing a mixture of literal and interpretive questions that suggested to me that they were beginning to apply their new knowledge to their own inquiries and understanding. Also, later in the unit, the students were spontaneously writing down questions while I was reading, without any prompting from me. I believe this indicates the students' engagement in the text and comfort in asking their own questions, truly seeking a deeper meaning for themselves. We used these questions to conduct our peer discussion groups during each session.

After meeting with her group regularly for a few weeks, Jessica felt she was still dominating the discussion, but she worked diligently to refrain, especially since her students were "apparently waiting for [her] to control, conduct, and ask all the questions." And her continual efforts to maintain the balance between leading and following paid off, "As the unit progressed, they stopped waiting for me to call on them and joined in when they were propelled by comments, insights, alternative perspectives, and further questions. They began to have more real discussions that flowed naturally, with interruptions and laughter and surprises!"

In one of their discussions, they had just finished reading the chapter that held Esperanza's experiences on the train. As they disembark, Esperanza's mother and Carmen exchange gifts and embrace each other as friends. Later, Esperanza and Miguel witness Carmen giving a crippled woman a coin as well as tortillas, even though the finely dressed passengers ignore her. Watching, Miguel comments, "The rich take care of the rich and the poor take care of those who have less than they have" (p. 79).

Jessica's group was eager to share their questions, and by this time their questions were "fat" and focused on more complex issues. For example, Matias's initial questions about the book were very literal and could be easily found within the text itself. However, as they read further into the book, Jessica wrote, "Matias's questions began to change, and he started asking more *how* and *why* questions." For example, in reflecting on the train scene Matias wrote, "Why does Carmen give money and chickens to people when she is poor too?" Several of the children had been similarly intrigued with the class issues raised by this scene. Seated in a circle with their desks facing one another, Angel began the discussion with his first question:

> **Angel:** Do you think that Miguel thinks that rich people have a poor soul?
> **Ms. Knorr:** Explain what you mean by a poor soul.
> **Angel:** Someone that's not a good person inside, like the Uncles.
> **Ms. Knorr:** Like Tío Luis and Tío Marco.
> **Branden:** Poor people are more thankful, and rich people aren't as thankful for what they have.
> **Matias:** Poor people *are* richer. Look at Carmen. She's poor, and she still gives the poor money and chickens and eggs. I think the rich people have a poor soul. They'll be like Esperanza and pull her doll away. They don't want to help the poor.
> **Ms. Knorr:** Why do you think Esperanza thinks like that?
> **Cristina:** She's not used to poor people or sharing with people who are different.

Angel's use of the term "poor soul" shows three insights. First, he is reading with deep comprehension, for when Jessica asks him to define the term he uses a textual example about the Uncles' behavior to support his claim. Second, he's analyzing character, but his analysis goes beyond a surface description and into the very "soul" of the characters. He clearly understands the Uncles' evil intentions, especially that of Tío Luis who proposes marriage to Esperanza's mother in a thinly veiled plot to garner her influence in the community and then burns her house to the ground when she resists.

Third, Angel is calling on his own background knowledge of rich and poor to understand character motivation.

Branden is equally interested in determining the motivation of the rich who aren't "thankful for what they have." In response, Matias becomes adamant, and he answers his own earlier question about why Carmen would give away precious resources when she obviously had little to spare. He even takes Esperanza's action and hypothetically applies it to what rich people in general might do if a poor child wanted to touch their belongings. Finally, Cristina contributes to the analysis of character by suggesting the reasoning behind Esperanza's actions.

Jessica's role in this conversation is particularly deft because, instead of focusing on her own questions and looking for parallel answers to her own reflections, her questions nudge the children into deeper explanations of their thinking. In fact, the conversation was so successful, Jessica wrote that it went well beyond this brief transcript as the children connected these ideas "to their own lives and cited people as well as reasons why they had 'rich' or 'poor souls.'"

Intriguingly none of the children were eager to lay too much blame at Esperanza's feet. As Cristina stated, the protagonist was "not used to poor people or sharing with people who are different." Indeed, Cristina seemed to have a great deal of empathy for Esperanza, and her compassion became even more evident a few weeks later when Jessica asked the children to communicate important themes of the story through the visual arts. While I'll devote the entirety of chapter 7 to children's artistic response, Cristina's representation can serve to foreshadow the importance of literary interpretation through the visual arts.

Based on the work of Patricia Enciso (1996) as well as some examples of cut paper work I had shown in class (Whitelaw & Wolf, 2001), Jessica provided the children with construction paper and scissors, and she asked them to "create a visual image—realistic, abstract, or a combination—that showed thoughtful interpretation of important textual events." While she gave them a fair amount of freedom in their use of materials, she made it clear that they should justify their artistic choices in their presentations, including decisions about shape and color.

During the activity, Jessica wrote, "Cristina was more focused than ever, not stopping to talk or interact with others." When the children met to share their renderings, Cristina carefully explained the art you see in Fig. 4.2—a portrayal of critical events in the first half of the book:

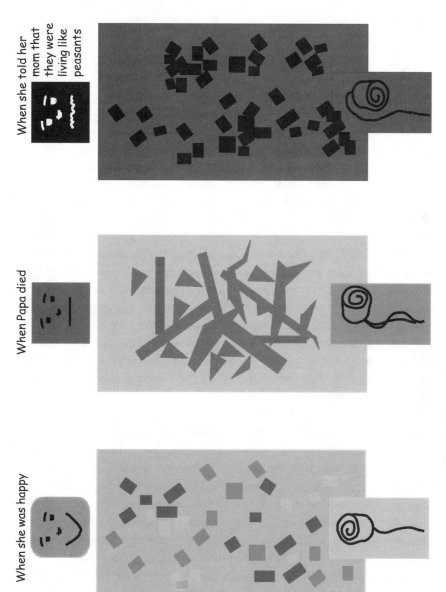

When she was happy

When Papa died

When she told her mom that they were living like peasants

FIG. 4.2. Cristina's Interpretation of the First Half of *Esperanza Rising*.

The first, blue rectangle represents the happy time in Esperanza's life. She was filled with joy and love from her family, especially Papa, which the pink represents; alive land and earth, which the brown represents; and yellow sunshine. The purple rose is standing strong and tall just like *she* was when the story began.

The second, purple rectangle shows the time in her life when Papa died. The orange shapes are daggers in her heart, and they have pointy, sharp tips. Her smile is gone, and the rose now has a bent-down head, in mourning, like she is now.

The third, red rectangle shows the time in her life when she realized she was living just like a peasant. Her face is black and her heart and insides are filled with darkness. The rose is completely bent over now, showing how much sadness she is feeling and hope lost. These images show the major events that made Esperanza's life change so much, and how she felt about them on the inside.

The clarity of Cristina's explanation reveals remarkable insight into Esperanza's character. Her brief annotations of the three rectangles ("When she was happy," "When Papa died," and "When she told her mom that they were living like peasants") serve to summarize much deeper aspects of the story. And Esperanza's faces, while simple, demonstrate the changing mood. Intriguingly, the "happy" face is rounded, while the next two faces are squares with sharp corners. The rose at the bottom of each rectangle moves from upright, to drooping, to completely downcast as more and more pain comes into Esperanza's life.

The shifting mood of the story is even more clearly demonstrated in Cristina's cut paper shapes within the rectangles. The colors in the "happy" rectangle are varied, and while she uses yellow for sunshine and pink for happiness, the use of brown for the earth goes beyond standard significance to represent Esperanza's father's attachment to the earth. In the opening scene of the novel, he and Esperanza lie on the ground to hear the earth's heart beating. With the death of her beloved father, represented in the second rectangle, the shapes are sharp and uniform in color. But Cristina saved the color black for her final rectangle, when Esperanza's troubles seem to multiply and "her heart and insides are filled with darkness." Not only is her father dead, but they have lost their land and their homeland and are working like peasants.

Perhaps another reason the children felt for Esperanza was because she grew through her experiences. She began to take notice of the political world in which she lived and realized that there was more to life than wealth. Indeed, Angel summed it up best in his final journal entry in response to Jessica's question, "What did you learn from the story?" Angel replied briefly, "Pretty much that life's a circle." However, in group, he expanded on this statement, explaining:

> I mean that life's a circle; that it comes back to where it started. Like Esperanza's hope that she would always be with her family. She was, when Abuelita came to America and Mama got better. And her family grew even bigger, with Isabel and her parents. Even though she lost Papa, she had her life again because she and Miguel felt the earth's heartbeat again.
>
> She was rich inside. Even though her life changed, and she lost the ranch and her Papa, she had love and family and a full heart. She ended up on the same side of the river as Miguel. That was different. That was a change. But it was better because she realized more important things. She wasn't spoiled anymore. Her birthday came around again like a circle, and she was a different, but better person because of what happened to her.

Angel's oral explanation provides a rich interpretation of the text. Leaning on a number of plot events, he states the theme for *Esperanza Rising* as well as for the consistent home-away-home pattern. Life is a circle, especially in children's literature, and characters set off from home only to come back again "different" but often "better." Just as she and her Papa lay on the earth to hear its heartbeat in the first chapter, Esperanza and Miguel hear it together at the end of the tale. And the river that initially divides Esperanza from Miguel no longer exists.

At this point, you might be tempted to think, "Well, these are 11- and 12-year-olds. No wonder they have so much to say." But I'd encourage you not to create a river between young children and talk about culture and class. They, too, have much life experience, and they are quite capable of insightful discussions about social worlds both on and off the page. In my university classes of practicing teachers, *Esperanza Rising* is one of their favorite books, and I've seen them use it for read alouds and book discussions, not just in intermediate and middle grades, but with children as young as second grade.

Talking About Amelia's Road
with 7-, 8-, & 9-year olds

In teaching *Esperanza Rising*, I often pair it with *Amelia's Road*, a picture book about a young migrant child who longs for a home of her own. I like this book because it further complicates the question of the "right to write."

The author, Linda Jacobs Altman (1993), is not Latina, nor does she claim direct experience as a migrant farm child in her own life. Instead, she spoke with the United Farm Workers and Labor committee as well as directly with migrant workers. The illustrator, Enrique Sanchez, is a former Pura Belpré honor winner, and he is originally from the Dominican Republic. I was introduced to this book by Unna Montoya-Trunkenbolz, a practicing teacher. Unna is biracial Mexican and Apache American whose parents were migrant field workers. She felt strongly that even though the author was "not Hispanic . . . her views were very accurate. Altman selected specific words and phrases that captured the ethnicity of Amelia in a detailed cultural setting." I also admire *Amelia's Road* because it is published by Lee & Low Books— a house that is devoted to publishing "multicultural literature for children" (http://www.leeandlow.com/home/). Lee and Low also encourages unpublished authors through their New Voices Award, and they have published over 50 first-time authors and illustrators of color.

After I read this book in class, Sandra Vazquez, a bilingual Spanish literacy teacher read it to her class of 8- and 9-year-olds. The children were extremely excited to read a book about "Mexicans," and when Sandra asked them why they made this prediction, they had many ideas. They shared their ideas in Spanish, but Sandra provided us with an English translation:

> **Alex:** Because they look like this. [He put his hands on his face.] Like Mexicans.
> **Atto:** Yes. Like us.
> **Crystal:** They look like Mexicans, and because they are working in the ranches.
> **Martha.** Working the hard jobs.
> **Crystal:** And they look tired.
> **Martha:** And because they have clothes like this [pointing to her own clothes]. Well—old.

Sandra was pleased that they immediately related to the story, especially since Martha was the daughter of a migrant worker and was eager to relate what life was like in the fields. After Sandra read the story, the conversation continued:

> **Ms. Vazquez:** I want to hear what you think about the story. Did you see any cultural aspects in the story that are the same as yours?
> **Crystal:** I think it was *beauuuutiful*.
> **Martha:** Me, too. But I felt sorry.

Ms. Vazquez: What did you feel sorry for?

Martha: Cause Amelia had to help her parents pull the carrots and other things. When you work like that, the mosquitoes bite you really ugly. [She pretended to scratch her arms and legs.]

Alex: Well, then why did you work there?

Martha: Cause my parents had to work to make money, not because they liked working on ranches.

Ms. Vazquez: And are there many children who help their parents?

Martha: Yes, my brothers and I help, and also the other sons of the other workers were working there.

Crystal: I also used to help my parents. But a long time ago. They don't work in the fields anymore.

Ms. Vazquez: Do you think that Amelia's parents taught her to help with the work?

Martha: Yes. My mom always says that we all have to help because we all eat.

Atto: I help my father. I know he gets tired, and if I help he finishes sooner.

Ms. Vazquez: Do you think it is part of our Mexican culture to teach the children to be hard workers and always help their parents?

Alex: I think so because my mother is always helping my grandmother. She sends her money to Mexico and food.

Crystal: Yes, my parents also help my grandparents. They send them money. A little. What they can. But they always help them.

Again, Sandra was happy that the book brought the children such an opportunity to discuss their lives, but she worried that without careful conversation she might be perpetuating stereotypes of Mexican Americans solely and consistently associated with work in the fields. These were stereotypes that she had had to suffer as a teen when her family came to the United States from Mexico. She explained to her children, "jobs don't represent our culture, but a way of living," and she read a variety of stories that showed Mexicans and Mexican Americans with a range of lifestyles, including *Family Pictures/Cuadros de Familia* (Lomas Garza, 1990), *My Very Own Room/Mi Propio Cuartito* (Pérez, 2000), and *¡Qué Montón de TAMALES!* (Soto, 1996), a Spanish edition of *Too Many Tamales* (Soto, 1993).

Later, however, she read the children *Radio Man: A Story in English and Spanish/Don Radio: Un Cuento en Ingles y Español* (Dorros, 1997). Sandra explained that she chose it for its similarity to *Amelia's Road*: "Just like *Amelia*, the book talks about the life of a child who has to help his family with the work in the fields. The literacy lesson after reading both stories was to make a Venn diagram and show cultural relationships between the two main characters of the stories." The children were quick to notice the similarities, but this time their understanding of the issues of culture and class ran deeper:

> **Crystal:**   Diego [the protagonist in *Radio Man*] also has to help his parents with the work in the fields.
> **Martha:**   It's also because he is Mexican.
> **Ms. Vazquez:**   And what about him being Mexican?
> **Martha:**   Well, that he was taught that he has to help to gain money and be able to buy food for everybody.
> **Alex:**   Everybody in the family works to help each other.

Sandra was thrilled to see the children's focus on the "cultural pieces of the stories" as well as their "deeper connections between the characters and themselves." She wrote:

> We all have respect for our parents, and even though not all of us have the experience of working in the fields like Martha and Crystal, we were able to understand that our culture is within ourselves, not in the jobs we do. We have it deep inside of us; we carry it with us everywhere we go. I know we still have a lot to work on, but we were pleased to find connections that united all of us together.

Sandra's insights help us to realize the beauty of multicultural literature and the power of talk about culture and class. Culture is not defined by employment, but exists in the myriad subtleties deep within us and in our families and communities. In sharing some of the stories they read in class with their parents, 8-year-old Alex told Sandra, "Mi mama dijo que nuestra cultura nos hace lo que somos. / My mother said that our culture makes us who we are." Still, Sandra's idea of using literature to unite all of us together need not be limited to only linking children with parallel texts. We all need to learn more about each other. As Bishop (1994) argued:

> Literature educates not only the head, but the heart as well. It promotes empathy and invites readers to adopt new perspectives. It offers opportunities for children to learn to recognize our similarities, value our differences, and respect our common humanity. In an important sense, then, children need literature that serves as a window onto lives and experiences different from their own, *and* literature that serves as a mirror reflecting themselves and their cultural values, attitudes, and behaviors. (p. xiv)

The same spring that Sandra Vazquez was working with her 3rd graders, another practicing teacher in my class, Amy Schackman, was helping her 2nd graders talk about culture and class. Her school's population was predominately European American and middle class. In a conversation with her students about an African American children's literature story, one of her children asked her why the people were so "dirty." Another student explained that they had dark skin because they were from Mexico. Worried by their comments, Amy wrote that her students had "formed obvious misperceptions about race and culture," and she felt that "introducing these students to children of other cultures through literature and discussion would hopefully prevent their creation of stereotypes resulting from their limited experience with non-white people."

One of the books she shared with them was *Amelia's Road*, and Amy asked her school's assistant principal, María Ramírez, to read the story to her class. María is Mexican American and "grew up in a family of migrant workers herself," and she agreed to read the story to the children in Spanish so they could "experience the discomfort of trying to understand something that is not presented in one's native language." While she read the story with panache, pointing to the illustrations to help the children make connections, they were understandably confused. At the end of the story, one child complained, "I didn't get it!" María responded, "It's a wonderful story. One of my favorites." And then she slyly added, "You didn't understand it?" The children moaned a chorus of "No!" and the following conversation ensued:

> **Ms. Schackman:**   How did you feel when Ms. Ramírez read this story to you in Spanish instead of English?
>
> **Johnny:**   It kind of made me feel weird because I didn't understand it.
>
> **Jessica:**   I felt weird and I guess stupid because I had no idea what you were talking about.
>
> **Joe:**   I wanted to lean more about Spanish and how to speak it.
>
> **Ms. Ramírez:**   You would understand the story better, wouldn't you?
>
> **Cindy:**   It made me feel kind of tired. I couldn't just sit back and relax and enjoy the story. I had to think really hard what it was about.
>
> **Ms. Ramírez:**   You're right. It takes a lot more effort, doesn't it? Well, I chose to read this book to you in Spanish because Amelia went to a school that spoke English, but she spoke Spanish . . . . Did you know that it happens a lot? In a lot of schools people come from Mexico and they do not know English. Sometimes they are the only one in the class that does not know the language. How do you think they feel?

Johnny: Embarrassed. Shy.

Joe: They probably wouldn't raise their hands a lot.

Katy: Weird. Odd.

Johnny: Lonely.

Ms. Ramírez: All of those describe what it is like when you go to school when you don't understand.

Both Amy and María felt that in this conversation the children moved toward a greater understanding of Amelia's story, but they had only begun.

Ms. Ramírez returned to the class and brought artifacts from her migrant childhood. She helped individual children strap on a belt with a large sack attached, and asked them to simulate picking vegetables. When they only made a slight sweep, María reminded them, "Bend over. The potatoes don't grow in the air!" Amy observed, "In just a few minutes the children complained that their backs hurt. They could only imagine how Amelia and her family felt doing this work all day in the hot sun."

Over the next few days the children dramatized the text in several ways, enacting short scenes and then discussing the character's feelings. When Amy asked them to write about their favorite character in the book, two boys intriguingly chose Amelia's father. Joey, for example, suggested that even though his family didn't have a lot of money, he "felt good because his family is with him." Jon wrote, "He loves his family because they help him out." And both boys wrote that the father had to spend a lot of time "thinking about roads" as he planned the family's next destination in following the crops.

As Bishop suggested, literature can be both a mirror and a window. But in looking through this window, we are often protected by the glass. We look out, we empathize, but we do not act. Megan Boler (1999), an expert in cultural studies, warned us against "passive empathy" which she defined as "instances where our concern is directed to a fairly distant other, whom we cannot directly help" (p. 159). Instead, she proposed "testimonial reading":

What, then distinguishes empathetic from testimonial reading? What might it mean for the reader to "take action"? I suggest that unlike passive empathy, testimonial reading requires a self-reflective participation: an awareness first of myself as reader, positioned in a relative position of power by virtue of the safe distance provided by the mediating text. Second, I recognize that reading potentially involves a task. This task is at minimum an active reading practice that involves challenging my own assumptions and world views. (p. 166)

The work that Amy and María did with these 7- and 8-year olds is more akin to testimonial reading than passive empathy. As teachers and administrators, they acted to make a change in children's thinking, to challenge their assumptions about cultural groups—specifically Mexican Americans. For the children, looking through *Amelia's Road* as well as María's stories of being a migrant worker as a child and an assistant principal as an adult, provided them with a partial view into lives quite different from their own. And rather than see Mexican Americans only for their skin color or for a specific kind of work, they began to see the richness of family life. These second graders spent some time "thinking about roads"—and perhaps the paths they will travel in their own lives will allow them to step beyond the glass and take in a wider view.

The words of Amy's children give us hope. At both the beginning and the end of their short unit, Amy asked her children to define the word "stereotype" and write about why it was important not to judge people by stereotypes. In response to both questions in the beginning, Joey wrote "I do not know." But after reading *Amelia's Road*, listening to discussions with María, his teacher, and his classmates, and enacting scenes from the story, Joey defined stereotypes as "someone who makes fun of someone who they don't even know." And in discussing the critical need to avoid stereotypes he wrote, "So we can have peace in the world."

Summary

In this chapter, I focus on multicultural children's literature in terms of "the right to write" as well as the need to talk with children about issues of culture and class. These are sensitive subjects, no doubt, but if we fail to address them in our classes, we may end up perpetuating stereotypes rather than defeating them. However, if you carefully select the literature you use based on both authenticity and aesthetic heat and ask your children to consider the deeper sociocultural issues, you can help them move well beyond "sympathy" and even "passive empathy" (Boler, 1999) to readings that help them reconsider their lives and the lives of others who they are only beginning to know. Together you and your children can look for deeper and richer portrayals of humanity, rather than poor substitutes. As Rudine Sims [Bishop] (1982) eloquently pointed out, there is a significant difference between shadow and substance.

At the end of *Esperanza Rising*, Esperanza asks Miguel to lie on the ground to hear the heartbeat of the earth, and when he shows impatience she reminds him of a phrase her father taught her, "*Aguántate tantito y la fruta caerá en tu mano*. Wait a little while and the fruit will fall into your hand" (p. 248). He smiles, nods, and soon feels the beat of the earth. As the sun rises, Esperanza feels as if she's rising with it. Although she has suffered many losses, she knows that with the strong support of her family, she too can rise like the phoenix: "She soared with the anticipation of dreams she never knew she could have, of learning English, of supporting her family, of someday buying a tiny house. Miguel had been right about never giving up, and she had been right, too, about rising above those who held them down" (p. 250).

There is a lesson in this for all of us who love literature and care about children. Literature should lift us and allow us to dream what we never thought we could. While we know that "life is a circle," we also come to know about the potential for change, for increasing wisdom, and for "peace in the world." If we select our literature with care and help children consider the world around them, and then wait a little while, the fruit will fall into our hands.

BOOKS FOR THE PROFESSIONAL

Bishop, R. S. (1994). *Kaleidoscope: A multicultural booklist for grades K-8.* Urbana, IL: National Council of Teachers of English. This is an early edition of a series devoted to reviewing the best multicultural children's literature for elementary and middle school readers. Junko Yokota (2001) edited the third and latest edition.

Harris, V. J. (1993). *Teaching multicultural literature in grades K-8.* Norwood, MA: Christopher Gordon. In this extraordinary collection, Violet Harris serves as editor and chapter author among many other well-known scholars of multicultural children's literature. Each chapter is devoted to a particular group and emphasizes that much of the literature written by outsiders often misses the subtle aspects of culture and, at its worst, upholds harmful stereotypes.

Harris, V. J. (1997). *Using multiethnic literature in the K-8 classroom.* Norwood, MA: Christopher Gordon. This second volume of chapters by scholars of note extends on the work of the first volume—clarifying issues, critically reviewing more titles, and continuing to offer counsel about the often-confounding issues surrounding the "right to write." As Harris explains, each chapter offers a "brief historical overview, current status, contemporary trends, analysis of problematic texts, exemplary texts, treatment of multicultural issues such as the elderly, and teaching strategies" (p. ix).

Slapin, B., & Seale, D. (1998). *Through Indian eyes: The Native experience in books for children.* Los Angeles, CA: American Indian Studies Center, University of California. This critical collection contains essays about Native Americans, poetry and art by Native peoples, as well as enlightening critiques of Native American children's literature.

Chapter Touchstone Texts

Altman, Linda Jacobs. (1993). *Amelia's road,* illustrated by Enrique Sanchez. New York: Lee & Low Books. Amelia Martinez hates roads, because every time her father takes out the map it means her migrant family will be on the move again. Longing for permanence—a tidy home with a big tree in the front yard—Amelia finally finds at least the tree of her dreams on an "accidental road." The sense of belonging it gives her, though brief, is enough to offer her hope, and she carries that hope with her when her family must move once again.

Erdrich, Louise. (1999). *The birchbark house.* New York: Scholastic. See chapter 1.

Ryan, Pam Muñoz. (2000). *Esperanza rising.* New York: Scholastic. Winner of the Pura Belpré Award, the Jane Addams Children's Book Award, and an Honorable Mention for the Américas Award, Pam Muñoz Ryan's tale of transformation is about a young girl from Mexico who moves from a sheltered and privileged life to one of labor, economic hardship, and racial prejudice in California during the Depression. Her father had taught her that "the land is alive," and she learns that this is true, even when the land is no longer your own.

Recommended Tradebooks for Culture & Class

Bruchac, Joseph. (1998). *The heart of a chief.* New York: Dial. An Honor book for the Jane Addams Book Award, Abenaki author, Joseph Bruchac, wrote this story as a gift to young Native people. The novel's protagonist is Chris Nicola, a sixth grader who is just beginning middle school off his Penacook reservation. Among the issues Chris faces, including his father's alcoholism and his reservation's debate on casinos, he takes a stand against his school's use of Indian names for sports teams. Chris argues, "It has been said that giving a sports team an Indian name is meant to honor Indians. But if real Indians don't feel honored by that name, what really is the honorable thing to do?" (p. 129).

Lomas Garza, Carmen. (1990). *Family pictures/Cuadros de familia*, as told to Harriet Rohmer, with a version in Spanish by Rosalma Zubizarreta. San Francisco: Children's Book Press. This lovely book is a set of captioned paintings that depict the author's childhood in Kingsville, Texas, near the Mexican border. The portrayal of family life—going to the fair, attending a birthday party, visiting the beach, and making tamales— are, like the watermelon the family shares one evening together, sweet slices of Mexican American culture. The book's publisher— Children's Book Press—is "one of the country's first publishers to focus exclusively on quality literature for children of Latino/Chicano, African American, Asian American, and Native American communities" (http://www.cbookpress.org/index.html).

Mora, Pat (Ed.). (2001). *Love to mamá*, illustrated by Paula S. Barragán M. New York: Lee & Low. With contributions from thirteen Latino/a poets, this tender collection is a celebration of the poets' Puerto Rican, Cuban, Venezuelan, and Mexican American mothers and grandmothers, making it a fine text-to-text link to *Esperanza Rising*. In her first picture book, Ecuadorian Paula Barragán's striking art makes the poems even more joyous. Brief bios of the poets and the Spanish glossary add to the text's authenticity.

Williams, Vera B. (2001). *Amber was brave, Essie was smart.* New York: Greenwillow. Beautifully illustrated by the author, Amber and Essie's story in poems and pictures perfectly captures the fragility of family life for two sisters. Their mother works long hours, their father is in jail, the radiator is too cold, and there's just not enough food. Still, the sisters find warmth curled in a "Best Sandwich," and their bravery and wit sees them through. This book won Honors from the Boston Globe/Horn Book Award and the Jane Addams Book Award. Williams also created the Caldecott Honor, *A Chair for My Mother* (1982), which highlights family love in tight times as they save precious coins for a much-needed easy chair.

5

Gender in Children's Literature

The sorceress cared for the baby, seeing to her every need. Rapunzel grew to be a child of rare beauty, with pale skin and an abundance of flowing red-gold hair. When she reached the age of twelve, the sorceress led her into the forest to live in a high tower.

The tower was a great column rising in the middle of the woods. Although it looked narrow on the outside, on the inside it was large, with many elegant rooms. Yet no door led into this tower, and its only window was at the very top.

When the sorceress wished to enter, she stood below the window and called, "Rapunzel, Rapunzel, let down your hair." Then Rapunzel would unpin her silky braids, wind them around a hook on the window frame, and let them tumble all the way to the ground. The sorceress would grab hold of them and hoist herself up.

For years, Rapunzel lived alone in her rooms above the treetops, visited only by the sorceress. Then one day a king's son came riding through the woods...

—Zelinsky (1997)

The princess in the tower is one of the enduring images of our time. Looking up at the window, the sorceress, the witch, the woman who is known in most versions as "Mother Gothel" calls, "Rapunzel. Rapunzel. Let down your hair." And as Anne Sexton (1971) reveals in *Transformations*, her famous book of fairy tale poetry, "Rapunzel's hair fell to the ground like a rainbow. / It was as yellow as a dandelion / And as strong as a dog leash" (p. 40).

What ties us so strongly to this tale and to other tales of women trapped in the tallest of towers? What is the pull of the passive princess waiting patiently for rescue from her prince? And when does this image become cemented in children's minds? Quite early, in fact. For my daughter, Lindsey, the story of

167

Rapunzel and the wondrous long braid of hair was a favorite throughout her early years of knowing children's literature (Wolf & Heath, 1992). To Lindsey, the braid was the symbol of the enchantment of story, the beauty of the fairy princess, and the rich luxury of the world of fantasy. In her youngest years, with the slightest suggestion of a prop that could substitute for a braid— toys clipped together, scarves, or ribbons—Lindsey would announce, "I'm Rapunzel and this is my braid, Mama." My youngest daughter, Ashley, also loved the tale of Rapunzel and her glorious hair. Once at age two, while she was bathing in the tub, I commented that when her hair was wet it was very long. "Yes," she replied, leaning her head back in the water to set the strands afloat, "just like Punzel."

My own daughters' love of the story, complete with stereotypes, is repeated with very young children's comments in school. A few years ago I had a teacher in class—Kirsten Ames—who read her 7- and 8-year-olds *The Kitchen Knight* (Hodges, 1990). This picture book is a retelling of "The Tale of Sir Gareth of Orkney" from Sir Thomas Malory's *Le Morte d'Arthur*. In the tale, a beautiful but surprisingly active heroine, Linette, comes to King Arthur's court seeking help to release her sister, Linesse, from imprisonment in the castle of the infamous Knight of the Red Plain. Arthur dispatches Gareth, his kitchen servant but secretly his nephew, to do the heroic deed, and along the way he has to put up with the very demanding Linette, who is not so sure that a lad from the kitchen is up to the task. Yet, he consistently proves himself along the way and is knighted to boot, so Linette comes to admire his pluck.

After several trials, they come to the castle where Linesse is captive, and she leans out her tower window to cheer Gareth on. The illustration is wonderfully rendered by Trina Schart Hyman. Linesse's dandelion hair flies out the window of her gray, stone prison as she offers a supportive wave to Gareth. The battle to win her freedom from her captor is a hard one, and at one point Gareth loses his sword and falls to the ground. Linette, ever watchful, goads him on with her characteristically straightforward style, "Sir Gareth, what has become of your courage? My sister is watching you." Indeed, Linesse is pictured in a small inset illustration observing the battle with some skepticism. But when Gareth hears Linette's challenge, he leaps up and strikes the evil Knight such a blow that the villain falls and begs for mercy. Still, the story of these very active sisters is not over. Linesse, while pleased with her release, is as cautious as her sister of her hero's background. She summarily dismisses him until she can learn more about his lineage. Then she captures the dwarf that always travels at his side and questions him closely.

Gareth, dismayed that his dwarf has been kidnapped, fights his way back to the castle and demands his diminutive friend's return. The lady agrees, but only if she can meet Gareth in disguise. The text continues to the end:

> He washed, and the dwarf brought him clothing fit for a knight to wear. And when Gareth went into the great hall, he saw the lady Linesse disguised as a strange princess. They exchanged many fair words and kind looks. And Gareth thought, "Would to God that the faraway lady of the tower might prove to be as fair as this lady!"
>
> They danced together, and the lady Linesse said to herself, "Now I know that I would rather Sir Gareth were mine than any king or prince in this world, and if I may not have him as my husband, I will have none. He is my first love, and he shall be the last.
>
> And she told him that she was the same lady he had done battle for, and the one who had caused his dwarf to be stolen away "to know certainly who you were."
>
> Then into the dance came Linette, who had ridden with him along so many perilous paths, and Sir Gareth took the lady Linesse by one hand and Linette by the other, and he was more glad than ever before.
>
> Thus ends the tale of Sir Gareth of Orkney.

The image of Linesse waving from her tower window is only one in a story full of exciting scenes. Yet when Kirsten asked her students to draw their favorite scene, two thirds of the class chose to draw the image of Linesse captive in the castle. When she asked her children why, many responded, "That's what always happens to the girls until the man comes to the rescue." They easily ignored other powerful pictures and words of women in charge and focused instead on the singular image of a woman trapped in a tower. Only one student had a suggestion for the princess, "I think that Linesse needs lipstick to kiss the prince more!" Kirsten rightly felt that their relatively uniform responses "reflected the idea of the female as an object of beauty, helpless and dependent." She then compared their responses to an essay she read about the ideal of the typically patient princess in traditional tales, particularly a story about a princess waiting on a glass hill:

> As Lieberman (1989) explains, "The Princess on the Glass Hill is the prototype of female passivity. The whole story is the title; the Princess has been perched somehow on top of a glass hill, and thus made virtually inaccessible. There she sits, a waiting prize for whatever man can ride a horse up the glassy slope.

So many of the heroines of fairy stories, including the well-known Rapunzel, are locked up in towers, locked into a magic sleep, imprisoned by giants, or otherwise enslaved, and waiting to be rescued by a passing prince, that the helpless, imprisoned maiden is the quintessential heroine of the fairy tale." (p. 192)

Even younger children, especially those who have been exposed to numerous fairy stories, have the prince and the princess pegged. For example, remember the mother and child I discuss in chapter 1? The mother was a former student and her daughter was the child who was so interested in the defeat of witches that she wanted to throw water on an angry woman in the post office yelling for her place in line. The two had read many fairy tales together, and one day they were reading *Little Red Riding Hood* (Grimm Brothers, 1983), another tale fabulously illustrated by Trina Schart Hyman. As they came to the part in the story where the woodcutter rescues Little Red from the belly of the wolf, the 5-year-old had a question as well as her own insightful response:

Child: Is Red Riding Hood going to marry the woodcutter now?
Mom: Red Riding Hood is a child. I don't think she can marry the woodcutter because he's a grown up. Why do you think they'd get married?
Child: Because after they rescue you, you get married. (Wolf, Carey, & Mieras, 1996, p. 149)

Ah, the wisdom of children! Since fairy tales often end with a young female marrying her rescuer, stretching the nuptial rule to a new situation is eminently logical. And the implied gender roles of this and other fairy stories allow a 5-year-old to quickly pick up the pattern.

Of course, in all this passive waiting, waiting, waiting, let's not forget the role of men riding to the rescue—an equally restrictive role considering the range of life possibilities. Over the last few decades, feminist scholars have worked hard to dispel the myth of girls' and women's passivity, but we also need to keep a balanced view of what happens to men and boys when they are relegated to fighting dragons and rescuing and then marrying fair maidens with more curls than character. Maybe, bottom line, she's not what he wants at all. In Linda de Haan and Stern Nijland's tale (2000) *King & King*, a wry take off on *The Princess and the Pea*, the young prince is forced by his mother to consider a number of young princesses, but it's only when his eye finally falls on the brother of one of the damsels that his heart begins to beat with love.

They become dual Kings of their kingdoms, and as the saying goes, everyone lived happily ever after. Indeed, it wouldn't be surprising if the prince wasn't what the princess was looking for either.

Still, in the traditional and very much heterosexual world of children's literature, both sexes are equally fated to fall in love with each other at a moment's notice. In *The Kitchen Knight*, the hesitation Linesse demonstrates while she pauses to question Gareth's dwarf is rare in the world of traditional love. Most often, the lightning bolt of love strikes before either prince or princess have time to consider the long term. Still, prose writers, playwrights, and poets are constantly reconsidering these old tales. For just one example, contemplate the final verse of Sara Henderson Hay's (1998) poem on "Rapunzel":

I knew that other girls, in Aprils past,
Had leaned, like me, from some old tower's room
And watched him clamber up, hand over fist . . .
I knew that I was not the first to twist
Her heartstrings to a rope for him to climb.
I might have known I would not be the last. (p. 23)

One of the best postmodern views of the prince's side of this story comes from Stephen Sondheim's and James Lapine's musical classic "Into the Woods." In one scene in the play, two handsome princes meet in a forest and discuss their latest amours. One is in love with Cinderella and the other with Rapunzel. In a classic song entitled "Agony" the first prince laments the unbearable pain of wanting something just beyond his grasp. The second prince agrees, for he has yet to figure out how to scale the tower to his longhaired love. But, predictably, after the princes have won their wives, they begin to look around. One now has his eye on Snow White and the other on Sleeping Beauty. When Cinderella questions her husband about his infidelity, he frankly admits, "I was raised to be charming, not sincere."

But is that the message we want to communicate? In the past it certainly seemed so, but that view has been changing over the years. Thus, in the sections to follow I first discuss typical and stereotypical gender patterns in traditional as well as 20th century children's literature. Then I turn to the shift from stereotypes and take a closer look at authors who are working hard to transcend the traditional roles. Finally, I discuss the essentials of talking with children about gender, for unless children are given ample opportunities to question and comment on gender bias in both old and new tales, they might be prone to ignore the range of roles available and focus instead on the princess trapped in the tower with the prince battling below.

Typical & Stereotypical Gender Patterns

Traditional Fairy Tales

Let's begin with traditional fairy tales. In the introduction to his enlightening book, *Don't Bet on the Prince,* Jack Zipes (1989) offered a list of the expected patterns in these tales:

1. Females are poor girls or beautiful princesses who will only be rewarded if they demonstrate passivity, obedience, and submissiveness.
2. Stepmothers are always evil.
3. The best woman is the housewife.
4. Beauty is the highest value for women.
5. Males should be aggressive and shrewd.
6. Money and property are the most desirable goals in life.
7. Magic and miracles are the means by which social problems are solved.
8. Fairy tales are implicitly racist because they often equate beauty and virtue with the colour white and ugliness with the colour black. (p. 6)

This list was originally crafted by Robert Moore (1975) in his essay, "From Rags to Witches: Stereotypes, Distortions, and Anti-humanism in Fairy Tales." While we've already extensively discussed the expected passivity in princesses and the rescue role of princes, let's look at a few of the other characteristics more closely. And I'll add a characteristic that is not on Moore's list:

9. Fairy tales assume heterosexuality as the normative and "natural" view (Evans, 2002).

Women Against Women. The evil of stepmothers is a given. The good, true mother dies—often in childbirth— leaving her daughter at the mercy of a stepmother who can hardly bear to look at her new daughter without envy. In *Snow White* (Grimm Brothers, 1974), she looks into a mirror instead, believing that in the child's death, her own youth and beauty will return. As Karen Rowe (1989) pointed out, "For the aging stepmother, the young girl's maturation signals her own waning sexual attractiveness and control. In retaliation [stepmothers] jealously torment the more beautiful virginal adolescent who captures the father's affections and threatens the declining queen" (p. 212).

Even if the stepmother is not in competition for the affection of a husband/father, she still tries to block the maturation of her adopted daughter. For example, in the story of *Rapunzel*, Zelinsky (2001), the author/illustrator, describes the women in the following way:

> [The story] begins with an almost independent story, telling of the mother who craves rapunzel the herb, and loses Rapunzel the daughter. This is a prologue for the tale of the girl and the sorceress, her mother-figure, an obsessive parent who won't let go, a woman, in my view, who can't bear her own loss of youth and beauty. Why else would she take Rapunzel away from the world except to subsume her, in a way to become her? (pp. 90–91)

To extend this idea, stepmothers often come with two daughters of their own who further victimize the heroine. Cinderella is a prime example. The stepsisters are not only physically ugly, but their actions are reprehensible as they vie for the affections of a prince who will never give them more than a passing glance. In the case of Beauty, there is no stepmother, but her own sisters take over the role of continual harassment. Indeed, if you were to track the sisters over several retellings of *Beauty and the Beast* you would find them described in the most damaging of terms. Thus, whether they appear as witches, evil fairies, stepmothers, stepsisters or very real sisters, in the fairy tale women are a woman's worst enemy.

The Fairest of Us All.   While the word "beauty" itself is given to *Beauty and the Beast* and *Sleeping Beauty*, it is a defining feature of fairy tale females. Almost any heroine you can name is marked by excessive good looks. As Lieberman (1989) explained, "The immediate and predictable result of being beautiful is being chosen, this word having profound importance to a girl. The beautiful girl does not have to *do* anything to merit being chosen; she does not have to show pluck, resourcefulness, or wit; she is chosen because she is beautiful" (p. 188).

But in actuality she does have to show her willingness to keep a clean house. In return for the dwarves' protection from the wicked queen, Snow White must agree to sew, cook, clean, and generally mop up after the men in her life. In the old Norwegian fairy tale of *East O' the Sun and West O' the Moon* (Lynch, 1992), the prince—in his attempt to avoid marrying a troll princess—sets a task that only his true love can accomplish. She must wash three drops of wax from his shirt. When the evil troll princess attempts the task, the shirt becomes blacker and ever more foul, but when the beautiful young girl begins to scrub, the shirt sparkles as white as snow. Thus, the fairest of them all also implies the racism noted by Moore (1975) when he suggested that fairy tales consistently equate beauty with white and ugliness with black.

The final marker of the fairest of them all is goodness, and this demands a lack of what Maria Tatar (1992) termed the "sins" of fairy tale heroines: "In harping on the evils of pride, disobedience, stubbornness, and curiosity, these tales indulge in the same need to promote a safe docility while also participating in the cultural project of stabilizing gender roles" (p. 96). In other words, good girls do what they're told. They do not protest their plights or even question their fates. They marry whom they're told to marry and remain faithful and true, no matter the antics of the groom. They stay out of rooms they are warned against, and when they don't the consequences are horrific. Tatar explained, "Even the harshest penalties remain unchallenged when women begin breaking all the rules in the book of feminine behavior by taking steps in the direction of acquiring knowledge and power" (p. 119).

From Incest to Innocence.   But power in princes pays off, or at least some of the time. In today's popular versions of fairy tales, this aggression translates most often into fighting dragons and hacking through the thorns of briar hedges, but in the tales that have not achieved such popular status, the real aggressors are fathers and husbands who victimize daughters and wives in alarming ways. *Bluebeard* is a prime example, but this is not a tale typically read in elementary classrooms nor is it often selected by parents for bedtime story reading. Indeed, images of male aggression against women—while rife in the old tales—are generally banned or much transformed in the new.

Cinderella offers a perfect case study. In earlier variants of this "animal bride" story, such as the Grimms' *Many Fur* (Segal & Sendak, 1973), the mother dies and her father casts his eye about for a new wife and it lands, low and behold, on his daughter. However, the father's incestuous culpability is often translated into innocence, and provides yet another opportunity to blame women. In *Many Fur,* the blame falls on his wife whose deathbed wish is that he only remarry when he finds a woman equal to her beauty and with her identical golden hair. Who else but his daughter could fit the bill? In Anthony Minghella's (1991) "Sapsorrow", the father blames the daughter because she tries on his dead wife's ring, and he is helplessly destined to marry the one who can wear the ring. In Charlotte Huck's (1989) *Princess Furball,* the father is not the groom, but he is willing to marry his daughter off to an ogre who looks like his identical twin. Dr. Huck (1995)—one of our foremost children's literature scholars—explained that the "psychological truth of incest" (p. 79) is thus retained.

Still, the most popular versions deny even a hint of such deeds. In the Disney version, for example, the father's innocence is undeniable, and he even dies, thus making him unavailable to Cinderella in her hour of need. As Maria Tatar (1992) perceptively pointed out, his "only mistake" (p. 138) is to marry a woman who will treat his daughter cruelly, but of course, once in the ground, he is in no position to stop it. Tatar elaborated:

> The Disney version does not, however, represent a revolutionary turn. . . but rather the logical culmination of a trend that diminished the part of the father even as it magnified the role of the mother. We have seen just how important it was to eliminate fathers and to write large the villainy of mothers as folktales were turned into storybooks. Since then, the invisible father and the monstrous mother have come to serve as twin anchors of many fairytale plots and will remain stationed there until the tellers of tales receive new messages to inscribe on their narratives. (p. 139)

Pluck & Sheer Dumb Luck.   Men in fairy tales are also marked by courage, but the stereotypical dragon slayer is rarer than you think. Indeed, Tatar (1987) explains that in the first version of the Grimm Brothers stories "there are exactly two dragon slayers and only one giant killer in the entire collection of some 150 tales" (p. 86). Instead, images of daring in the very face of a dragon's fire are more often modern media creations. While the prince does battle with a dragon in Disney's *Sleeping Beauty,* in the Grimm Brothers' (1977) tale, retold by Trina Schart Hyman, there is no dragon. Even the thick hedge of briars transforms into welcoming roses before the prince has to hack too far because the 100 year period is up and the time for rescue is nigh.

Many fairy tale heroes are the third and youngest sons—the simpletons of their families, or at least less significant than the first two sons. Still, underneath their lack of intelligence or easy dismissal stands a core of goodness. For example, in the Grimm Brothers' (1986) tale of *The Water of Life*, three brothers set off one by one to find a cure for their father's illness. Along the way each meets a dwarf. The first two treat the dwarf with disrespect and are cursed, but the youngest, who chats politely with the small fellow, is rewarded with clear directions to the water of life and a princess to boot. Of course, they fall in love there and then, but since the young prince is on a mission, the princess tells him to return to wed her in one year. On his way home, he meets with many adventures and then falls victim to the evil plotting of his older siblings. They try to get to the princess first, but she has built a road of gold up to her palace and has warned her servants that they should not admit any prince but the one who rides directly up the straight and narrow of the road. The two brothers, wishing to avoid damage to the gold, ride on either side and are refused admittance. Yet, the young prince, his thoughts only of his love, doesn't even see the gold and rides right up the road to his waiting bride.

Not really looking where you're going pays off time and again in the classic tales. The prince in *Snow White* is so dazzled by her beauty that he bargains with the dwarves for her as she lies in her glass coffin—stilled by the stepmother's poisoned apple. But as he and his servants cart the coffin off to his castle, they stumble and the piece of apple is dislodged. Snow White wakes and the two immediately fall in love and wed. Even the prince in *Rapunzel*, after being hurled to the ground and blinded by the thorns below, wanders in the forest for over a year before he happens on his lady love. Hearing her voice, he staggers towards her and falls to his knees, and her tears of joy restore his sight so that he can see clearly on his wedding day. Thus, even though Moore (1975) characterized men in fairy tales as "shrewd," they often seem to win their fortunes through a combination of luck and true love, no matter how short the courtship.

Men & Women Say, "I do".   In the world of the traditional fairy tale, courtship and marriage ceremonies are reserved for men and women. Other possible pairings simply don't occur. Sleeping Beauty marries her prince, Beauty weds her Beast, and the clever soldier in *The Twelve Dancing Princesses* claims the eldest for his bride. In his famous as well as infamous analysis of fairy tales, Bruno Bettelheim (1977) wrote:

> Snow White's story teaches that just because one has reached physical maturity, one is by no means intellectually and emotionally ready for adulthood, as represented by marriage. Considerable growth and time are needed before the new, more mature personality is formed and the old conflicts are integrated. Only then is one ready for a partner of the other sex.... (p. 213)

Even if the union is a disaster—consider Bluebeard's unlucky bride or the unhappy partnership of Hansel and Gretel's parents—the implication is that a long-term relationship is strictly a male-female arrangement.

20th Century Children's Literature

The traditional fairy tale is not the only genre to uphold stereotypical gender roles, so let's look at children's literature in the latter half of the last century. In the '60s and '70s, a plethora of studies emerged that showed the prominence of gender stereotypes in children's literature. Peterson and Lach (1990) summed them up well, "Males always outnumbered females by a significant proportion, regardless of whether the characters depicted were humans, animals, machines, or fantasy characters. In addition, males were most likely to be portrayed as positive, active and competent, while females were likely to be portrayed as negative, passive and incompetent" (p. 185).

These patterns occurred in both longer works of fiction as well as in picture books. For example, Weitzman, Eifler, Hokada, and Ross (1972) studied character images in Caldecott award-winning picture books of the '40s, '50s, and '60s, and they found that males were overwhelmingly the focus of stories. In fact, out of a five-year sample of winners and honor books, males were pictured 261 times compared with 23 images of women. The researchers concluded that females were nearly invisible in these early books.

It would be wonderful to think that these abysmal numbers are shifting, but a change in the headcount doesn't cancel all the stereotypes. For example, Kortenhaus and Demarest (1993) conducted a study of randomly selected nonaward picture books as well as 25 Caldecott winners and honor books for the fifty years between the '40s and the '80s. They analyzed the books based on several characteristics including the central characters' gender as well as the number of times they were portrayed in the illustrations. Their conclusions showed positive results in terms of more recent texts, for the number of times girls appeared in stories was nearly equivalent to that of boys. But their analysis showed continuing discrepancies in how the two were portrayed:

> While it is encouraging to note that the instrumental role of females in children's literature has increased twofold between the 1960s and 1980s, even this progress seems inconsequential when taken in the context of overall male activity. In the last two decades, boys were still shown engaging in active outdoor

play three times as often as girls, and they solved problems five to eight times as often. Girls, it would seem, are still busy creating problems that require masculine solutions. These characterizations provide children with a strong message as to the gender appropriateness of active and passive roles.

The increased female representation in titles, central roles, and pictures would appear to indicate that authors of the 1980s are more aware and sensitive to women's changing roles; however, the way in which these females are pictured is still sexist and biased. (p. 230)

As one example from their study, Kortenhaus and Demarest found that of the 60 books they examined from the years between 1970 and 1986, only one portrayed a working mother, which is in striking contrast to the very real numbers of women working in today's society. Bumping up into the '90s, Peggy Albers (1996) studied issues of representation in Caldecott Gold Medal winners from 1984 to 1995 and still found women represented less frequently than men. When they did appear, they were often characterized as the nurturers and the helpers; their identities were in constant relationship with white, male role models.

Turning to gay and lesbian literature, the issues are even more problematic. First of all, these books are very rare, particularly for young children. Second, when they do exist, they come under constant attack. Books like *Heather Has Two Mommies* (Newman, 1989) and *Daddy's Roommate* (Willhoite, 1990) are both published by Alyson Publications, one of the first gay presses. They are censored so often that in 1993, the American Library Association showed them holding the first two spots in their list of books people attempted to ban. It was extraordinarily difficult to convince outraged readers that the books were about families and not about sex. You can read more about the firestorm of protest surrounding these two texts at http://www.alyson.com/html/00_files/00_ednote/0400/0400heather10_03_int.html.

While there are more books for young adults, they are often rife with stereotypes. Christine Jenkins (1998) studied young adult novels with gay and lesbian content from 1969 to 1997. She analyzed these books along a number of intriguing theoretical lines, including a comparison with Sims [Bishop's] (1982) categorization of books with African Americans from "social conscience," to "melting pot," to "culturally conscious" literature. Jenkins concluded that books with gay and lesbian content in the first two categories were still far more prevalent. She asked, "Could a young reader not simply feel for gay/lesbian people but feel with them? With rare exceptions, it appears that this literature has yet to be written" (p. 315). In terms of Bishop's (1994) vision of literature as a mirror and a window into diverse lives, when the content concerns gay or lesbian lives, the glass is more than a little clouded.

The Shift from Stereotypes

The combination of uneven numbers, unequal roles, and unwritten literature has served as a wake up call to some of today's authors and illustrators. Mem Fox (1993a) is a well-known example. Sitting in a children's literature lecture in the early '70s, she was astonished to hear the state of affairs and determined that she would work for change in her own writing:

> Girls can do anything, or so we are told. They can be anything. They can feel anything. Why is it, then, that in children's literature they are still portrayed more often than not as acted upon rather than active? As nurturers rather than adventurers? As sweetness and light rather than thunder and lightening? As tentative, careful decision makers rather than wild, impetuous risk takers? Could children's literature be partly to blame for the fact that we grown-up girls have been denied in our womanhood the excitement and power so readily available to boys and grown-up boys?
>
> Let's flip the coin for a moment. Boys can do anything, too, and be anything, and feel anything, or so we have assumed. Why is it then that they aren't allowed to cry? Why is it that ballet dancing and painting are seen as less fit occupations for them than being machine gunners, for example, or baseball players? Why should they live, as most of them do, with the idea that it is, in the main, their crippling responsibility to provide for a family when they become grown-up boys? Don't boys and men need liberating too? Could children's literature be partly to blame for trapping males in a frightful emotional prison and demanding intolerable social expectations of them? (pp. 84–85)

In other words, girls aren't the only gender stifled by societal expectations.

Over the last few years authors and illustrators have been hard at work to add more windows, doors, stairs, and at least a better view for both male and female characters trapped in metaphorical towers. While the fairy tale is one of the most popular places for change, much modern fiction is undergoing transformation as well. Still, it's best to stress caution. While the next sections will discuss some brave attempts towards change, it's critical to remember that "achieving balance in gender is more easily said than done" (Louie, 2001, p. 143).

Feminist, Gay & Lesbian, Fractured, & Multicultural Fairy Tales

The fairy tale has always been a critical site for shifting perceptions. Jack Zipes (2001) called this "the contamination of the fairy tale," but he meant it in the best of possible interpretations. Using the Grimm Brothers tales as a "pre-text" Zipes argued, "contemporary writers... are contaminating the Grimm legacy while enriching it and forging new concepts of the fairy tale" (p. 108). In my own reading of current fairy tales, I see this contamination taking place in four central forms: feminist, gay and lesbian, fractured, and multicultural fairy tales. While I briefly discuss each of these in turn, it's important to realize that some tales are a blend of two or even three areas.

Feminist Fairy Tales.   As a result of the women's movement, particularly in the United States and England, both women and men are rewriting the traditional tales to offer non-sexist stories. Jack Zipes' (1989) book, *Don't Bet on the Prince*, is a collection of feminist fairy tales. However, while much rewriting through prose and poetry has been done for adults, there are a number of non-sexist tales for children as well. One famous example for older children and young teens is *Beauty,* Robin McKinley's (1978) glorious retelling of *Beauty and the Beast.* Although there are a number of changes, some of the prominent features include a very active heroine with sisters who support rather than malign her as well as a thoughtful, complex Beast.

Another well-known author of feminist fairy tales is Gail Carson Levine (1997). She is most famous, perhaps, for her Newbery Honor winner *Ella Enchanted.* Ella (as in Cinder...) is a spunky, intelligent protagonist who bends gender lines in surprising and humorous ways, and her prince (Char, short for Prince Charmont or *Charming)* loves her more for her wit than her beauty. Although Levine keeps several fairy tale staples—such as the two ugly and laughable step sisters—she makes Ella's father much more culpable for the difficulties in her life. Levine has also written several other charming retellings under the rubric of *The Princess Tales.*

Picture books have also been a site for feminist rewriting. One example is *Rumpelstiltskin's Daughter* by Diane Stanley (1997). In this clever recreation, the miller's daughter, Meredith, decides to marry Rumpelstiltskin rather than weave a roomful of gold for a cruel king. Later, Rumpelstiltskin and Meredith have a daughter themselves, and she is captured by the same King. Rather than wilt under the King's will and become his wife, she becomes his prime minister. Looking at two passages—one from a traditional retelling by Zelinsky (1986) and one from Stanley—will demonstrate their differences.

Rumpelstiltskin	Rumpelstiltskin's Daughter
When the king had left, the little man appeared for the third time. "What will you give me if I spin for you yet once more?" he asked. "I have nothing else," the girl replied. "Then promise that when you become queen, your first child will belong to me." The miller's daughter gasped. How could she promise such a thing? Then she thought, But who knows whether that will ever happen? And as she could think of no other way to save herself, she promised. . .	"Okay, here's the deal," he said. "I will spin the straw into gold, just like before. In return, once you become queen, you must let me adopt your firstborn child. I promise I'll be an excellent father. I know all the lullabies. I'll read to the child every day. I'll even coach Little League." "You've got to be kidding," Meredith said. "I'd rather marry you than that jerk."

Even the pictures have telltale differences. In *Rumpelstiltskin*, the nameless miller's daughter sits hunched over, weeping into her hands. Yet when *Rumpelstiltskin's Daughter*, whose name is appropriately Hope, is faced with the same dilemma as her mother, she leans back in her chair, props her feet up on a stool, crosses her arms in concentration, and *thinks* up her own solution.

Still, some sacrifices are made in the name of feminism, for the cruel king is portrayed as a fop, who out dresses Hope in ribbons, jewels, and even curls. As Diane Starkey, a teacher in one of my classes wrote, "It isn't enough for Hope to be presented as a strong, smart female character, the male character of the king is presented as an emasculated, inept, foolish leader. In essence, because she is the strong character, he is presented as the weaker—the female—figure Rather than combat sexist stereotypes, this book underscores sexist and heterosexist images." Perhaps the lesson here is that when you work to combat certain images, you sometimes end up damaging others.

Gay & Lesbian Fairy Tales.   Though rare, there are some wonderful examples of gay and lesbian fairy tales. *King & King* (de Haan & Nijland, 2000), which I mentioned previously, upends the typical portrayal of romance, and this book is a finalist for a Lammy, more formally known as the Lambda Award, which among a range of categories has a literary award for children's and young adult books (see http://www.lambdalit.org/lammy.html). A very famous collection of short stories by young adult authors, some gay and some not, is *Am I Blue? Coming Out from the Silence* edited by Marion Dane Bauer, which won the Lammy in 1994. The title of the book is also the title of the first short story by Bruce Colville—a clever and campy tale of a boy who is aided by a fairy godmother to consider with wonder the sexual orientation of those around him. Perhaps the most famous collection of feminist/lesbian fairy tales is *Kissing the Witch: Old Tales in New Skins* by Emma Donoghue (1997). In thirteen interrelated tales, with a question at the end of one tale leading to the next, Cinderella abandons the prince and runs away with her fairy godmother, the Beast turns out to be a woman, and Snow White forsakes both prince and dwarves to return to her stepmother's castle.

Fractured Fairy Tales.   Like gay and lesbian tales, fractured fairy tales tend to bend or even break the routine rules of traditional stories, particularly along gender lines, but they suffer no censorship for their efforts. On the contrary, they are hugely popular for their humor and their alternative points of view. For example, *The Three Little Pigs* (Zemach, 1988) is a very old tale, but it's been rewritten myriad times for humorous effect. The most recent rendition—*The Three Pigs* by David Wiesner (2001)—won the Caldecott award. In this postmodern portrayal, the pigs are puffed right off the page, where they pal around with other story book characters in search for a better home. In another modern retelling, *The Three Little Wolves and the Big Bad Pig* (Trivizas, 1993), the central characters are reversed. Three cuddly wolf cubs are persecuted by a pig who knocks off their first home with a sledgehammer, crumbles their second with a pneumatic drill, and blasts through their third with dynamite. Only when they build a flower house does the porcine menace settle down and join them for a dance.

The most famous retelling of this old tale is by Jon Scieszka (1989), or perhaps I should say Alexander T. Wolf, who tells his side of the story. He's innocent, after all. He was just trying to borrow a cup of sugar, and when he sneezed and the house fell down and a ham dinner presented itself, what could he do? Scieszka likes these tongue-in-cheek questions. He went on to write *The Frog Prince Continued* (1991) where the hero's sticky tongue-out-of-cheek proves so annoying to his Princess wife, he heads off into the woods to seek a new spell from some well-known witches. Then Scieszka (1992) wrote *The Stinky Cheese Man and Other Fairly Stupid Tales* that included "The Princess and the Bowling Ball." In this retelling the Prince gets fed up with his parents' demands that the girl he marries must feel a pea through one hundred mattresses, so he decides to take matters into his own hands and substitutes a bowling ball.

While gender bending is less obvious in these tales, plays on the nature of wolves and the possibilities of marriages being not so happily-ever-after or not so honest help to make the point. But multiple points are made in James Garner's (1994) *Politically Correct Bedtime Stories: Modern Tales for Our Life & Times*. In these side-splitting spoofs on a variety of tales, Garner upends racist, classist, and sexist stereotypes. The dwarves in *Snow White* are vertically challenged, the guests arriving in their carriages at the ball in *Cinderella* are criticized for not carpooling, and when the prince and the witch plot together on a recording contract for *Rapunzel*, she caustically notes that greed doesn't always depend on gender!

Multicultural Fairy Tales. While the Grimm Brothers worked hard to smooth away "any trace of specific locality, nation, or character" (Zipes, 2001, p. 103) in their fairy stories, today's multicultural writers work to infuse their tales with highly diverse and culturally unique variations while simultaneously stressing universal qualities. Two lovely examples will serve to demonstrate this category. The first is the Caldecott award-winning *Lon Po Po: A Red-Riding Hood Story from China* by Ed Young (1989), a tale with many links to the Grimm's tale, but with critical differences. In Young's story, three sisters are left at home while their mother goes to visit their grandmother. When the wolf arrives, the sisters have no need for a woodcutter's intervention. Instead, they use collaboration and cunning to bring about his demise. Young's illustrations are beautifully rendered: "The drawings are split into sections that give the art the appearance of Chinese decorative panels; however, strong color and dramatic angles transform the art, giving it a thoroughly contemporary look" (Silvey, 1995, p. 703). Young dedicated the book "To all the wolves of the world for lending their good name as a tangible symbol for our darkness," quite a different take on the big, bad wolf.

The second example is John Steptoe's (1987) *Mufaro's Beautiful Daughters, An African Tale.* The book not only won the Coretta Scott King Award for illustration, but it also won the Boston Globe-Horn Book Award and was a Caldecott Honor Book. With links to *Beauty and the Beast*, the story tells of two African sisters, Manyara and Nayasha, only one of whom will to be chosen to marry the King. Although both girls are equal in beauty, only Nayasha has a good heart. She not only passes the tests set before her through her generosity, but when the king disguises himself in various animal forms she sees through the guise to the equally good nature of the king. The glorious illustrations carefully deliver the flora, fauna, clothing, and cultural artifacts of Zimbabwe, though Steptoe used his daughter Bweela to pose for the sisters.

Modern Fiction

Modern stories, even those quite distant from the genre of fairy tales, are also shifting away from stereotypical gender patterns, though more attention has been paid to girls than boys (Nodelman, 2002). While the list of stories pushing on these edges could go on and on, here I'll discuss just a few of the most well-known authors. In thinking about picture books, Mem Fox's (1993a) work immediately comes to mind. She explained,

> Of the 24 books I have written for children, 14 are deliberately dominated by main characters who are either girls, or female animals, or dynamic elderly women. Three of the 24 books have no gender stated at all. In the remaining 8, 4 of whose titles are unequivocally male. . . , I have embedded counter-sexist attitudes intentionally. (p. 85)

One of my favorites is *Wilfrid Gordon McDonald Partridge* (Fox, 1985), the story of a boy well in tune with his sensitive side who seeks to restore the missing memory of an elderly woman friend.

Another famous gender-sensitive example is *William's Doll* by Charlotte Zolotow (1972), in which a boy desperately wants a doll. While his brother teases him and his father tries to dissuade him and distract him with railroad sets and basketballs, his grandmother understands, explaining that he needs it in order to learn how to be a good father. Judith Viorst is also well-known for her portrayals of boys in gentle relationships with others. *The Tenth Good*

Thing About Barney (1971) is about a young boy's devastation with the loss of his cat and his search to find the right words to commemorate his pet. And Viorst (1974) was one of the first to show friendship between the sexes in *Rosie and Michael,* who are equally devoted to one another.

Turning to longer pieces of fiction, Katherine Paterson's (1977) *Bridge to Terabithia,* a Newbery winner, is also the story of a boy–girl friendship, but the gender issues are everywhere. When Jess first meets Leslie, he can't tell if she's a girl or a boy, because her cut-offs and tank-top don't look like the apparel most girls wear. And then she has the temerity not only to enter into the boys' 4th- and 5th-grade races, but to win her heat. Jess defends her right to participate, though he was planning to win himself. When Leslie admits that she doesn't have a TV and the kids at school take it as another opportunity to tease her, Jess begins to feel sorry for her. After all, he knows what it's like to be an outsider, for he loves art and music, and his family picks on him for such interests. Together Jess and Leslie build a friendship in Terabithia, a mythical forest land, where they are King and Queen and in charge of their fates. Leslie, however, is killed on the rope swing to Terabithia, and Jess must face a new destiny. Through denial, rage, and finally tears he learns to value the gift of friendship, and he passes it on to his sister May Belle when he builds a bridge to Terabithia in what Paterson (1986) calls "an act of grace" (p. 44).

Another author famous for her lyrical writing as well as her willingness to take on life's complexities is Jacqueline Woodson. Two of her many fine novels address gay and lesbian issues. The first, *From the Notebooks of Melanin Sun* (1995), was an Honor book for the Jane Addams Book Award as well as a winner of the Lambda Literary Award. It details the life of a 13-year-old African American boy whose life is turned upside down when his mother tells him that she is a lesbian, and even more complicated, she is in love with a white woman. Melanin's initial anguish—especially his agony over what will happen when his friends find out and his worries over his changing relationship with his mother—slowly gives way to acceptance. In another Lammy award winner, Woodson (1997) tells of young Staggerlee, a 13-year-old biracial child, who begins to question her own sexual identity. Woodson's willingness to leave things open and unanswered makes the novel all the more compelling, for when the questions circle around "Who am I?" and "Who will I become?", the answers are never simple.

Several of the novels we've already discussed—such as *The Watsons Go to Birmingham—1963* (Curtis, 1995), *The Birchbark House* (Erdrich, 1999), and *Esperanza Rising* (Ryan, 2000) show the complexity of gender roles in boys, girls, men, and women. As the list of "gender bending" books in Fig. 5.1

Girls

Picture Books

- *Piggybook* (Browne)
- *Her Stories* (Hamilton)
- *Seven Brave Women* (Hearne)
- *Harriet and the Promised Land* (Lawrence)
- *The Paper Bag Princess* (Munsch)
- *Kate and the Beanstalk* (Osborne)
- *Brave Irene* (Steig)
- *The Serpent Slayer* (Tchana)
- *Clever Beatrice* (Willey)
- *Heckedy Peg* (Wood)
- *Roses Sing on New Snow* (Yee)

Chapter Books

- *Speak* (Anderson)
- *The Midwife's Apprentice* (Cushman)
- *Kissing the Witch* (Donaghue)
- *The Birchbark House* (Erdrich)
- *The Hero and the Crown* (McKinley)
- *Scooter* (Williams)
- *The House You Pass on the Way* (Woodson)

Girls & Boys Together

Picture Books

- *Virgie Goes to School With Us Boys* (Howard)
- *The King's Equal* (Paterson)
- *The Frog Prince Continued* (Scieszka)
- *Caleb & Kate* (Steig)
- *Rosie and Michael* (Viorst)
- *Timothy Goes to School* (Wells)

Chapter Books

- *The Secret Garden* (Burnett)
- *The BFG* (Dahl)
- *The Tiger Rising* (DiCamillo)
- *Guests* (Dorris)
- *Politically Correct Bedtime Stories* (Garner)
- *The View from Saturday* (Konigsburg)
- *Ella Enchanted* (Levine)
- *Baby* (MacLachlan)
- *Anne of Green Gables* (Montgomery)
- *Bridge to Terabithia* (Paterson)
- *His Dark Materials Trilogy* (Pullman)
- *Esperanza Rising* (Ryan)

Boys

Picture Books

- *My Dad* (Browne)
- *King & King* (De Haan & Nijland)
- *Tough Boris* (Fox)
- *Wilfrid Gordon McDonald Partridge* (Fox)
- *Owen* (Henkes)
- *The Mariposa* (Jiménez)
- *My Rows and Piles of Coins* (Mollel)
- *The Three Questions* (Muth)
- *Pete's a Pizza* (Steig)
- *The Tenth Good Thing About Barney* (Viorst)
- *William's Doll* (Zolotow)

Chapter Books

- *Love That Dog* (Creech)
- *The Seeing Stone* (Crossley-Holland)
- *Silent to the Bone* (Konigsburg)
- *The Giver* (Lowry)
- *A Single Shard* (Park)
- *Wringer* (Spinelli)
- *From the Notebooks of Melanin Sun* (Woodson)

FIG. 5.1.   Recommended Gender-Bending Books.

indicates, the lines separating responsibilities, careers, attitudes, and emotions are no longer so clear. Still, the progress we see in these books is slowed by stereotypical patterns that continue to crop up throughout the world of children's literature. One of the most popular books of our age, *Harry Potter and the Sorcerer's Stone* (Rowling, 1998) presents a vivid example. Although critic Deborah Thompson (2001) began with the disclaimer that she loved the Harry Potter books, she argued, "From ghosts to wizards, the subtext of Harry's novels is that boys have great adventures and girls are studious, weepy, or simpering" (p. 43). Jack Zipes (2001) agreed, though he made no disclaimer about loving the books. When he called the novels "formulaic and sexist" on a radio show, he was attacked by callers. Still, Zipes quoted Christine Schoefer to support his own opinions:

> From the beginning of the first Potter book it is boys and men, wizards and sorcerers, who catch our attention by dominating the scenes and determining the action. . . . Girls, when they are not downright silly or unlikable, are helpers, enablers and instruments. No girl is brilliantly heroic the way Harry is, no woman experienced and wise like Professor Dumbledore. In fact, the range of female personalities is so limited that neither women nor girls play on the side of evil. (p. 179)

Zipes argued that the *Harry Potter* books tend to repeat many of the same sexist stereotypes we see in traditional fairy tales.

Thus, we come full circle, in a typical home-away-home pattern back to the fairy tale, and if I've done my job in this chapter, I hope that through the last two sections on stereotypes and the shift from stereotypes, your attitude toward the innocence of children's literature along gender lines is changed. This is critical because as you'll see in the upcoming section, talking about gender with children can sometimes make a difference in their lives.

Talking With Children About Gender

A few years ago, I had a teacher in my class—Erika Norman—who was fascinated by the reading she'd been doing on adolescent girls. She'd read several popular texts including Mary Pipher's (1995) *Reviving Ophelia: Saving the Selves of Adolescent Girls* and Peggy Orenstein's (1995) *Schoolgirls: Young Women, Self-Esteem and the Confidence Gap*, and Erika wondered how soon understandings of gender roles really began. She decided to put gender on the table of her class of seven and eight-year-olds. In an experiment designed to check her children's perceptions, she brought in a number of objects from her home—all things that belonged to her, though she didn't tell the children their origin. Instead, she asked them to separate the objects according to whether they thought they belonged to boys or girls. The children took turns placing the items, and if they couldn't decide, they could place them between the two piles.

When they were finished, the piles were almost uniformly separated along traditional gender lines. The girls' pile contained all the cooking materials, the barrette, the Christmas stocking, the sewing kit, the make-up, a brush, and *Bridge to Terabithia* (Paterson, 1977). The boys' pile had the road map, the pocketknife, the hammer, the rubber snake, the plastic car, flies for fly fishing, the motor oil, and *Baseball in April and Other Stories* (Soto, 1990). The one thing placed in between the piles was a watercolor set. Lucy began the conversation by pointing with exasperation to the boys' pile:

Lucy: I would rather be in this pile! I go fishing. I make things with my Dad. I like snakes.
Phoebe: I would move a lot of things. I would move all the cooking stuff to the boys' pile.
Charlie: Hey! I don't like cooking.
Phoebe: Boys should get the chance to cook!
Charlie: No! I don't like cooking. I really don't like to cook. Boys don't like to cook!
Phoebe: They have to *learn* to cook.
Charlie: I don't want to!
Phoebe: Not fair. Not fair! It's not fair! Girls do all the work. They cook, they— [Looking directly at Charlie] When you get holes in your pants, we fix them!
Charlie: Oh, yeah?!
Phoebe: We do everything!"

I think Lucy's opening words, "I'd rather be in this pile!" serve as a metaphor for the way we feel when we see ourselves strapped to a stereotype that is at odds with our own perceptions. Lucy is looking at the objects for girls and can't find herself, but when she studies the boys' pile she sees many more links. She fishes, she makes things, and she's unafraid of snakes.

The cooking argument between Charlie and Phoebe exemplifies the resistance that often occurs when we try to make a shift in stereotypes. Charlie clearly doesn't like to cook, nor does he feel it's a responsibility for his gender. Phoebe makes an escalating argument, moving from the opportunity to cook to the necessity of learning how. But her reasoning falls on deaf ears. When Charlie continues to flatly reject the notion of boys' involvement in the culinary arts, Phoebe explodes. In her anger, she makes a critical pronoun shift—"When *you* get holes in your pants, *we* fix them!"—stressing solid protest as well as the solidarity of her gender.

But the argument between Phoebe and Charlie was far from over. Indeed, it expanded when Erika began to explore traditional as well as feminist, fractured, and multicultural fairy tales with her children. Ultimately she brought the discussion around to a central question:

Ms. Norman: Is it important for girls to see other girls in stories that are strong?
Charlie: No.
Ms. Norman: Why not?
Charlie: I'm not sure, but princesses are supposed to be saved.
Phoebe: No! They can save the prince. I'm the fastest girl in our class.
Charlie: No, I don't think so. We'll see in P.E.

Yes, and Charlie's words help us to see the necessity of talking about gender in our classrooms.

Still, research shows that interrupting gender stereotypes may be "easy to think about," but "difficult to do" (Alvermann, Commeyras, Young, Randall & Hinson, 1997). Children receive messages about gender through myriad sources—comments their parents and community members make, media messages, toys they receive, and, of course, books they read. Even when they read gender-bending books, they can sometimes ignore the message. For example, Greever, Austin, and Welhousen (2000) compared classrooms of 4th-grade children in 1975 and in 1997 responding to *William's Doll* (Zolotow, 1972), and they found continuing resistance among boys and girls to the idea that William wanted a doll. While some children were positive, others were definitely not. One boy wrote, "I think the story was good but I never saw a kid that wanted a doll more than a basketball the boy was like a girl because I never wanted a doll befor accept maybe when I was a baby." And a girl wrote, "I liked it but Willuum don't need a doll he needs boy toys

to play with like a basketball a alatik [electric] car that you can play with"
(Greever, Austin, & Welhousen, 2000, p. 328).

Another teacher in one of my classes, Jennifer Mayer, asked her 8- and
9-year-old children to study traditional fairy tales and then list the typical
activities of males and females:

What Girls Do	What Boys Do
• Girls are told what to do. • Girls are always threatened and in trouble. • Fairies have magic. • Spells are usually cast on the girl. • Girls are usually lonely and bored, so they talk to little animals. • Kisses and love solve the problem.	• Boys are brave. • Boys always save the girl. • Boys get magic. • Boys fall in love with girls. • The Prince is sometimes an animal (a frog or beast). • Boys are in control 'cause they are husbands.

Jennifer was startled to discover that even though her students were able
to list the stereotypes, they didn't "comment on how ridiculous some of
them were. They just seemed to accept them." But after working with her
children for several weeks, discussing the contrasts between traditional and
non-traditional tales, the children decided to write a play entitled *Cinderella—
A Fractured Tale*. They invited their parents to see their performance. In the
program, Jennifer explained, "In our classroom, we have been talking about
gender stereotypes in literature, especially fairy tales. We decided to create
this classroom play in an attempt to make the characters more like 'real'
people." The children wrote the following program summary:

> Our story starts with the announcement of a fabulous dance. Everyone wonders
> if Cinderella will get to go. Cinderella's evil stepfather locks her in the castle.
> Thankfully, her fairy godfather comes to the rescue and helps her get to the
> dance where she meets the prince. They fall in love after seven years of dating.
> They get married and live happily ever after.

The script for the play is quite humorous because the children wanted the
play to be enjoyable, but underneath the laughter many serious conversations
occurred.

Inspired by Mem Fox's (1993a) admonition that both boys' and girls' roles should be considered, Jennifer encouraged her children to discuss their decisions about character with care. Her guiding question was, "Would a real boy/real girl do that?" As a result, the children debated the role of the stepmother and the fairy godmother, which they ultimately transformed into male characters. They decided to make both Cinderella and the prince a bit clumsy, so they wouldn't come off as such perfect personalities. They deliberated over how long the two would date before marriage, and they even argued whether Cinderella would wear jeans or a dress to the ceremony. Jennifer wrote, "One of the most powerful aspects of the play is that the children created it with very little help from me. They were forced to explore, agree, and disagree with each others' views and opinions about gender." At the end of the unit, they went back to their original chart and now recognized the "ridiculous" nature of the stereotypes in contrast with their own work to create "real" characters. One girl remarked, "Real girls don't have to get rescued before they fall in love." While Jennifer was pleased with their insights, she felt they still needed "to continue working on why stereotypes are harmful."

Another teacher in my class, Susan Kandyba, worked closely with her 10- and 11-year-olds to instigate some changes in their thinking. However, like Erika and Jennifer, she wanted to see where her students were before she made gender issues the center of their literature discussions. One of her first activities focused on *The Paper Bag Princess* (Munsch, 1980). Leaning on research conducted by Janet Evans (1998), Susan told her children she would be reading them a story about a prince, a princess, and a dragon that was conquered. She then divided her class into three groups and "asked the members of each respectively to draw a picture of the person who had been saved, the person who did the saving, and the last page of the text." She asked them to include a description of what the person in each picture was feeling. Susan wrote, "With only one exception, the children had the prince as the savior, the princess as the person saved, and the last page as 'They lived happily ever after.'"

Susan described Cassie's drawing as typical, "The crowned prince stands victoriously, bow overhead, next to the arrow-riddled body of the dragon. High above in the distant tower, the tiny princess calls 'Help!'" And Cassie wrote the following explanation of her character's feelings, "The prince conquered the dragon, and he is happy, joyous, excited, prideful and ready to go to the next step of his journey." Her illustration with the prince in the foreground and the princess almost invisible in the background except for the large bubble with the word "Help!" shows that the action is all on the prince. The princess is just the next step of his journey.

Sathya followed the classroom pattern by showing a princess as the one who was rescued, but her written description of the woman's feelings were more complex, "I think she was so relieved. She'd been in that castle for so long. But I think she feels like maybe she doesn't really want to spend her whole life with this man. Or she doesn't want to marry him." Her picture reflects this hesitation, for the princess—though dressed in full princess regalia—stands stiffly with her arms to her side and her expression is more depressed than delighted.

Susan then read *The Paper Bag Princess* to her children—the tale of a princess who outwits a dragon and rescues the prince. But when Prince Ronald chides Princess Elizabeth for her disheveled attire, she decides not to marry the "bum" after all. Susan's children defended their original views because they were based on typical fairy tale patterns. They argued that a tale like this one was a rarity. Paul wrote a lengthy summary detailing his surprise:

> I thought that the story, *The Paper Bag Princess*, would be about a prince saving a princess guarded by a dragon, but it turned out different. I wrote what I wrote before the story because in most fairy tales I read it's usually the prince saving the princess. It also surprised me when the prince just put down the princess when she saved him.
>
> When the princess was going to save the prince I thought she would try killing the dragon, but instead she asked him questions to tire him out. I thought in fairy tales like that it would always be the prince and the princess living happily ever after, and they would have a baby or something, but I guess not. When Ms. Kandyba read it, I got really surprised. I thought everything would turn out perfect.

But as the children worked over the next few weeks analyzing fairy tales, they came to realize that happily-ever-after, where everything turns out perfect is not always the case. Moreover, they began to see the potential power of alternative patterns.

Indeed, when Ms. Kandyba asked them to write their own fairy tales with a prince, a princess, and a dragon at the end of their unit, the results were quite distant from the children's original interpretations. One child wrote a story where the prince and princess joined forces to defeat the dragon. Another also had the prince and princess pair up, but instead of killing the dragon they lulled him to sleep and took him to "a distant land where he could reek havic [wreak havoc]" to his heart's content. Paul, who had initially been so surprised by the fractured tale of *The Paper Bag Princess*, wrote a story about a prince captured by an evil warlock who locks the prince in an "old, abandoned, run down, no good, rotten, stinky, smelly, ugly, really small castle." But the princess, "who was even stronger than the prince," comes to the rescue armed with her trusty toolbox. On the way she meets a "mean dragon" and knocks him out. Then she hurls the dragon into the castle where he lands on the warlock and the prince. Paul's story continued to the end, "She rushed to the prince and got him to the good castle. He barely made it. He married the princess and they lived happily for two years and then they got divorced. As for the warlock, he lays under the dragon till this day."

Summary

This chapter focuses on the gender issues that have lain under the weight of stereotypes nearly till this day. Beginning with traditional fairy tales, I examine the prevalent patterns—particularly the princess trapped in the tower with the prince battling below. I then survey more modern literature to demonstrate the gender problems that continue to exist in today's tales. Even though boys no longer outnumber girls in stories, they are still more active. However, this scene is shifting in several ways. Feminist, gay and lesbian, fractured, and multicultural fairy tales provide a more balanced as well as more realistic look at girls, boys, men, and women. And many modern authors are writing non-fairy tale fiction that portrays a more equitable view.

But why do these patterns and shifts in stereotypes matter? Quite simply, they matter to children who receive their notions of gender roles from a variety of sources including the books they read. If we put gender on the table for literature discussion, looking closely at the designated roles and asking about the potential harm in typecasting characters, perhaps we can help to further the shift from stereotypes in real life.

In the foreword to Sara Henderson Hay's (1998) marvelous collection of fairy tale poetry, *Story Hour,* Miller Williams remarked that "a generation of readers can go with her through the back doors of these old houses we thought we knew so well" (p. xi). Her final poem—"The Formula"—is one of my favorites:

> It isn't easy, being the ugly one,
> Or an orphan with the cruelest of stepmothers,
> Or a foundling, or the dull-witted youngest son
> Competing with eleven brilliant brothers.
> But if you've a magic stone, or a wishing ring
> Some old crone gave you for helping her son cross the road,
> And if you follow the rules in everything,
> And if you're kind, and don't mind kissing a toad,
>
> You'll scale the slope that nobody else could climb
> And kill whatever giant disputes your way,
> And reach the impossible goal in record time,
> And win the bride or the groom, as the case may be,
> For this is the formula which never fails,
> (At least, that's how it works in fairy tales.) (p. 53)

But the "formula" rarely works in real life. And though we might hope in our heart of hearts for a wishing stone or a wise old crone to help us along the way, we might be better off taking action than waiting for the action to come to us. This is not to diminish the sheer wonder of fantasy tales that offer hope and possibility, but potential exists in reality as well.

Hay's poem begins with "It isn't easy...," and she's right. It isn't easy to shift stereotypes. Research has shown time and again that it's easier to fall back on set patterns. Just as one final example, Peggy Rice (2000) conducted a study where she read 6th-grade children the Japanese story "Three Strong Women" (Barchers, 1990), a feminist tale of a daughter, mother, and grandmother who help to train a wrestler, though he will never equal their strength. Rice asked the children to retell the story in writing within minutes of her reading as well as a week and a month later. She found that the children veered from the actual telling of the tale over time, and they reverted to old patterns depicting the "physical strength of men and the dependence of women on men" (p. 211). While Rice saw "some movement away from stereotypical gender positioning for the girls," the boys were less likely to disrupt predictable patterns.

When Susan Kandyba repeated this study with her children, she found similar results. But she took the work a step further by placing her children's rewritings against the original tale and asking them why they "rewrote them in their memories over time." She explained, "In the reflection that followed, the children began to consider their own deep-seated beliefs about gender. Many were surprised that they had remembered the girl as attractive when in fact she was not and that they had failed to mention the strength of the women." Though she saw shifts in her children's thinking as her unit progressed, she knew that for "lasting change to occur, gender equity should be taught over long periods of time." Susan's right as well. Fracturing "the formula" of gender does take time, but it's essential work for our children's future.

BOOKS FOR THE PROFESSIONAL

Lehr, S. (Ed.). (2001). *Beauty, brains, and brawn: The construction of gender in children's literature.* Portsmouth, NH: Heinemann. This unique collection offers an alternative view of boys and girls in literature who have options in determining who they will be. Edited by Susan Lehr, a Professor of reading and children's literature at Skidmore, the essays are written by well-known scholars of children's literature as well as renowned children's book authors and illustrators.

Tatar, M. (1992). *Off with their heads! Fairy tales and the culture of child-hood.* Princeton, NJ: Princeton University Press. A Professor of German Literature at Harvard University, Maria Tatar provides an extraordinary exploration of traditional fairy tales as well as a few modern pieces to demonstrate the service of these stories in the socialization of children. She stresses the importance of reading against the grain of these tales to question their formulaic patterns.

Zipes, J. (1989). *Don't bet on the prince: Contemporary feminist fairy tales in North America and England.* New York: Routledge. Jack Zipes is a Professor of German at the University of Minnesota and one of our nation's foremost scholars of the fairy tale. In this classic text, he provides a comprehensive anthology of essays as well as feminist fairy tales and poetry that question expected gender roles for children and adults in literature.

Zipes, J. (2001). *Sticks and stones: The troublesome success of children's literature from Slovenly Peter to Harry Potter.* New York: Routledge. Zipes' most recent text is a collection of essays questioning the very foundation of children's literature, and asking if the tales we tell our children are really for them or merely what we think they should have. Are the books designed to give flight to their creativity and possibility? Or do we actually clip their wings by repeating predictable and limited patterns?

Chapter Touchstone Texts

Zelinsky, P. O. (1997). *Rapunzel.* New York: Dutton. This tale is a traditional retelling of the young Rapunzel trapped in a tower by a witch. The Caldecott Award-winning illustrations are based on Italian Renaissance art, and the image of Rapunzel looking out from her tower window, with her red-gold tresses framing her face and body, are a perfect portrayal of a woman passively waiting for her rescue by a handsome prince.

Munsch, Robert. (1980). *The paper bag princess*, illustrated by Michael Martchenko. Toronto: Annick Press. This was one of the first gender-bending tales for young children. It turns traditional costuming inside out (the princess wears a paper bag), reverses rescue protocol (the princess rescues the prince), and upends the happily-ever-after ending (no wedding). My daughter Lindsey loved this tale as a child because Princess Elizabeth defeated the dragon with "her ideas" and "thinking strength." As for the prince, Lindsey's clear assessment was, "He didn't deserve her!"

De Haan, Linda, & Nijland, Stern. (2000). *King & King.* Berkeley, CA: Tricycle Press. One of the finalists for the 2003 Lambda Literary Award proves that when it comes to fracturing fairy tales, there are still traditions to be broken. In this marvelously illustrated story, the young prince is berated by his mother who laughably tells him that by the time she was his age she'd already been married twice. Although she brings in a parade of princesses, it's not till he sees the brother of one that his heart begins to stir. They are married and become King & King of the land with a happily-ever-after ending that is truly for everyone.

Recommended Tradebooks for Gender

Anderson, Laurie Halse. (1999). *Speak.* New York: Farrar Straus Giroux. A face floats up through the leaves. First the eyes appear, green eyes with leaves for eyebrows, then the nose, and finally the... No. There is no mouth. Though the eyes speak volumes, the missing mouth says even more. This is how we are first introduced to Melinda Sordino, who is outcast, despised by her peers because she called the cops at a summer party and several teens were arrested. But we don't learn until much later in the novel that Melinda was raped at that party. Both the National Book Award and the Michael L. Printz Award for excellence in young adult literature gave *Speak* Honors. Although this novel takes place in high school, the gender issues are critical for discussion with younger teens.

Gaiman, Neil. (2002). *Coraline*, with illustrations by Dave McKean. New York: HarperCollins. This tale begins with a perceptive quote, "Fairy tales are more than true: not because they tell us that dragons exist, but because they tell us that dragons can be beaten." But the dragons in this gender-bending story take on an even more menacing form as Coraline walks through a door in her house and into another world. Still, Gaiman's attempt to deliver a female protagonist who defeats her nemesis through wit and bravery still relies on the traditional roles of fairy tale parents, for "the other mother" is an evil harridan, and "the other father" is at the mercy of his wife's terrible plotting.

Konigsburg, E. L. (2000). *Silent to the bone.* New York: Atheneum. Like *Speak*, this novel is about a youth who is "silenced by sex" (Wolf & Maniotes, 2002), but here the protagonist is a 13-year-old boy. Branwell has chosen silence over revealing the truth of his baby sister's nearly fatal accident, but his silence is not caused by another's sexual aggression. Instead, Branwell is muted by his own shame. He was too infatuated with Vivian—the au pair who actually shook the baby into unconsciousness—to speak when he should have spoken. Throughout the novel, Branwell's friend, Connor, works to break the mystery of his friend's silence, as well as show him that being struck dumb has only temporary advantages.

III

Ways of Doing Literature

6

Interpreting Literature Through Writing

Winn-Dixie lay down on the couch. He put his nose in the preacher's lap and his tail in mine.

"Ten," said the preacher.

"Nine," I told him.

"Nine," said the preacher. "She drank. She drank beer. And whiskey. And wine. Sometimes, she couldn't stop drinking. And that made me and your mama fight quite a bit. Number ten," he said with a long sigh, "number ten, is that your mama loved you. She loved you very much."

"But she left me," I told him.

"She left us," said the preacher softly. I could see him pulling his old turtle head back into his stupid turtle shell. "She packed her bags and left us, and she didn't leave one thing behind."

"Okay," I said. I got up off the couch. Winn-Dixie hopped off, too. "Thank you for telling me," I said.

I went right back to my room and wrote down all ten things that the preacher had told me. I wrote them down just the way he said them to me so that I wouldn't forget them, and then I read them out loud to Winn-Dixie until I had them memorized. I wanted to know those ten things inside and out. That way, if my mama ever came back, I could recognize her, and I would be able to grab her and hold on to her tight and not let her get away from me again.

—DiCamillo (2000, pp. 29–30).

Why would a child want to write? What would persuade a small person to pick up a pencil and put it to paper? For years, process writing experts have told us it comes from personal motivation—the need to write. And this certainly seems to be the case for India Opal Buloni, the protagonist of *Because of Winn-Dixie*. Abandoned by her mother and living with her father, a preacher whose own pain causes him to retreat like a turtle to his shell, Opal finds solace in her dog, Winn-Dixie, and in writing down the ten things her father shares about her mother. Perhaps inscribing her mother on the page and memorizing her characteristics inside and out will allow her to hold on tight if she ever gets the chance to hold her mother again.

The author of this Newbery Honor Book is Kate DiCamillo, and Kate believes in writing. She believes in the power of print on the page to conjure up the potential magic in life. She once wrote an essay about a childhood incident in her own life when she found a bone in the ground. Holding it tight, she transformed it in her mind into a "wishing bone," and she conjured up an honest-to-goodness, real live pony. Now it's true that the pony was an escapee from a local carnival, but her wish on the bone and the simultaneous appearance of the pony was serendipity she never forgot. And to Kate, that's the link to writing:

> It did not matter that I knew already that the bone would never work again. What mattered was this: somehow, through sheer audacity, through dumb luck, through will power, through instinct, through defiance, through faith, through something unknowable, inexplicable, magical, I had conjured something from nothing.
> And that is what writing is. (2000–2001, p. 15)

Yes and no. Yes, in that when the muse is with you writing seems like a magical gift. But no, in that writing has its very real foundation in careful crafting and extensive reading. Annie Dillard (1989) summed it up beautifully. "At its best, the sensation of writing is that of any unmerited grace. It is handed to you, but only if you look for it" (p. 75). And the best place to look for writing is in reading. Indeed, just about any well-known writer will tell you that they are readers first and foremost.

In her Newbery acceptance speech for *Jacob Have I Loved*, Katherine Paterson (1986) explained, "Those who know me best will testify that I am far more of a reader than I am a writer" (pp. 76–77). She acknowledged the work of Jane Langton and Madeleine L'Engle—"writers whose extraordinary vision lighted many of those dark days when I was still struggling to write fiction that someone would find worth publishing" (p. 77). Paterson's testimony matches that of other authors. In reflecting on her own writing, Natalie Babbit acknowledged her debt to Joseph Campbell. Virginia Hamilton felt inspired by the sociological writing of W.E.B. Du Bois and Shirley Graham. E. B. White tipped his hat to Thoreau.

Thus, professional writers often pay tribute to exemplars of the craft both as fonts of inspiration and as sources of critical analysis. Authors read widely and analyze what they read, allowing these reflections to help shape their own writing. As Annie Dillard (1989) explained:

> The writer studies literature, not the world. He lives in the world; he cannot miss it. If he has ever bought a hamburger, or taken a commercial airplane flight, he spares his readers a report of his experience. He is careful of what he reads, for that is what he will write. He is careful of what he learns, because that is what he will know. (p. 68)

So it is, or at least can be, with children.

In earlier years, the trend of writing process classrooms was to encourage young authors to write-what-you-know, to take life experience and put it on paper. Yet, professional writers like those mentioned above, seem to suggest alternative advice, implying that writers are often inspired by what they know about literature. Still, a caution is in order because "the difference between a Tolstoy and you or me is not the amount of fiction we have read" (Freedman, 1993, p. 238). Good writers have important things they want to say, and many of these things stem from their own life experience and creative imagination. However, I believe children will be better equipped to say these things if they are given multiple opportunities to read and to talk extensively and analytically about text.

In the '80s and early '90s, the write-what-you-know model resulted in a preponderance of personal narrative writing. Much of it was good because kids were writing from the heart, but there were at least two hitches. First, because children had little chance to write in other genres, their range was restricted. And second, even if they did study the features of particular genres, they were often denied the opportunity to see literature as a resource for their own writing. Teachers held literature apart, fearing that children would copy rather than craft their own ideas. Shelley Harwayne (1992) explained the effect of this stance on topic generation:

> Over the years the teachers I know best have been reluctant to focus on litera-ture as a means of helping students find their own topic for writing. Literature was fine if it helped students study a genre or revise a draft, but it was not supposed to give them topics. That was their responsibility. Suggesting that a

piece of literature might help our students find their own topics was somehow connected to "story-starter" activities.

. . . Now our stomachs don't tighten when we hear Tom Newkirk say, "Stories enable stories." And we don't shrink in our seats when we hear Jane Yolen say, "Stories lean on stories." Instead, we nod our heads in agreement. We know it to be true. We've not only come to appreciate that responding to literature can help students find their own topics for writing, we've come to value literature as a major resource for generating topics. (pp. 60–61)

Paying attention to literature, however, extends far beyond the focus on topic. It's true that you could read *Because of Winn-Dixie* and then compose a list of 10 things you want to remember about your mother, or write about the way your father has withdrawn from your life, or even pen a picture of the way your dog greets you at the door, with a smile like nobody's business. And these would be good things to write about. But *Winn-Dixie* offers so much more, for the craft of DiCamillo's exquisite writing is there for the taking.

Now this last statement may make you uncomfortable. "Isn't that cheating?" you ask. No. I don't mean taking in the literal sense—copying and claiming it to be your own. I mean "literary borrowing," a term Peter Lancia (1997, p. 470) coined to capture how children borrow plots, characters, genre features, and even information from stories they've read to put into their own prose and poetry. Even more important, they borrow from authors' stylistic choices. When children take up literature, they learn to live in the language of another and then reshape it to make it their own. Mem Fox (1993b) said it best, "structures are but useless skeletons until we have gathered a hoard of life-giving words and the knowledge of where best to put them" (p. 109). This is what happens in children's literary engagement through writing.

In the sections that follow, I focus on literary response journals—places where children draw or write down their questions, predictions, feelings, and observations about the texts they read, especially the language of literature. Then I turn to look at children's writing as they lean on literature to craft their own expressions.

Literary Response Journals

Literary response journals have been with us long enough to become a mainstay in many classrooms. These journals serve as places for children to put down their thoughts about texts, and the first value lies in providing children an opportunity to think about their thinking. You've no doubt heard some version of the phrase, "I don't know what I think until I write it down." Literary response journals help us communicate what we think about literature. As Julia Wollman-Bonilla (2000) suggested, "Writing can facilitate learning; composing slows down thought processes, inviting consideration of ideas and questions. Writing also nudges students to articulate, shape, and organize ideas in their own words . . ." (p. 37).

A second value lies in your ability to track children's thinking about text by reading and responding to children's journal writing. As your children inscribe their ideas about a book, you'll be able to follow their progression through the story. When do they pause and question? How does their thinking change over time? What are the quotes—phrases, metaphors, vocabulary words—they note? What characters, plot points, and themes connect to people, events, and messages in their own lives? While there are a number of ways for students to respond to literature through writing, some are more enlightening than others. Let's look at three kinds of response in turn.

Summing Up

Some children use their response journals to summarize what they've read, and this can be helpful in demonstrating comprehension. Indeed, the "retell" is a valuable assessment tool to check on children's abilities to reconstruct the vital aspects of a text. But in terms of literary interpretation, this is only a first step. For example, Christy Shoemaker, a third grade teacher, read *Because of Winn-Dixie* to her 8- and 9-year-old students and asked them to keep response journals because she wanted to "learn about their thoughts, feelings, and understandings of the text while teaching them about the essential link between reading and writing."

They had just finished reading chapters 3 and 4 in which Opal had already found her dog in the local grocery store and named him Winn-Dixie after the store. She decided he could use some grooming and went to work with the hose and her own hairbrush.

> The whole time I was working on him, I was talking to him. And he listened. I told him how we were alike. "See," I said, "you don't have any family and neither do I. I've got the preacher, of course. But I don't have a mama. I mean I have one, but I don't know where she is. She left when I was three years old.

I can't hardly remember her. And I bet you don't remember your mama much either. So we're almost like orphans."

Winn-Dixie looked straight at me when I said that to him, like he was feeling relieved to finally have somebody understand his situation. (DiCamillo, 2000, pp. 20-21)

As Opal talks, she comes to the conclusion that she really wants to know more about her Mama, and Winn-Dixie seems to agree. Together they go in and Opal asks the preacher to tell her 10 things about her Mama, one for each year Opal's been alive.

Christy's group listened closely to these chapters and then went to their response journals to write down their thoughts. One boy, Luis, veered slightly from his initial pattern of simple restatements of the story's events using as many of DiCamillo's words as he could remember. Indeed, Christy called this entry a "transitional piece." Even though he again summarized the main events, he was "beginning to use more of his own words." Luis wrote:

Ople was giving a bath to Winn-Dixie. Also she was talking to Winn, and she told him something about orphins—which means that your family left you. So she came inside and said Papa. I decided since I'm 10 years old you should tell ten things about my mama. OK said the preture. So she said Sit down. So they started to talk all the way to ten! And Ople said, Just like me! Except for the drinking beer stuff! And the preacher said And your mama loved you!

Although Luis recounted most events in order with little personal connection, Christy saw his own opinions begin to creep in, especially when he described the mother's alcoholism as "drinking beer stuff." Christy wrote, "His reaction to this section during discussions made his opinion of this issue clear. As he read his description of the problem, he shook his head with a concerned look on his face, as if wanting to tell Opal's mother why drinking beer is not a good idea." Still, Christy felt that Luis hesitated to elaborate on his own opinions, so she commented positively on his ability to retell the story, but also nudged him "to write about some of the personal reactions and connections that he had shared during group discussions." When he persisted in summarizing the text more than offering his own insights, she asked him "to think about which of the events he recounted were the most important."

Christy's emphasis on the most important events is critical. As Keene and Zimmermann (1997) stressed, "Proficient readers make instantaneous decisions about what is important in text" (p. 94). But children who are learning this strategy need opportunities to debate and defend their ideas about importance, because what one child deems the most vital element in a passage may be different from another child's view. While Luis focused on the "drinking beer stuff," another child might concentrate on the turtle image for the preacher, while still another might hone in on Opal's growing relationship with Winn-Dixie. None of them are wrong if they can support their decisions about significance.

Puzzles & Predictions

Deliberating over significance leads us to another way that children respond to literature in their journals, for they often have questions and make guesses about text. Looking at another book with a canine character, *Love That Dog* by Sharon Creech (2001), will allow us to see how children's puzzles and predictions about a text play out. In this lovely book, Jack, the protagonist, is resistant to his teacher's emphasis on children's poetry writing. Indeed, Jack's opening journal entry indicates his gendered take on poetry in general, "I don't want to / because boys / don't write poetry. / Girls do" (p. 1). Slowly, using example after example from published poets as well as encouraging his every attempt, Miss Stretchberry convinces Jack to express himself in rhythmic language. One of the first poems she uses is by William Carlos Williams (1938), and it's entitled "The Red Wheelbarrow":

So much depends
upon

a red wheel
barrow

glazed with rain
water

beside the white
chickens.

Cathy Glaab, a 4th grade teacher in one of my classes, decided to have her 9- and 10-year-old children respond to this poem in writing before she read them the beginning of *Love That Dog*. The children were decidedly perplexed and responded in their journals with a number of questions. Kenny asked,

"Why are the chickens there? Why is it a *red* wheelbarrow? Why does so much depend on a wheelbarrow?" Jordan responded in a similar vein: "What's with the chickens? Why is it a red wheelbarrow instead of a black or a blue one? *What* depends on the red wheelbarrow?" Indeed, Jordan concluded "I think that the poem doesn't really have a purpose!"

Purpose or not, Cathy's children were eager to discuss their written responses in group, and their puzzles with the poem led to some intriguing predictions:

> **Kenny:** I don't get this poem. What's it talking about?
>
> **Alva:** I don't get it either. Why does anything depend on a wheelbarrow?
>
> **Jordan:** I don't get the part about the chickens.
>
> **Bob:** And why does the wheelbarrow have to be red?
>
> **Kenny:** I think the wheelbarrow is supposed to be important or something. Maybe it brings feed to the chickens.
>
> **Bob:** Nah, wheelbarrows aren't that important. Farmers can use tractors to carry stuff on farms.
>
> **Kenny:** Maybe this poem was written a long time ago like when farmers did use wheelbarrows a lot.
>
> **Karen:** But why did it have to be red? A neighbor of mine has a wheelbarrow on her porch, and it's blue. I don't think I've ever seen a red wheelbarrow.
>
> **Peter:** So maybe it's like what Kevin said—that the poem is from a long time ago and maybe wheelbarrows used to be red.
>
> **Karen:** [sarcastically] Yeah. Right. And all the chickens were white, too.
>
> **Jordan:** I kind of like the red wheelbarrow and the white chickens. I think this guy wanted them to stand out against each other, like if we pictured it in our mind.

In taking their written puzzles to their literary discussion group, the children were able to voice their conjectures about textual meaning. They wondered if the time the poem was written might have impact, and they brought in their personal understandings of wheelbarrows to justify or counter Williams' verse. Jordan's final insight is a long way from her initial view that that poem lacked purpose. She is beginning to see an image in her mind—a picture of how seemingly insignificant things gain significance when they "stand out against each other."

After their discussion, Cathy read them the beginning of *Love that Dog*. She wanted her children's responses to stand against Jack's so they could see that their perplexity was repeated in the protagonist's confusion. Cathy wrote, "The entire group burst out laughing when I read the part where Jack said, 'I don't understand / the poem about / the red wheelbarrow / and the white chickens / and why so much / depends upon / them' [p. 3]. I believe they all totally identified with Jack." But even more important than their character identification is that their puzzles and predictions led them to some synthesis of textual meaning. As Harvey and Goudvis (2000) suggested, "Synthesizing at the highest level goes beyond merely taking stock of meaning as one reads. A true synthesis is achieved when a new perspective or thought is born out of the reading" (p. 144), and it also occurs in the potent combination of writing and literary discussion.

Critiquing Craft

Even when the children in Cathy's class questioned the Williams' poem, they admired his ability to create vivid images. In her journal, Jordan noted that she liked the "awesome language" in "glazed with rain water." And Kenny admitted that he liked the phrase "so much depends upon a red wheel barrow," though he still puzzled over its significance. In learning to become better writers, so much depends on children's attention to the language of a text and their willingness to critique it. Katie Wood Ray (1999) called this "reading like a writer" and suggested, "Writing well involves learning to attend to the *craft* of writing, learning to do the sophisticated work of separating *what it's about* from *how it is written*" (p. 10).

In reading *Love That Dog* to her class, Cathy decided to read them some other poems by poets cited in the text, including Robert Frost's "The Road Not Taken." In her journal Jordan wrote, "I think this should have been called 'The Road Less Traveled' because it isn't about the road he didn't take, it's about the one he did take." In her literary discussion group, she read her critique and the following conversation ensued:

Karen: [nodding her head] I agree with Jordan. The one he took made the difference, not the one he didn't take.

Kenny: Yeah, but it doesn't sound as good. "The Road Not Taken" sounds a lot better. It makes you want to read the poem.

Bob: Maybe it should be "The Road Less Ventured." It'd be better word choice. He's already used the word traveled.

Cathy was surprised by her children's willingness to critique a master poet. She wrote, "I grew up with a reverence for Robert Frost and would never have thought to criticize his work, but my children do not hold him in that same elevated position. In fact, they loved the part in *Love the Dog* when Jack suggests that Mr. Frost 'has a little too much time on his hands' [p. 21]. They wanted to make sure that I noticed that Jack felt pretty free to criticize Robert Frost too."

In encouraging children to critique craft, however, it's important to help them emphasize the effective as well as the ineffective. Indeed, the word "critique" need not dwell in the negative, but takes on a more analytic aura as children try to figure out how an author crafts a piece of prose or poetry, and what makes it so accomplished. Katie Wood Ray (1999) believes that one way to do this is to identify an aspect of craft and give it a name. She has a variety of unique terms that refer to particular kinds of craft. But she's clear that you don't have to use her names. You and your children can make up your own. The important thing is to name it so you can use it when you come across this kind of craft again.

Still, many stylistic terms are already established, and they are also there for you and your students' use—alliteration, metaphor, irony, personification, just to name a few. You can return to Table 2.1 in chapter 2 if you want to review some common technical terms. The idea is that in giving children the opportunity to use well-recognized terms or ones you've created together, you are providing them with a chance to critique craft. In my own classes, I often take a text passage and ask my students to analyze the craft. Figure 6.1 offers an example with an excerpt from *Because of Winn-Dixie* that describes the dog's terror of thunderstorms. As Winn-Dixie races around the house, knocking the preacher to the ground, DiCamillo strategically sprints through several stylistic devices including imagery, onomatopoeia, simile, sophisticated word choice, and personification.

Over my years of watching teachers at work, I've seen them heighten children's attention to craft by asking them to take note of the use of language in their response journals. And children are eager to write down the words, sentences, and structures that intrigue them—the alliteration that allows for rhythm, the metaphors that lift a character off the page, the shift in line length that delivers a critical break in the flow. You can also ask your children to conduct author studies, choosing favorite authors to be their mentors in writing. They can lean on these mentors for inspiration, in the same way that Jack in *Love That Dog* learned to lean on Mr. Walter Dean Myers for help in crafting his own poetry.

But then you can take it a step further, as you encourage your children to bring their comments about passages or favorite authors into group or

"You want the door open?" I said. "Huh? Is that what you want?" I stood up and opened the door and Winn-Dixie flew through it like **something big and ugly and mean was chasing him.**

"Winn-Dixie," I hissed, "come back here." I didn't want him going and waking the preacher up.

But it was too late. Winn-Dixie was already at the other end of the trailer, in the preacher's room. I could tell because there was a *sproi-i-ing* sound that must have come from Winn-Dixie jumping up on the bed, and then there was a sound from the preacher like he was real surprised. But none of it lasted long, because Winn-Dixie came tearing back out of the preacher's room, panting and running like crazy. I tried to grab him, but he was going too fast.

"Opal?" said the preacher. He was standing at the door to his bedroom, and his hair was all kind of wild on top of his head, and he was looking around like he wasn't sure where he was. "Opal, what's going on?"

"I don't know," I told him. But just then there was a huge crack of thunder, one so loud that it shook the whole trailer, and Winn-Dixie came right past me and I screamed, "Daddy, watch out!"

But the preacher was still confused. He just stood there, and Winn-Dixie came barreling right toward him **like he was a bowling ball and the preacher was the only pin left standing, and *wham*, they both fell to the ground.**

"Uh-oh," I said.

"Opal?" said the preacher. He was lying on his stomach, and Winn-Dixie was sitting on top of him, panting and whining.

"Yes sir," I said.

"Opal," the preacher said again.

"Yes sir," I said louder.

"Do you know what a pathological fear is?"
"No sir," I told him.

The preacher raised a hand. He rubbed his nose.

"Well," he said, after a minute, "it's a fear that goes way beyond normal fears. It's a fear you can't be talked out of or reasoned out of."

...

"The storm won't last long," the preacher told me. "And when it's over, the real Winn-Dixie will come back."

After a while, the storm did end. The rain stopped. And there wasn't any more lightning, and finally, the last rumble of thunder went away and Winn-Dixie quit running back and forth and came over to where me and the preacher were sitting and cocked his head, **like he was saying, "What in the world are you two doing out of bed in the middle of the night?"** (DiCamillo, 2000, pp. 73-77)

Imagery:
The image of something so threatening and yet so intangible helps us feel Winn-Dixie's fear.

Onomatopoeia:
Sproi-i-ing is a sound-packed word that captures the sheer surprise of the jump as well as the weight of Winn-Dixie on the bed springs .

Simile:
The bowling ball and pin image is perfect for portraying the preacher's vulnerability in the face of Winn-Dixie's panic.

Word Choice:
Using a sophisticated vocabulary word works well when you can figure out a way to define it. The preacher's question and Opal's "No" serve this purpose well.

Personification:
Notice how having Winn-Dixie seem to talk enhances his character as well as highlights his confusion from the storm.

FIG. 6.1.   Analyzing Craft in *Because of Winn-Dixie.*

classroom conversation, for it is often in the discussion of the writing that children's reasoning comes out. And in collaborative conversation, they learn things they didn't think of themselves or help another to see their point. By noting language in their journals—especially the techniques of writing mentors—and discussing it in group, they come to read like writers, and this helps them with their own writing in turn.

Leaning on Literature

When children are learning to write well, authorial mentors are there to offer advice—plot lines, settings, characters, and stylistic techniques—but only if the children have learned to listen. When we run across children in our classrooms that have an ear for language, we need to recognize that their talents are often deeply connected to years of reading and being read to. However, we mustn't forget that children's capacity with language is also influenced by experiences with storytellers in their family and community life as well as multiple media messages in music, film, and TV.

Whether oral or written texts are the influence, the idea is that language has rushed in to expand children's repertoires. They have more words, phrases, images, and structures at their fingertips, and when they pick up the pen they do it with more power than if they were working alone. Because this book concentrates on literary engagement, I'll focus on the influence of the written word, but keep in mind that published authors are only part of a large range of voices available to children as they learn to tune into language.

Mentors Standing in the Shadows

Authorial mentors are often hidden in the shadows. A child will lean on the language of an author without really acknowledging a direct contact. I first learned this from my own children, and my eldest daughter, Lindsey, was the first to teach me. When she was young she often wrote fairy tales—both traditional and fractured—leaning heavily on the ones we read together as well as the ones she read in school. Lindsey knew that literary language could evoke images and emotions far beyond the capacity of ordinary language. Between once-upon-a-time and happily-ever-after, the words of story describe a world where life is non-ordinary—often more formal and elegant than everyday life. Thus, in Lindsey's literary renditions there was often "a golden castle of great beauty" where servants love a princess "as they would their own daughter." When an evil fairy "storms in" with a voice that sounds "like stones falling from a cliff" and later screams "I've got you now!", the princess and all her courtiers sleep "for a hundred years." The prince, on his way to the rescue, enters into a "quiet castle" where his "footsteps echo in the halls" and the walls seem to be "holding their breath."

Just as the prince's footsteps echo in the halls, there were often echoes of published literature throughout her texts. Sometimes she borrowed directly, such as when she wrote a tale of an ugly princess based on Jane Yolen's (1981) *Sleeping Ugly.* But much more often she borrowed plot structures and larger chunks of language from the many tales she had read as a child. And this pattern continued throughout her elementary years.

One of my favorite examples of Lindsey's literary borrowing occurred when she was in the 5th grade. She decided to use an illustration from Chris Van Allsburg's (1984) *The Mysteries of Harris Burdick.* The book is essentially a set of distinct pictures each with a title and a brief caption, but they are joined by an introductory frame story. Lindsey selected an illustration of a young woman asleep with an open book—a book from which mysterious vines grow up and over the pages. The title of the illustration is "*Mr. Linden's Library*" and the caption reads, "*He had warned her about the book. Now it was too late.*" But in writing her story, Lindsey also wove in her love of Patricia MacLachlan's (1993) *Baby.* In this extraordinary story, Ms. Minifred, a school librarian, sweeps her arm toward the library shelves and says, "In this room, in these books, there is the power of a hundred hurricanes. Wondrous words" (p. 43). Combining Van Allsburg's title, image, and enticing caption with MacLachlan's emphasis on wondrous words, Lindsey's story of "Mr. Linden's Library" began:

> Amy Satchel was at the young age of ten. She was a curious girl, and my next-door neighbor. I am Samantha Witicor, and I was Amy's best friend until Mr. Linden moved into the vacant house across the dirt road. Mr. Linden was an elderly man with a white beard that hung down to about his Adam's apple. His white hair was piled on the top of his head like a wild bird's nest. He liked to walk with a hollowed out carved shotgun for a cane. He used it to help the problems with his back, as he always told Amy and me.
>
> Mr. Linden was a bookworm, for that is what the littler children called him. If he did not have us to bother him, he would probably get lost in all the words in all his wondrous books. Mr. Linden would tell Amy and me stories of his travels all over the world. Some were scary and some were adventurous. But what we loved most was when he read us stories. Mr. Linden said we could read or borrow any story in his whole library except the tale called *The Book of Secrets*.

Because Lindsey, too, was a book borrower, she was able to braid together three texts—Van Allsburg's, MacLachlan's, and her own. The emphasis is on reading stories and the potential of literally losing oneself in books. Words in books are wondrous, secretive, and ultimately powerful. And just as Little Red Riding Hood is destined to disobey her mother's admonitions and go off the path, Amy, a "curious girl" is bound to disregard Mr. Linden's warning.

Indeed, Amy steals the book, and it leads to dire consequences, as Sara is about to discover:

> . . . When I rushed into Amy's room, she was sprawled across her bed. In the flickering candlelight I could see the book across her chest. It was open to the twenty-second page, to a story entitled "The Secret Garden." But it was not the story I knew, for twisted vines grew out of the pages. Mr. Linden entered the room and stood by me with tears glistening on his cheeks.
>
> "There's only one way to save her. I have to take her place," said Mr. Linden in a shaking voice. Before we could stop him, he took a piece of the plant and rubbed it across his tear-stained cheeks. Suddenly, Mr. Linden started to shake. Then he fell to the ground, his cane breaking in two. Amy sat up quickly. The book fell to the floor and vanished. She looked at Mr. Linden and burst into tears. The End

Here Lindsey introduced a fourth text, Burnett's (1910) *The Secret Garden*, but as she suggests it was not the familiar story. Instead, it is intertextual play which allowed her to introduce a much more ominous tale. Although these references make obvious links to specific texts, a part of the power as well as the somewhat clichéd nature of Lindsey's writing comes from other textual sources. These sources are not named, but phrases like "flickering candlelight" and "tear-stained cheeks" are found in multiple texts. When we talked about her story, Lindsey could not name any specific citation for these phrases, but she explained, "They might have been borrowed 'cause sometimes I borrow without even thinking."

Literary borrowing occurs when children have authors to lean on. Sometimes they hear them quite clearly and call on them for aid. Lindsey knew that her title and plot turn came from Van Allsburg and the idea of "wondrous words" came from MacLachlan. But other times the borrowing was subtler, as unseen authors whispered to her from the shadows. Still, many children do not hear the authors' voices because they don't have a repertoire of extensive reading. But that doesn't mean that books are closed for them. Instead, you can help your children learn to listen when you purposefully move authorial mentors out of the shadows.

Moving Mentors Out Into the Open

It is no accident that Lindsey loved Patricia MacLachlan's *Baby*, with her emphasis on "wondrous words" for it is an extraordinary book, and one that I use with my practicing teachers just about every year. I leaned on it to write an article for *The New Advocate* on Lindsey's literary borrowing (Wolf & Heath, 1998), where I detailed her stories of "Sleeping Ugly" and "Mr. Linden's Library" among others. Katie Wood Ray (1999) leaned on MacLachlan's text to write her book on the necessity of literary mentors in children's writing. Coincidentally, both of us titled our pieces "Wondrous Words" demonstrating the impact of literary borrowing even on adult academic authors. We all borrow, but what's becoming increasingly clear is how important it is to make this option available to children.

Expert teachers tune up the volume of authorial voices by asking children to listen in highly specific ways. A few years ago, a 4th grade teacher in my class, Kerri Therriault, decided to try to enhance her children's ability to lean on authorial mentors. She noticed that while her children read books utilizing a variety of writing techniques, they rarely commented on them except in the most general of terms. They would read a story and when Kerri asked them what they noticed about the writing, her 9-year-olds would respond with "It has lots of details" or "I can see what's happening in my head." But they couldn't take their comments any further to explore how those details enhanced their mental images. They were stuck in generalities, and because they hadn't done closer analysis they didn't know how to apply similar stylistic devices in their own writing.

Kerri was intrigued by the advice of children's literature expert Glenna Sloan (1991) who argued that "writing grows out of reading" and stressed the importance of teaching particular genres or forms. She suggested children "must first be caught by pleasure in language as it is used in [the short story] or any other form. Then, through extensive experience followed by reflection and discussion—criticism—they are taught by the form itself" (p. 158). Kerri was convinced that if she made this criticism a more explicit part of her instruction, the children would begin to incorporate more creative uses of language in their own texts.

One of Kerri's first assignments was open-ended—to write about experiences her children had had "that were just dangerous enough to be thrilling without being terrifying." Travis produced two sentences in less than two minutes and was perfectly satisfied that he was done, "At my neighbor's house there is a ramp that I like to jump, and then I fall down. I still want to do it but my mom doesn't want me to."

Not surprisingly, Kerri was disappointed with Travis's effort, but rather than give him generalized and unhelpful directions like "write more," she assembled her children and read them the "swing passage" from E. B. White's *Charlotte's Web* (you can reread this passage in chapter 1 of this book). She read the passage with panache, and the children launched into a discussion of "how their mothers worried about them needlessly" when they were off on their adventures, especially when they were having the "best time of their life." Then Kerri took them through the passage, asking them to comment on how White helped them feel the swing, the nervousness of the jump, the thrilling ride with wind in your hair, and the clever punch line about how "Children almost always hang onto things tighter than their parents think they will" (p. 69). Then she set them to their task again—asking them to pay particular attention to the *sensation* of their adventure, and the results were very different. Travis switched to another activity altogether, but more important to another style of writing:

> When I pull the go-cart out of the garage, I wonder if I should because my mom says that I could get hurt if I ride it. After I make up my mind to ride it, I pull the starter on the motor. It revs up. I sit down in it and put on my helmet and seat belt. I rev it up a couple more times and ease off the brake, and I start to move forward. For a minute you're really scared, and then you realize it's not hard at all. The next thing you know you're OFF, and the wind is in your hair and you're having the best time of your life.

This was more like what Kerri was hoping for. She wrote:

> Travis's growth is evident. Using the information he gained from *Charlotte's Web* as well as from the language used in peer discussion about the best time of your life, he is much more effectively able to communicate his own message. Vygotsky (1978) believes that what a child can do with others today, he can do alone tomorrow. That is so true!

It is also true that children can borrow not only from the sensation that language provides, but the structure of a text as well. To continue the discussion of adventures or activities that children enjoy though their parents protest, Kerri read them Judith Viorst's (1990) marvelously funny tale *Earrings!* It is the story of a young girl who wants pierced ears and cajoles, begs, and pleads with her parents, promising all sorts of responsible behavior if only she can get earrings! A chorus runs throughout the text about the beauty and glory of earrings, but her parents are tired of hearing her nonsense and reject her plea.

The discussion following Kerri's reading was passionate, "Every student in the group had experienced the same feelings as the young girl in the story, and was excited to have a venue in which to vent." Figure 6.2 shows the text and some of the illustrations from Ann Marie's story "Stay Up Late!!!!"—a tale of Ann Marie's nightly argument with her parents about her early bedtime. She knows her parents' reasoning is "so they can have their privacy," and her illustration shows how much she knows, as she peeks over the balcony at her mom snuggled in dad's lap with hearts, flowers, and even a prince approaching a castle tower on the bookcase in the background. But what good is privacy, she asks, when they don't seem to do much with it! "Why do they need privacy so Mom can do her afghan and Dad can fall asleep in the chair at 8:00 at night?" with his mouth wide open to let the ZZZZZZs of sleep escape.

Ann Marie writes of her resistance with her radio, playing it "just loud enough so they can hear it, but I don't get in trouble." But her parents ignore this as well, as they head to the kitchen for their nightly snack. Even when Ann Marie falls forgetfully asleep, the next night brings the same story and "a bell goes off in [her] head"—a phrase she admitted borrowing from Kenny in *The Watsons Go to Birmingham—1963*. Then she remembers, "what happened the night before, and that it will happen again."

What's most marvelous about Ann Marie's text is the opening and the matching coda at the end: "Stay up late / till 10:00, / till Dad's sacked out! / I don't need ten hours of sleep! / I only need eight!" Ann Marie's verse contains echoes of Viorst's chorus on beautiful, glorious earrings, and even though the parents in both stories reject their daughters' requests, Viorst's continuation of the chorus and Ann Marie's duplication of the verse show that the arguments are far from over. These two children will persist until they get what they want!

Ann Marie got what she wanted from Viorst's text as well. She clipped and changed words, images, and structures to communicate her own critical message. She took a parents' dismissal of a child's passionate plea as her subject, but her entreaty is all the more effective because of her wry observations on parental activity and her cleverly repeated rhyme. Because Kerri,

Stay up late,
   till 10:00,
      till Dad's sacked out!
I don't need ten hours of sleep!
   I only need eight!

   My parents say, "You need your sleep, and I'm not bargaining with you!" But I know they want me to go to sleep, so they can have their privacy.

   They say, "We work all day. Then we come home and deal with you, and we hardly get to see each other all day."

   Why don't they go up to their room and watch their TV? Why do they need privacy so Mom can do her afghan and Dad can fall asleep in the chair at 8:00 at night?

   I think it's mean! When I am just about to drift off to sleep, I can hear my whole family in the kitchen getting a snack.

   I want them to know that I know what they're up to, so I shut my door and turn on my radio just loud enough so they can hear it, but I don't get in trouble.

   The next morning, my parents act like nothing happened. I don't say anything, because every night I fall into a deep sleep and can't remember what happened the night before.

   However, each night, when my mom tells me to get my PJs on, a bell goes off in my head. I remember what happened the night before, and that it will happen again.

Stay up late,
   till 10:00,
      till Dad's sacked out!
I don't need ten hours of sleep!
   I only need eight!

FIG. 6.2.   Stay Up Late!!!! by Ann Marie.

her teacher, knows how to bring authors out into the open, Ann Marie can follow her own path, but still has a mentor to guide her.

Mentors Leading From the Heart

One of the most powerful passages in *Because of Winn-Dixie* occurs when Opal visits the town library, and Miss Franny, the librarian, tells her the tale of her great-grandfather, Littmus W. Block, who lost his entire family as well as his youth in the Civil War. After the war, he decided that a world so full of sorrow needed more sweetness, and he opened up a candy factory featuring the Littmus Lozenge. When Miss Franny gives Opal and another girl, Amanda, a piece, they both are overcome by a feeling of sadness, and Miss Franny explains:

> "There's a secret ingredient in there," Miss Franny said.
> "I know it," I told her. "I can taste it. What is it?
> "Sorrow," Miss Franny said. "Not everybody can taste it. Children, especially, seem to have a hard time knowing it's there."
> "I taste it," I said.
> "Me, too," said Amanda.
> "Well, then," Miss Franny said, "you've probably both had your share of sadness." . . .
> "But how do you put that in a piece of candy?" I asked her. "How do you get that taste in there?"
> "That's the secret," she said. "That's why Littmus made a fortune. He manufactured a piece of candy that tasted sweet and sad at the same time." (pp. 114–115)

When I teach *Because of Winn-Dixie*, I often open my class reading the chapters that hold this passage. At the point where Miss Franny Block opens her old desk drawer and offers Opal and Amanda a Littmus Lozenge, I open the drawers of a small wooden chest I've brought to class and offer my students candy, which they sample while I finish the chapter. Although I've had no luck finding a candy that is truly "sweet and sad at the same time," my students swear they can almost taste it as they listen to DiCamillo's lovely text.

A teacher in one of my classes, Jeannie Finch, was moved enough by the experience that she decided to repeat it in her own class of 14-year-olds. She was trying to show her students how literature taps on the heart and once it comes in, its words, images, and emotions can dwell there for quite a while. A student in her class had been trying to write about the death of her dog, but she was having a hard time of it. In conferences, Jeannie had brought Alice *The Tenth Good Thing About Barney* (Viorst, 1971), hoping that the story of a boy's list of 10 good things about his cat, Barney, might provide a helpful structure for Alice to follow. When Jeannie began reading *Because of Winn-Dixie*, Alice noted how Opal's list of 10 things about her mother was like the boy's list about Barney; both characters "listed things they wanted to remember about their loved ones." Still, though she liked the idea of talking about her dog's characteristics, the structure of the list didn't appeal to Alice. She was searching for something better. However, when Jeannie read the passage about the Littmus Lozenge, Alice quietly told her, "I think I've got it," and still sucking on her candy she headed back to her desk to write. After several drafts, conversations with Jeannie, and much consideration, Alice crafted the following piece:

Rags

She came in a box with a big, blue bow on my 5th birthday. I can still remember lifting the cardboard lid, peeking in at her adorable face. She was a mutt, a rascal, a rag of a dog that we called Rags in her scruffy honor, and she was my sidekick for years. My mom never had to wonder where I was. All she had to do was look out the door and down the street and see Rags sitting on the stoop of a neighbor's house, and she'd know right away where to find me.

Rags had many talents. She was a rodeo dog, for one thing. Not really, but sometimes when we called her in, our cat Zinger would leap on her back, dig in, and get a wild ride down the hill for their supper. She was also a newspaper boy. My dad would open the garage and say "get the paper," and Rags would leap out the door. Standing in the driveway, she would nose the paper around and around till she could grab it in her jaw and then drop it at my dad's feet. We all admired this trick, and we learned to ignore the soggy wet spot in the fold of the front page. It dried soon enough.

Rags knew a lot more than "get the paper." She had her own stuffed bear named Teddy, and when we'd say, "find Teddy" she'd run down her toy and wrestle it to the ground. She knew "let's go for a walk" and "wait" and "give me your paw." But the word she knew best was "cookie." Rags would do anything for a treat. She'd come from anywhere in the house and from anywhere in the neighborhood if she heard us call "cookie." She'd balance it on the tip of her nose or "wait" for it till we gave the okay. She'd stare at it on the floor, waiting and watching it, like it might just jump up and take off if she took her eyes off it for a second.

When Rags died, I could hardly stand it. Our rodeo dog was gone, and Zinger slunk into supper on his own. Our newspaper boy was gone, and the front page was so dry it ached. Teddy lay abandoned in a corner of the living room, and the cookies stayed in the cupboard. Finally, Mom asked me to take the treats down to a neighbor's who had a dachshund, and I did. But on the way I got to wondering what Rags saw in those bone-shaped biscuits. So I reached inside the box and grabbed one and took a bite. It was the oddest flavor, dryer than our newspaper. But as I chewed, I thought I tasted something sweet—something sweet and sad at the same time. Rags up and left us. We took our eyes off her for a second, and she was gone. But somehow she's still here, sitting on the stoop of my heart, watching over me and waiting for a cookie.

Children and adolescents, writing to express themselves, watch and wait for the mentors they need. For Alice, Viorst came in with a cat and a list of characteristics, but it wasn't quite right. Then DiCamillo came in with her own scruffy dog and yet another list, but it still didn't provide what she needed. But then came DiCamillo's Littmus Lozenge—a candy that held both sweetness and sorrow—and Alice found her muse. As teachers, we don't really know which author, which passage, which phrase will provide what our students need. But as Alice's teacher, Jeannie, wrote, "If we read them a wide range of stories and show them how authors hone their craft, children will meet the mentors they need to write well."

Summary

In this chapter, I show how children learn to pay attention to craft in their literary response journals. Children often begin by summarizing text, but with encouragement they soon move to noting their own puzzles and predictions. With more time and focused instruction, they begin to analyze the craft of established authors, especially when their teachers make the combination of criticism and creativity the center of the conversation. An emphasis on both the effective and ineffective aspects of text helps children learn to borrow from literature in their own writing. For those who have an extensive reading background, authors often serve as mentors in the shadows, calling out ideas and images, though it's clear that all children call on the language available in their lives, from grandma's tales to MTV.

But capable teachers move literary authors out into the open, and encourage their children to listen well and lean in for the support they need in their own writing. In the book *Love That Dog*, Jack borrows from a well-known writer of prose and poetry to write his own poem about the death of his dog. But he worries that this might be cheating. His teacher, Miss Stretchberry, shows Jack that the author, "Mr. Walter Dean Myers / is not the sort of person / who would get mad / at a boy / for using some of his words." She explains that when Jack does this, he is not "copying"; instead, he is "*inspired by* / Mr. Walter Dean Myers" (pp. 50–51).

Critic Glenna Sloan (1991) agreed, "Ideas of what originality is are often exaggerated; the best writers have always used the forms and conventions, and even the ideas, of those who came before them. Child writers may be encouraged to do the same" (p. 169). But if we want our children to lean on authorial mentors and expand their literary interpretation through writing, we've got to supply opportunities for creativity and critique through authors who will inspire them. And such inspiration—both the sweet and the sorrowful—most often comes from the heart.

BOOKS FOR THE PROFESSIONAL

Dillard, A. (1989). *The writing life.* New York: HarperCollins. Annie Dillard's remarkable little book is packed with profound ideas about writing. My own copy sits underneath my computer where I can see it, reach for it, and lean on it for absolute inspiration. Whenever I'm stuck in my own writing life, Annie's prose commiserates briefly, but then propels me into forward movement.

Harwayne, S. (1992). *Lasting impressions: Weaving literature into the writing workshop.* Portsmouth, NH: Heinemann. This helpful and often lyrical text was one of the first to bring the writing workshop back to literature. Founding Principal of the Manhattan New School and now a New York Superintendent, Shelley Harwayne has spent over thirty years bringing children together with fine literature, and her voice is both passionate and unfailingly practical for classroom teachers eager to help children express themselves through writing.

Lensmire, T. J. (1997). *Powerful writing, responsible teaching.* New York: Teachers College Press. Timothy Lensmire cares about children as writers enough to take the smoothly standard definition of writing workshop and deconstruct it in a more democratic light. Deft with tough theory from Dewey to Bakhtin, Lensmire's prose is wry, witty, and sharp as a tack as he captures the carnival of the writing classroom.

Ray, K. W. (1999). *Wondrous words: Writers and writing in the elementary classroom.* Urbana, IL: National Council of Teachers of English. One of the latest in the line of academics currently advocating literature's place in the writing workshop, Katie Wood Ray believes that our students need to read like writers and to develop habits of inquiry about the craft of writing, especially since the "wondrous words" of mentor authors are available and ready for children's use if they can learn to listen.

Chapter Touchstone Texts

Creech, Sharon (2001). *Love that dog.* New York: HarperCollins. The subtle powers of a gifted writing teacher (wonderfully named Miss Stretchberry) shine in this short novel in free verse about a boy named Jack who shifts from disdain to a love of poetry. Several of the poems Miss Stretchberry uses in her teaching are appended, including "Love That Boy" by Jack's authorial mentor, Mr. Walter Dean Myers.

DiCamillo, Kate. (2000). *Because of Winn-Dixie.* Cambridge, MA: Candlewick. New to town, India Opal Buloni walks into a grocery store and comes out with a dog. Although "mostly he looked like a big piece of old brown carpet that had been left out in the rain," the two new friends have a knack for bringing people together. More than a dog story, this 2001 Newbery honor tale by Kate DiCamillo is about redemption and salvation. It's also an exemplar of writer's craft.

Recommended Tradebooks for Writing

Adedjouma, Davida (Ed.). (1996). *The palm of my heart: Poetry by African American children*, illustrated by Gregory Christie. New York: Lee and Low. These twenty poems were the result of a writing workshop for children led by the editor to celebrate Black culture and creativity. The illustrations are stunning and won a Coretta Scott King Honor Award.

Grimes, Nikki. (1998). *Jazmin's notebook.* New York: Dial. Another Coretta Scott King Award Honor Book, this is the story of the power of the written word in the life of a 14-year-old. With her father dead and her mother institutionalized, Jazmin now lives with her older sister, CeCe, but she lives to baptize blank pages with her own special mark.

The lovely combination of prose and poetry is a pattern that Grimes continued in her current Coretta Scott King Award Winner. In *Bronx Masquerade*, Grimes (2002) delivers the reflections, raps, and rhythms of teenage life in Mr. Ward's secondary class of Open Mike Fridays.

MacLachlan, Patricia. (1993). *Baby.* New York: Delacorte. As an award-winning writer and accomplished word smith, MacLachlan's voice is always poetic, but this text is particularly beautiful as she reveals one family's intricate dance to avoid painful talk, and how poetry ultimately serves as a healing force in their lives. MacLachlan's "wondrous words" will always be a part of my own family's writing life.

Myers, Tim. (2000). *Basho and the fox*, illustrated by Oki S. Han. New York: Marshall Cavendish. The Japanese poet, Basho, was renowned for his extraordinary haiku. In this tale, Basho tries to create a haiku worthy of a fox's listening, but the first two he offers are ridiculed by the fox. Basho finally succeeds in a desperate last attempt, because his haiku features a fox. In addition to the clever story, writing teachers appreciate the time and care that Basho puts into his poetry. The fact that a master must work so hard as well as the power of the inspirational flash of a new idea will make for an effective discussion with children about the art of writing. Illustrator Oki Han's aerial view of the master at work surrounded by discarded drafts makes the point even stronger.

Skármeta, Antonio. (2000). *The composition*, pictures by Alfonso Ruano. Buffalo, NY: Groundwood Books. A picture book winner for the Américas Award in 2000 and the Jane Addams Book Award in 2001, this tale shows the power of not writing what you know. Set in a police state in Latin America, a boy and his classmates are challenged by an army captain to write a composition on what their parents do at night. Instead of revealing how his parents listen to the radio, eager for news against the dictatorship, Pedro writes an ingenious story of how his parents play chess every night, thus protecting his parents with his writing.

7

Interpreting Literature Through
the Visual Arts

In the picture book tale of *Olivia* (Falconer, 2000), the porcine protagonist wears fire engine red and takes equally flamboyant control of her world. A city girl, whose father no doubt works on Wall Street, Olivia orders her brother about and manipulates her mother with a mastery that many mainstream children maintain. She wants to be an opera star like Maria Callas, or perhaps a ballet dancer like one in a Degas painting. On a trip to the museum, she admires Degas' work, though she puzzles over the abstract renderings of Jackson Pollock. Thinking that she could accomplish such art in no time flat, she decides to try it at home. She flings paint on her bedroom wall in an attempt at abstract composition that is not half bad (at least that's what a review by artist David Hockney on the back book cover implies). And while Olivia earns a time out from her indulgent mother who makes her sit briefly on the stairs, she also earns a place in the hearts of all those who encourage children's expression through the visual arts.

Understatement is one of author/illustrator Ian Falconer's qualities. For example, when Olivia's mother teaches her how to build sandcastles, the text only implies that she did okay. But the sleek, sharp-cornered Empire State sandcastle she builds belies the oversimplified claim. Indeed, the juxtaposition of seemingly simple statements with stylish, urbane artwork is what makes this picture book so successful, and what, no doubt, caught the attention of the Caldecott committee who awarded it a silver medal in 2001.

Perry Nodelman (1988) argued that the essence of the picture book lies in just this combination of the childlike with the sophisticated:

Picture books are clearly recognizable as children's books simply because they do speak to us of childlike qualities, of youthful simplicity and youthful exuberance; yet paradoxically, they do so in terms that imply a vast sophistication in regard to both visual and verbal codes. Indeed, it is part of the charm of many of the most interesting picture books that they so strangely combine the childlike and the sophisticated—that the viewer they imply is both very learned and very ingenuous. (p. 21)

Innocent, yet experienced. Simple, yet complex. Ingenuous, yet ingenious. A children's picture book is an oxymoron, which means "pointed foolishness" in its original Greek. Yet, foolishness is not really the point, for seemingly self-contradictory pairings of words ("to make haste slowly" and "cruel kindness") result in a fresh idea. So it is with picture books, for the words say what the pictures cannot reveal, and the pictures show what the words do not tell. The verbal and the visual speak and show, show and speak, and together they construct new meaning.

Still, this meaning is often untouched in K–8 classrooms today. Intermediate and middle school classrooms avoid picture books with the misguided perception that children have probably outgrown them. And in primary classrooms, where picture books continue to hold a prominent position, they are often seen as more amusing than a goldmine for analysis. As Barbara Kiefer (1995) explained, "few teachers spend time helping children sort out, recognize, and understand the many forms of visual information they encounter, certainly not in the same way teachers deal with print literacy" (p. 10). Kiefer argued that teachers all too often ignore the "potential of picturebooks." Equally disturbing, children's uptake of literature through their own art is pushed further out the classroom door as you go up in grade level. While primary teachers have long understood how children's art supports their writing, all too quickly children are asked to leave their artistic expression behind and learn to communicate with words alone. Art is seen as a frill, an extra, something to be done down the hall in art class, or in special classes for the gifted and talented.

Yet, limiting access to art doesn't make sense. First of all, some of the best art in America is present in children's picture books. And second, all children—not just the "gifted and talented" kids—are well served when they are allowed to express their interpretations through the visual arts. Denying children a range of materials from paints, brushes, scissors, charcoal, chalk, and construction paper to the astonishingly available graphic possibilities offered by computers would be a critical mistake, especially since these tools have a remarkable capacity for enriching children's cognitive activity.

Rather than take away the potential in such materials, you should encourage their use. As Anne Haas Dyson (1993) suggested, children are "symbol makers," and they need access to multiple modes of expression. In the last chapter, I focused on writing as one way of expanding literary engagement, but here I want to argue that any mode of expression can be substantially enhanced when it works in collaboration with other modes. Dyson explained:

> Children's interest in one kind of symbol making, writing, is best viewed within the context of children's artistic and social lives, as that writing is couched within their drawing, talking, and playing.... Stories, pictures, dramas—these are children's ways of giving shape to their experiences, of figuring out who they are in relationship to the world and to each other. These are also children's ways of making their own the tools that will serve them throughout their lives. Humble and great, we doodle and sketch, share stories, and play out possibilities in our minds, enriching our adult lives with the child still within us. (p. 56)

Just as great authors and illustrators of children's literature well remember their own childhoods and infuse their texts with the words, images, and feelings of what it's like to be a child, capable teachers have a real understanding of the child within. They know how to encourage a blending of alternative modes of expression—writing with art, art with talk, and talk with writing. And these modes cycle in the same ways that picture books spin in an "eternal circle" (Nikolajeva & Scott, 2001) where the visual sets the stage for the verbal and the verbal draws out the discourse of the visual. Indeed, the dialogue between the words and the pictures is where the action is.

Analyzing the interaction of the verbal and the visual is a vital part of literary interpretation, but children can benefit from guidance here as much as they do in any kind of interpretive work. Just as children need the tools for talking about prose and poetry with access to technical vocabulary and kinds of criticism, they similarly require the means for viewing text. They need to learn new ways of seeing or perceiving the pictures in relationship with the words. Karla Kuskin (1998) called the picture book "thirty-two pages of graphic drama starring pictures and words" (p. 161), and children need to see how it plays.

In the sections to follow, I begin by showing the play of picture books, providing you with a variety of ways to see how illustrated texts work both in relationship to the words as well as through artistic means. Then I move to children's ways of interpreting text through their own art as they envision, compose, and critique the texts they view as well as those they read. Here the emphasis will move out from picture books to chapter books as children work to express what they see in their mind's eye through their art and then take it to their literary discussion groups for further interpretation. Literary interpretation through the visual arts ultimately uses all three processes—envisioning, composing, and critiquing. A child reads a text and envisions an image, puts it to paper, and then brings it to his or her class for discussion. In seeing, creating, and talking, the three processes blur, intermingle, and cycle back and forth. Discussion about a piece of art creates new images in the mind, and these in turn are taken back to the drawing board.

Seeing Picture Books

The first way to think about picture books is to see them as illustrations and words in relationship. The images do not decorate the text, and the words do not caption the illustrations. Instead, they work hand-in-hand and sometimes in opposition to deliver two kinds of information that together make up a unique message. Maurice Sendak (1988) called the relationship between pictures and words "seamless," and he argued that in the best of picture books the artist brings the words to life:

> *Vivify, quicken*, and *vitalize*—of these three synonyms, *quicken*, I think, best suggests the genuine spirit of animation, the breathing to life, the swing into action, that I consider an essential quality in pictures for children's books. *To quicken* means, for the illustrator, the task first of comprehending the nature of his text and then of giving life to that comprehension in his own medium, the picture. (p. 3)

Picturing Words

While you might think that the ability to quicken a text is something akin to translation, it is not. Picturing words is deeply interpretive work, packed with information that is often not present in the words. The text might say something simple like "the stepmother went to her room to make a poisoned apple," but nothing in that text indicates the shape of the room, the arcane and mysterious herbs hanging from the ceiling, the vials and potions that might be within, the low fire, the bubbling cauldron, the black cat that slinks by the stepmother's side. No, the words say "stepmother" and "room" and "poisoned apple," and it's up to the illustrator to decide what it all looks like. Indeed, the myriad decisions an illustrator makes in the creation of a text suggest where to look, what to look for, and how to feel. Although I'll separate out these three directions in the sections to follow, in truth they all work in tandem.

Where to Look. Helping the viewer decide where to look is critical because an illustrator only gets 15 to 18 opportunities to communicate an interpretation. With the average picture book at 32 pages, the illustrator chooses the moments for imaging with care. I once heard Trina Schart Hyman explain that she just couldn't bring herself to illustrate the moment in *St. George and the Dragon* (Hodges, 1984) when George thrusts his sword into the mouth of the monster and kills him. She also doesn't show the wolf in *Little Red Riding Hood* (Grimm Brothers, 1983) actually attacking the child. Instead, she shows Little Red looking shocked as the wolf leaps from the bedcovers, but the image on the next page is a comforting view of the woodcutter with rifle at the ready. Of course, what Trina does show often exceeds the 15 to 18 picture limit, for she likes to surround the facing page of print with border work and additional illustrations. She's not about to let her hours of research into the particulars of a period's art, flora, and fauna be lost. Instead, she infuses her border work with accurate details that add even more information, but do not detract from the central images she has chosen to tell the story.

Whether artists comply with or veer from the number of images typically allowed, their central illustrations stay with the action of the text. Nodelman (1988) argued "the pictures are always on the trajectory. They must be where they are and show what they show at exactly that moment; even though they stop the action, they must be an integral part of our sense of the story as a whole while we read it" (p. 248). Still, staying on the trajectory sometimes means that some images are more important than others. For example, in *Pink and Say*, Patricia Polacco (1995) tells of two boys, one black and one white, who become friends during the Civil War. The European American boy, Say, has once touched Mr. Lincoln's hand, and Pink and his African American mother touch Say's hand in wonder at being so close to a president they admire.

When the boys are later captured and dragged off to the infamous prison at Andersonville, they reach for each other with hands stretched out even as they are being torn apart, and Pink's desperate face shows how much he wants to touch the potential of freedom and friendship once more. The first image of the reach shows adults pulling on the boys, struggling to lead them off to their separate fates. On the next page, Polacco takes us in for a close up of the hands as the boys complete their final grasp. We see more of Say this time, while Pink's hand, black on white, is literally being pulled off the page. Polacco's decision to spend two of her very few illustrations on the image of the boys' hands provides us with a moment of hope in a cruelly racist world, though it is only a moment, for Pink is hung within hours of the boys' separation while Say lives on to tell the story. Thus, the repeated view of the hands is extraordinarily effective in delivering the emotional weight of the story.

Emotional weight is often aligned with visual weight. The most famous example is Maurice Sendak's (1963) *Where the Wild Things Are*, as the pictures begin as small images surrounded by white space and grow and grow just as the land of the wild things grows, and Max's dream gets larger and larger in his mind. The wild rumpus commands not one, but three full double-page spreads, and it's clear that Sendak is saying this is the moment when the child is king, for Max is pictured swinging from trees and clearly in command as he rides the back of a wild thing with a crown on his head and scepter held high. But after the rumpus, the pictures shrink smaller and smaller in size in the face of the encroaching white space and the realistic return to home.

Another example of visual weight comes from Polacco (1990) in *Just Plain Fancy*—a tale of two Amish girls who discover an unusual egg and put it in their hen's nest. When the chick hatches, the girls name him Fancy in honor of his special qualities. But then they begin to worry, because their community places value on what is plain rather than fancy. Fearful that they will be shunned for raising something so showy, they hide Fancy in the henhouse at a community gathering. But he escapes, springs to the clothesline, and from this vantage point unfurls his tail feathers in all their magnificence. While there are several hints as to Fancy's species in the story, the double page spread of the peacock provides the visual delight we've been waiting for. And rather than being shunned, the girls are rewarded for raising a creature of such beauty.

Raising images off the page also demands our attention, especially when illustrators use two- and three-dimensional effects. In *My Name is Georgia*— the story of Georgia O'Keeffe's life—Jeanette Winter (1998) shows the artist painting a landscape that blends into the actual countryside she's painting.

But what catches our attention are the birds that fly off the dual landscape and into the white space, drawing the eye beyond the boundaries and indicating the freedom from restrictions that O'Keeffe's work represents.

Another example of dimensional effects has to do with dominance, for we often focus on larger objects. In *Piggie Pie!* (Palatini, 1995), Howard Fine shows the witch exploding in a major temper tantrum with a huge picture of her angry face in the foreground. In this portrayal, her body pushes past the illustration's border, elbowing into the surrounding white space. But then, moving left to right from this first frenetic image, we see three smaller pictures of the witch winding down and beginning to think more rationally about how she will get pigs for her pie.

Where to look has much to do with movement and time. Since pictures cannot really show movement, there are a number of illustrative conventions that provide the sensation of movement (a character is pictured running with one foot off the ground) and the passage of time (a moon outside the window shifts higher in space). In the double-page spread of the witch's tantrum in *Piggie Pie!*, the quadrupling of the witch image is not meant to show four different witches, but the same witch doing four different things. Multiplying images of characters in a variety of poses is called continuous narrative, and one of the most famous examples comes from Leo and Diane Dillon's Caldecott award-winning *Why Mosquitoes Buzz in People's Ears* (Aardema, 1975). On one page, a rabbit that hears a snake entering her underground home pricks her ears and looks cautiously back at the entrance to her warren. But the image of the rabbit's face is overlaid on a second image of a rabbit springing to life and escaping out the back door. Again, this is not a portrayal of two rabbits, but one, who sees the danger and makes a run for it. The fact that she makes her run from the left to the right also makes sense because English readers are used to letting their eyes travel in this direction.

Helping readers know where to look comes through the careful selection of images, visual weight, two- and three-dimensional effects, continuous narrative, and left-to-right movement, just to name a few techniques. Children can benefit from clear instruction in these visual conventions for they are not givens. They are learned. A book that uses almost every convention I've mentioned is *Dance*, a collaboration of Bill Jones, the dancer, and Susan Kuklin, the photographer (1998). Through her photographs, Susan communicates Bill's extraordinary energy as he twirls and twists his body into amazing shapes. Continuous narrative is a constant feature as multiple images of Bill unfold from a bend to standing stretch. Still, nothing in the book is more dramatic than the half image of Bill as he literally leaps off the page. But why would a photographer only show half a man? Because her decision demonstrates movement. And in this case, telling us where to look means turning the page for more.

What to Look For.   Illustrators not only tell us where to look, but what to look for, and they do this through a variety of techniques, some more subtle than others. Quite often they tell us through the details of their work. For example, in the Caldecott Honor Book (Andersen, 1999) *The Ugly Duckling*, the illustrator, Jerry Pinkney, redelivers this time-honored tale through realistic details. When an man of African descent rescues the ugly duckling from his trap in the ice, the man is portrayed on his knees, gently tucking the bird into the warm depths of his coat for protection. The frost on his beard and eyebrows as well as on the swan's feathers tell us just how cold it is, but the inner lining of his sheepskin coat is frost free and secure. Although the swan is frightened, it's clear that while the man's grasp is firm, it is also gentle, and the expression of compassion on his face makes us feel all the more that the duckling is safe.

Details draw the eye because they are so intriguing and packed with information. In *The Fortune-Tellers*, Trina Schart Hyman took a tale by Lloyd Alexander (1992) that came with no specifics as to setting and time, and she set the entire tale in Cameroon. The details of dress, jewelry, food, and materials as well as the minutiae of the fortune-teller's dwelling all call for a closer look. Having just returned from a visit to Cameroon to meet her son-in-law's family, Trina was no doubt fascinated by the details herself.

Indeed, her choice leads us to another important point about what illustrators subtly ask us to look for, for they are often filling their texts with personal statements. Trina, for example, pictured herself as one of the seven dwarves in *Snow White* (Grimm Brothers, 1974). In one illustration she sits behind the protagonist arranging her hair. Trina dedicated *The Fortune-Teller* (Alexander, 1992) to her grandson Michou, and the baby is pictured on both the front and back cover of the text. More recently, Trina's family is featured in her Caldecott Honor book, *A Child's Calendar.* Though John Updike (1999) wrote the poems in the text for any and all children, Trina's grandchildren, Michou and Xavier, are the stars of these illustrations.

Many illustrators put their family members, friends, and pets as well as their memories into their texts. For example, in Maurice Sendak's (1970) *In the Night Kitchen*, the New York skyline is made up of baking products and utensils that were standard in the kitchen of Sendak's youth. Indeed, this book is rife with Sendak's personal statements. In addition to comments on his mother's cooking, Sendak reveals his love of early comic art. The bakers are all Oliver Hardy, one of the two comedians in the team of Laurel and Hardy. And Sendak's admiration for Mickey Mouse is reflected in his protagonist's name, Mickey. Even the point of the book—that children want to be up, active, and in control of their world in defiance of adult-mandated bedtimes—is reflected in Sendak's annoyance with an advertisement from his youth about the Sunshine Bakers, whose motto was, "We Bake While You Sleep!" Nothing doing, Sendak implies. Children like Mickey want to be where the action is! But Sendak's artistic choices go far beyond personal statements and become highly symbolic. As Joseph and Chava Schwarcz (1991) explained, "The artistic styles, derived from comics and including pop art's insistence on the symbolic force resting within commonplace objects, are combined to great effect" (p. 199).

Looking for symbolism in images is fabulous fun, but illustrators are often muted in their messages. How would a reader know that the goblins in Sendak's (1981) *Outside Over There* are meant to recall the Dionne quintuplets? How would the reader realize that the kidnapping of Ida's sister by these very goblins and her eventual safe return is Sendak's fictional wish for the impossible recovery of the Lindbergh baby? How would a reader come to understand that the Wild Things are really metaphors for Sendak's Jewish aunts and uncles, who came to Maurice's house when he was a boy and pinched his cheeks and said he looked good enough to eat? Quite simply, a reader wouldn't, unless she or he had read one of the many biographical articles and books on Sendak (e.g., Lanes, 1980) or an essay by the artist himself (Sendak, 1993).

Thus, what to look for in illustrations is often something seen only after viewing further research. But this information used to be a lot more elusive than it is today. With the proliferation of online sites on the World Wide Web, especially illustrator home pages, as well as chat rooms dedicated to detailed discussions, teachers and children have a much stronger chance of searching out the visual symbols of story. Even without such insider information, children often have a field day ferreting out the finer details and signs. With a good pair of eyes and your encouragement, they will see the gilt faces changing in the frame of the magic mirror in *Snow White* (Grimm Brothers, 1974) as the stepmother gets more and more vindictive. They can pay close attention to the cover page of *Just Plain Fancy* (Polacco, 1990) and see the egg bounce out of a truck that is marked for exotic birds. They can ponder the portrayal of two women—the stepmother and the witch—in *Hansel and Gretel* (Grimm Brothers, 1981) and confirm their similarity. And they can witness the African American characters in Pinkney's illustrations of *The Ugly Duckling*, and attest to the fact that even in such a traditionally Eurocentric story (Andersen, 1999), the potential for viewing it with more diverse characters is not only possible, but powerful.

How to Feel.   Illustrators tell us where to look and what to look for because they want to guide us in how to feel, and they use a number of pictorial elements including size, color, shape, and line as well as varying media and artistic styles to enhance the feeling. From the very first look at a book, you get a message about its content. For example, Tom Feelings' (1995) masterpiece, *The Middle Passage*, communicates through the sheer size of the book. It's massive in its message. The somber cover shows the triangular tip of a boat packed with enslaved Africans and headed across stormy seas towards the ghostly white and waiting ship. Feelings' choice of using black and white instead of color, magnifies the serious message and reiterates the subtitle of the text: *White Ships/Black Cargo.*

In opposition, a little book often communicates a more tender message. For example, all of Beatrix Potter's books were designed to fit the size of a child's hand. A more recent book, *Grandmother Bryant's Pocket* (Martin, 1996) tells the story of a child recovering from the death of her dog. Sarah is sent to visit her grandmother, who wears a pocket tied like an apron around her waist. The book itself is the size of such a pocket, and it contains words of comfort, just as grandmother Bryant's pocket holds herbal cures. The cover illustration by Petra Mathers resembles deep blue fabric with tiny flowers stitched upon it. An oval in the center reveals a pastoral picture of Sarah leaning happily against her grandmother, and the shape is reminiscent of that of the embroidery hoop grandmother uses to stitch designs on her own pockets.

Just as the size and cover of a book reveal much of what's to come, color and lack of color helps us understand how to feel. Black and white, in addition to communicating a somber tone, can also suggest mystery. Chris Van Allsburg uses black and white for his more mysterious books such as *The Widow's Broom* (1992) and color for his brighter tales like *The Polar Express* (1985). Illustrators often mix black and white with color within a single text. For example, in *Olivia* (Falconer, 2000), all the characters are portrayed in black and white. Only Olivia is allowed her signature red. In another Caldecott

Honor book, *The Gardener* (Stewart, 1997), David Small shows the colorful but tiny protagonist standing alone in an ominously black and white railway station, sending off a cold, industrial chill. But the increasing color in this text adds warmth, as Lydia Grace creates a rooftop garden on top of her uncle's drab bakery and symbolically brings color into their lives.

Shape and line also tell us how to feel. In Yumi Heo's illustrations for *Yoshi's Feast* (Kajikawa, 2001), the lines of Yoshi's body literally undulate across the page, and the fact that the design of the text allows the print to follow the shape of Yoshi's dance makes the image even more musical. In Molly Bang's (1999) *When Sophie Gets Angry—Really, Really Angry ...*, we can tell just how angry by the thick red and orange lines that emanate off her body like waves of volcanic lava. Yet when she finally calms down, she is outlined in soft yellow, and the lines are thinner and more uniform in thickness.

Molly Bang—one of our foremost children's book illustrators—has spent a lifetime studying the effects of color, shape, and line on mood. In *Picture This* (1991), she provides a perfect art lesson in illustrating Little Red Riding Hood, showing us how the slightest shifts in pictorial elements make enormous changes in tone. Molly's choice of medium is simple—cut paper—but the meaning is significant. For example, Little Red is a small red triangle, a form that seems to suggest the shape of her cloak and its pointed hood. Her size and the fact that she is partially hidden by thick black rectangles for trees, some at a tilt, makes her seem especially vulnerable. Then Molly shows us how to make the wolf's character clear. When she changes the wolf's snout from rounded to sharp he becomes more menacing. When she makes his eye a flat red diamond, he reflects Little Red, his prey, and his sinister motives are even more evident. But the final addition of a lolling red tongue and stark white teeth against the deepening twilight of the purple background reveals just how much trouble Little Red is truly in.

Molly's use of cut paper leads us to media, for the materials an illustrator uses—watercolors, woodcuts, scratchboard, collage, photography, sculpture, drawing, and computer-generated graphics—send further signals about how we should feel. Some believe that the choice of media clearly impacts what can and cannot be communicated, for materials have their limits (Stewig, 1995). Conversely, Perry Nodelman (1988) argued, "The medium is never the message. Having chosen a medium to help them achieve the attitude they want to communicate toward their subject, artists must then use their knowledge of the various techniques ... to make the medium evoke that attitude" (p. 76). In other words, skillful artists manipulate their chosen media to accomplish their messages. Just looking at several Caldecott winners will help to make this point. Look at the detailed drawings of Chris Van Allsburg (1981) in *Jumanji*, the cut-paper miracles of David Wisniewski (1996) in *The Golem*, or the wondrous woodcuts of Mary Azarian in *Snowflake Bentley* (Martin, 1999). Or study the combination of thickly textured acrylics with mixed-media collages in David Diaz's *Smoky Night* (Bunting, 1994), and you'll understand how media can be artfully adjusted to communicate an astonishing array of images and ideas.

Just as artists choose from a range of available media to communicate a way to feel, they also select specific artistic styles, and these styles evoke emotions. The cartoon wolf wearing a straw hat in James Marshall's (1987) *Red Riding Hood* lets children know that the story will be good for a laugh. In contrast, the much more realistic wolf painted by Ed Young (1989) in *Lon Po Po* makes most young children's eyes widen in terror.

Artists also lean on historical and cultural movements in art that often come with their own conventions. For example, Paul Zelinsky's (1997) oil paintings for *Rapunzel* are beautifully reminiscent of Renaissance art and richly portray the romance of this timeless tale. Maurice Sendak used impressionism in his creation of *Mr. Rabbit and the Lovely Present* (Zolotow, 1962), and the spontaneity of light and color loans itself well to a young girl's desire to find her mother a unique gift. Leo and Diane Dillon studied eighteenth-century Japanese woodcuts in a form called ukiyo-e to create *The Tale of the Mandarin Ducks* (Paterson, 1990), and the supposed limitations of block printing still manage to reveal a love with no restrictions. Finally, Carmen Lomas Garza (1999) used her understanding of papel picado, cut-paper art from Mexico, to create *Magic Windows/Ventanas Mágicas* and allow her readers to press against the clean edges of the paper to unfold an unparalleled view of the artist's studio, life, and culture.

Selecting an artistic style meshes with other artistic choices. In his most recent book, *Zathura*, Chris Van Allsburg (2002) chose to use striking surrealism to finally reveal what happened to the Budwing boys after they ran out of the park with the game, Jumanji. Young Danny, much persecuted by his older brother, Walter, finds another game tucked underneath the first, and it looks much more intriguing than a game of jungle animals, for Zathura is a planet in outer space. With Danny's first toss of the dice, everything starts to go awry, and Walter joins in, trying to put a stop to the mayhem. But there is no stopping it, and meteors crash through the roof, a robot goes on the rampage, and long-tailed, scale-covered pirates invade.

Surrealism is an art form that emerged in the 20th century, and it's designed to deliver distorted images, oddly real and yet irrational. What better form for *Zathura*, a space age game that turns the Budwing boys' world off kilter. When Walter loses his gravity to a roll of the dice, he lies pinned to the ceiling, and his distorted view matches the theme of a world turned upside down. But Van Allsburg's choice to combine surrealism with black and white drawings adds even more to the mystery, for his finely detailed pencil work is reminiscent of old photographs as well as more modern science fiction movies. Thus, the black and white, the old and new, the real and the surreal combine to help the reader feel the bizarre antics of this time-warped adventure combined with an old-fashioned tale of two brothers who come together in new ways.

As we study the images created by illustrators—their choices of color, shape and line, as well as varying media and artistic styles—we fall into story just as the Budwing boys tumble into another world. But how much we see depends on what we have learned. Thus, you need to talk with your children about artistic techniques, for such knowledge enhances the view. And prepared with an eye toward the potential in art, your children can then turn to their own creations, demonstrating literary engagement through their personal artistic visions.

Creating Images

The picture books we discuss in this chapter come with their own images, but many books don't. True, the visuals are in the imagery of the words, but it's up to the reader to see his or her own vision of text while being guided by those words. However, envisioning words is only the beginning of interpretation through the visual arts, for children also need opportunities to compose their own art as well as critique it. In the sections to follow, I concentrate on how children envision, compose, and critique their own images, and although I concentrate here on how children create pictures for books without illustrations, it's important to remember that children can take what they've seen in picture books and design their own original images.

Envisioning Words

The first process, envisioning, is often associated with comprehension. Here the reader calls on his or her bank of stored visual imagery in order to understand the words on the page. Whether the image comes from personal experience, more distanced background knowledge, or is created on the spot to illustrate a character or concept, mental imagery helps the reader envision what's being said. As Keene and Zimmerman (1997) suggested, good readers "take possession of the books they read by creating, being aware of, and describing their own mental images" (p. 135). As a comprehension strategy, elaborated images—rich in detail—are the most effective.

One way for you to begin is to ask your children to consider what they see in their literary response journals, to note in writing what they sense of the images, and then bring their ideas to group for literary discussion. Such assignments help children analyze the text more closely, and see where they have a vision of the text and where they do not. And these considerations can run from the straightforward to the highly sophisticated.

On the straightforward side of things, two teachers in one of my classes, Sybil Hall and Stephanie Brown, read *Because of Winn-Dixie* (DiCamillo, 2000) to their 6-year-olds. They found that the children loved the story, but there were places where they couldn't envision the scene. For example, in initially reading the section where Winn-Dixie runs frantically about the trailer in fear of the thunderstorm, some of the children thought he must be outside. They weren't sure of the meaning of the word "trailer," and thought Winn was running back and forth from a house to a recreational camper. But if he was outside, how did he leap up on the preacher in bed? Expressing their confusion, the children asked Sybil to read the text again, but before she did she brought in photos off the Internet of trailer homes, and she and the children discussed the layout of the bedrooms. With this additional information, they were able to see Winn-Dixie's frenetic run from Opal's to the preacher's bedroom within the confines of the trailer.

Turning to more sophisticated envisioning, a sixth-grade teacher, Jessica Whitelaw, read *The Giver* by Lois Lowry (1993) to her 11- and 12-year-old students. In this beautiful text, a young boy named Jonas lives in a Utopian community where "Sameness" is cherished. However, he is chosen to be the "Receiver of Memory"—to hold the visions of all past times—and studying the memories allows him to see an alternative to "Sameness." To help her students understand Jonas's society, Jessica gave them multiple opportunities to think about and envision different ways of organizing a community. They started by looking at the word "Utopia," for none of her students were familiar with the concept. They first looked at the dictionary definition: "an ideal place or state with perfect laws." They explored its origins in ancient Greece where the word has a dual meaning: perfect place/no place. They then discussed the implications of this dichotomy and asked, "Could a perfect society really exist?" As a class, they listed out the features of their own utopia—envisioning a place where the values included: "family," "love," "fun," "humor," "brains," "books," "kindness," "dance," "peace," and "my dog." The list provided something tangible to revisit as they read *The Giver*, and Jessica encouraged her students to go up and add new thoughts as the unit progressed, which they often did.

Thus, envisioning words runs from the straightforward (e.g., "trailer") to the complex (e.g., "Utopia"), and you can encourage such envisionments to help your children see a text. As Jeffrey Wilhelm (1996) argued, "reading *is* seeing"(p. 467). Having studied young adolescents with a history of reading difficulty, Wilhelm well knew the pain that children suffer when they can't visualize what they're reading. Once, as he was questioning one of the seventh-grade boys in his study about his interpretation of a text, Tommy exclaimed, "I can't think about it, talk about it, do anything about it, if I can't see it!" (p. 476). But as Wilhelm made clear, and I concur, envisioning stands a better chance when children are encouraged to compose their own images.

Composing Images

Composing involves students responding to written texts through their own art. While "envisioning" implies the images in the head, "composing" means getting these pictures on paper. As Anderson, Kauffman, and Short (1998) explained, "composing art involves constructing meaning through 'authoring' a piece of art" (p. 148). A variety of researchers have explored this process, asking students to "Sketch to Stretch" (Short & Harste, 1996) or create more complex artistic representations (Wilhelm, 1996). Enciso (1996) is known for developing the Symbolic Representation Interview (SRI) "which gives children a way to both talk about and depict their engagement with a story" (p. 180). One aspect of the SRI involves creating character and reader cutouts which children "manipulate . . . to demonstrate the movement, relationships, images, and ideas they experienced" (p. 181). In this process, students make decisions in the creation of a piece of art in terms of both the ideas it represents as well as in the practical execution of the piece. As students create visual art to respond to text, they are essentially creating a new text.

In Sybil Hall and Stephanie Brown's class, a 6-year-old girl named Ellianna decided to create a representation of Winn-Dixie running around in the thunderstorm. After seeing pictures of trailers and discussing the layout of the bedrooms in her group, Ellianna now understood that the dog was running back and forth from one end of the trailer to another. In the top illustration of

FIG. 7.1.   Children's Visual Art From *Because of Winn-Dixie*.

Fig. 7.1, you can see Ellianna's portrayal of panic. She explained to her teachers, "When you read the book over again, it made more sense. Winn-Dixie was not supposed to be outside, so I drew him inside. Here's Winn-Dixie, and now he is running over there."

In Ellianna's illustration, the trailer is surrounded by black sky, gray clouds, heavy rain, and flashes of lightening all around. Winn-Dixie moves against the typical left-to-right movement in most picture books, and his right-to-left dash shows his confusion in the storm. The tripling of the dog adds time and motion. As Ellianna explained, "I showed Winn-Dixie three times so you could see he's running." Running, indeed. As Winn takes off from Opal's room, he gives one look backwards, but the direction of his ears signal that he's heading out the door. In the second picture of Winn-Dixie, he's in between bedrooms, possibly in a hallway, and his ears again give clues about his panic. It's almost as if he's just heard another crash of thunder, and his ears stand straight up in terror. In the third picture he's just landed—"sproi-i-ing"—on the preacher in bed, and though his ears are still up in the air, they tip down as if looking for comfort in the storm.

Ellianna's composition shows deep envisionment, communicating the heart-racing horror Winn-Dixie felt, especially in the continuous narrative of drawing three dogs on the page. The shifting of the ears is yet another indication of Winn's anxiety as is the hair raised on his back, which stands up taller with each image. While the white space of the trailer against the black of the storm would seem to indicate some comfort, the ears signal that it is not the sights but the sounds of the storm that are driving Winn-Dixie to distraction. And the nearly identical forms of Opal and the preacher show they are equally shocked by Winn's actions. As Stephanie and Sybil wrote, "When Ellianna drew this image, we had been studying visualization for a couple of months. It just shows that time, practice, discussion, and rich literature are the key to success!"

Just as children can create images of singular scenes, they can also capture the themes of an entire book or dynamic shifts of character in even more symbolic representations. Another teacher in my class, Kathryn Buhler, read *Because of Winn-Dixie* to her 4th graders, and she provided multiple opportunities for them to create their own images from the text. She began by asking them to sketch character portrayals, but their initial work was relatively basic. She then decided to demonstrate with her own artwork, and although Kathryn is very artistic, she made her rendering "non-artistic" because she "didn't want to shut them down" by modeling too much talent. However, even with her plain portrayal, what wasn't elementary was her description of how she thought about her art in terms of the color, symbolism, size, and placement of objects within a character outline that would significantly illustrate that character's traits.

After her demonstration, her 9- and 10-year old children went back to work, but again, their art was somewhat static. Still, one of her children, Sasha, showed promise in her presentation—less in terms of the art than in the thought behind the art. The children had an extended conversation about Sasha's picture, and began to see the potential in the careful selection and placement of objects. Based on the group conversation, Kathryn decided to have them now work in small clusters to create a collaborative "group vision" of the character of their choice.

One group decided to demonstrate the shift in the preacher's personality from the beginning to the end of the story. In the bottom half of Fig. 7.1, you can see their portrait, which the children created with construction paper, drawing materials, magic markers, and brass brads for holding specific pieces together. The brads turned out to be especially important, for in deciding to attach the preacher's U-shaped mouth on his face with a brad, the children could show him in two emotional states—unsmiling at first and then smiling at the end of the tale. They also used a brad to hook a turtle shell to his tie and show how "the preacher is unhappy" at the beginning of the story. Yet, they could swing the shell away to reveal his later personality. Thus the children's creation is movable art, which I've tried to capture in Fig. 7.1 by showing the two versions of the preacher that can be achieved by shifting pieces with the brads.

When the preacher's turtle shell is on, the children said that his stomach is his "lonely place," for he is in pain over Opal's "mother with beer." His heart is small in size, and "there is only room for Opal, the church, and Winn-Dixie in the preacher's heart." In the second view, however, the children used the brads to shift the preacher's unhappy face into a smile as well as move the turtle shell away to disclose a more optimistic interior. Though his lonely place is still there, it is smaller, and the list of things he can hold in his much larger heart now includes Opal's mother. As the children explained, "now it's easier for him to talk about her a little." Finally, the children kept the brads as a constant in the preacher's eyes in both portrayals because they symbolized "his glimmer of hope that his wife will come back someday."

All this with a few art materials! Still, looking closely at the art along with the children's talk is where the action is. Indeed, Kathryn felt, "Children at this age are just learning about deep discussion, and sometimes they can stray from the topic. But art can serve as an essential prop to focus the children's discussion. They can agree and disagree, but they stay with a central train of thought. I don't think their conversation would have been as deep without the prop. Making the character of the preacher visual, makes it more powerful." The triple use of the brads makes this point. Without the children's verbal account, a viewer who knew the book might be able to look at their preacher and understand the shifting smile and perhaps even see the potential in moving the turtle shell on or away from the preacher. But the brads as a "glimmer of hope" might have slipped by unseen without the children's explanation. In addition, the children's use of the brads shows how generative art materials can be, for they might serve one purpose here but an entirely different one elsewhere. The enlargement of the preacher's heart as well as the additional space for "mother" therein, might also have been missed without focused discussion. Thus, children's articulation of their artistic creations is essential, and it leads us to the final process in literary interpretation through the visual arts: critique.

Critiquing Images

Anderson, Kauffman, and Short (1998) explained, "Interpreting art involves constructing meaning through 'reading' illustrations and artwork" (p. 148). Typically, this process refers to opportunities for students to interpret illustrations in published texts—in other words, the artwork of professional children's book illustrators. However, here I am concentrating on students involved in critiquing their own artwork as well as the artwork of other students in the class. In responding to textual images, reflection is essential, for it is in the process of rethinking that ideas are sorted, synthesized, and thus, interpreted.

Still, any kind of critique implies risk, so the wise teacher often demonstrates initial forays into critique using artwork from sources other than the children's. An 8th grade teacher, Shannon Suedkamp, took a risk in showing her young teens her own artwork. She wanted to demonstrate how envisioning and composing images helped her to get to deeper levels in text interpretation, and this was especially important to her group, for many read far below grade level.

She began by showing two images she had drawn. The first was a black and white, deeply shadowed rendering of a man writing at his desk, and the second was a simpler picture of a turtle. You can view the first image in Fig. 7.2. Shannon started the conversation by reviewing the meaning of metaphor and simile, and then, "using the images on the overhead as a catalyst," she asked them "to explore how a person could be like a turtle." Her students' "ideas came fairly easily, but were pretty basic in their interpretation." Shannon then read them the first two chapters of *Because of Winn-Dixie* that reveal the

Shannon Suedkamp's portrait of the preacher

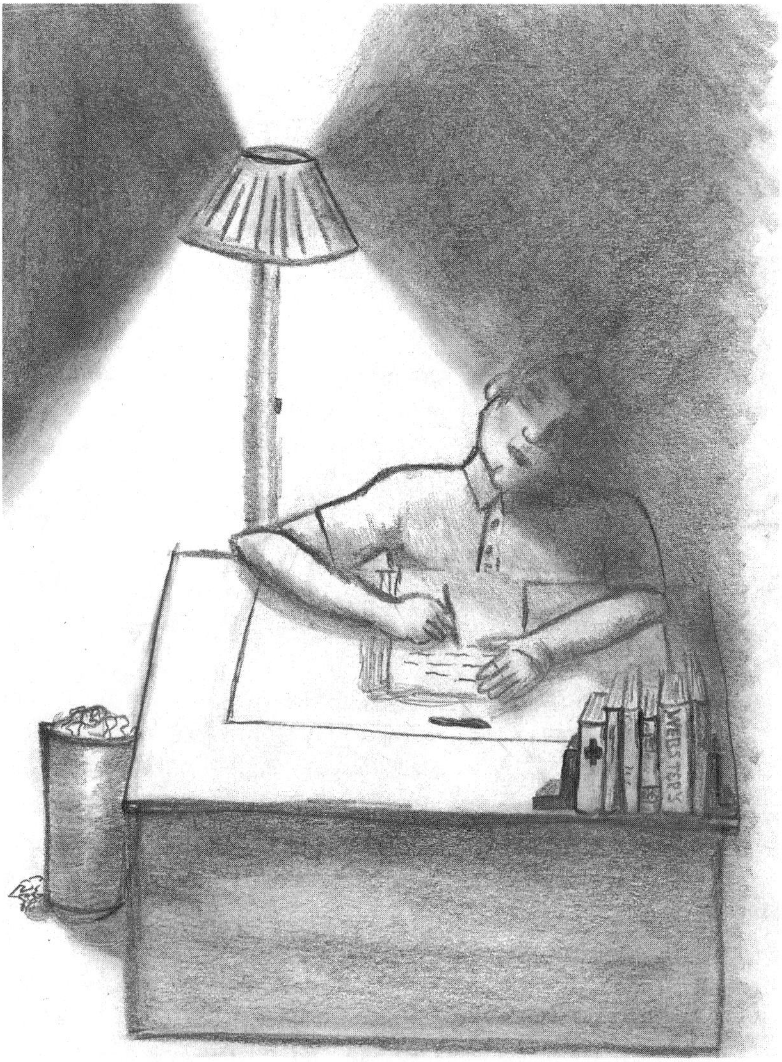

FIG. 7.2.   A Teacher's Visual Art From *Because of Winn-Dixie*.

symbolism of the preacher sitting at his desk, writing his sermons, and hiding his loneliness like a turtle in his shell. After the reading, she put her first picture back on the overhead, and her students jumped right in:

Mike: So it's the Dad who's the turtle. My dad is like that. Only sometimes he is more like a snapping turtle.

Rosa: Yeah, Opal says he keeps pulling his head in and out of his shell.

Aaron: That's why you drew the light in the picture that way. Right, Ms. Suedkamp? It's his shell.

Maria: That's not all though. Look at his desk. It's hiding him too. And his back is all hunched over like he's protecting himself.

Ahmed: I think it's his work. Opal says that he is always being a preacher, or preparing to preach. His work is what he uses to keep Opal out.

Aaron: Yeah, but—[Aaron leaps up and goes to the overhead where he traces the lines of the shadow.] Look at the picture. See how dark it is. Which room would you go in to talk to someone? One that the lights were on or ones that are dark? Light, right? It's like a sign to other people to stay out when you sit alone in the dark.

Rosa: I do that. I turn off the lights if I want to be alone. You know how he looks like he's cut in half. [She motions to Aaron to point to the division she's describing.] When you do that, you feel that way, like you are cut in half.

Ms. Suedkamp: From the text, what could be some reasons that the preacher feels like he's cut in half, or that he hides inside a shell?

Ahmed: He's hiding because his wife left him.

Mike: Because his daughter reminds him of his wife, I'll bet. My dad does that with my half sister.

Maria: I think he'll come out of his shell. Something will happen to the girl and he'll have to.

Ahmed: No, I bet the dog does something.

Aaron: Yeah, totally. Like the title, *Because of Winn-Dixie*. [He runs his finger over the title on the cover of his book.] He's going to have to stop writing all this stuff and come out of his shell.

It's clear from the conversation that the students' level of critique is enhanced by the combination of literature with art. The illustrations started them thinking, and then the text sparked more specific understandings. But these understandings evolved and expanded even further as the students began to notice links between the symbols of the illustration and the metaphor of the turtle as well as to experiences in their own lives. The darkened room, the cut of the lamplight, the shield of the preacher's desk, and the endless writing responsibilities (with a trashcan full of discarded drafts) that create a second shield are all signs of how far the preacher has drawn into his shell. Even the bend of his back signals his self-protection.

This is what Marjorie Siegel (1995) stressed in her discussions of transmediation—"the act of translating meanings from one sign system to another" (p. 455). Siegel argued that moving among alternative sign systems encourages the learner to see the commonalities in different expressive modes, but since the commonalities are not givens, they must be explored and justified, which asks the learner to work at a more metaphorical level. Thus, "crossing the gap between different *sign systems* is . . . a generative process." As a result, "juxtaposing different ways of knowing . . . [is] a way to position students as knowledge makers and reflective enquirers" (pp. 472–473). And this is the stance that Shannon's students are taking.

The idea of the creative power of transmediation came through clearly in Jessica Whitelaw's class as well, as her 6th grade students began to construct their own visual representations of *The Giver* (Lowry, 1993). To heighten her students' ability to cross between sign systems, Jessica asked them to create similes and metaphors that illustrated characters and concepts in the novel. David, an 11-year-old who often saw intriguing connections among texts, created one of the illustrations that sparked the most discussion. For his representation, David chose to look closely at the early beginnings of Jonas's assignment as the Receiver of Memory, especially when the memories moved from a thrilling sled ride to more devastating scenes of hunger, pain, and war. Jonas comes to realize that as he receives remembrances from the Giver, he alleviates some of the weight that the Giver carries as the sole keeper of these memories. At the same time, he realizes that he alone will have to carry these painful scenes once the Giver is gone. If Jonas is unwilling to take on the responsibility of holding these memories, they will escape into and affect the entire community.

David's attention to the burden the Giver carried was revealed in his illustration of Atlas carrying the world on his back (see the top illustration in Fig. 7.3). Jessica explained, "His artwork demonstrates both a close and careful reading of *The Giver* as well as his attention to our recent unit in Social

David's comparison of the burden Jonas has to carry with Atlas carrying the world on his back.

Riley's cut-paper illustration of the final scene of the novel.

FIG. 7.3.   Children's Visual Art From *The Giver.*

247

Studies class on Greek myths." When David brought his drawing to the group, the following discussion ensued:

> **David:**   Jonas is like Atlas having to carry the weight of the world because Jonas has to carry all of the memories of the world since the beginning of time—war, the bad things and good things. And he was never brought up with the bad things.
>
> **Ms. Whitelaw:**   Can you tell us a bit about Atlas?
>
> **David:**   Atlas is a man in Greek legend. . . I think he did something wrong and the gods said that you have to carry the weight of the world for the rest of your life.
>
> **Bailey:**   I agree, because you're right about Jonas having to—He has to hold everything and once he's done, he's gonna feel so weighted. He's gonna feel like the world is on his shoulders and—
>
> **Riley:**   Like the Giver. . .
>
> **Ms. Whitelaw:**   What about the way the carrier of the world *feels* in this picture?
>
> **Bailey:**   He's unhappy. It's special. But you know, still, it's exhausting. And he knows he has a job to do.
>
> **Chelsea:**   I think another thing is—He's bowing down to the weight of the memories. Exhaustion. But still knows that he can't sit down or lay down, or apply for release [The community term for euthanasia.] He still knows he has stuff to do.
>
> **Ms. Whitelaw:**   How does this relate to the end of the novel?
>
> **David:**   Well, I think this relates to the end of the book 'cause he'd want to escape. Jonas wanted to escape, too. He didn't feel like the memories were right, but if he left, the memories would be released on to the whole community and so—
>
> **Bailey:**   Everybody would share the weight, which would make him feel better about it.
>
> **David:**   So, I think escaping was good, but somewhat bad too. But now people will know the memories. Atlas would want to escape holding the world, just like Jonas would want to escape from holding all the memories. The same as Atlas, he wanted to escape holding the world. (Whitelaw & Wolf, 2001, pp. 62)

In this discussion, Jessica was struck with how the talk switched back and forth between Jonas, the Giver, and Atlas. The word "he" was used almost interchangeably to refer to all three characters when talking about "carrying the weight," for the students didn't seem to feel it necessary to distinguish who they were referring to every time. As Jessica drew the students' attention back to David's illustration to look at the details in the face, they recognized the emotional "exhaustion" Jonas felt as well as his personal desire to "escape" the responsibility. But then they debated what would happen to the community if Jonas did leave. They realized that the sheer weight of Jonas's decision made it hard to know whether to stay or go.

While Jessica was impressed with David's metaphor and her students' conversation, she felt they only briefly looked at David's art. She wrote, "I had to draw their attention to the facial expression, and their discussion included no comments about Atlas's awkward position—his bent back and ungainly grip, the size of the world on his shoulders. Thus, I felt that if my students were going to go even deeper in their analysis they had to know more about art."

Jessica's observation makes great sense, for if students are provided with technical vocabulary as well as shown the techniques that artists use, they will be better equipped to critique both professional and personal art with perception. Indeed, in teaching *The Giver*, Jessica saw the training of the novel's protagonist to see the memories as a metaphor for the training she needed to provide to her students to help them see the value of working and reworking, creating and critiquing their own artistic representations. She wrote:

> Similar to the way Jonas received training from the Giver to fine tune his own capacity to see beyond, I felt that my students could benefit from more instruction in the elements of art in order to hone their own visual skills. To enhance the depth and quality of response, we needed to build a shared language for dialogue and a common framework for interpretation, which we did by examining line, shape/form, value, texture, space, and color. With a common language in place, we then looked at Molly Bang's (1991) *Picture This: Perception and Composition*. Recalling the elements of art previously discussed, we studied the author's choices in color, shape, line, value, and positioning.
>
> We then concentrated on Bang's process of reworking, making changes and adapting the results to craft her illustrations. I emphasized the simplicity of Bang's visual representation of Little Red Riding Hood as well as the achieved power in this simplicity. I then asked my students to create their own cut-paper creations (Enciso, 1996) based upon their interpretive ideas from *The Giver*. I wanted them to pay particularly close attention to the elements of art we had discussed as well as how they positioned their shapes on the page, reminding them of the power of overall simplicity. After completing their construction paper illustrations, the students composed an accompanying paragraph explaining their artistic choices.

Thus, Jessica felt that helping students generate critique of professional illustrators' art helps to prepare them to critique their own.

In the cut-paper creations that followed, the students were not only able to represent scenes from *The Giver* that they found personally memorable, but they were also able to explain their artistic decisions in detail. Riley was particularly intrigued with Jonas's decision to leave the community with his baby brother, Gabriel. The baby had not been thriving well, and was marked for release, the community's term for euthanasia. Rather than release his brother to such a fate, Jonas feels the time has come to go. He and Gabriel escape on a bicycle, traveling for many days through harsh weather and rough terrain. At the end of their journey, they come to a lighted place of hope, and while it might be the Elsewhere Jonas is seeking, Lois Lowry, the author, doesn't make it clear that the ending for Jonas and Gabriel will be a happy one. Still, Riley saw the final scene of the novel as hopeful. His cut-paper creation appears in the bottom half of Fig. 7.3, and in his accompanying caption, Riley wrote:

> In my symbolic representation, many of the symbols stand for more than one thought. The red oval at the bottom of my picture represents a bicycle being ridden by the purple triangle, Jonas, and the pink circle, Gabriel. The red oval signifies sturdiness and being strong enough to handle the task of a long journey. Purple usually means wisdom and courage, two of Jonas's traits, and pink stands for calmness and babies. The black triangles symbolize the trees in the forest that Jonas rides through. These objects also represent the obstacles in Jonas's path to Elsewhere. The yellow squares going across the screen symbolize the shining path to freedom. In the upper right hand corner, the shiny rectangle [which Riley illustrated with tin foil] stands for Jonas's final destination, a city in Elsewhere. The brightness of the paper shows the importance of the object to Jonas. Finally, the colorful rectangles at the top of the picture represent life out of Sameness, which is unpredictable and full of great dreams and expectations.

Riley's interpretation is multi-layered and complex. By transferring his knowledge into visual symbols, he was able to have his shapes stand for more than one idea. For example, black triangles represent trees on the journey to Elsewhere as well as obstacles in Jonas's path. As Siegel (1995) explained, "transmediation . . . increases students' opportunities to engage in generative and reflective thinking because learners must invent a connection between the two sign systems, as the connection does not exist a priori" (p. 455).

Riley also added the element of texture to his paper cutout. In addition to the construction paper Jessica provided, Riley found a piece of shiny tin foil to use at the top of his creation, reflecting his positive outlook on the end of the novel. The switch in medium, moving from the colored paper to the foil, suggests that Jonas will reach Elsewhere and that it is a desirable place. Even Riley's use of the construction paper was uniquely symbolic—the yellow squares for the "the shining path to freedom" and the "colorful rectangles" for "life out of Sameness, which is unpredictable and full of great dreams and expectations." Thus, Riley manipulated the medium to expand on the meaning of the text and create an image that captured the hope ahead.

Riley's insightful explanation shows the power of personal critique, and taking his work to the group for discussion gave him more ideas for how to refine his composition. While it is essential for students to envision and compose, literary uptake through the visual arts is incomplete without critique. As Jessica explained, "By drawing attention to the elements of art, my students were able to see the many imaginative possibilities for visual response."

Summary

In this chapter, I showcase literary interpretation through the visual arts. I begin by taking a close look at picture books, analyzing the relationship of pictures and words. The words *say*, the pictures *show*, but together the verbal and the visual suggest what neither could do alone. As David Lewis (2001) explained, "The words are pulled through the pictures and the pictures are brought into focus by the words" (p. 48). I then explore how images "quicken" a text (Sendak, 1988), for illustrators choose their moments carefully, giving more visual weight to some aspects of a text than others. Through a combination of artistic choices including dimensional effects, time and movement, detail, personal statements, symbolism, size, shape, line, color, media, and artistic styles, illustrators help the viewer see where to look, what to look for, and how to feel.

In the Caldecott Honor book, *Olivia* is entranced by a Degas painting of ballerinas on stage. As she stares up at the painting, the narrator of the story wonders what in the world Olivia is thinking about. Knowing Olivia, a child with real artistic flair, she could be thinking about the artist's technique, the brush strokes, the interplay of light and dark that shines on the dancers in their white tutus. But the next page reveals Olivia's thoughts in a full-page picture—for she sees herself on stage in her own white tutu, with a tiara on her head and her leg flung back in an artful arabesque. And when she later sees an abstract by Jackson Pollack, she tries his technique on her bedroom wall.

Just as the images from professional artists lead Olivia to her own imaginative creations, literature with and without pictures can lead children to their own visual interpretations. Still, they need opportunities for thinking about art, and you can provide it. Through the three processes of envisioning, composing, and critiquing, your children will come to understand how the combination of words and art enhances not only what they see, but how they feel.

BOOKS FOR THE PROFESSIONAL

Bang, M. (1991). *Picture this: Perception & composition.* Boston: Little, Brown. Molly Bang is a gifted illustrator whose picture books are often award winners. In this small but power-packed book, she explores artistic choices and how they affect our emotions. By carefully adjusting shape, size, line, and color, her alternative versions of Little Red Riding Hood offer a perfect introduction to art for both children and teachers alike.

Kiefer, B. Z. (1995). *The potential of picturebooks: From visual literacy to aesthetic understanding.* Englewood Cliffs, NJ: Merrill. When I teach classes on the art of the picturebook, this is the text I assign. A professor at Teachers College Columbia, Barbara Kiefer not only clearly explains the intricacies of illustrated children's literature, but she also offers a unique exploration of how children talk about picture books.

Marcus, L. S. (2002). *Ways of telling: Conversations on the art of the picture book.* New York: Dutton. Leonard Marcus is one of our best children's book biographers. In this delightful new volume, he interviews fourteen famous illustrators—including Mitsumasa Anno, Robert McCloskey, Jerry Pinkney, Maurice Sendak, and Charlotte Zolotow—as they share insights into their artistic processes and motivations. This book, as well as Marcus' own "picturebooks," *Side by Side* (2001) and *A Caldecott Celebration* (1998b), really deliver the stories behind the art.

Nodelman, P. (1988). *Words about pictures: The narrative art of children's picture books.* Athens, GA: University of Georgia Press. In this brilliant book, Perry Nodelman demonstrates the interplay of the verbal and visual aspects of picture books. His central argument is that rather than "simple" books, picture books are marked by "childlike sophistication," and the value of analyzing them with children is immeasurable.

Chapter Touchstone Texts

DiCamillo, Kate. (2000). *Because of Winn-Dixie.* Cambridge, MA: Candlewick. See chapter 6 for an annotation of this image-filled novel.

Falconer, Ian. (2000). *Olivia.* New York: Atheneum. A Caldecott Honor book, Olivia is an irrepressible pig with a flair for fashion design and artistic expression. After a visit to the museum, where she studies Degas and Jackson Pollack, she creates a copy of the latter's drip painting on her bedroom wall. Following a brief time out, Olivia has a bath, a meal, and is then tucked in with several bedtime stories read by her loving, but worn-out mother.

Lowry, Lois. (1993). *The Giver.* Boston: Houghton Mifflin. Chosen to become the next Receiver of Memory because of his "Capacity to See Beyond," Jonas must leave his childhood behind. He is selected, singled out from his community—a seemingly Utopian society that has rejected choice, color, pain, and even love in order to achieve "Sameness." He begins his training with the Giver, who transmits memories of the past through visual scenes. Through these experiences, Jonas comes to see his community in new ways, and comes to perceive alternatives to "Sameness" in the possibilities of Elsewhere.

Recommended Tradebooks for the Visual Arts

Feelings, Tom. (1995). *The middle passage: White ships/black cargo.* New York: Dial. This book is a masterpiece, visually detailing the crossing of enslaved Africans to America in illustrations that took almost 20 years to make. It won both the Coretta Scott King Award and a special commendation from the Jane Addams Book Award. I was fortunate enough to see Tom speak at our local library, where he explained the long journey he had undertaken in the book's creation and related his own mother's reaction to the text once it was completed—slowly turning the pages and rhythmically beating her fist against her heart.

Giff, Patricia Reilly. (2002). *Pictures of Hollis Woods.* New York: Wendy Lamb Books/ Random House. A Newbery Honor in 2003, this lyrical tale travels with Hollis, a young girl who is able to find a family and her place in the world through art. Indeed, her pictures help her understand that, ". . . sometimes what you see is so deep in your head you're not even sure of what you're seeing. But when it's down there on paper, and you look at it, really look, you'll see the way things are."

Greenberg, Jan, & Jordan, Sandra. (2002). *Action Jackson*, illustrated by Robert Andrew Parker. New York: Harry N. Abrams. This gloriously active book captures the vibrant artistic technique of Jackson Pollack. The text won an Honor Award from the Robert F. Sibert Informational Book Award for distinguished informational books for children.

Park, Linda Sue. (2001). *A single shard.* New York: Clarion. As the first Korean American to win the Newbery, Linda Sue Park delivers a fascinating story of early Korea. The young protagonist, Tree Ear, is an orphan apprenticed to Min, the village's master potter. On a trip to deliver two of Min's superb vases to an important emissary, he is robbed by thieves who hurl the vases from a cliff. Tree Ear considers making the same leap in shame, but instead retrieves a single shard from one of the vases and continues on his way. Rather than reject the shard, the emissary sees the quality of the artistic work. Like celadon pottery, Park's prose shows exquisite clarity and craft, and her helpful Author's Note, which explores the history of celadon pottery, only enhances the tale.

Winter, Jonah. (2002). *Frida*, illustrated by Ana Juan. New York: Scholastic. The life of Frida Kahlo is presented in this extraordinary picture book. Overcoming both illness and injury, Frida is a symbol for women whose lives are saved by art. The illustrations by Ana Juan are stunning— reminiscent of Kahlo's work, yet rich with original images.

8

Interpreting Literature Through Drama

My mom: "When are you going to stop moping and go out and play?"

Me: "<u>Who</u> am I going to play with?"

My mom: "I see lots of kids down there. All colors and sizes. They look great to me."

Me: "But I don't <u>know</u> any of those kids...."

My mom: "Well, you never will if you don't go out. Kids won't come to our door just seeking out the famous and beautiful Elana Rose Rosen."

Me: "I didn't say they would."

My mom: "Elana, please! Did I say <u>you</u> said it? And don't start to cry! I have too much to do to get involved in scenes with you. I have to get us settled. Find a job. Get ready for my courses."

Me: "Just leave me here alone then."

My mom: "But it breaks my heart to see you standing on that scooter, moping."

Me: "I'm not moping."

Finally my mom came right up behind me and put her hands on the handlebars and pushed me and the scooter out our front door and down the hall and into the elevator and out the elevator and through the lobby. Then she gave me a big push that sent me out the front doors . . .

—Williams (1993, pp. 2-3)

In raising the curtain on this final chapter that features literary interpretation through drama, it's symbolic that the spotlight shines on the "famous and beautiful Elana Rose Rosen"—the heroine of Vera B. Williams' extraordinary novel, *Scooter.* Elana is perfect because she is such a dramatic soul. Even more important, she's an honest one, and drama is all about truth, or at least,

255

as Constantin Stanislavski—an actor and artistic director of the Moscow Art Theatre—explained, imagined truth:

> The actor says to himself:
>
> "All these properties, make-ups, costumes, the scenery, the publicness of the performance, are lies. I know they are lies, I know I do not need any of them. But *if* they were true, then I would do this and this, and I would behave in this manner and this way towards this and this event."
>
> I came to understand that creativeness begins from that moment when in the soul and imagination of the actor there appears the magical, creative *if* . . . that is, the imagined truth which the actor can believe as sincerely and with greater enthusiasm than he believes practical truth, just as the child believes in the existence of its doll and of all life in it and around it. From the moment of the appearance of *if* the actor passes from the plane of actual reality into the plane of another life, created and imagined by himself. Believing in this life, the actor can begin to create. (Cole & Chinoy, 1970, pp. 494–495)

Still, such creativity is rare, for drama, even more than the visual arts, is all too often missing from the classroom stage and relegated to behind-the-scenes work in gifted and talented classes and after-school programs. Classroom teachers feel pressed by time, space, and curricular constraints, especially with the focus on state-wide and nation-wide assessment, and when pressed, they tend to let drama go.

Even more problematic is the fact that teachers often feel unprepared to take on an art form that demands a certain level of expertise. As Betty Wagner (1998) pointed out, "Since most school districts do not have a team of drama specialists, the future of drama in the classroom lies increasingly with regular classroom teachers, most of whom have never had even a course in educational drama" (p. 10). Yet, the greatest reluctance on the part of teachers is the over-inflated idea of drama as THE PLAY—words in bold on a marquee—with scripts to be prepared, lines to be learned, sets and costumes designed, invitations sent out, and parents and other audience members in attendance. No wonder you might avoid it! But let me emphasize just how accessible drama can be. While there are certainly wonderful possibilities in productions, working with drama in your classroom will be less daunting if you place more stress on dramatic moments—opportunities for smaller interpretive scenes and scenarios.

For example, let's look at a short scene in *Scooter* where Elana Rose Rosen and her mother have another altercation. In this scene, Elana is enraged over the fact that a young friend of hers won't be able to participate in Field Day because there is no somersaulting contest, even though it seemed to be advertised as an event. Petey has been practicing his rolls all summer and is sure to be heartbroken. Elana's mother tries to argue with the officials, but to no avail, and Elana storms up the stadium steps and wedges herself tightly into an opening in the stadium's back wall. As much as she is sympathetic, Elana's mother is not about to allow her daughter's histrionics to ruin Field Day for the other children, especially those on her relay team. She marches up the steps after Elana, pulls her out of her corner, and drags her down:

> She said I <u>had</u> to be in the Field Day, especially after I practically broke my head practicing on that scooter. "You can't go through life sulking," she said.
>
> "I'm <u>not</u> sulking," I told her. And I said that I liked it up there where you could see everything and that if Petey couldn't be in <u>his</u> race I certainly wouldn't...
>
> "No sacrifices, please," she said. It wouldn't help Petey one bit! If I cared to get off my high horse and look, she would show me Petey running along the bleachers and he was just fine. She reminded me there was Nanette, who was my guest, to think of, too. She braided my hair and pinned it back up tight. I screamed.
>
> "That hurts!" I told her.
>
> "Run!" she said. "Just shut up and run!" Just then the woman with the megaphone called out, "Elana Rose Rosen to the 514 Melon Hill Avenue relay team immediately!" (p. 128)

In considering this scene, let's look across a continuum of dramatic possibilities. For example, you might begin by sticking closely to the text. You could assign your children the roles of Elana, her mother, and the woman with the megaphone, and they'd need to decide what to do with the voice of the narrator, especially since *Scooter* is written in Elana's first person narrative. You could advise them to mark up their photocopied passages (since they can't write in their books), eliminating words that might be unnecessary in a dramatic interpretation such as the "she said" in the sentence "Run!" she said. "Just shut up and run." Then you could ask them how they plan to read the text. Will they read it as a readers theatre piece with eyes on the audience, or will they take it into classroom theatre and exchange eye gaze among characters and perhaps add gestures? Ask them to consider the vocal qualities in either choice. Will they emphasize certain words and phrases? What tone will they adopt to reflect their character's attitude?

This kind of work is called "text-centered" because the text is central to the interpretation. But after their performances in this mode, you could take them further and further out the continuum to "text-edged drama." In my own research over the years, I've studied text-centered drama much more, but when I collaborated with Brian Edmiston and Pat Enciso, they taught me the value of text-edged work (Wolf, Edmiston, & Enciso, 1997). In the edgier drama for *Scooter*, you could begin with a *tableau*—a frozen moment—asking your children to show the scene where Elana's mother pulls her daughter from her wedged-in space in the stadium wall. Actors can't talk or move once they finalize their tableaux (the plural for the singular tableau), so they have to negotiate what moment they'll freeze, what their body positioning will be, and what facial expression they will use. From tableaux, you could move your children into *unwritten conversations*, and ask them to create an exchange among characters that was *not* in the book. For example, how might Elana explain the stadium argument to Nanette—her guest, cousin, and best buddy? On the other hand, how might Elana's mother talk over the scene with her neighborhood friend, Mrs. Greiner? Although these conversations are unwritten by the author, your students will know enough of the characters in the novel to create conversations that they feel are true to the characters as written by Vera Williams.

Both text-centered and text-edged dramas are prepared for an audience of peers—your children perform for their class colleagues—and after each mini performance, both move into *critical space*, which is an essential opportunity to debrief the drama and discuss process as well as product. In the upcoming sections, I follow this line of thinking beginning with text-centered drama and then moving out to text-edged drama. In both, I stress the need for critical space. Throughout these sections, I argue that whatever the form of drama, all involve rich cognitive work as well as much-needed opportunities for multiple modes of communication through the voice and body in interaction with others' interpretations. I also try to make a convincing argument for the accessibility of drama in classrooms when teachers are not too preoccupied with the notion of THE PLAY. Like Elana Rose Rosen's mother, I try to persuade you to head out and introduce yourself to new and always dramatic ideas, and if that means I have to come right up behind you and put my hands on the handlebars of your scooter and push you down the hall and through your school and in through the front doors of classroom drama, I'll do it!

Text-Centered Drama

Text-centered drama can take on many forms, but as McCaslin (1990) explained, in all of these forms, "the primary virtue is the text" (p. 280). The author's words are not sacrosanct, but interpreting the words on the page is the driving force. One form is *story theatre* in which a narrator—often the classroom teacher—reads a story with her or his children seated in a semicircle. As she or he reads, the children move to the inner circle to take on a variety of parts, and then they move quickly out again to make room for other children and other interpretations as the story progresses. Another form is *readers theatre* in which children orally present a piece of literature reading from hand-held scripts. Rather than interact with each other, they tend to face the audience, and they bring their characters to life through vocal choices. Still another form is *classroom theatre* which Brian, Pat, and I defined in the following way:

> Classroom theatre is a blend of creative drama and readers theatre that has much in common with regular theatre. Classroom theatre takes and reshapes the best from both worlds—offering children opportunities to (a) participate in theatre games to exercise their voices and bodies as well as build concentration, and (b) collaboratively produce theatrical interpretations of selected scenes in published texts. Children are encouraged to think like actors, using the theatre's technical vocabulary and the strategies of those on the stage—marking their scripts to note body movement and intonation, arranging for a prompter if needed, and running their lines repeatedly, though they can enact the final performance with hand-held scripts. (Wolf, Edmiston, & Enciso, 1997, p. 494)

I'm most familiar with this last form, having studied children both in regular theatre as well as in classrooms preparing for a final performance. In one study, I was privileged to watch an experienced high school theatre teacher—whose pseudonym is Bill after William Shakespeare—lead a group of 9-, 10-, and 11-year-old children in the preparation and ultimate performance of classroom theatre pieces (Wolf, 1994; 1995).

His work was especially important, because the children involved were disengaged from school. They had had few opportunities for literary uptake, and several even told me they thought reading was "the devil." Bill and I wanted to see if we could turn some of this around through drama, and Natasha—the classroom teacher—was in enthusiastic agreement. Thus, in the sections to follow, I take you through a typical classroom theatre process beginning with the warm up and moving to scene selection and scripting. Then we look at rehearsal followed by critical space and, finally, performance. Although I try to emphasize that THE PLAY is not necessarily the endpoint—indeed it rightly scares a lot of teachers off—I thought it would be best to take you there so you can see the value in performance. In your own classrooms, you can visit each stop along this route without going to the final destination of major performance, and you and your children will still have a dramatic and delightful journey. I primarily use examples from Bill's work in Natasha's classroom, but I also add several examples from practicing teachers I've known who have made drama a part of their classroom life.

Warming Up

Because drama is so reliant on the "instruments" of voice and body, it's essential to warm them up. Bill began most drama sessions with a "vocal warm-up," often a fast-paced tongue twister. He followed with a "physical warm-up" to engage the entire body: "Sticky goo" might be removed from the skin or an imaginary pencil placed on the head to write numbers in the air. In some sessions he returned to a warm-up used in a previous session and reshaped it to make it more demanding. For example, the normal recitation of a Lewis Carroll poem one week would be transformed the next to build in increasing speed.

In the beginning sessions, theatre exercises followed. Some were designed to help the children apply their understanding of theatre vocabulary. To build their concentration, the children played the "mirror game" in which two partners worked together, one mimicking the other's actions. Other exercises led them into an understanding of the classroom theatre work to come. Prior to a classroom theatre interpretation of some Æsop's fables, the children performed an exercise entitled "Whose Zoo" to practice speaking thoughts aloud in animal voices.

Readying the voice and body comes from a long tradition of theatre activity. I spent three years in "Highcastle," a pseudonym for one of the oldest children's theatres for children and by children in America, as well as a year and a half with "Walk with Warriors," a teen improvisational troupe. In these two very different theatrical sites, warm-ups and acting exercises were held at the start of every class and/or rehearsal. Sometimes the children and youth practiced "London Guards," standing as stiff and straight as a soldier at the queen's palace, trying to "keep their focus" in spite of other actors' antics. Another exercise was "Name that Channel," where young actors were assigned to create specific radio channels—a country western show, a call-in show with a psychiatrist, etc.—while the director channel switched among them, calling out "Click!" and pointing to individual channels in random, rapid-fire order. In such an exercise, the young actors learned to be verbally ready for anything. And in terms of collaboration, they took turns falling backwards into each other's arms in a "Trust Fall" to ensure that they could depend on each other in performance. They learned to neither literally nor metaphorically let a fellow actor down.

Skill, concentration, and control mark these exercises. The goals are clear, the feedback immediate, and the enjoyment apparent. The actors take risks and heighten their trickery to control their role in the game. Yet, above all, as Tillie—the director of the teen improvisational troupe—told me, these exercises are "clearly about relationship. I have to look you directly in the eye. I have to be speaking right to you. This is about you and me."

Warm-ups and theatre exercises are also about the whole person. Children need to use all their resources, to express their thinking physically as well as vocally in interaction with others. We've now known for years about Howard Gardner's (1983) theory of multiple intelligences, with linguistic, bodily kinesthetic, and interpersonal as three of his beginning seven. Warm-ups and acting exercises use all three, with the voice, the body, and actors working and playing in relationship. And the play aspect cannot be ignored, for it is often in play that the child's mind is working the hardest. As Vygotsky (1978) suggested, "In play a child always behaves beyond his average age, above his daily behavior; in play it is as though he were a head taller than himself. As in the focus of a magnifying glass, play contains all developmental tendencies in a condensed form and is itself a major source of development" (p. 102).

And it's fun! Children love these opportunities to play, yet they don't have enough of them in school. Still, a teacher in one of my classes, Rebecca Ervin, decided to provide them. She wrote:

Sadly, my classroom has not served as a stage for my students' dramatic response to literature in the last few years. My first decade of teaching, however, I clearly remember the annual production of "The Goose that Laid the Golden Egg" and a host of other stories created and enacted by my second graders. My enthusiasm ignited children's creativity and their insistence to perform. The daily activities were easily enhanced as my students' response to literature enveloped them in dramatic play. What prompted me to orchestrate their lessons and take a central role? And what ever happened to that lovely bag of hats and capes? In answer to both of these questions, I just don't know. However, I can say in earnest, my rationale for choosing drama as literary response is personal. *I want it back.* I want to see my children dancing, singing, and carrying on, thoroughly involved with literature. And I want my days filled with engagement and satisfaction. As it now stands, my students have become complacent. I hope that by combining literature with drama, I can rekindle their creativity and sense of expression.

In an effort to get it back, Rebecca introduced several acting exercises. Her children recited exaggerated vowels, tongue twisters, and nursery rhymes in Australian animal voices to prepare for roles from a variety of Australian trade books including Mem Fox's (1983) *Possum Magic.* They wrote numbers in the air with their noses to increase flexibility and played the mirror game to enhance concentration. They rehearsed slow motion for gestures and slow speech for voice control. Rebecca found these playful activities paid off, "Aside from the obvious voice and body preparation, warm-ups allowed my students to feel more skillful at an actors' trade."

Scene Selection & Script Writing

Although actors in the theatre are usually given their scenes and the scripts are set, this is not so with classroom drama. Once children have selected the story they wish to enact, they usually have to pair it down to a scene or two, because performing the entire story would be too time consuming. And because they are performing literature, they need to rewrite it into the format of a play to match the requirements of the genre. When Bill began to work in Natasha's classroom, he started with excerpts from the basal reader, using stories that the children had already read in class. Each week he came with a prepared excerpt from the textbook—a script that the children could follow. But he quickly found ways for them to rewrite the scripts, either by changing the gender of the characters to match their own, adding additional creative episodes, stitching two scenes together with a helpful transition, or writing new endings for the story.

From this supportive beginning, he placed increasing emphasis on the children's decision-making roles, ultimately inviting them to select their own texts and prepare their own scripts. One of the first things to go was the "he said/she said" in prose, which was deemed unnecessary in script format and interrupted the flow of the dialogue. The children also made decisions for revising the prose based on what they felt they could and could not do. For example, Tomás and Stella, who played the mouse dentist and his wife in *Dr. De Soto* (Steig, 1982), refused to follow the words of the original text and kiss each other. They ignored advice offered by Bill to rewrite the script as "hug each other" and after much discussion finally eliminated the phrase all together. "I ain't gonna touch him!" Stella declared, keeping Tomás at a distance.

As the children worked on their scripts, I helped them to prepare polished copies, typing up their scenes using a different font for each child's role. For children who typically had trouble with reading, it was critical to help them locate their parts easily with distinctive, large print fonts. For the *Dr. De Soto* play, I provided the children with a key at the bottom of their script.

KEY

Tomás: **Reads Dr. De Soto's part in this type of print.**
Bart: Reads the fox's part in this type of print.
Stella: Reads the narrator's part in plain print and plays Mrs. De Soto.

Bill encouraged the children to do even further script work. He explained, "When I'm acting in a play, I take the script and I think about how I want to emphasize certain words. If I really want to make a word stronger with my voice, I underline it. Or maybe I highlight it in a different color or I draw a circle around it." Bart, who played the role of the fox created his own system, circling the words on the script he wanted "to say loud" and drawing a light pencil line through those he wanted "to say soft." He explained that the fox says some things about eating Dr. and Mrs. De Soto that he doesn't want the mice to hear: "See, you don't want them to hear that you're gonna eat 'em, and they shouldn't hear you talkin' about it, so you gotta say it low."

Rehearsal

For children who are typically at a distance from literature, the activity of scripting is essential literacy work that invites them into the writing and rewriting of language. They learn to attend to the subtle nuances of phrasing and word choice. But rehearsal takes them even further, for children who usually duck their heads when it's their turn to read are eager to practice their drama pieces because the text becomes more familiar with each rereading. While it may seem obvious that children's fluency would increase with each rehearsal, practice in traditional reading groups all too often consists of reading many of the same words in different story contexts. The emphasis is on turning pages, attempting to master certain skills, and moving on to the next story. In classroom theatre, however, children immerse themselves in a story and become more enthusiastic with every practice.

Part of their enthusiasm is the result of character analysis. As children experiment with vocal choices in intonation, accent, and stress as well as physical choices in gesture and facial expression, they find that each rereading brings something fresh to the interpretation. And each interpretation is heavily dependent on negotiated character analysis. Individual readings, in other words, have to meet with group expectations. Following an early rehearsal, Bart summarized the character of the fox in *Dr. De Soto* in his journal, writing, "I look like a cocky fox with bad teeth. Next I act like a smart aleck and I love mice." Bart subsequently decided that a smart aleck would have his own distinct mode of discourse. In the next rehearsal, he added a flippant tone to his character's voice and ended some lines with "baby" or "honey," explaining that since the fox was "sly" he ought to talk this way. His group agreed. His first attempt in practice sent them into high giggles, and they encouraged him to keep his sarcastic tone.

Interpretive work in rehearsal often goes hand in hand with individuals' journal writing or artwork. In the attempt to discover character, your students can work out some of their thoughts privately and then bring them to the group for discussion. Thus, rehearsal is not only what's done in group, repeating lines over and over again, but what is rehearsed in the head as children consider their characters. For example, in Rebecca Ervin's class, the children were creating and rehearsing their plays of Australian trade books. In an attempt to discover her character in *Koala Lou* (Fox, 1989), Caroline, a 7-year-old, brought her own background knowledge to her art, which you can see in the picture on the left in Fig. 8.1. The story is about a young koala who wishes her mother would speak to her with the same affection as she did before all her other children arrived. Caroline comes from a family with many siblings, and her portrayal of the mother unhappily looking at her first born brings life to her caption, "Koala Lou's Mom felt busy around the babys" [babies]. The jagged lines of her fur seem to highlight her distress, and Koala Lou seated on a separate branch from her clamoring siblings drives home the point.

Caroline's portrayal of Koala Lou's Mom   Sistine's portrayal of Hush

FIG. 8.1.   Young Children's Character Portrayals for Classroom Theater Rehearsals.

In rehearsing ideas about the character of Hush in *Possum Magic* (Fox, 1983), another child, Sistine, went deep into the story's theme. In this tale, the young possum Hush is made invisible by Grandma Poss to protect her from the dangers of the outback, especially snakes. But ultimately Hush doesn't really want to be invisible, and over the course of the story, the two possums try to reverse Hush's invisibility by trying out an assortment of Australian foods. In Fox's story there are few words to describe Hush's desire to return to visibility. She tells her Grandma Poss not to worry, that she doesn't really mind, but in reality she does. Sistine, who played Hush in the play, tried to capture the small possum's feelings, but instead of attempting to draw a realistic portrayal of a possum, she chose to create something much more symbolic. She colored a red and blue spiral with a soft, brown circle at its core and labeled her picture "difrint," which you can see in the picture on the right side of Fig. 8.1. Observing the presentation of her art in rehearsal, Rebecca wrote: "Sistine's rendition of Hush no longer wanting to be invisible is impressive. Her caption 'different' was visualized as a dark spiral. While discussing her interpretation with the group, I overheard her explain, 'It's like an animal's hole in a tree. You can see out, but you can never really get out.'"

The subject of Hush's invisibility came into larger play in a later rehearsal with Sistine's group and proves that some individual interpretations do not

meet with others' visions of how the story should be played. Joey, playing the part of the snake in the story, turned his character into the poi-
sonous death adder, a snake he had been researching in the Australia unit
and much admired. His group began to discuss his adder's interaction with
Hush.

Ms. Ervin: Joey, you're going to slink around a lot and try to sneak up on
  Hush?

Joey: Yeah, but she's invisible, so . . .

Sistine: Joey, maybe you saw me once while I was visible, but I got away
  just in time. But then the next time you came, you couldn't find me.

Ms. Ervin: How are you going to see her if she's invisible?

Joey: Ah. Ooooooh. That's a good one, Ms. Ervin!

Caroline: He could like smell her.

Sistine: Yeah. Your sense of smell.

Joey: And I could watch things move, like the branches or something and
  take a chance she's there and #@!!##@! [Joey makes a mouth-crunching
  sound].

Caroline: How about Hush discovers the death adder and can turn invisible when he's around?

Sistine: Yeah. That's what I mean. I'm only invisible when the death adder
  is near. See here in the book? [Turns to the page in the book.] Grandma
  Poss is sprinkling her magic around to make Hush invisible.

Caroline: Invisible, to protect her from danger.

Sistine: Yeah. So she doesn't get hurt.

Joey: But now you're making her visible when she *wants* to be. That's
  changing what's in the story!

Sistine: [Acting offended] I know! I know!

Rehearsals are marked by experimentation and much discussion to justify
choices. The language of rehearsal is often in the hypothetical with "maybe"
and "how about?" leading children further into "the magic if." A suggestion
might be picked up and played out or it might be rejected, and children base
their criticism on what's on the page as well as what they've discovered in
their research. Could the death adder, as Caroline and Joey suggest, find Hush
through his sense of smell or from her movement in the branches? If they
follow Caroline and Sistine's suggestion that Hush control her invisibility,
have they strayed too far from the text? Joey certainly seems to think so.

This kind of informal criticism is an inherent part of the rehearsal process and helps to prepare children for the more formal debriefing that typically follows rehearsal.

Critical Space

In the theatre, directors provide "notes" or commentary on the effectiveness of any performance—whether in rehearsal or in production. These notes range from the smallest detail to the largest concept, and it's an opportunity for the director and the actors to debrief the performance and consider possible changes. In classroom theatre, I call this "critical space." Though the performance is over, the discussion is just beginning, and actors stay "on stage" while their classmates remain as an audience—but this time in a more participatory role. Critical space can begin with the actors discussing their process as well as their product or it can begin with audience commentary. Who begins doesn't matter nearly as much as what gets accomplished in the conversation, as both actors and audience consider the effective aspects of the performance as well as discuss suggestions for improvement.

Although teachers sometimes shy away from criticism, it's essential to growth. Just as peer and teacher conferences are a vital feature of writers workshop, classroom drama demands critical discussion. And just as with writers workshop, the more specific the criticism, the more helpful it will be to the actors on stage, especially if some simple rules are followed. In the critical space discussions that Bill conducted, he felt that children should start with the positive. Still, positive comments had to be specific, for he would always respond to a generalized "I like it" comment with, "What did you like about it?" He also made it clear that negative criticism should consistently be accompanied by new suggestions.

Entering into critical space as an insightful, yet comfortable conversation asks children to question whether their performance was believable. Their conversations are marked linguistically through conditional constructions, "If we do it that way, it won't work" and "If we do it this way, it just might." Play with the imaginary world is thus formed in language that calls on hypotheticals to toy with ideas—build hypotheses, test propositions, compare events and scenes, and weigh the consequences of various decisions. The central "what if" is "what if they don't believe in us as we play?"

Believability is often attached to particular features of characters as they respond to the situation around them. For example, in the scenes enacted from *Dr. De Soto*, Bart played the role of the fox determined to eat the mouse dentist and his wife as soon as they repair his tooth. But the De Sotos trick the fox into testing out a new product designed to rid him of tooth decay for life. Instead of a miracle formula, however, they use glue, and the fox cannot open his mouth to devour his targeted delicacies. Stunned, he can only mouth words of thanks through his clenched jaws and stagger out of the office. In discussion with Bart, Bill had emphasized that the line, though said through clenched teeth, had to be clearly articulated in order to be understood. He explained that it was a part of the "actor's responsibility" to ensure that the audience could hear all lines, and Bart would have to take care that the line was not "thrown away." Bart repeatedly practiced the line, setting his jaw in a tight grin, and forcefully breathing out the words. His practice paid off, for in an evaluation of a rehearsal, both Bill and the children paid high compliments to the group, but particularly Bart:

> **Bill:**   [to Tomás who played Dr. De Soto] I *really* liked that first line that you had about '*BE SERIOUS*.' You really said that with such good interpretation.
>
> **Greg:**   Um, I like the part where Bart says "*Thank you very much*." 'cause he wanted to eat the mice so he says [clenching his teeth and repeating the line] OOOGH! So like that, "*Frank oo berry mush*."
>
> **Bill:**   That was really good frustration that he was putting into his interpretation.
>
> **Greg:**   Still, maybe next time you could face the audience more. You kinda had your head down, and I think you need to tilt it more to us.

The effectiveness of Bart's interpretation was the result of the reflection provided by critical space as his director, Bill, and the children offered specific feedback on his creation of a believable fox as a cocky, but frustrated character. Still, as Greg pointed out, while the frustration seemed real, facing the audience would help them feel it even more.

Critical space can be established with even more formality. Lorynda Sampson, a 4th grade teacher, asked her 9- and 10-year-olds to create small scenes from the fairy tales they were reading. Together they developed a rubric based on the believability of character. The children held a discussion after each mini performance and gave their feedback. Then they wrote their compliments and criticisms on sticky notes. Even the actors provided their own self-assessments. The children then gave the stickies to Lorynda to help her make her final rubric evaluations.

Two girls chose to do a scene from *Rumplestiltskin*, and Ying Ying, a Chinese American child, played the queen while Rachel, who is European American, played Rumplestiltskin. The girls had raided Rachel's mother's closet and dressed Ying Ying in a glittery cocktail dress with a tiara on her head. They enacted the scene where the queen is trying to guess Rumplestiltskin's name, and Ying Ying held a wrapped baby doll that Lorynda said, "cried at just the right moments at the threat of being taken away from her mother." After their performance, the children discussed and wrote up their feedback, emphasizing the effectiveness of the costumes and the use of the baby doll. But a couple of the children felt that the character of the queen needed work. In Fig. 8.2, you can see several of the children's sticky note compliments and criticisms as well as Lorynda's rubric evaluation and commentary. Like the children, she admired the costumes, but felt that the character of the queen was lacking. She wrote, "I didn't feel the queen's desperation. It would've been nice to have heard you put more expression into your presentation, instead of just reading the parts." Ying Ying was pleased, but realized that if they had worked more "on learning our lines," perhaps she would have been better able to show the queen's state of mind.

Formal as well as informal opportunities for critical space are essential to growth in dramatic interpretation as children weigh the consequences of their interpretive decisions in conversations with teachers and peers. If consistently and effectively done, these opportunities help children self assess their own interpretations. Critical space also offers reflective occasions for defining character, sequencing plot, symbolizing setting, and delivering theme, as well as communicating these narrative essentials through language. And criticism is vital if you decide to move to the next level of classroom theatre and take your children into performance for an outside audience.

Performance

I caution you not to think of classroom theatre only in terms of creating a big production. However, playing for audiences other than classmates can be a powerful motivator for children to up the ante on their performance. Knowing that children from other classrooms and family members and friends will

Character Presentation Rubric

4 Advanced

Really shows the character's personality, not just the story
Powerful expression
Excellent—clear, creative presentation
Very well rehearsed   *Beautiful costumes*

Work on telling more about the character. You sort of showed some of the story, but you could show a tad more character.

③Proficient

✓ Good character description
   Good expression   *Could use more expression*
✓ Presentation is good, but may be a little hard to follow or hear in parts
   Well rehearsed

2 Partially Proficient

   More story than character in the presentation
✓ 1 or 2 "flashes" of character expression
   Might not be loud or clear enough, and it seems disorganized
✓ Could use a bit more rehearsal

1 Not Proficient

   Not focused on the character, just on the story
   Little or no expression
   Silly, off topic, and/or confusing
   Doesn't seem rehearsed

You showed good humor and you got me hooked. The costumes were great!

I loved your costumes. It was clear that you really thought about them. I also liked the names you chose for the parts when the queen is trying to guess Rumplestiltskin's name.

I didn't feel the queen's desperation. It would've been nice to have heard you put more expression into your presentation, instead of just reading the parts. Did you practice enough to go without your script?

Ms. Sampson

It was a well-organized play because you split the characters up. I also liked when you used the baby.

TRY TO SHOW, NOT TELL. BUT, HEY, I LOVED YOUR COSTUMES.

Ying Ying's Response
The best part was when the baby cries while I'm guessing. We needed to work on learning our lines.

FIG. 8.2.   Written Response in Critical Space.

be witnessing their work, often compels children to take their interpretations more seriously. In addition, a performance provides even more opportunities for alternative modes of expression as sets have to be built, costumes considered, and programs designed. These additional tasks help to diversify the available roles, for children who are not eager to perform in front of a more high-stakes audience can take on the positions of stage manager or program designer, bringing their talents in art and/or organizational skills to the fore.

When the children in my study decided they wanted to have a big performance, Natasha was careful to focus more on the process of what the children had been learning about drama rather than simply on the product of scene interpretation. To ensure this, she interspersed the scenes from books with some of the theatre activities they had learned, and the children voted on the order of events. Small groups of children opened with a vocal warm-up, followed by a physical warm-up. They then did two scenes from two books. Four children then partnered to do the mirror game, and two more scenes followed, including the one from *Dr. De Soto.* The children closed with a whole class performance of the "sound machine." Bill acted as conductor while the children made a resounding assortment of noises on cue. The audience went wild!

Still, you need to establish some limits to safeguard your children from catastrophe, especially when they are taking risks in reading. For example, in a classroom discussion about who they would invite, Natasha's 9-, 10-, and 11-year-olds were very clear that they did not want to invite any of the older-aged classes, for they felt that the older children would know when they "messed up" and never let them forget it. Instead, they invited some classes of their own age and almost all of the primary classes of "little kids." Their planning paid off, for these children were eager to believe, and their response was attentive as well as joyous. Bart's interpretation of the fox in *Dr. De Soto* was particularly well received. In a critical space discussion following the final performance, Bart proudly related, "I really like the part where I kept on saying 'honey' and stuff like that. The audience kept on laughing and laughing!"

Still, the actors had to take the youth of their audience into careful consideration. For example, Jewel, Catalina, and Maia were performing a scene from *Mirandy and Brother Wind* (McKissack, 1988). Jewel suggested that they should all wear gloves and their "Sunday best dresses" on the day of the school performance. Although the characters in the story did not wear gloves, Jewel explained, "My mama's mama wore gloves to church when she was little." While the girls readily agreed to this suggestion, when Maia recommended that they bring a real cake for one of the props, Catalina rejected the idea, "No. A fake one's better. It can look real. But if it was real the little kids in the audience would be watchin' the cake, not us."

The audience members who were sure to watch the actors, however, were their relatives. The children were nervous to perform in front of them, but even prouder to have their families see them so involved in school. Grand-mothers, parents, cousins, and siblings attended; over two thirds of the children had a family member in the audience. After the show, they hugged their children, and several parents approached Natasha, Bill, and me with compliments. Jewel's mother told me that classroom theatre made a "big difference" in her daughter's attitude about reading. Bobby's mother said that her son was now considering a "career in the theatre." Most important, the performance was one of the first times many parents had been invited to the school when their child was not in trouble, which in itself was a cause for celebration.

Text-centered work puts the emphasis on literature, but within classroom theatre there is ample room for theatre games and activities to warm-up the voice and body for the work to be done. The choice of a final performance is unnecessary, but it does have tremendous advantages in raising children's investment in their interpretive decisions. Still, as Natasha wisely recognized, the action is often in the process not the product, and with an eye towards process we now turn to even edgier work.

Text-Edged Drama

Both text-centered and text-edged dramas are art forms as well as learning processes, but Brian Edmiston (1993) suggested that there is a distinctive difference in drama that hovers on the edge. "Rather than putting our energies as teachers into getting the story right, we can work with our students to create dramatic situations in which they may all take up perspectives on certain aspects of the story" (p. 252). Like text-centered drama, dramatizing at the edges of the text may take many forms. One form is *story drama* (Booth, 1995) in which the story serves as a pre-text to imagined alternative scenarios both in and beyond the text, and children can combine these scenarios with personal experiences they've actually encountered. Another form is *process drama* (O'Neill, 1994), which relies on the teacher's ability to aesthetically structure imaginary scenes using improvisation and theatrical as well as film processes. These dramas begin with the text's intial dilemma, but they quickly expand to include "curricular topics, teacher objectives, and students' personal experiences" (Schneider & Jackson, 2000, p. 38). The central text is not absent, but it is being created as the drama progresses.

Brian Edmiston and Pat Enciso (2003) explained that a common feature in the varying text-edged forms is their emphasis on a dialogic approach to drama. In their work, they leaned on Bakhtin (1984) who suggested, "To live means to participate in dialogue: to ask questions, to heed, to respond, to agree, and so forth" (p. 293). In classroom dramas on the edge, children are not so much assigned roles as they are provided opportunities to try out social positions and their accompanying discourses. For example, in working at the edges of the *Dr. De Soto* text, Brian led primary students to imagine they were all mice dentists wondering what to do about foxes and other dangerous animals in need of dental care. The children had to enter into the social positions of being a dentist and weigh professional discourses of attention to patients in pain with the contrasting discourses that swirled around the risk of their own personal safety. As the children balanced these discourses, they used language in multiple ways, making signs for their offices and a television commercial that made clear that their services were for all "nice animals." They even practiced what to do if a fox came to them for care. Brian and Pat argued that in these and other text-edged dramas:

> All of these inventions of dialogue, interactions, presentations, and plans enable children to participate in the authoring of the text. As they invent and elaborate on the text's potential, they generate multiple perspectives based on their knowledge of stories and life. Rather than moving through the text in a linear, literal, and ultimately monologic manner, the text's narrative is reshaped to make room for additional narrative pathways, perspectives, images, and positions. These pathways enable the teacher to actively engage children with the problems of conflicting viewpoints and discourses without taking children directly to the enactment of the moment of conflict when Dr. De Soto and his wife begin their repairs on the fox's tooth.
>
> If and when the children do eventually want to face that moment, they will bring a more fully elaborated understanding of the decisions and worries accompanying the action. (Edmiston & Enciso, 2003, p. 870)

The pathways created in text-edged drama are marked by three main features: (a) multiple roles/multiple forms, (b) the teacher-in-role, and, as with text-centered dramas, (c) critical space. In the sections to follow, I take you through each of these features to demonstrate how you and your students can move to the edges of text.

Multiple Roles/Multiple Forms

The roles in text-edged work are not as clear as those that exist in text-centered drama where children are assigned or select character roles from the story to play. Role boundaries in text-edged work are more porous, and they can appear in multiples. For example, in Brian's work with primary students, all the children played the role of the mouse dentist, even though they chose different discourses to communicate their character's dilemma. In later work, Brian and Pat used the novel *Out of the Dust* (Hesse, 1997), and they asked 9- and 10-year-olds as well as 13- and 14-year-old students to play the roles of photojournalists researching and writing the stories of the 1930s Oklahoma dust bowl. Using Hesse's poetic novel as a pre-text, the children studied some of the famous photographs of the time, especially those of Dorothea Lange, whose black and white images of the pain and poverty of the time are hauntingly beautiful. Through tableaux as well as artwork, the children illustrated a variety of scenes:

> One group depicted a person receiving a foreclosure notice from the bank, another group showed a family looking at a charred farmhouse, another represented a family on the road headed west. As these depictions were shared, the students talked about why the sorrows had happened, why the people kept struggling, and how journalists, in their writing, might acknowledge the complexity of the story. (Edmiston & Enciso, 2003, p. 871)

As the drama progressed, more students took on the roles of bankers delivering foreclosure notices and farmers receiving such blows. As Brian and Pat argued, "Students role-playing the dust bowl period might imagine and enact only one of these positions, yet it is crucial to the experience of that time to appreciate the struggle among competing discourses embedded in different social positions" (p. 873).

Competing discourses do not have to be aligned with larger historical events, but can occur within a single-family structure. For example, in *Joey Pigza Loses Control* (Gantos, 2000), Joey has Attention-Deficit Hyperactivity Disorder (ADHD) and wears a daily-medicated patch to control his frenetic behavior. Under court order, his mother must send him to spend the summer with his father, who is an alcoholic, and his grandmother, who is a chain smoker and has many of the symptoms of emphysema. These conflicted and conflicting goals make the novel a controversial one. Indeed, in chapter 3, I explained how practicing teachers either avoided the novel because they found it too "exhausting" or praised it because they felt that novels like *Joey* are essential for children with similar life circumstances. If you'll recall, Lorynda Sampson and her children were "incredulous" that some teachers might not see the value of the piece. Spring boarding from their many discussions, Lorynda's 9- and 10-year-old students chose to enact a number of text-edged pieces to portray the novel's themes.

Two girls decided that Joey might keep a diary, and they wrote and enacted diary entries to capture Joey's internal conflict as his dad takes away his patches and encourages him to go it alone, though he himself can't stop drinking. Another girl created an interpretive dance which she performed to the Jeopardy game show song because, like the song, "Joey was in jeopardy," especially after his father took away his patches. Two boys created a large paper sculpture of Joey, which they hung by a string. Using an instrumental with a frenzied drumbeat as background music, they made the figure jump like a puppet on a string to communicate the craziness and lack of control in Joey's life without his patch. Through their writing, their dances, and their puppet shows, all the children played Joey in crises, but the ways in which they communicated his life took their own creative pathways. They also entered into some of the scientific and emotional discourses surrounding alcoholism and ADHD, as they explored the impact of the disease and the disability on the lives of families today.

Teacher-in-Role

As much as Lorynda felt thrilled by her students' interpretations, she regretted that she had not played a more participatory role in their dramas. And Dorothy Heathcote (1995) might agree with her lament. Heathcote pioneered the strategy of "teacher-in-role"—the practice of teacher structuring from within the drama by participating in fictional encounters alongside the students. Johnson and O'Neill (1984) explained Heathcote's position, ". . . the teacher, as the most mature member of the group, has not merely a right but a responsibility to intervene, since learning is the product of intervention" (p. 12).

Still, a teacher's intervention and her or his willingness to structure and play alongside the students does not mean a domineering position. Indeed, Heathcote wanted to give her students the "mantel of the expert" so they could interact from positions of strength and competence:

> Teacher-in-role is a feature of much classroom drama, but a mantle of the expert approach demands a particularly mercurial version (!), with the teacher frequently engaged in hopping deftly, sliding elliptically, switching abruptly, or

even bestriding the two worlds of fiction and reality. It may be just a matter of *seconds* that a role is held and then dropped—and then assumed again. It is even possible to convey with a word and the raising of an eyebrow a deliberate ambiguity between the two. It is also something of a paradox that the *in-role* usage breeds a healthy teacher/student relationship, whereas *out-of-role* talk and actions foreshadow the adventure and power of the drama. Both are essential. (Heathcote & Bolton, 1995, p. 30).

Lorynda's out-of-role structuring led her students to construct their own interpretations of Joey's dilemma, but if she had chosen to enter in-role, she might have been able to push the drama to even more intriguing levels.

For example, she might have entered the interpretive dance of Joey in Jeopardy as the father, questioning Joey's unwillingness to try life without a patch. On the other hand, she could have entered as Joey's mother and attempted to reapply Joey's patches. In the children's enactments of Joey's diary entries, she might have questioned why, if Joey was so worried, he didn't take on a more proactive role and call his mother for help. Or she might have pretended to be the father's girlfriend who notices Joey's behavior and questions him about why he is no longer taking his medication. The possibilities are endless, but each challenges the thinking of the children's original interpretations and represents competing discourses.

When Brian Edmiston worked with 10- and 11-year-olds, they dramatized at the edges of *The Journey: Japanese Americans, Racism and Renewal* (Hamanaka, 1990), a picture book about the experience of Japanese Americans who had been interned during World War II. Brian's goal was to bring the children to a decisive point in U.S. history when Japanese American citizens had to decide whether or not to sign a Loyalty Questionnaire. Those who signed renounced their allegiance to the Japanese emperor and effectively to Japanese culture, but then were faced with conscription into the U.S. Army. Those who refused faced being branded as traitors and being sentenced to prison. In the so-called "relocation centers," the children and Brian all adopted positions of internees. Brian told them that he had heard that they would be let out of the camp if they all signed a piece of paper and renounced allegiance to Japan. A heated discussion among the students followed, but it intensified when Brian repositioned himself as the camp commander demanding a response. Brian explained:

By structuring and interacting in role with the group, I was able to ... press them to reflect more deeply than they might have without my presence in role. Those who remained silent were pressed to decide whether or not to speak out. One person asked whether they might be sent to fight their family in Japan if they were drafted. I answered that they would be sent to fight the enemies of the United States. Many scoffed in reply and asked me if I would kill my own relations. . . . The intensity of these students' feelings and the range of their thoughts did not occur by accident. Just as with all significant moments in classrooms, careful teacher structuring, both externally and internally, in all cases brought the students to situations in which they were challenged in their thinking about aspects of a piece of literature. (Edmiston, 1993, p. 256)

Brian's emphasis on internal and external structuring, and Heathcote's and Bolton's (1995) reiteration that classroom dramas need teachers to be both in-role and out-of-role bring us to the final feature in any kind of text-edged work, for critical space is essential in the continual need to challenge children's thinking as they take up pieces of literature.

Critical Space

In text-edged work, critical space allows children and their teachers to live in the life of the drama and then step out into real life to critique it. Gavin Bolton (1999) explained, "There is a mercurial inside-outside dialectic that heightens awareness. Thus 'Living through' implies continually arresting the process of living to take a look at it, and it is the '*spectator*' as much as the '*participant*' that re-engages with that 'living" (p. 232).

One effective analogy for this inside-outside, spectator-participant view is to think about how we see. Each of our eyes brings a slightly different vision, and it is only in the balance of the two versions that depth perception is accomplished. The same is true for children in drama, for they balance stepping back with a critical eye and stepping in to create the vision. They simultaneously doubt and believe their interpretation and enactment of text, and the balance of doubt and belief makes the experience all the more compelling.

Critical space in text-edged work tends to be informal and ongoing, and it often appears in the questions that teachers and children might ask as they are living through the work itself. In Brian and Pat's work with *Out of the Dust* (Hesse, 1997), they wrote:

As the students observed one another's depictions they evaluated. We asked open-ended, though pointed, questions such as "I wonder how the people lived with such sorrow and yet continued to help each other?" Some of the students' evaluations were initially detached and prescriptive, as when they argued,

"They should have paid their bills." However, as students became more engaged and discourses were dialogized, evaluations became more double-voiced: "I don't trust those flyers about California, but if we stay we might not all survive another summer." With these words, this student expresses an evaluation of meaning that refers to yet another text, and she also assesses the tensions in her own and an Oklahoman's troubled situation. (p. 873)

No matter how edgy the work, criticism is essential.

Text-edged critical space can also come in more formal evaluations. In Lorynda Sampson's class, her 9- and 10-year-olds performed their interpretations of Joey, and then held a group discussion to highlight their "comments, criticisms, and concerns." Many of the comments were positive. For example, the children felt that the girl who did the interpretive dance was "really brave." Another child complimented the use of the theme song from the game show, Jeopardy, "I think the song went really well. Joey was really scared and that's kind of a spooky song." Indeed, the girl's choice to perform her dance while robotically and repetitively humming the central tune did add to the frightening aspects of Joey's dilemma.

At the end of all the enactments, Lorynda commented, "Could you feel the confusion and the chaos in Joey in each of these performances?" The children heartily agreed, and Lorynda closed the session saying, "It's fascinating how many different ways you can respond to and interpret the same theme. The human mind is truly amazing." And what's even more amazing is how the combination of being in the life of the drama and out in real life critical space can enhance the learning to be had. In evaluating the effectiveness of drama in her classroom, Lorynda stressed critique: "It truly was through the critique that my students and I came to know exactly what was learned. The critiques were great discussion starters for what I, as a teacher, need to do as well as what my students need to do to be more effective. All of these thoughts tell me that I will, like my creative, artistic, intelligent, thinking students, continue to grow and learn."

Summary

In this chapter, I take you along the multiple pathways of drama in the classroom. In text-centered work, the focus is on the literature, but within classroom theatre—beginning with the warm up and moving to scene selection and scripting, as well as rehearsal, critical space, and performance—there is always more attention to the process than the product. Text-edged work is even more process-oriented, and using literature as a pre-text allows for the multiplicity of roles, the teacher to be in- and well as out-of-role, and critical space as a place for ongoing and insightful critique that presses students to look carefully at the intersections of text with their lives.

Figure 8.3 offers ideas for text-centered as well as text-edged work using the touchtone texts from chapter 2—*The Watsons Go to Birmingham— 1963* (Curtis, 1995) and *Hansel and Gretel* (Grimm Brothers, 1981). My suggestions are only a beginning list, but they will give you an idea of the many ways children could enact these stories both on and off the page. As Brian Edmiston (1993) explained, "If [students] reflect on those experiences, they may well discover new insights into the characters, the themes, and themselves" (p. 252).

Drama is all too often seen as a frill, something tacked on to the day if only there is time, but this stance ignores the rich cognitive work that children accomplish when they play. To illustrate this point, let me return to Vera B. Williams' lovely book, *Scooter.* At the end of Field Day, Elana Rose Rosen and her pals celebrate their day with its small defeats and larger victories.

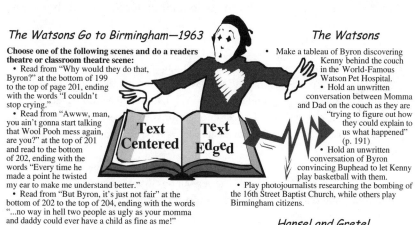

The Watsons Go to Birmingham—1963

Choose one of the following scenes and do a readers theatre or classroom theatre scene:

• Read from "Why would they do that, Byron?" at the bottom of 199 to the top of page 201, ending with the words "I couldn't stop crying."

• Read from "Awww, man, you ain't gonna start talking that Wool Pooh mess again, are you?" at the top of 201 and read to the bottom of 202, ending with the words "Every time he made a point he twisted my ear to make me understand better."

• Read from "But Byron, it's just not fair" at the bottom of 202 to the top of 204, ending with the words "...no way in hell two people as ugly as your momma and daddy could ever have a child as fine as me!"

Hansel and Gretel

• Read from "The woodcutter lay fretting in bed at night, tossing and turning" to "But I am grieved for the poor children."

• Read from "All the best food was now cooked for poor Hansel, while Gretel got nothing but scraps" to "He rushed out, like a bird set free, and they hugged and kissed each other with joy."

• Choose your own scene.

Text Centered   **Text Edged**

The Watsons

• Make a tableau of Byron discovering Kenny behind the couch in the World-Famous Watson Pet Hospital.

• Hold an unwritten conversation between Momma and Dad on the couch as they are "trying to figure out how they could explain to us what happened" (p. 191)

• Hold an unwritten conversation of Byron convincing Buphead to let Kenny play basketball with them.

• Play photojournalists researching the bombing of the 16th Street Baptist Church, while others play Birmingham citizens.

Hansel and Gretel

• Make a tableau of the children as they return home the first time, and their stepmother greets them at the door.

• Play children discussing the delicious qualities of the witch's house when the teacher enters in-role as the wicked witch!

• Hold an unwritten conversation between Hansel and Gretel and their father after their return.

• Play wicked witches in therapy with their psychiatrists, or play fathers and stepmothers with their marriage counselors.

FIG. 8.3.   Dramatic Possibilities for Chapter 2 Touchstone Texts.

They're about to head home, moving across the Gretel Green, the large lawn in their city park, when Petey, who had been denied his own contest, begins to somersault across the Green. Elana watches for a moment and then joins in, and the rest of the kids follow suit. Though their parents yell admonitions about supper, the children just keep rolling on.

> None of us stopped till Petey stopped. When Petey couldn't make another somersault I didn't make another and neither did Nanette. No one did. We just lay there catching our breath.
>
> I was looking up at the moon. I thought how it would be to be the face in the moon looking down right then on Melon Valley Park. If I were that face in the moon I would be able to see kids from all over our borough, hundreds of kids spread out just whichever way we landed, lying there catching our breath, resting as though our parents were a million miles away.... (p. 141)

But the parents enter the now and imminent time of the children soon enough and bring them back to reality. Some are laughing and some are angry, but no matter their reaction, they begin to guide their children towards home once more.

> Still, Elana's mother stops to question her daughter's actions:
> "Elana, I'll just never understand you. We had a whole big ample Field Day. Right?.... But that wasn't enough for you. You had to add a whole field Day of your own on top of it. It's just never enough for you." She shook her head and had that expression meant to tell me I am a person beyond any normal mother's comprehension.
> So of course I didn't try to explain how truly ultimately necessary it was for me to follow Petey and how somersaulting out on Gretel Green was enormously a different thing than the real Field Day. (pp. 142–143)

Though drama is an enormously different thing than the real School Day, it's well worth explaining. Whether at the center or at the edges of text, drama stretches and somersaults the mind and body to new thinking. Children take on perspectives quite different than their own, and they live in the story rather than talk about it. Through multiple roles and new experiences, all carefully crafted through critique, they take up literature in profound ways and prove that drama is truly and ultimately necessary.

BOOKS FOR THE PROFESSIONAL

Bolton, G. (1999). *Acting in classroom drama: A critical analysis.* Portland, Maine: Calendar Islands. Gavin Bolton, a distinguished drama educator, provides an overview of five British pioneers of drama education. His historical and developmental perspective yields rich insights into the value of a variety of acting behaviors both on and off the stage.

Heathcote, D., & Bolton, G. (1995). *Drama for learning: Dorothy Heathcote's mantle of the expert approach to education.* Portsmouth, NH: Heinemann. Dorothy Heathcote is one of the pioneers Gavin Bolton celebrates in the text above. In this book, the two join together to explore Dorothy's central tenet that in drama, teachers need to simultaneously support and challenge their students if they are to become experts in their learning.

Stanislavski, C. (1989). *An actor prepares.* New York: Routledge/Theatre Arts Books. An actor and artistic director of the Moscow Art Theatre, Constantin Stanislavski's books on the theatre are treasures. This is the first volume in his famous trilogy on the art of acting and focuses on the inner preparation an actor must attend to in the creation of realistic character.

Wagner, B. J. (1998). *Educational drama and language arts: What research shows.* Portsmouth, NH: Heinemann. When you are challenged to justify using drama in your classroom, this volume can help you do it. Betty Jane Wagner does a great service for drama education by clearly delineating what drama actually teaches.

Wilhelm, J. D., & Edmiston, B. (1998). *Imagining to learn: Inquiry, ethics, and integration through drama.* Portsmouth, NH: Heinemann. This is a powerful book on drama that balances profound theory with practical plans for how to do drama with children and young teens. Jeff and Brian's work clearly demonstrates that when children take on different discourses, they learn to create and critique story as well as very real worlds.

Chapter Touchstone Texts

Hesse, Karen. (1997). *Out of the dust.* New York: Scholastic. A Newbery Award winner, Hesse's novel gives poetic voice to the Oklahoma dust bowl of the Great Depression. In the novel, 14-year-old Billy Jo must not only learn to survive the drought, dust, and wind, but a tragic family accident that results in the loss of her mother and brother as well as the use of her hands. The first-person narrative poems are as spare as the land and ideal for a variety of text-edged dramas.

Steig, William. (1982). *Dr. De Soto.* New York: Scholastic. The dentist in this wonderful picture book is a rodent who refuses to treat animals dangerous to mice. In a moment of weakness, the Doctor and his wife decide to extract a tooth from a dapper, but devious fox. Under the influence of gas, the fox dreamily voices his plans for the De Sotos' ultimate demise. Professional courtesy turns to fear in the face of such a threat, and the De Sotos spend a worrisome night wondering how they will be able to insert a new gold tooth without self-sacrifice. The humorous ending makes this story perfect for dramatic enactment.

Williams, Vera B. (1993). *Scooter.* New York: Greenwillow Books. This story's heroine is a dramatic child who lives with her mother and beloved scooter in a diverse, urban setting. Her active, poetic life is made for the stage, for everything Elana Rose Rosen does is done with panache! Her emotional ups and downs are at the heart of the novel, but it is perhaps best captured in the "zigzag" of field day as she defends her friend Petey's right to a somersault contest. This text won the Boston Globe-Horn Book Award in 1994.

Recommended Tradebooks for Drama

Aardema, Verna. (1977). *Who's in rabbit's house?: A Masai tale*, illustrated by Leo and Diane Dillon. New York: Dial. In this tale a rabbit returns to her abode one day to discover it occupied by a mysterious animal called "The Long One." She enlists the help of several powerful friends—an elephant, a rhinoceros, and a cheetah among others—but none manage an eviction. In desperation, the rabbit agrees to let a small frog make his attempt. He's able to oust the intruder with a trick, but "The Long One" turns out to be a caterpillar who was playing a joke of his own. The frame for the telling of this story is an artistic invention as Masai villagers perform the tale, combining the intricacies of African art with the theatre.

Aliki. (1999). *William Shakespeare & the Globe.* New York: Harper-Collins. This Boston Globe-Horn Book Award Honor illustrates Sam Wanamaker's ambitious project to rebuild the Globe theatre. The central story is enhanced with details of Shakespeare's life and times as well as a number of quotations from his plays. The intricate illustrations range from small portraits of figures from Elizabethan England to the technical details of a Tudor theatre. A terrific text-to-text connection would be Diane Stanley's (1992) *Bard of Avon*.

Cooper, Susan. (1999). *King of shadows.* New York: McElderry. This novel is yet another tribute to the Bard. Young Nat Fields travels to London to play the part of Puck in a Globe production of *A Midsummer Night's Dream*, but after a bout of dizzy spells, he falls into a time warp that takes him back to Shakespearean England. Once there, he meets the master himself, and together Nat and Will Shakespeare come to terms with their own personal losses. The novel provides vibrant detail into the life of the theatre, both past and present.

Myers, Walter Dean. (1999). *Monster*, illustrated by Christopher Myers. New York: HarperCollins. Winner of the Coretta Scott King Award and the Michael L. Printz award, this powerful drama—in journal form and film script—portrays a young protagonist, Steve Harmon, as he stands trial, accused of being an accomplice in a murder. Whether he is the "monster" the prosecutor describes or innocent is left for the reader to decide.

Epilogue: How Like the Mind

In Russell Freedman's (1998) marvelous book on the life and work of Martha Graham, he explains that Martha was quite close with Helen Keller, the famous blind and deaf author and advocate for the handicapped:

> Keller would visit Martha's studio and "watch" the dancing by feeling the vibrations of the dancers' feet on the wooden floor. Once she asked Martha to describe jumping to her. "What is jumping?" she asked. "I don't understand."
>
> Martha asked Merce Cunningham to demonstrate. She placed Helen's hands on Merce's waist as everyone in the studio looked on. When Merce jumped into the air, Helen's hands rose and fell with his body. Her face lit up with a joyous smile. She threw up her arms and exclaimed, "How like thought! How like the mind it is!" (pp. 95–96)

Putting the jump together with the mind is a complex blend that perfectly captures what I've been trying to say in this book. The sheer physicality and activity in leaping up and down—the push off from the floor, the short but thrilling suspension in space, the return to firm ground with the flexibility required to spring once more into the air is so like the mind.

Indeed, putting two things together—even two entire systems like a jump in a dance and thought—is a key characteristic of the mind. As Fauconnier and Turner (2002) explained, "the exceptional cognitive abilities of human beings [lies] in their capacity to put two things together. Aristotle wrote that metaphor is the hallmark of genius" (p. 175). Yet Fauconnier and Turner are very clear that Aristotle also wrote that "'all people carry on their conversations with metaphors.' . . . The various schemes of form and meaning studied by rhetoricians can be used by the skilled orator, the everyday conversationalist, and the child" (p. 17).

Here, I have worked to bring two things together—literature and the child. Literature has much more in common with the skilled orator than the everyday conversationalist. Even when the writing captures everyday talk, it is crafted to play on the sound properties of language, to make metaphor, and to construct the structure of a story, building an event, an idea, or a character ever higher in the mind. Even more important, literature is there for the taking. It stands ready on the page for the resourceful reader, and children are, if anything, resourceful. And they can certainly learn to become readers if given half the chance.

But the kind of readers I hope children will become goes far beyond unlocking the black and white on the page. Instead, interaction with literary language implies lifting the words off the page to new levels of creativity, connections, and criticism in collaboration with others. As Barbara Kingsolver (1995) suggested, "Literature is a collaborative act—especially fiction—more than any other art form I can think of. When I've written a book, it's half done. When a reader takes it, reads it, forms the pictures in his or her mind and has an emotional response to it, that's the moment of art" (http://archive.salon.com/16dec1995/departments/litchat.html).

Moments of art occur in the classrooms of exemplary teachers who recognize the powerful combination of literature and children, and these moments come in many forms. They come in a variety of critical stances as children learn about authors and close readings, investigating the intersection of the narrative components (genre, theme, character, setting, plot, point of view, style, and tone) and the life of the author behind it. They come when children learn to make connections in an ever-widening net—connections to other written texts, to personal life experience, and to the cultural, political, and social-historical issues of the larger world.

To make these connections, children bring to bear their language, their culture, their class, and their gender. In other words, they carry their lives with them when they enter the pages of a story. It's only when children are asked to leave their lives at the door of exalted literary interpretation, that they stop on the threshold, watch for a while, and then turn away from reading. A teacher can be a wizard with words, waving a magic wand over the nuances of criticism, shooting out sparks of significance, dazzling the viewer with technical terms and tropes. But spectators tire. And if they are never given opportunities to participate in the leap of the dance, children may walk away.

But when they are invited in, that's when uptake begins. Using talk as the "tool of tools" (Cole, 1996), children can articulate their literary interpretations, giving voice to experiences they've not even met themselves. For example, a few years ago, a teacher in one of my classes, Karen Musick, read her 8- and 9-year-olds a picture book by Eve Bunting (1992). In the story, a father brings his son to see the name of his grandfather on the Vietnam Veterans Memorial. Toward the end of *The Wall*, Karen read about how the boy wished his grandfather were with him, and then she paused to make room for her students' comments:

> **Monica:** I don't understand why the grandpa's name is on the wall.
> **Pat:** 'Cause he died in the war.
> **Brenda:** And they wanted to remember him.
> **Kyle:** I wonder if his dad goes to war like the grandpa.
> **Jerry:** I wonder if his dad dies.
> **Annie:** War makes people sad.
> **Kyle:** They shouldn't have war.
> **Pat:** My uncle says that. My uncle says that us bombing over in Kosovo will be like Vietnam.
> **Monica:** What's Vietnam?
> **Jerry:** That's what that wall's about. The Vietnam War.
> **Ms. Musick:** I wonder why the author chose to write a story about the wall?
> **Kyle:** I wonder why the ending had to be so sad.
> **Brenda:** I think it's so kids could know how sad war is.

What's important about this conversation is the children's exchange of questions and comments, as together they wonder over the world and its workings. Indeed, in a snippet of conversation that took less than a minute, the word "wonder" occurs four times. And one of those times comes from the teacher, as Karen joins her students in speculating about story and life.

In children's literature, wonder is typically associated with fairy tales. Jack Zipes (1991) called them oral wonder tales, and Peter and Iona Opie (1974) made clear the critical link between magic and wonder:

> The magic sets us wondering how we ourselves would react in similar circumstances. It encourages speculation. It gives a child license to wonder. And this is the merit of the tales, that by going beyond possibility they enlarge our daily horizon.... A child who does not feel wonder is but an inlet for apple pie. (p. 16)

Yet, license to wonder comes in many books, fanciful and realistic, and the license gains even more credence when fine teachers make ample room for talk.

Karen called her read-aloud sessions "Talk Club," emphasizing that within "our wonderfully rich conversations, we went back to the books over and over again. It was as if time stopped during our time together." But the thinking never stopped, as her children demonstrated their deep comprehension of texts, their questions, their puzzles, their connections to the world around them, and their willingness to weigh interpretations. As one of her students explained when asked about the value of their discussions, "Talk Club is like reading . . . only better!"

Yet, talk gets better and better when it's combined with children's writing, visual arts, and drama. When Christy Shoemaker asked her 8- and 9-year-olds to create a "visual map of *Because of Winn-Dixie* (DiCamillo, 2000) as a culminating activity, three of [her] students began with an outline picture of a dog and then added smaller sketches that represented specific events, characters, or themes from the story." And as they drew, they talked.

Luis: Hey, we should add lightning!

Jesse: Yeah, 'cause Winn-Dixie was so scared of it!

Luis: Yeah. Ms. Shoemaker, what was the name of that fear?

Ms. Shoemaker: Do you mean a pathological fear?

Luis: Yeah, that's it.

Tristan: Put the lightning big over here because it was really important 'cause he was so scared of it.

Jesse: How about if I put the thunder too?

Tristan: How are you gonna draw thunder?

Jesse: I'll just put the words.

Luis: Yeah!!! [Both Jesse and Luis start adding words like "crash," "crack," and "thwack" interspersed between their drawn raindrops and flashes of lightening.]

Ms. Shoemaker: Do you think Winn-Dixie will always be afraid of storms?

Luis: Probably. Unless Opal always keeps him safe.

Tristan: Maybe his old owners didn't take care of him and let him be scared of lightning.

Jesse: Yeah. Probably. I think they were mean.

In her reflection on this conversation, Christy commented, "This was an effective dialogue because it was the students who led the discussion, not me asking test-like questions." She elaborated:

> Listening to the thoughtful discussions and watching the careful drawing demonstrated how well my students knew this book. Their conversations built on some of the ideas they had explored in their individual response journals and expanded their thinking on specific parts of the story, such as when they began to surmise why Winn-Dixie feared storms. This activity was a wonderful celebration of how this unit, focused on written response journals, also incorporated opportunities to sketch and talk about the story. We created an environment where students truly understood the story on a much deeper level than if we'd used traditional worksheets, testing, or teacher-dominated conversations. In addition, it is evidence of the ways in which mental imagery is essential to the enjoyment, comprehension, and interpretation of text.

Christy's commentary demonstrates the intriguing blend that occurs when children come together with books. They talk, they write, they dramatize, and they represent themes with imaginative and generative images. They exchange ideas, compare and contrast characters and themes, and agree as well as argue, all in an effort to expand their understandings and justify their claims. They look deeply into the text, and they look beyond to the experiences of their lives and those of the larger world. And no matter the beginning focus, their interpretations spring up from the page and out into multiple worlds of expression, including those I've only touched on in this book—through technology, through music, and though dance. How like the mind it is to find new forms for thought.

Without rich literary interpretation through talk and alternative modes of expression, there is little chance for children to learn to love reading and to learn to love thinking about literature. Indeed, Dennis Sumara (2002) recently wrote a book entitled, *Why Reading Literature in School Still Matters*. He argued that on the map of reading, literary engagement represents a rich site for cognition, including "representing, imagining, and interpreting knowledge." He also emphasized that if teachers and schools are willing to try, they have the power to help their children reach these destinations, "By creating pedagogical structures that include shared interpretations of literary engagements, I believe schools can continue to push the boundaries of what is considered true about the world" (p. xiii). Still, pushing the boundaries and traveling out beyond typical traditions is brave work indeed.

I began this book with dragons, explaining that in olden times, the folk felt that danger lay beyond the edges of the earth. I also began with a classroom tale of a 10-year-old boy who knew how to recognize dragons both in life and in literature. I challenged you then to journey out from your current and comfortable pedagogies to discover the rich, round world of children's literary engagement, and I've tried to arm you with intriguing texts and inspiring classroom examples to help you make your way. So it seems most fitting to end with a dragon and with the tale of Bilbo Baggins, who did venture out in J. R. R. Tolkien's (1966) *The Hobbit*. In the edition I own, *The Horn Book Magazine* review on the back cover reads, "All those, young or old, who love a finely imagined story, beautifully told, will take *The Hobbit* to their hearts."

And one young boy who did, made all the difference in the world. Rayner Unwin was 10-years-old when his father, a publishing partner at the British firm Allen & Unwin, gave him the manuscript and paid him a shilling for his opinion. Rayner's review—hand written on a single page—was enthusiastic and promoted the publication of what is now considered a classic story of Hobbits and wizards, elves, goblins, dwarves and, of course, a dragon. In his own summary of his famous tale, Tolkien wrote, "If you care for journeys there and back, out of the comfortable Western world, over the edge of the Wild, and home again, and can take an interest in a humble hero (blessed with a little wisdom and a little courage and considerable good luck), here is a record of such a journey and such a traveler." Tolkien explained that the journey was "all the more remarkable. . . perhaps because [Hobbits] as a rule preferred comfort to excitement."

This book is a record of teachers and their children heading there and back again. The teachers could have stayed with the comfortable curriculum they knew. And their children could have listened or not, especially in classrooms where the questions are set and the answers predetermined. But, as a rule, the children and teachers described here preferred excitement to comfort, and they stepped out beyond the edges of the known to create their own questions and craft their own interpretations. If it's a journey you're willing to take, I wish you wisdom, courage, and considerable good luck. The adventure is here for the taking, and you will gain much in the end.

References

ACADEMIC REFERENCES

Albers, P. (1996). Issues of representation: Caldecott gold medal winners 1984-1995. *The New Advocate, 9* (4), 267-283.

Almasi, J. F., O'Flahavan, J. F., & Arya, P. (2001). A comparative analysis of student and teacher development in more and less proficient discussions of literature. *Reading Research Quarterly, 36* (2), 96-120.

Alvermann, D. E., Commeyras, M., Young, J. P., Randall, S., & Hinson, D. (1997). Interrupting gendered discursive practices in classroom talk about texts: Easy to think about, difficult to do. *Journal of Literacy Research, 29,* 73-104.

Anderson, C., Kauffman, G., & Short, K. G. (1998). Now I think like an artist: Responding to picture books. In J. Evans (Ed.), *What's in the picture? Responding to illustrations in picture books* (pp. 146-165). London: Paul Capman.

Applebee, A. (1991). Literature: Whose heritage? In E. H. Hiebert (Ed.), *Literacy for a diverse society: Perspectives, practices, and policies* (pp. 228-236). New York: Teachers College Press.

Appleman, D. (2000). *Critical encounters in high school English: Teaching literary theory to adolescents.* New York: Teachers College Press and the National Council of Teachers of English (NCTE).

Aronson, M. (2001, May/June). Slippery slopes and proliferating prizes. *The Horn Book Magazine,* 271-278.

Atleo, M., Caldwell, N., Landis, B., Mendoza, J., Miranda, D., Reese, D., Rose, L., Slapin, B., & Smith, C. (1999). A critical review of Ann Rinaldi's *My heart is on the ground: The diary of Nannie Little Rose, a Sioux girl.* Retrieved May 15, 2003, from http://www.oyate.org.

Bakhtin, M. M. (1981). *The dialogic imagination.* Austin, TX: University of Texas Press.

Bakhtin, M. M. (1984). *Problems of Dostoevsky's poetics.* Minneapolis, MN: University of Minnesota Press.

Barrera, R. B., & Garza de Cortes, O. (1997). Mexican American children's literature in the 1990s: Toward authenticity. In V. J. Harris (Ed.), *Using multiethnic literature in the K-8 classroom* (pp. 129-153). Norwood, MA: Christopher Gordon.

Barrera, R. B., Liguori, O., & Salas, L. (1993). Ideas a literature can grow on: Key insights for enriching and expanding children's literature about the Mexican-American experience. In V. J. Harris (Ed.), *Teaching multicultural literature in grades K-8* (pp. 203-241). Norwood, MA: Christopher-Gordon.

Bennett, W. (1993). *The book of virtues.* New York: Simon & Schuster.

Bettelheim, B. (1977). *The uses of enchantment: The meaning and importance of fairy tales.* New York: Alfred A. Knopf.

Bishop, R. S. (Editor), and the Multicultural Booklist Committee. (1994). *Kaleidoscope: A multicultural booklist for grades K-8.* Urbana, IL: National Council of Teachers of English.

Bishop, R. S. (1997). Selecting literature for a multicultural curriculum. In V. J. Harris (Ed.), *Using multiethnic literature in the K-8 classroom* (pp. 1-19). Norwood, MA: Christopher Gordon.

Boler, M. (1999). *Feeling power: Emotions and education.* New York: Rutledge.

Bolton, G. (1999). *Acting in classroom drama: A critical analysis.* Portland, Maine: Calendar Islands.

Booth, D. (1995). *Story drama.* Markham, Ontario: Pembroke.

Bruner, J. (1986). *Actual minds, possible worlds.* Cambridge, MA: Harvard University Press.

Bruner, J. (2002). *Making stories: Law, literature, life.* New York: Farrar, Straus and Giroux.

Bush, E. (2001). A conversation with Ann Rinaldi, author. *The New Advocate, 14* (4), 311-319.

Calkins, L. M. (2001). *The art of teaching reading.* New York: Longman.

Chambliss, M. J., & McKillop, A. M. (2000). Creating a print- and technology-rich classroom library to entice children to read. In L. Baker, M. J. Dreher, & J. T. Guthrie (Eds.), *Engaging young readers: Promoting achievement and motivation* (pp. 94-118). New York: The Guiford Press.

Cole, M. (1996). *Cultural psychology: A once and future discipline.* Cambridge, MA: Harvard University Press.

Cole, T., & Chinoy, H. K. (1970). *Actors on acting: The theories, techniques, and practices of the world's great actors, told in their own words.* New York: Crown.

Commeyras, M., & Sumner, G. (1995). *Questions children want to discuss about literature: What teachers and students learned in a second grade classroom.* (NRRC Year 2 Project 1.9.2 Research Report). Athens, GA: U. of Georgia and U. of Maryland, National Reading Research Center.

Daniels, H. (1994). *Literature circles: Voice and choice in the student-centered classroom.* York, Maine: Stenhouse.

DiCamillo, K. (2001-2002, Winter). The wishing bone. *Riverbank Review,* 14-16.

Dillard, A. (1989). *The writing life.* New York: HarperCollins.

Dorris, M. (1992). "I" is not for Indian. In B. Slapin & D. Seale (Eds.), *Through Indian eyes: The Native experience in books for children* (pp. 27-28). Philadelphia, PA: New Society.

Dresang, E. T. (1999). *Radical change: Books for youth in a digital age.* New York: H. W. Wilson.

Dyson, A. H. (1993, January). Symbol makers, symbol weavers: How children link play, pictures, and print. *Young Children,* 50-57.

Eagleton, T. (1983). *Literary theory: An introduction.* Minneapolis, MN: University of Minnesota Press.

Edmiston, B. (1993). Going up the beanstalk: Discovering giant possibilities for responding to literature through drama. In K. E. Holland, R. A. Hungerford, & S. B. Ernst (Eds.), *Journeying: Children responding to literature* (pp. 250-266). Portsmouth: Heinemann.

Edmiston, B., & Enciso, P. (2003). Reflections and refractions of meaning: Dialogic approaches to classroom drama and reading. In J. Flood, D. Lapp, J. R. Squire, & J. M. Jensen (Eds.), *Handbook of research on teaching the English language arts, Second edition* (pp. 868-880). Mahwah, NJ: Lawrence Erlbaum.

Enciso, P. (1996). Why engagement in reading matters to Molly. *Reading and Writing Quarterly: Overcoming Learning Difficulties, 12,* 171-194.

Evans, J. (1998). "Princesses are not into war 'n things, they always scream and run off" Exploring gender stereotypes in picture books. *Reading, 32* (3), 5-11.

Evans, K. (2002). *Negotiating the self: Identity, sexuality, and emotion in learning to teach.* New York: RoutledgeFalmer.

Evans, K. S. (2002). Fifth-grade students' perceptions of how they experience literature discussion groups. *Reading Research Quarterly, 37* (1), 46–69.

Fauconnier, G., & Turner, M. (2002). *The way we think: Conceptual blending and the mind's hidden complexities.* New York: Basic Books.

Flores, B., Tefft Cousin, P., & Díaz, E. (1998). Transforming deficit myths about learning, language, and culture. In M. F. Opitz (Ed.), *Literacy instruction for culturally and linguistically diverse students* (pp. 27–38). Newark, DE: International Reading Association.

Fowler, A. (1982). *Kinds of literature: An introduction to the theory of genres and modes.* Cambridge, MA: Harvard University Press.

Fox, M. (1993a). Men who weep, boys who dance: The gender agenda between the lines in children's literature. *Language Arts, 70* (2), 84–88.

Fox, M. (1993b). *Radical reflections: Passionate opinions on teaching, learning, and living.* San Diego: Harcourt Brace.

Franklin, R. W. (Ed.). (1999). *The poems of Emily Dickinson.* Cambridge, MA: Harvard University Press.

Freedman, A. (1993). Show and tell? The role of explicit teaching in the learning of new genres. *Research in the Teaching of English, 27,* 222–251.

Gardner, H. (1983). *Frames of mind: The theory of multiple intelligences.* New York: Basic Books.

Goldenberg, C., Reese, L., & Gallimore, R. (1992). Effects of literacy materials from school on Latino children's home experiences and early reading achievement. *American Journal of Education, 100,* 497–536.

Greever, E. A., Austin, P., & Welhousen, K. (2000). *William's doll* revisited. *Language Arts, 77* (4), 324–330.

Harris, V. J. (1993). *Teaching multicultural literature in grades K-8.* Norwood, MA: Christopher Gordon.

Harris, V. J. (1997). *Using multiethnic literature in the K-8 classroom.* Norwood, MA: Christopher Gordon.

Hartman, D. K., & Hartman, J. A. (1993). Reading across texts: Expanding the role of the reader. *The Reading Teacher, 47* (3), 202–211.

Harvey, S., & Goudvis, A. (2000). *Strategies that work: Teaching comprehension to enhance understanding.* York, Maine: Stenhouse.

Harwayne, S. (1992). *Lasting impressions: Weaving literature into the writing workshop.* Portsmouth, NH: Heinemann.

Hearn, B. (1993). *The Zena Sutherland lectures 1983–1992.* New York: Clarion.

Hearn, B. (1993, July). Cite the source: Reducing cultural chaos in picture books, Part one. *School Library Journal,* 22–27.

Heathcote, D., & Bolton, G. (1995). *Drama for learning: Dorothy Heathcote's mantle of the expert approach to education.* Portsmouth, NH: Heinemann.

Hirsch, E. D. (1987). *Cultural literacy: What every American needs to know.* Boston: Houghton Mifflin.

Holton, L. (2001, September/October). Letters to the editor. *The Horn Book Magazine,* 503–504.

Huck, C. S. (1995). *Princess Furball:* The writing, illustrating, and response. In S. Lehr (Ed.), *Battling dragons: Issues and controversy in children's literature* (pp. 79–86). Portsmouth, NH: Heinemann.

Huck, C. S., Hepler, S., Hickman, J., and Kiefer, B. Z. (1997). *Children's literature in the elementary school* (Sixth edition). Dubuque, IA: Brown & Benchmark.

Hurley, S. R., & Chadwick, C. D. (1998). The images of females, minorities, and the aged in Caldecott award-winning picture books, 1958–1997. *Journal of Children's Literature, 24* (1), 58–66.

Jefferson, M. (2002, January 20). Harry Potter for grown-ups. *The New York Times Book Review*, 23.

Jenkins, C. (1998). From queer to gay and back again: Young adult novels with gay/lesbian/ queer content, 1969-1997. *Library Quarterly, 68* (3), 298-334.

Jenkins, C. B. (1999). *The allure of authors: Author studies in the elementary classroom.* Portsmouth, NH: Heinemann.

Johnson, L., & O'Neill, C. (1984). Introduction. In L. Johnson & C. O'Neill (Eds.), *Dorothy Heathcote: Collected writings on education and drama* (pp. 9-13). Evanston, IL: Northwestern University Press.

Keene, E. O., & Zimmermann, S. (1997). *Mosaic of thought: Teaching comprehension in a reader's workshop.* Portsmouth, NH: Heinemann.

Keesey, D. (1987). *Contexts for criticism.* Mountain View, CA: Mayfield.

Kiefer, B. Z. (1995). *The potential of picturebooks: From visual literacy to aesthetic understanding.* Englewood Cliffs, NJ: Merrill.

Kingsolver, B. (1995, December 16). Lit chat: "I'm a horrible eavesdropper." Retrieved May 15, 2003, from http://archive.salon.com/16dec1995/departments/litchat.html.

Kleinfield, N. R. (2002, June 2). The elderly man and the sea? Text sanitizes literary texts. *The New York Times,* YNE1, YNE30.

Kohl, H. (1995). *Should we burn Babar? Essays on children's literature and the power of stories.* New York: The New Press.

Kortenhaus, C. M., & Demarest, J. (1993). Gender role stereotyping in children's literature: An update. *Sex Roles, 28* (4), 219-232.

Kuskin, K. (1998, March/April). To get a little more of the picture: Reviewing picture books. *The Horn Book Magazine,* 159-165.

Lancia, P. J. (1997). Literary borrowing: The effects of literature on children's writing. *The Reading Teacher, 50* (6), 470-475.

Lanes, S. G. (1980). *The art of Maurice Sendak.* New York: Abradale Press/Harry N. Abrams.

Langer, J. A. (1995). *Envisioning literature: Literary understanding and literature instruction.* New York: Teachers College Press.

Larrick, N. (1972). The all-white world of children's books. In D. MacCann & G. Woodard (Eds.), *The black American in books for children: Readings in racism.* Metuchen, NJ: Scarecrow Press.

Lasky, K. (1996). To Stingo with love: An author's perspective on writing outside one's culture. *The New Advocate, 9,* 1-7.

Lehr, S. (Ed.). (2001). *Beauty, brains, and brawn: The construction of gender in children's literature.* Portsmouth, NH: Heinemann.

Lensmire, T. J. (1997). *Powerful writing, responsible teaching.* New York: Teachers College Press.

Lewis, C. (2001). *Literary practices as social acts: Power, status, and cultural norms in the classroom.* Mahwah, NJ: Lawrence Erlbaum.

Lewis, D. (2001). *Reading contemporary picturebooks: Picturing text.* New York: Routledge/ Falmer.

Lieberman, M. K. (1989). "Some day my prince will come": Female acculturation through the fairy tale. In J. Zipes (Ed.), *Don't bet on the prince: Contemporary feminist fairy tales in North America and England* (pp. 185-200). New York: Routledge.

Livingston, M. C. (1991). *Poem-making: Ways to begin writing poetry.* New York: HarperCollins.

Louie, B. Y. (2001). Why gender stereotypes still persist in contemporary children's literature. In S. Lehr (Ed.), *Beauty, brains, and brawn: The construction of gender in children's literature* (pp. 142-151). Portsmouth, NH: Heinemann.

Lukens, R. J. (2003). *A critical handbook of children's literature.* Boston, MA: Allyn and Bacon.

Marcus, L. S. (1998a). *Dear genius: The letters of Ursula Nordstrom.* New York: HarperCollins.

Marcus, L. S. (1998b). *A Caldecott celebration: Six artists and their paths to the Caldecott medal.* New York: Walker.

Marcus, L. S. (2001). *Side by side: Five favorite picture-book teams go to work.* New York: Walker.

Marcus, L. S. (2002). *Ways of telling: Conversations on the art of the picture book.* New York: Dutton.

Marshall, J. (2000). Research on response to literature. In M. L. Kamil, P. B. Mosenthal, P. D. Pearson, & R. Barr (Eds.), *Handbook of reading research Volume III* (pp. 381–402). Mahwah, NJ: Lawrence Erlbaum.

McCaslin, N. (1990). *Creative drama in the classroom.* New York: Longman.

McClure, A. (1995). Censorship of children's books. In S. Lehr (Ed.), *Battling dragons: Issues and controversy in children's literature* (pp. 3–30). Portsmouth, NH: Heinemann.

McGinley, W., & Kamberelis, G. (1992). Personal, social, and political functions of children's reading and writing. In C. K. Kinzer & D. J. Leu (Eds.), *Literacy research, theory, and practice: Views from many perspectives* (pp. 403–413). Chicago, IL: National Reading Conference.

Medina, C. L., & Enciso, P. (2002). "Some words are messengers/Hay palabras mensajeras": Interpreting sociopolitical themes in Latino children's literature. *The New Advocate, 15* (1), 35–47.

Moll, L. (2000). Inspired by Vygotsky: Ethnographic experiments in education. In C. D. Lee & P. Smagorinsky (Eds.), *Vygotskian perspectives on literacy research: Constructing meaning through collaborative inquiry* (pp. 256–268). Cambridge, UK: Cambridge University Press.

Moore, R. (1975). From rags to witches: Stereotypes, distortions, and anti-humanism in fairy tales. *Interracial Books for Children, 6,* 1–3.

Morrison, T. (1992). *Playing in the dark: Whiteness and the literary imagination.* Cambridge: MA: Harvard University Press.

National Reading Panel. (2001). *Teaching children to read: An evidence-based assessment of the scientific research literature on reading and its implications for reading instruction.* [Online]. Available: http://www.nichd.nih.gov/publications/nrp/smallbook.htm.

National Research Council. (1998). *Preventing reading difficulties in young children.* C. E. Snow, M. S. Burns, & P. Griffin (Eds.). Washington, DC: National Academy Press.

Neider, C. (Ed.) (1961). *Mark Twain: Life as I find it.* Garden City, NY: Hanover House.

Neumeyer, P. F. (1994). *The annotated Charlotte's web.* New York: HarperCollins.

Nieto, S. (1997). We have stories to tell: Puerto Ricans in children's books. In V. J. Harris (Ed.), *Using multiethnic literature in the K-8 classroom* (pp. 59–93). Norwood, MA: Christopher Gordon.

Nikolajeva, M., & Scott, C. (2001). *How picturebooks work.* New York: Garland Reference Library of the Humanities, Vol. 2171.

Nodelman, P. (1988). *Words about pictures: The narrative art of children's picture books.* Athens, GA: University of Georgia Press.

Nodelman, P. (1996). *The pleasures of children's literature.* New York: Longman.

Nodelman, P. (2002). Who the boys are: Thinking about masculinity in children's fiction. *The New Advocate, 15* (1), 9–18.

O'Neill, C. (1994). Here comes everybody: Aspects of role in process drama. *NADIE Journal, 18* (2), 37–44.

Opie, I., & Opie, P. (1974). *The classic fairy tales.* Oxford: Oxford University Press.

Orenstein, P. (1995). *Schoolgirls: Young women, self-esteem and the confidence gap.* New York: Alfred A. Knopf.

Paterson, K. (1986). Newbery medal acceptance (1981) for *Jacob have I loved.* In L. Kingman (Ed.), *Newbery and Caldecott medal books 1976–1985* (pp. 76–85). Boston: Horn Book.

Pearson, P. D., & Fielding, L. (1991). Comprehension instruction. In R. Barr, M. L. Kamil, P. B. Mosenthal, & P. D. Pearson (Eds.), *Handbook of reading research, Volume II* (pp. 815–860). New York: Longman.

Peterson, R., & Eeds, M. (1990). *Grand conversations: Literature groups in action.* New York: Scholastic.

Peterson, S. B., & Lach, M. A. (1990). Gender stereotypes in children's books: Their prevalence and influence on cognitive and affective development.*Gender and Education, 2* (2), 185–196.

Pinkney, A. D. (2001, September/October). Awards that stand on solid ground. *The Horn Book Magazine,* 535–539.

Pinsky, R. (1998). *The sounds of poetry: A brief guide.* New York: Farrar, Straus and Giroux.

Pipher, M. (1995). *Reviving Ophelia: Saving the selves of adolescent girls.* New York: Ballantine Books.

Raphael, T. E., & McMahon, S. I. (1994). Book club: An alternative framework for reading instruction. *The Reading Teacher, 48,* 102–116.

Ray, K. W. (1999). *Wondrous words: Writers and writing in the elementary classroom.* Urbana, IL: National Council of Teachers of English.

Reese, D., & Caldwell-Wood, N. (1997). Native Americans in children's literature. In V. J. Harris (Ed.), *Using multiethnic literature in the K-8 classroom* (pp. 155–192). Norwood, MA: Christopher Gordon.

Rice, P. S. (2000). Gendered readings of a traditional "feminist" folktale by sixth-grade boys and girls. *Journal of Literacy Research, 32* (2), 211–236.

Ríos, F. A. (1996). *Teacher thinking in cultural contexts.* Albany, NY: State University of New York Press.

Roller, C.M., & Beed, P. L. (1994). Sometimes the conversations were grand, and sometimes.... *Language Arts, 71,* 509–515.

Rosenblatt, L. M. (1994). *The reader, the text, the poem: The transactional theory of the literary work.* Carbondale, IL: Southern Illinois University Press.

Rothstein, M. (1988, October 19). From the very busy Sendak, a book of a rare Grimm tale. *The New York Times,* C19, C24.

Routman, R. (2000). *Conversations: Strategies for teaching, learning, and evaluating.* Portsmouth, NH: Heinemann.

Rowe, K. E. (1989). Feminism and fairy tales. In J. Zipes (Ed.), *Don't bet on the prince: Contemporary feminist fairy tales in North America and England,* (pp. 209–226). New York: Routledge.

Santman, D. (2002). Teaching to the test?: Test preparation in the reading workshop. *Language Arts, 3* (3), 203–211.

Schneider, J. J., & Jackson, S. A. W. (2000). Process drama: A special space and place for writing. *The Reading Teacher, 54* (1), 38–51.

Schwarcz, J. H., & Schwarcz, C. (1991). *The picture book comes of age: Looking at childhood through the art of illustration.* Chicago: American Library Association.

Schwartz, L. S. (1996). *Ruined by reading.* Boston, MA: Beacon Press.

Sendak, M. (1988). *Caldecott & Co. Notes on books & pictures.* New York: Farrar, Straus and Giroux.

Sendak, M. (1993). Sources of inspiration. In Betsy Hearne's (Ed.) *The Zena Sutherland lectures* (pp. 1–25). New York: Clarion Books.

Shepard, L. A. (1991). Negative policies for dealing with diversity: When does assessment and diagnosis turn into sorting and segregation? In E. H. Hiebert (Ed.), *Literacy for a diverse society: Perspectives, practices, and policies* (pp. 279–298). New York: Teachers College Press.

Short, K. G., & Harste, J. with Burke, C. (1996). *Creating classrooms for authors and inquirers.* Portsmouth, NH: Heinemann.

Short, K. G., & Pierce, K. M. (1990). *Talking about books: Creating literate communities.* Portsmouth, NH: Heinemann.

Siegel, M. (1995). More than words: The generative power of transmediation for learning. *Canadian Journal of Education, 20* (4), 455–475.

Sikora, F. (1991) *Until justice rolls down: The Birmingham church bombing case.* Tuscaloosa, AL: The University of Alabama Press.

Silvey, A. (1995). *Children's books and their creators.* Boston, MA: Houghton Mifflin.

Silvey, A. (2002). *The essential guide to children's books and their creators.* Boston, MA: Houghton Mifflin.

Sims [Bishop], R. (1982). *Shadow and substance: Afro-American experience in contemporary children's fiction.* Urbana, IL: NCTE.

Slapin, B., & Seale, D. (1998). *Through Indian eyes: The Native experience in books for children.* Los Angeles, CA: American Indian Studies Center, University of California.

Sloan, G. D. (1991). *The child as critic: Teaching literature in elementary and middle schools.* New York: Teachers College Press.

Soter, A. (1999). *Young adult literature & the new literary theories: Developing critical readers in middle school.* New York: Teachers College Press.

Spandel, V. (2000). *Creating writers through 6-trait writing assessment and instruction* (3rd Edition). New York: Longman.

Stanislavski, C. (1989). *An actor prepares.* New York: Routledge/Theatre Arts Books.

Stewig, J. W. (1995). *Looking at picture books.* Fort Atkinson, WI: Highsmith Press.

Sullivan, J. (1997). On "Ballad of Birmingham." In *On the walls and in the streets: American poetry broadsides from the 1960s.* University of Illinois. Retrieved May 11, 2003, from http://www.english.uiuc.edu/maps/poets/m_r/randall/ballad.htm.

Sumara, D. J. (2002). *Why reading literature in school still matters: Imagination, interpretation, insight.* Mahwah, NJ: Lawrence Erlbaum.

Sutton, R. (2001, May/June). An interview with Virginia Euwer Wolff. *The Horn Book Magazine,* 280–286.

Takaki, R. (1993). *A different mirror: A history of multicultural America.* Boston, MA: Little Brown.

Tatar, M. (1987). *The hard facts of the Grimm's' fairy tales.* Princeton, NJ: Princeton University Press.

Tatar, M. (1992). *Off with their heads! Fairy tales and the culture of childhood.* Princeton, NJ: Princeton University Press.

Taylor, M. D. (1986). Newbery medal acceptance (1977) for *Roll of thunder, hear my cry.* In L. Kingman (Ed.), *Newbery and Caldecott medal books 1976–1985* (pp. 21–30). Boston: Horn Book.

Temple, C., Martinez, M., Yokota, J., & Naylor, A. (2002). *Children's books in children's hands: An introduction to their literature.* Boston, MA: Allyn and Bacon.

The Horn Book Association for Library Service to Children. (2001). *The Newbery & Caldecott medal books 1986–2000: A comprehensive guide to the winners.* Chicago: American Library Association.

Thompson, D. L. (2001). Deconstructing Harry: Casting a critical eye on the witches and wizards of Hogwarts. In S. Lehr (Ed.), *Beauty, brains, and brawn: The construction of gender in children's literature* (pp. 42–50). Portsmouth, NH: Heinemann.

Villaume, S. K., Worden, T., Williams, S., Hopkins, L., & Rosenblatt, C. (1994). Five teachers in search of a discussion. *The Reading Teacher, 47* (6), 480–487.

Vygotsky, L. S. (1978). *Mind in society: The development of higher psychological processes.* Cambridge, MA: Harvard University Press.

Vygotsky, L. S. (1986). *Thought and language.* Cambridge, MA: MIT Press.

Wagner, B. J. (1998). *Educational drama and language arts: What research shows.* Portsmouth, NH: Heinemann.

Weich, D. (2000, April 5). *Christopher Paul Curtis goes to Powell's - 2000.* Retrieved May 11, 2003, from http://www.powells.com/authors/curtis.html.

Weil, D. K. (1998). *Towards a critical multicultural literacy: Theory and practice for education for liberation.* New York: Peter Lang.

Weitzman, L. J., Eifler, J., Hokada, E., & Ross, C. (1972). Sex-role socialization in picture books for preschool children. *American Journal of Sociology, 77,* 1125-1150.

Welty, E. (1952, October 9). Life in the barn was very good. *The New York Times Book Review,* 49.

Wertsch, J. V. (1991). *Voices of the mind: A sociocultural approach to mediated action.* Cambridge, MA: Harvard University Press.

Whitelaw, J., & Wolf, S. A. (2001). Learning to "see beyond": Sixth-grade students' artistic perceptions of *The Giver. The New Advocate, 14* (1), 57-67.

Wilhelm, J. D. (1996). Reading *is* seeing: Using visual response to improve the literary reading of reluctant readers. *Journal of Reading Behavior, 27* (4), 467-503.

Wilhelm, J. D., & Edmiston, B. (1998). *Imagining to learn: Inquiry, ethics, and integration through drama.* Portsmouth, NH: Heinemann.

Winner, E. (1982). *Invented worlds: The psychology of the arts.* Cambridge, MA: Harvard University Press.

Wolf, S. A. (1994). Learning to act/Acting to learn: Children as actors, characters, and critics in classroom theatre. *Research in the Teaching of English, 28* (1), 7-44.

Wolf, S. A. (1995). Language in and around the dramatic curriculum. *The Journal of Curriculum Studies, 27* (2), 117-137.

Wolf, S. A., Ballentine, D., & Hill, L. (1999). The right to write: Preservice teachers' evolving understandings of authenticity and aesthetic heat in multicultural literature. *Research in the Teaching of English, 34* (1), 130-184.

Wolf, S. A., Ballentine, D., & Hill, L. (2000). Only connect!: Cross cultural connections in the reading lives of preservice teachers and children. *Journal of Literacy Research, 32* (4), 533-569.

Wolf, S. A., Carey, A. A., & Mieras, E. L. (1996). "What is this literachurch stuff anyway?": Preservice teachers' growth in understanding children's literary response. *Reading Research Quarterly, 31* (2), 130-157.

Wolf, S. A., Edmiston, B., & Enciso, P. (1997). Drama worlds: Places of the heart, head, voice, and hand in dramatic interpretation. In J. Flood, D. Lapp, & S. B. Heath (Eds.), *A handbook for literacy educators: Research on teaching the communicative and visual arts* (pp. 474-487). New York: Macmillan.

Wolf, S. A., & Heath, S. B. (1992). *The braid of literature: Children's worlds of reading.* Cambridge, MA: Harvard University Press.

Wolf, S. A., & Heath, S. B. (1998). Wondrous words: Young children's rewritings of prose and poetry. *The New Advocate, 11* (4), 291-310.

Wolf, S. A., & Maniotes, L. (2002). Silenced by sex: Hard truths & taboos in teaching literature. *The New Advocate, 15* (3), 197-204.

Wollman-Bonilla, J. (2000). Teaching science writing to first graders: Genre learning and recontextualization. *Research in the Teaching of English, 35* (1), 35-65.

Woodson, J. (1995, November/December). A sign of having been there. *The Horn Book Magazine, 711*-715.

Yamate, S. S. (1997). Asian Pacific American children's literature: Expanding perceptions about who Americans are. In V. J. Harris (Ed.), *Using multiethnic literature in the K-8 classroom* (pp. 95-128). Norwood, MA: Christopher Gordon.

Yokota, J. (Editor), and the Committee to Revise the Multicultural Booklist. (2001). *Kaleidoscope: A multicultural booklist for grades K-8, Third Edition.* Urbana, IL: National Council of Teachers of English.

Zarin, C. (2001, November 18). Once upon their times. *The New York Times Book Review,* 29.

Zelinsky, P. O. (2001). Illustrator profile: Paul O. Zelinsky. In S. Lehr (Ed.), *Beauty, brains, and brawn: The construction of gender in children's literature* (pp. 88–91). Portsmouth, NH: Heinemann.

Zipes, J. (1987). *Don't bet on the prince: Contemporary feminist fairy tales in North America and England.* New York: Routledge.

Zipes, J. (1991). *Spells of enchantment: The wondrous fairy tales of western culture.* New York: Viking.

Zipes, J. (2001). *Sticks and stones: The troublesome success of children's literature from Slovenly Peter to Harry Potter.* New York: Routledge.

ADULT LITERATURE REFERENCES

Erdrich, L. (2001). *The last report on the miracles at Little No Horse.* New York: HarperCollins.

Hay, S. H. (1998). *Story hour.* Fayetteville, AR: University of Arkansas Press.

Randall, D. (1969). Ballad of Birmingham. In Margaret Danner and Dudley Randall (Eds.), *Poem counterpoem.* Detroit, Michigan: Broadside Press.

Sexton, A. (1971). *Transformations.* Boston: Houghton Mifflin.

Tolkien, J. R. R. (1966). *The Hobbit.* Boston: Houghton Mifflin.

Tolkien, J. R. R. (1967). *The lord of the rings.* Boston: Houghton Mifflin.

Whitman, R. (1968). *The marriage wig and other poems.* New York: Harcourt.

Williams, W. C. (1938). *Collected poems: 1909–1939.* New Directions.

CHILDREN'S LITERATURE REFERENCES

Aardema, V. (1975). *Why mosquitoes buzz in people's ears,* illustrated by L. and D. Dillon. New York: Dial.

Aardema, V. (1976). *Ashanti to Zulu: African traditions,* illustrated by L. and D. Dillon. New York: Dial.

Aardema, V. (1977). *Who's in rabbit's house?: A Masai tale,* illustrated by L. and D. Dillon. New York: Dial.

Ada, A. F. (1991). *The gold coin,* illustrated by N. Waldman. New York: Atheneum.

Ada, A. F. (1998). *Under the royal palms: A childhood in Cuba.* New York: Atheneum.

Ada, A. F., Harris, V. J., & Hopkins, L. B. (1993). *A chorus of cultures: Developing literacy through multicultural poetry.* Carmel, CA: Hampton-Brown.

Adedjouma, D. (Ed.). (1996). *The palm of my heart: Poetry by African American children,* illustrated by G. Christie. New York: Lee and Low.

Aesop. (1988). *Aesop's fables,* illustrated by C. Santore. New York: JellyBean.

Aesop. (1999). *Aesop's fox,* retold and illustrated by A. Sogabe. San Diego, CA: Browndeer.

African American poets. (1997). *In daddy's arms I AM TALL: African Americans celebrating fathers,* illustrated by J. Steptoe. New York: Lee and Low.

Alarcón, F. X. (1997). *Laughing tomatoes and other spring poems / Jitomates risueños y otros poemas de primavera,* illustrated by M. C. Gonzalez. San Francisco: Children's Book Press.

Alexander, L. (1992). *The fortune-tellers,* illustrated by T. S. Hyman. New York: Dutton.

Aliki. (1999). *William Shakespeare & the Globe.* New York: HarperCollins.

Altman, L. J. (1993). *Amelia's road,* illustrated by E. Sanchez. New York: Lee & Low Books.

Alvarez, J. (2002). *Before we were free.* New York: Alfred A. Knopf.

Andersen, H. C. (1999). *The ugly duckling,* adapted and illustrated by J. Pinkney. New York: Morrow.

Anderson, L. H. (1999). *Speak.* New York: Farrar Straus Giroux.

Babbitt, N. (1975). *Tuck everlasting.* New York: Farrar, Straus, & Giroux.

Bang, M. (1991). *Picture this: Perception & composition.* Boston: Little, Brown.

Bang, M. (1999). *When Sophie gets angry—Really, really angry...* New York: Blue Sky Press.

Barchers, S. I. (Ed.). (1990). *Wise women: Folk and fairy tales from around the world,* illustrated by L. Mullineaux. Englewood, CO: Libraries Unlimited.

Barrie, J. M. (1988). *Peter Pan.* Quebec, Canada: Tundra.

Bauer, M. D. (Ed.). (1994). *Am I blue? Coming out from the silence.* New York: HarperCollins.

Baum, L. F. (1900). *The wizard of Oz,* illustrated by W. W. Denslow. Chicago: Reilly & Lee.

Begay, S. (1992). *Ma'ii and cousin Horned Toad: A traditional Navajo story.* New York: Scholastic.

Berry, J. (1991). *Ajeemah and his son.* New York: HarperCollins.

Bontemps, A. (1948). *Story of the Negro.* New York: Knopf.

Bridges, R. (1999). *Through my eyes.* New York: Scholastic.

Browne, A. (1986). *Piggybook.* New York: Alfred A. Knopf.

Browne, A. (2001). *My dad.* New York: Farrar Straus Giroux.

Bruchac, J. (1998). *The heart of a chief.* New York: Dial.

Bruchac, J., & London, J. (1992). *Thirteen moons on turtle's back: A Native American year of moons,* illustrated by T. Locker. New York: Philomel/Putnam.

Bunting, E. (1992). *The wall,* illustrated by R. Himler. Boston, MA: Houghton Mifflin.

Bunting, E. (1994). *Smoky night,* illustrated by D. Diaz. New York: Harcourt.

Burnett, F. H. (1910). *The secret garden,* illustrated by M. Hague. New York: Henry Holt.

Carle, E. (1990). *The very quiet cricket.* New York: Philomel.

Carlson, L. M. (1994). *Cool salsa: Bilingual poems on growing up Latino in the United States.* New York: Henry Holt.

Casanova, M. (2000). *The hunter: A Chinese folktale,* illustrated by E. Young. New York: Atheneum.

Cleary, B. (1975). *Ramona the brave,* illustrated by A. Tiegreen. New York: Avon.

Coles, R. (1995). *The story of Ruby Bridges,* illustrated by G. Ford. New York: Scholastic.

Cooper, S. (1999). *King of shadows.* New York: McElderry.

Creech, S. (2001). *Love that dog.* New York: HarperCollins.

Crossley-Holland, K. (2000). *The seeing stone: Arthur trilogy book one.* New York: Scholastic.

Curtis, C. P. (1995). *The Watsons go to Birmingham—1963.* New York: Delacorte.

Curtis, C. P. (1999). *Bud, not Buddy.* New York: Delacorte.

Cushman, K. (1995). *The midwife's apprentice.* New York: Harper.

Dahl, R. (1982). *The Twits,* illustrated by Q. Blake. New York: Bantam Books.

Dahl, R. (1984). *The BFG,* illustrated by Q. Blake. New York: Puffin.

Dahl, R. (1988). *Matilda,* illustrated by Q. Blake. New York: Viking Kestrel.

Dahl, R. (1996). *James and the giant peach,* illustrated by L. Smith. New York: Penguin.

De Brunhoff, J. (1931). *The story of Babar, the little elephant,* translated from the French by M. S. Haas. New York: Random House.

De Haan, L., & Nijland, S. (2000). *King & King.* Berkeley, CA: Tricycle Press.

De Regniers, B. S. (1988). *Sing a song of popcorn, every child's book of poems,* selected by B. S. de Regniers, E. Moore, M. M. White, & J. Carr, illustrated by nine Caldecott medal artists. New York: Scholastic.

DiCamillo, K. (2000). *Because of Winn-Dixie.* Cambridge, MA: Candlewick.

DiCamillo, K. (2001). *The tiger rising.* Cambridge, MA: Candlewick.

Donoghue, E. (1997). *Kissing the witch: Old tales in new skins.* New York: HarperCollins.

Dorris, M. (1992). *Morning Girl.* New York: Hyperion.

Dorris, M. (1994). *Guests.* New York: Hyperion.

Dorros, A. (1997). *Radio man: A story in English and Spanish/Don Radio: Un cuento en ingles y español.* New York: HarperCollins.

Erdrich, L. (1999). *The birchbark house.* New York: Scholastic.

Falconer, I. (2000). *Olivia.* New York: Atheneum.

Farmer, N. (1994). *The ear, the eye, and the arm: A novel.* New York: Orchard Books.

Farmer, N. (2002). *The house of the scorpion.* New York: Atheneum.

Feelings, T. (1993). *Soul looks back in wonder.* New York: Dial.

Feelings, T. (1995). *The middle passage: White ships/black cargo.* New York: Dial.

Fleischman, P. (1988). *Joyful noise: Poems for two voices,* illustrated by E. Beddows. New York: Harper & Row.

Fox, M. (1983). *Possum magic,* illustrated by J. Vivas. New York: Harcourt Brace.

Fox, M. (1985). *Wilfrid Gordon McDonald Partridge,* illustrated by J. Vivas. Brooklyn, NY: Kane/Miller.

Fox, M. (1989). *Koala Lou,* illustrated by P. Lofts. San Diego: Harcourt Brace Jovanovich.

Fox, M. (1994). *Tough Boris,* illustrated by K. Brown. San Diego: Harcourt Brace Jovanovich.

Freedman, R. (1998). *Martha Graham: A dancer's life.* New York: Clarion.

Gaiman, N. (2002). *Coraline,* with illustrations by D. McKean. New York: HarperCollins.

Gantos, J. (1998). *Joey Pigza swallowed the key.* New York: Farrar, Straus and Giroux.

Gantos, J. (2000). *Joey Pigza loses control.* New York: Farrar, Straus and Giroux.

Gantos, J. (2002). *What would Joey do?* New York: Farrar, Straus and Giroux.

Garner, J. F. (1994). *Politically correct bedtime stories: Modern tales for our life & times.* New York: Macmillan.

Geras, A. (2001). *Troy.* San Diego, CA: Harcourt.

Giff, P. R. (2002). *Pictures of Hollis Woods.* New York: Wendy Lamb Books/Random House.

Giovanni, N. (1996). *Shimmy shimmy shimmy like my sister Kate: Looking at the Harlem Renaissance through poems.* New York: Henry Holt.

Goble, P. (1978). *The girl who loved wild horses.* New York: Bradbury Press.

Greenberg, J. (2001). *Heart to heart: New poems inspired by twentieth-century American art.* New York: Harry N. Abrams.

Greenberg, J., & Jordan, S. (2002). *Action Jackson,* illustrated by R. A. Parker. New York: Harry N. Abrams.

Greenfield, E. (1978). *Honey, I love,* illustrated by L. & D. Dillon. New York: Crowell.

Grimes, N. (1994). *Meet Danitra Brown,* illustrated by F. Cooper. New York: Lothrop Lee & Shepard.

Grimes, N. (1998). *Jazmin's notebook.* New York: Dial.

Grimes, N. (2002). *Bronx masquerade.* New York: Dial.

Grimes, N. (2002). *Talkin' about Bessie: The story of aviator Elizabeth Coleman,* illustrated by E. B. Lewis. New York: Scholastic.

Grimm Brothers. (1973). *Grimm's fairy tales, twenty stories,* illustrated by A. Rackham. New York: The Viking Press.

Grimm Brothers. (1974). *Snow White,* freely translated from the German by P. Heins, illustrated by T. S. Hyman. Boston: Little, Brown.

Grimm Brothers. (1977). *The sleeping beauty,* retold and illustrated by T. S. Hyman. Boston: Little, Brown.

Grimm Brothers. (1981). *Hansel and Gretel,* illustrated by A. Browne. New York: Alfred A. Knopf.

Grimm Brothers. (1983). *Little Red Riding Hood,* retold and illustrated by T. S. Hyman. New York: Holiday House.

Grimm Brothers. (1986). *The water of life,* retold by B. Rogasky, illustrated by T. S. Hyman. New York: Holiday House.

Grimm Brothers. (1988). *Hansel and Gretel,* translated by E. D. Crawford, illustrated by L. Zwerger. Saxonville, MA: Picture Book Studio.

Grimm, W. (1988). *Dear Mili,* translated by R. Manheim, illustrated by M. Sendak. New York: Farrar, Straus and Giroux.

Hamanaka, S. (1990). *The journey: Japanese Americans, racism and renewal.* New York: Orchard Books.

Hamilton, V. (1968). *The house of Dies Drear,* illustrated by E. Keith. New York: Macmillan.

Hamilton, V. (1971). *The planet of Junior Brown.* New York: Macmillan.

Hamilton, V. (1974). *M.C. Higgins, the great.* New York: Macmillan.

Hamilton, V. (1983). *Sweet whispers, brother rush.* New York: Philomel.

Hamilton, V. (1985). *The people could fly: American Black folktales.* New York: Alfre A. Knopf.

Hamilton, V. (1988). *In the beginning: Creation stories from around the world,* illustrated by B. Moser. San Diego, CA: Harcourt Brace Jovanovich.

Hamilton, V. (1995). *Her stories: African American folktales, fairy tales, and true tales,* illustrated by L. and D. Dillon. New York: Scholastic.

Hearn, B. (1997). *Seven brave women,* illustrated by B. Andersen. New York: Greenwillow.

Henkes, K. (1993). *Owen.* New York: Greenwillow.

Henry, M. (1948). *King of the wind,* illustrated by W. Dennis. New York: Rand McNally.

Hesse, K. (1997). *Out of the dust.* New York: Scholastic.

Hoban, R. (1960). *Bedtime for Frances,* illustrated by G. Williams. New York: Harper & Row.

Hodges, M. (1984). *Saint George and the dragon,* illustrated by T. S. Hyman. Boston: Little, Brown.

Hodges, M. (1990). *The kitchen knight,* illustrated by T. S. Hyman. New York: Holiday House.

Horvath, P. (1999). *The trolls.* New York: Farrar Straus Giroux.

Howard, E. F. (2000). *Virgie goes to school with us boys,* illustrated by E. B. Lewis. New York: Simon & Schuster.

Huck, C. (1989). *Princess Furball,* illustrated by A. Lobel. New York: Green Willow Books.

Hughes, L. (1994). *The dream keeper and other poems,* illustrated by B. Pinkney. New York: Alfred Knopf.

Igus, T. (1998). *I see the rhythm,* paintings by M. Wood. San Francisco: Children's Book Press.

Jiménez, F. (1997). *The circuit: Stories from the life of a migrant child.* University of New Mexico Press.

Jiménez, F. (1998). *La mariposa,* illustrated by S. Silva. Boston, MA: Houghton Mifflin.

Johnston, B. (1978). *How the birds got their colors/Gah w'indinimowaut binaesheenhnyuk w'indinauziwin-wauh,* illustrated by D. Ashkewe. Toronto: Kids Can Press.

Jones, B. T., & Kuklin, S. (1998). *Dance,* photographed by S. Kuklin. New York: Hyperion.

Kajikawa, K. (2001). *Yoshi's feast,* illustrated by Y. Heo. New York: DK Ink.

Konigsburg, E. L. (1996). *The view from Saturday.* New York: Atheneum.

Konigsburg, E. L. (2000). *Silent to the bone.* New York: Atheneum.

Lawrence, J. (1993). *Harriet and the promised land.* New York: Simon & Schuster.

L'Engle, M. (1962). *A wrinkle in time.* New York: Farrar, Straus and Giroux.

Lester, J. (1968). *To be a slave.* New York: Dial.

Lester, J. (1994). *John Henry,* illustrated by J. Pinkney. New York: Dial.

Levine, G. C. (1997). *Ella enchanted.* New York: HarperCollins.

Lobel, A. (1980). *Fables.* New York: Harper & Row.

Lomas Garza, C. (1990). *Family pictures/Cuadros de familia,* as told to H. Rohmer, with a version in Spanish by R. Zubizarreta. San Francisco: Children's Book Press.

Lomas Garza, C. (1999). *Magic windows/Ventanas mágicas.* San Francisco: Children's Book Press.

Lowry, L. (1993). *The giver.* Boston: Houghton Mifflin.

Lunge-Larsen, L. (1999). *The troll with no heart in his body and other tales of trolls from Norway,* woodcuts by B. Bowen. Boston, MA: Houghton Mifflin.

Lyons, M. E. (1992). *Letters from a slave girl.* New York: Charles Scribner's Sons.

Lynch, P. J. (1992). *East o' the sun and west o' the moon.* Cambridge, MA: Candlewick.

MacLachlan, P. (1993). *Baby.* New York: Delacorte.

Marshall, J. (1987). *Red Riding Hood.* New York: Dial.

Mathis, S. B. (1975). *The hundred penny box.* New York: Viking.

Martin, A. M. (2002). *A corner of the universe.* New York: Scholastic.

Martin, J. B. (1996). *Grandmother Bryant's pocket,* illustrated by P. Mathers. Boston: Houghton Mifflin.

Martin, J. B. (1999). *Snowflake Bentley,* illustrated by M. Azarian. Boston: Houghton Mifflin.

Martinez, A. C., Zubizarreta, R., Rohmer, H., & Schecter, D. (1991). *The woman who outshone the sun: The legend of Lucía Zenteno—La mujer que brillaba áun más que el sol: La leyenda de Lucía Zenteno,* illustrated by F. Olivera. San Francisco, CA: Children's Book Press.

McKinley, R. (1978). *Beauty: A retelling of the story of Beauty and the Beast.* New York: HarperCollins.

McKinley, R. (1984). *The hero and the crown.* New York: Greenwillow.

McKissack, P. (1988). *Mirandy and brother wind.* New York: Alfred A. Knopf.

McKissack, P. (1992). *The dark-thirty: Southern tales of the supernatural,* illustrated by B. Pinkney. New York: Knopf.

Minghella, A. (1991). *Jim Henson's "The storyteller",* illustrated by D. May. New York: Alfred A. Knopf.

Mochizuki, K. (1993). *Baseball saved us,* illustrated by D. Lee. New York: Lee & Low.

Mollel, T. (1999). *My rows and piles of coins,* illustrated by E. B. Lewis. New York: Clarion.

Montgomery, L. M. (1908). *Anne of Green Gables,* illustrated by J. Lee. New York: Grosset & Dunlap.

Mora, P. (Ed.). (2001). *Love to mamá,* illustrated by P. S. Barragán M. New York: Lee & Low.

Mukerji, D. G. (1927). *Gayneck, the story of a pigeon.* New York: Dutton.

Munsch, R. (1980). *The paper bag princess,* illustrated by M. Martchenko. Toronto: Annick Press.

Muth, J. J. (2002). *The three questions.* New York: Scholastic.

Myers, T. (2000). *Basho and the fox,* illustrated by O. S. Han. New York: Marshall Cavendish.

Myers, W. D. (1992). *Somewhere in the darkness.* New York: Scholastic.

Myers, W. D. (1997). *Harlem: A poem,* illustrated by C. Myers. New York: Scholastic Press.

Myers, W. D. (1999). *Monster,* illustrated by C. Myers. New York: HarperCollins.

Na, A. (2001). *A step from heaven.* Asheville, NC: Front Street.

Namioka, L. (1992). *Yang the youngest and his terrible ear,* illustrated by K. de Kiefte. Boston: Little, Brown.

Naylor, P. R. (1991). *Shiloh.* New York: Atheneum.

Nelson, M. (2001). *Carver, a life in poems.* Asheville, NC: Front Street.

Newman, L. (1989). *Heather has two mommies.* Boston: Alyson.

Nye, N. S. (2002). *19 varieties of gazelle: Poems of the Middle East.* New York: Greenwillow Books.

Opie, I. & P. (Eds.). (1992). *I saw Esau: The schoolchild's pocket book,* illustrated by M. Sendak. Cambridge, MA: Candlewick.

Osborne, M. P. *Kate and the beanstalk,* illustrated by G. Potter. New York: Atheneum.

Palatini, M. (1995). *Piggie pie!,* illustrated by H. Fine. New York: Clarion.

Park, L. S. (2001). *A single shard.* New York: Clarion.

Paterson, K. (1977). *Bridge to Teribithia,* illustrated by D. Diamond. New York: Harper & Row.

Paterson, K. (1978). *The great Gilly Hopkins.* New York: Crowell.

Paterson, K. (1980). *Jacob have I loved.* New York: Avon.

Paterson, K. (1990). *The tale of the mandarin ducks,* illustrated by L. and D. Dillon. New York: Lodestar.

Paterson, K. (1992). *The king's equal,* illustrated by V. Vagin. New York: HarperCollins.

Pérez, A. I. (2000). *My very own room/Mi propio cuartito,* illustrated by M. C. Gonzalez. San Francisco, CA: Children's Book Press.

Perrault, C. (1954). *Cinderella,* illustrated by M. Brown. New York: Charles Scribner's Sons.

Polacco, P. (1988). *The keeping quilt.* New York: Simon and Schuster.

Polacco, P. (1990). *Just plain fancy.* New York: Bantam Doubleday Dell.

Polacco, P. (1995). *Pink and Say.* New York: Scholastic.

Potter, B. (1902). *The tale of Peter Rabbit.* London: Frederick Warne.

Potter, B. (1903). *The tailor of Gloucester.* London: Frederick Warne.

Prelutsky, J. (1993). *The dragons are singing tonight,* illustrated by P. Sis. New York: Greenwillow.

Pullman, P. (1996). *The golden compass.* New York: Alfred A. Knopf.

Rappaport, D. (2001). *Martin's BIG words: The life of Dr. Martin Luther King, Jr.,* illustrated by B. Collier. New York: Jump at the Sun/Hyperion.

Rinaldi, A. (1999). *My heart is on the ground: The diary of Nannie Little Rose, a Sioux girl. Carlisle Indian School, Pennsylvania, 1880.* New York: Scholastic.

Ringgold, F. (1991). *Tar beach.* New York: Crown.

Rosenberg, L. (Ed.). (1998). *Earth-shattering poems.* New York: Henry Holt.

Rowling, J. K. (1998). *Harry Potter and the sorcerer's stone.* New York: Scholastic.

Ryan, P. M. (2000). *Esperanza rising.* New York: Scholastic.

Sachar, L. (1998). *Holes.* New York: Farrar, Straus, & Giroux.

Saldaña, R. (2001). *The jumping tree.* New York: Delacourt.

Say, A. (1993). *Grandfather's journey.* Boston: Houghton Mifflin.

Scieszka, J. (1989). *The true story of the 3 little pigs!,* illustrated by L. Smith. New York: Viking Kestrel.

Scieszka, J. (1991). *The frog prince continued,* illustrated by S. Johnson. New York: Viking.

Scieszka, J. (1992). *The stinky cheese man and other fairly stupid tales,* illustrated by L. Smith. New York: Viking Penguin.

Segal, L., & Sendak, M. (Selection and Arrangement). (1973). *The juniper tree and other tales from Grimm,* translated by L. Segal and R. Jarrell, illustrated by M. Sendak. New York: Farrar, Straus and Giroux.

Sendak, M. (1963). *Where the wild things are.* New York: Harper & Row.

Sendak, M. (1970). *In the night kitchen.* New York: Harper & Row.

Sendak, M. (1981). *Outside over there.* New York: Harper & Row.

Silverstein, S. (1964). *The giving tree.* New York: Harper & Row.

Silverstein, S. (1981). *A light in the attic.* New York: Harper & Row.

Sisulu, E. B. (1996). *The day Gogo went to vote: South Africa 1994,* illustrated by S. Wilson. Boston: Little Brown.

Skármeta, A. (2000). *The composition,* pictures by A. Ruano. Buffalo, NY: Groundwood Books.

Snicket, L. (2000). *The miserable mill (A series of unfortunate events—Book the fourth),* illustrated by B. Helquist. New York: HarperCollins.

Sobol, D. (1973). *Encyclopedia Brown takes a case,* illustrated by L. Shortall. New York: Nelson.

Sones, S. (1999). *Stop pretending: What happened when my big sister went crazy.* New York: HarperCollins.

Soto, G. (1990). *Baseball in April and other stories.* San Diego: Harcourt Brace Jovanovich.

Soto, G. (1992). *Neighborhood odes,* illustrated by D. Diaz. New York: Harcourt Brace Jovanovich.

Soto, G. (1993). *Too many tamales,* illustrated by E. Martinez. New York: G. P. Putnam.

Soto, G. (1996). *¡Qué montón de TAMALES!,* translated by A. F. Ada & F. I. Campoy, illustrated by E. Martinez. New York: Putnam & Grosset Group.

Spinelli, J. (1997). *Wringer.* New York: HarperCollins.

Stanley, D. (1997). *Rumpelstiltskin's daughter.* New York: Morrow Junior Books.

Stanley, D., & Vennema, P. (1992). *Bard of Avon: The story of William Shakespeare,* illustrated by D. Stanley. New York: Morrow Junior Books.

Steig, J. (2001). *A gift from Zeus,* illustrated by W. Steig. New York: HarperCollins.

Steig, W. (1971). *Amos & Boris.* New York: Farrar, Straus and Giroux.

Steig, W. (1976). *Abel's island.* New York: Farrar, Straus and Giroux.

Steig, W. (1977). *Caleb & Kate.* New York: Farrar, Straus and Giroux.

Steig, W. (1982). *Dr. De Soto.* New York: Scholastic.

Steig, W. (1986). *Brave Irene.* New York: Farrar, Straus and Giroux.

Steig, W. (1998). *Pete's a pizza.* New York: HarperCollins.

Steptoe, J. (1987). *Mufaro's beautiful daughters, an African tale.* New York: Lothrop, Lee & Shepard Books.

Stewart, S. (1997). *The gardener,* illustrated by D. Small. New York: Farrar Straus Giroux.

Strauss, G. (1990). *Trail of stones,* illustrated by A. Browne. New York: Alfred A. Knopf.

Taylor, M. D. (1976). *Roll of thunder, hear my cry.* New York: Dial Books.

Taylor, M. D. (2001). *The land.* New York: Phyllis Fogelman Books/Penguin Putnam.

Tchana, K. (2000). *The serpent slayer and other stories of strong women,* illustrated by T. S. Hyman. Boston: Little, Brown.

Trivizas, E. (1993). *The three little wolves and the big bad pig,* illustrated by H. Oxenbury. New York: Margaret K. McElderry Books.

Updike, J. (1999). *A child's calendar,* illustrated by T. S. Hyman. New York: Holiday House.

Van Allsburg, C. (1981). *Jumanji.* Boston: Houghton Mifflin.

Van Allsburg, C. (1984). *The mysteries of Harris Burdick.* Boston: Houghton Mifflin.

Van Allsburg, C. (1985). *The polar express.* Boston: Houghton Mifflin.

Van Allsburg, C. (1992). *The widow's broom.* Boston: Houghton Mifflin.

Van Allsburg, C. (2002). *Zathura.* Boston: Houghton Mifflin.

Viorst, J. (1971). *The tenth good thing about Barney,* illustrated by E. Blegvad. New York: Aladdin Books, Macmillan.

Viorst, J. (1974). *Rosie and Michael,* illustrated by L. Tomei. New York: Atheneum.

Viorst, J. (1990). *Earrings!,* illustrated by N. L. Malone. New York: Atheneum.

Wells, R. (1981). *Timothy goes to school.* New York: Dial.

White, E. B. (1952). *Charlotte's web,* illustrated by G. Williams. New York: Harper & Row.

Wiesner, D. (1999). *Sector 7.* New York: Clarion Books.

Wiesner, D. (2001). *The three pigs.* New York: Clarion/Houghton Mifflin.

Willard, N. (1991). *Pish, posh, said Hieronymus Bosch,* illustrated by the Dillons. New York: Harcourt Brace Jovanovich.

Willey, M. (2001). *Clever Beatrice,* illustrated by H. Solomon. New York: Atheneum.

Willhoite, M. (1990). *Daddy's roommate.* Boston: Alyson.

Williams, V. B. (1982). *A chair for my mother.* New York: Scholastic.

Williams, V. B. (1993). *Scooter.* New York: Greenwillow Books.

Williams, V. B. (2001). *Amber was brave, Essie was smart.* New York: Greenwillow.

Winter, J. (1998). *My name is Georgia.* San Diego: Harcourt Brace.

Winter, J. (2002). *Frida*, illustrated by A. Juan. New York: Scholastic.

Wisniewski, D. (1996). *The Golem.* New York: Clarion.

Wolff, V. E. (1997). *Bat 6.* New York: Scholastic.

Wood, A. (1987). *Heckedy Peg*, illustrated by D. Wood. San Diego: Harcourt Brace Jovanovich.

Woodson, J. (1994). *I hadn't meant to tell you this.* New York: Delacorte.

Woodson, J. (1995). *From the notebooks of Melanin Sun.* New York: The Blue Sky Press.

Woodson, J. (1997). *The house you pass on the way.* New York: Delacorte.

Woodson, J. (1999). *Lena.* New York: Delacorte.

Yee, P. (1992). *Roses sing on new snow, a delicious tale,* illustrated by H. Chan. New York: Macmillan.

Yep, L. (1975). *Dragonwings.* New York: Harper.

Yep, L. (1993). *Dragon's gate.* New York: HarperCollins.

Young, E. (1989).*Lon Po Po: A Red-Riding Hood story from China.* New York: Philomel.

Yolen, J. (1981). *Sleeping Ugly,* illustrated by D. Stanley. New York: Coward McCann & Geoghegan.

Zelinsky, P. O. (1986). *Rumpelstiltskin.* New York: E. P. Dutton.

Zelinsky, P. O. (1997). *Rapunzel.* New York: Dutton.

Zemach, M. (1988). *The three little pigs, an old story.* New York: Farrar, Straus and Giroux.

Zolotow, C. (1962). *Mr. Rabbit and the lovely present,* illustrated by M. Sendak. New York: Harper & Row.

Zolotow, C. (1972). *William's doll,* illustrated by W. Péne Du Bois. New York: Harper & Row.

Credit List

Index

Note: (fig) after a page number indicates a figure on that page; (tab) after a page number, indicates a table on that page